Interdisziplinäre Verortungen
der Angewandten Linguistik

Band 11

Herausgegeben von
Sylwia Adamczak-Krysztofowicz, Silvia Bonacchi,
Przemysław Gębal, Jarosław Krajka, Łukasz Kumięga
und Hadrian Lankiewicz

Die Bände dieser Reihe sind peer-reviewed.

Łukasz Kumięga /
Magdalena Nowicka-Franczak (eds.)

Analysing Discourse,
Analysing Poland

The Case of a Political Interview

With 5 figures

V&R unipress

Bibliografische Information der Deutschen Nationalbibliothek
Die Deutsche Nationalbibliothek verzeichnet diese Publikation in der Deutschen
Nationalbibliografie; detaillierte bibliografische Daten sind im Internet über
https://dnb.de abrufbar.

Gedruckt mit freundlicher Unterstützung der Universität Łódź, der Universität Gdańsk und
der Schlesischen Technischen Universität in Gliwice.

© 2023 Brill | V&R unipress, Robert-Bosch-Breite 10, D-37079 Göttingen, ein Imprint der Brill-Gruppe
(Koninklijke Brill NV, Leiden, Niederlande; Brill USA Inc., Boston MA, USA; Brill Asia Pte Ltd,
Singapore; Brill Deutschland GmbH, Paderborn, Deutschland; Brill Österreich GmbH, Wien,
Österreich)
Koninklijke Brill NV umfasst die Imprints Brill, Brill Nijhoff, Brill Schöningh, Brill Fink, Brill mentis,
Brill Wageningen Academic, Vandenhoeck & Ruprecht, Böhlau und V&R unipress.

Druck und Bindung: CPI books GmbH, Birkstraße 10, D-25917 Leck
Printed in the EU.

Vandenhoeck & Ruprecht Verlage | www.vandenhoeck-ruprecht-verlage.com

ISSN 2749-0211
ISBN 978-3-8471-1647-9

Contents

Magdalena Nowicka-Franczak / Łukasz Kumięga
Introduction: Single case, multiple interpretations. Methodological
challenges of discourse studies   7

Marek Czyżewski
The single case as an object of analysis: In defence of a species threatened
with extinction 25

Magdalena Nowicka-Franczak
The elite and their privilege to speak about themselves and others in
public. Post-Foucauldian discourse analysis meets post-Marxist
studies 57

Jerzy Stachowiak
Media performance. Remarks on the possibility of its analysis and
critique 87

Artur Lipiński
Interactional strategies of journalistic neutralism and political
equivocation. The case of "Tomasz Lis na żywo" TV show 117

Waldemar Czachur / Marta Wójcicka
Analysis of one text from the perspective of discourse linguistics 139

Agnieszka Budzyńska-Daca / Marcin Kosman
Political interview or debate – the clash of ethoses from the perspective of
rhetorical genre studies 161

Magdalena Steciąg / Kaja Rostkowska-Biszczanik
"You can't speak Polish?" The disintegration of the idea of natural
language in public debate (based on the material from an interview of
Tomasz Lis with Jarosław Kaczyński) 191

Łukasz Kumięga / Przemysław Gębal
From autonomy to inclusion. Discourse studies and constructivist
teaching of Polish as a second language in the 'pretext' of Tomasz Lis'
interview with Jarosław Kaczyński 209

Violetta Kopińska
The potential of interdisciplinarity in Discourse-Historical Approach.
The example of the interview of Tomasz Lis with Jarosław Kaczyński in
educational perspective 229

Agnieszka Kampka
The eyes, the smile, the audience. A multimodal analysis from a rhetorical
perspective 249

Łukasz Kumięga / Magdalena Nowicka-Franczak
Weighing discourse in a single-case study. An attempt at an appraisal . . 269

Notes on Contributors 275

Magdalena Nowicka-Franczak / Łukasz Kumięga

Introduction: Single case, multiple interpretations. Methodological challenges of discourse studies

The present volume has been inspired by an online methodological workshop called "Homogeneous research subject, heterogeneous research process, and inquisitive meta-reflection. An interdisciplinary approach to studying discourse" (24–25 June 2021), organized jointly by the Silesian University of Technology and the University of Łódź. The very cooperation between two centres of such distinct characteristics may pose certain methodological dilemmas, which come down to the questions of the status, relevance, and scope of quantitative and qualitative modes of research, although some preferences in modern academia (regardless of its particular institutional embodiments) are rather evident. Consequently, the workshop and the texts included in the present volume essentially offer insights of methodological nature, which are discussed at greater length in the latter part of this introduction. Our intention has been for this collection to provide an added value by way of exploring a number of methodological perspectives which arise from the appreciation of the qualitative approach and its potential.

We also hope to be offering observations of cognitive and critical character that will reach out to a wider audience thanks to the language of publication. The authors of the texts collected in this volume chose as their research subject – or as the point of departure for the study proper – a televised interview, which at the time of its broadcast was hotly debated by all those invested in Poland's political life. This interview was granted by Jarosław Kaczyński, leader of the rightist-conservative party Law and Justice [Pol. PiS], to Tomasz Lis, back then Poland's most recognizable and influential political journalist, during the latter's show "Tomasz Lis na żywo" [Tomasz Lis live], which aired on Channel 2 of the Polish public broadcaster (TVP 2) on 3 October 2011[1].

Magdalena Nowicka-Franczak, University of Łódź (Poland), ORCID: 0000-0002-4535-4246, m.nowicka_franczak@uni.lodz.pl.
Łukasz Kumięga, University of Gdańsk (Poland), ORCID: 0000-0002-8034-3593, Lukasz.Kumiega@ug.edu.pl.
1 The show is available at https://www.youtube.com/watch?v=0jKUsSgvx0I.

Ten years on, from a present-day perspective, it is easier to notice the significance of this interview and its dual character. On the one hand, this conversation stands out against Polish political discourse, both contemporarily and at present. It owes its uniqueness to the very fact that Jarosław Kaczyński, leader of the rightist-conservative wing of Polish politics, agreed to an interview with a liberal journalist, who was openly critical of him. After the heavy defeat of PiS in the 2007 general election, and especially after the 10 April 2010 plane crash which killed, among others, his brother Lech, the sitting president, Jarosław Kaczyński was increasingly reluctant to appear in the media which were not in sympathy with his political party. The 3 October 2011 interview is his final conversation with Lis to date. It immediately preceded the still ongoing period of political and media polarization, which ushered in a tradition of refusing to speak to unfriendly media outlets in an effort to create the impression that Poland is split in half by an unbridgeable rift. The politicians' model of "speaking to our very own" was soon adopted by the media, which have since rarely invited proponents of political beliefs that are out of keeping with the outlet's leanings, and do not even profess impartiality. Such avoidance of pluralistic public debate is presently characteristic of the majority of the actors of Poland's political life.

The uniqueness of the 2011 interview also follows from its association with the strategic goals of both interlocutors. Just a few days later, on 9 October, parliamentary election was held. Kaczyński's party was bidding to return to power, having ruled the country between 2005 and 2007. Kaczyński served as Prime Minister between 2006 and 2007 and was ousted following the snap election of 21 October 2007. Kaczyński was hoping that PiS would form a majority government, without having to again forge problematic coalitions. However, the 41.51% of the vote went to his main rival, the centrist Civic Platform [Platforma Obywatelska, PO], with PiS scoring just 32.11%. PO president Donald Tusk formed a coalition government with the conservative Polish People's Party [Polskie Stronnictwo Ludowe, PSL], while PiS moved to the opposition. Many factors contributed to that defeat: from scandals and frictions in the PiS coalition government, to ignoring social and professional groups' demands for improved standard of living, to popular concerns about the international perception of Poland under the rule of parties holding ultra-conservative views on ethical issues. Kaczyński did himself no favours with a televised debate with Donald Tusk on 12 October 2007, having performed considerably worse than his opponent. In 2011, Kaczyński refused to take part in another debate with Tusk, but during the election campaign, he avoided radical antagonism toward PO. By speaking to Lis, he was hoping to sway the undecided voters of centrist persuasion. Lis, in turn, through his criticism of PiS, was trying to shatter Kaczyński's persona of a moderate politician, which the latter had created for the purpose of the campaign.

Yet another argument testifying to the uniqueness of this interview is its polyvocality. It is a consequence of the aforesaid strategic goals which the interlocutors hoped to achieve by its means. During the conversation, its participants refer to each other and to what was said by third parties (political allies and opponents), assume the roles of spokespersons for antagonistic social groups, and on two occasions, Lis quotes Kaczyński's past statements to prove that his guest is being dishonest. This property of communication between Lis and Kaczyński has little to do with Mikhail Bakhtin's polyphony, since the voices invoked in the course of the interview are neither autonomous nor independent. These voices – referring to a variety of issues and axioms – are being constantly validated, invalidated, decontextualized, recontextualized, and then, crucially, instrumentalized. This polyphonous interview touches upon multiple aspects of social, cultural, and economic conflicts, and encourages attempts to review the dynamics of Poland's political conflict and to make predictions as to its future shape.

On the other hand, this is an interview typical of Polish political discourse. We are looking at two flamboyant speakers standing on the opposite sides of the barricade. They are not interested in exchanging substantive arguments, but in claiming a rhetorical victory and publicly discrediting the other interlocutor. Another reason to analyse this interview ten years on is its relevance. The topics raised and the dividing lines drawn were, are, and will long be crucial for Polish political discourse – this is particularly true about the conflicting views on Poland's European relations: do we go hand in hand with the West, or do we go alone? Thus, looking at this interview, one can – as suggested by the title of this volume – research a variety of topics, from the discursive picture of Poland, the Poles, or Polishness, to political and national interests, diverging paths of modernization of a post-socialist state, to the condition of Polish elites.

The social and political context of the interview

It is 2011 again. Poland has been a member of the European Union for six years and the country's modernization is mostly subsidized through EU funds. Two thirds of Polish households have internet access (GUS 2012), but the primary source of information for middle-aged and elderly Poles is still television. Since 2007, the country has been ruled by the PO-PSL coalition, which is implementing neoliberal economic and social policies, and in foreign relations, the government favours close cooperation with the European Union and the United States. The authorities take pride in the fact that Polish economy has been largely unscathed by the economic crisis, which has been ravaging the EU, and the eurozone in particular, since 2008. Following the tragic death of Lech Kaczyński, the new president is Bronisław Komorowski, supported by PO.

However, large sections of the political and social stage are sceptical of the pro-European and neoliberal reforms of the country. The public discourse of the post-transition period has rekindled the dissensus concerning the proper axiological order and the preferable modernization path, a controversy which goes back to the 18th century (see Jedlicki 1988, Krasnodębski 2003). On top of that, the discourse-manifested social antagonism has set in. In the course of the political transition period, three main narratives concerning Poland's modernization developed: the neoliberal model, the conservative model, and the social-democratic model (Anioł 2015). In the discourse of the proponents of a particular narrative, those who did not espouse it appeared as the (a)moral civilizational enemies, or even an inferior human "race" (see Buchowski 2006, Bobako 2010, Kubiak 2017).

This "civilizational" antagonism came in multiple installments. In 2005, in the context of the election rivalry between PiS and PO, the notion of the "solidary Poland" was pitted against that of the "liberal Poland". By means of the nomenclature promoted by PiS, the rhetorical division into the bourgeois, market-oriented Poland and the provincial, prosocial Poland – or into the so-called "Poland A" and "Poland B" – acquired a political dimension (Popielarz 2011, Obacz 2018). Polish public discourse and social rifts were also greatly affected by *the Smolensk tragedy*, that is, the 10 April 2010 crash of the presidential plane carrying Lech Kaczyński, his wife Maria, and a few dozen representatives of Polish political and military elites. The Polish delegation was traveling to commemorate the 70th anniversary of the Katyn massacre. The tragic aviation incident was promptly mythologized by the rightist political camp, providing foundations for the so-called Smolensk myth and the conspiracy theory of a political assassination, allegedly carried out by the Russian Federation in collusion with Polish liberals. This legend channelled a number of other divisions running in Polish society, including the distinction between the *victims* and the *beneficiaries* of the political transition (mostly in its economic dimension), and between the advocates of Catholic traditionalism and lay progressiveness, giving political subjectivity to the former (see Jaskułowski 2012). Moving to the forefront of the conflict was the issue of aligning oneself with a particular political camp. According to sociologist Jacek Raciborski (2019), since 2011, Polish politics and its discourse have been revolving around the binary division into PiS and its loyal supporters, and anti-PiS, that is, the opposition parties and vocal critics of PiS. Since 2015, when PiS reclaimed power and won the election again in 2019, its government has introduced a number of systemic changes which infringe the Polish constitution of 1997. The PiS vs. anti-PiS division is no longer a mere partisan antagonism, having transformed into a civilizational-axiological division along the lines of who is right about the institutional framework of the Polish state, what the condition of Polish society is, and which direction it should take.

Dramatis personae

But in 2011, Jarosław Kaczyński's party was facing an uphill struggle, trying to reclaim power, and his participation in Tomasz Lis' popular show was one of many elements of the election campaign. Kaczyński is a symbolic figure and the grey eminence of modern Polish politics. He was already a notable figure in the 1990s, serving as editor-in-chief of "Tygodnik Solidarność" [Solidarity Weekly] and then as chairman of the Christian-democratic party Porozumienie Centrum [Centre Agreement]. His career accelerated in 2001, when he co-founded Law and Justice with his twin brother Lech Kaczyński. In 2006, he went on to become Prime Minister of the coalition government of PiS, the national-Catholic Liga Polskich Rodzin [League of Polish Families], and national-popular Samoobrona [Self-Defence]. It was then that words such as 'the network' ['układ' in Polish, an alleged conspiracy of post-communist political, economic, and media elites toward taking control of the state affairs] or 'the Fourth Republic' ['Czwarta Rzeczpospolita', the project of a new state, free from 'the network', based on conservative republicanism and the West-independent modernization strategy] became part of public discourse. Linguists argued that Poland was witnessing the re-emergence of the magical language of communist propaganda, i.e., new-speech (Głowiński 2009, Polkowska 2015). After the coalition collapsed in 2007, PiS lost the snap election, but the narrative promoting the suspiciousness of the democratic Third Polish Republic became a fixture of the mainstream debate.

After Lech Kaczyński and his wife were killed in a crash involving the presidential aircraft in Smolensk, Russia, Jarosław's political stature grew as he went into public mourning and legitimized a conspiracy theory about the Smolensk political assassination. In 2011, the year of a parliamentary election, he would repeatedly accuse the ruling liberals of "annihilating the opposition", that is, of resorting to institutionally-supported oppressive measures and curbing political freedom. His party came in second, having garnered just shy of 30% of the vote. Kaczyński's outlook on the government-opposition relations shifted when a second PiS government was formed in 2015, its focus being on the institutional solidification of its own power and replacing the liberal elites with those loyal to the new rulers. In the general election of fall 2015, PiS ran in a coalition with lesser right-wing and Christian-conservative parties, won almost 38% of the ballot, and formed a coalition government under the brand of the United Right (Zjednoczona Prawica). Jarosław Kaczyński opted against becoming prime minister. The job went to PiS vice-chairwoman Beata Szydło, in office between 2015 and 2017, who was replaced by Mateusz Morawiecki in December 2017. Kaczyński still had the casting vote in shaping the government policies and appointing top officials in public administration. What is more, he holds major sway over the cabinet and policies of president Andrzej Duda, who was elected thanks to the backing of PiS in May 2015, and won his second term five years later (this influence was particularly strong during Duda's inaugural term). Kaczyński is clearly the gray eminence of the post-2015 Polish politics.

The year 2015 also marked a change in the ideological and strategic aspects informing Kaczyński's political activity. Between 2005 and 2007, when PiS was Poland's ruling party for the first time, Kaczyński already started to be perceived as a right-wing populist, rather than a conservatist or Christian democrat. In today's Central-Eastern Europe, Kaczyński, aside from Victor Orbán, is the chief proponent of the so-called non-liberal democracy, which means an evolution toward authoritarianism based on Euroscepticism and moral conservatism (see e.g. Lewandowski / Polakowski 2018, Krastev / Holmes 2019, Kim 2021). The backseat driver of the government and the parliamentary majority, Kaczyński authorized a number of systemic reforms violating the constitutional rule of law (e.g. with regard to appointing judges to the Constitutional Tribunal and the Supreme Court). His party has also made frequent (albeit so far unsuccessful) attempts to muzzle the media outlets unfavorably disposed to PiS. Since 2016, the activities of the party have drawn criticism from the European Union, which has issued formal reminders to the Polish government concerning the restoration of the rule of law.

Additionally, Kaczyński's party has stirred up the existing axiological conflicts surrounding human and civil rights. In particular, it has targeted sexual minorities, transgender persons, refugees, and women. On 22 October 2020, the Polish constitutional court, *de facto* controlled by PiS, ruled on the invalidity of one of the three scenarios permitting abortion, i.e. the severe and irreversible fetal defect. As a result, Polish abortion law has become one of the strictest such laws in the world. The ruling sparked mass demonstrations in Warsaw and other Polish cities. Protesters had camped in front of Kaczyński's Warsaw residence for many days. According to a poll conducted two years after the ruling, 27% of the respondents believe that Kaczyński is directly responsible for curbing women's rights (arb 2022).

The discourse of the leader of PiS has often been the subject of critical analysis (see: e.g. Jakubowska 2011, Dziekan 2018, Paluchowski / Podemski 2019). Kaczyński has repeatedly spoken about ideological subjects, perpetuating a patriarchal, anti-emancipatory, and discriminatory discourse, which has radicalized over the years. It introduces a basic social division into "us" (i.e. the Poles supporting PiS and the traditional values anchored in Catholic ethics) and the cultural aliens, "them" (i.e. the opposition parties, their supporters, feminists, and sexual, religious, and ethnic minorities). This volume's release date coincides with Polish general election. Given the increased opprobrium heaped upon PiS, Kaczyński's party seems unlikely to command the support of the 2015 and 2019 levels, but it is still polling relatively strong (between 32 and 38%, according to various polls of August 2023).

∗ ∗ ∗

During the 2011 interview with Lis, some of Kaczyński's contemporary associates and allies are mentioned. At that time, a figure of considerable influence was Antoni Macierewicz. In communist Poland, he was a notable activist of the democratic opposition and one of the founders of the Workers' Defence Committee (KOR). In post-communist Poland, he was a member of a number of national-Christian parties and a tireless denunciator of former informants of the communist secret service. Many of his accusations were completely unfounded. He had served on Kaczyński's government as a Deputy Minister of National Defence and was subsequently appointed head of the Military Counterintelligence Service. He presided over a parliamentary subcommittee for ascertaining the facts surrounding the crash of the government Tu-154 aircraft in Smolensk and made a major contribution to popularizing the conspiracy theory as to the assassination of President Lech Kaczyński. For the liberals and the leftists, Macierewicz stands for right-wing dogmatism and the conspiracy-tainted perception of the world. An equally controversial figure, also mentioned during the interview, is Zbigniew Ziobro, back then a vice-chairman of PiS, who served in the dual role of Minister of Justice and Public Prosecutor General between 2005 and 2007 and used his office for political struggle (he was expelled from PiS in November 2007, and has been a coalition partner of PiS since 2015, as leader of the Solidary Poland [Solidarna Polska] party). Anna Fotyga, Kaczyński's Foreign Minister, was a symbol of incompetence for the opponents of PiS. Enjoying somewhat more favourable perception was Zyta Gilowska, who served as a Deputy Prime Minister and Minister of Finance on the first government of PiS. During the interview, Lis also asks Kaczyński about father Tadeusz Rydzyk, a Catholic media mogul and a clergyman-businessman, who openly supported PiS, but at the same time publicly admonished the party. Lis mentions a situation from 2007, when Rydzyk called First Lady Maria Kaczyńska "a witch" after she spoke against the tightening of Poland's abortion law (which was already very stringent). Toward the end of the interview, mention is also made of "Staruch" [old man], which is the nickname of Piotr Staruchowicz, the leader of the supporters of Legia Warsaw football club. He embodied the problem of radical and aggressive football hooligans. In 2011, Donald Tusk publicly accused him of inciting physical and verbal violence among supporters and of acts of criminal damage, and promised that his government would crack down on hooligans.

* * *

Let us now have a closer look at the host of the show. Tomasz Lis became a professional journalist for TVP, the state-owned television company, at the inception of the democratic Poland in 1990. His career was synonymous with success in the new capitalistic meritocracy. He interviewed top politicians and was a US correspondent before transferring to the commercial liberal outlet, TVN, where he was a leading opinion journalist. In 2004, following media speculation concerning his candidacy in a presidential election, which he did not dismiss, TVN terminated his contract. He became channel executive at Polsat, TVN's fiercest competitor. In 2008, he returned to TVP and for eight years hosted the program "Tomasz Lis na żywo", as part of which he interviewed Kaczyński in 2011. "Tomasz Lis na żywo" is a chronicle of the eight years of Civic Platform's rule. Even though Lis did not openly support Donald Tusk's administration, his program was consistent with the agenda of the liberals.

For many years, he was the embodiment of information media's mainstream and its political and class profile: the pro-European inhabitants of big cities who adopted a paternalistic approach to the lower classes and the countryside, but at the same time, they held rather traditional moral values. Although Lis has received numerous accolades, he sparks negative emotions among the right- and left-leaning audiences alike. In 2019, he suffered a stroke and returned to the media after completing rehabilitation, but his stature has diminished. This trend was already visible in his losing ground among the young generations of Poles: toward the end of its lifespan, "Tomasz Lis na żywo" was the preferred choice of one in ten spectators between 16 and 49 years of age (eight years before, this figure stood at one in seven, see Pallus 2016). Since 2015, Lis has supported the citizens protesting against PiS, the women demonstrating after the tightening of the abortion law, and the LGBT+ movement; however, all these groups perceive his stance as overly cautious.

Around the time when we were editing this volume, a scandal erupted with Tomasz Lis at its centre. On 24 May 2022, without any previous indication and to the surprise of his closest associates, he stepped down as editor-in-chief of the "Newsweek Polska" weekly, owned by the Ringier Axel Springer company. A month later, the Wirtualna Polska online news service published an article by Szymon Jadczak (2022). Based on documents, mails, and anonymous statements from the employees of the weekly, he claimed that Lis had repeatedly mobbed his subordinates, and that these cases were reported to the owners of "Newsweek Polska" from 2018. Soon afterward, rumours started to circulate in media circles that the efficient cause of Lis' dismissal was his texts to a female employee of Ringier Axel Springer, which potentially amounted to sexual harassment (Głuchowski 2022). Lis has denied all accusations. He has not been officially charged on either count. Under Polish law, the case of Lis – who is no longer a "Newsweek" employee – can be decided in court only if he himself brings a suit, citing his baseless dismissal or libel (Orliński 2022). However, he has not taken this step, which provokes even more questions about his integrity. Some of the media outlets for which he worked as a political commentator have put their cooperation on hold. In August 2022, the Society of Journalists (Towarzystwo Dziennikarskie), one of the associations of Poland's media people, published an open letter to all the parties involved, calling for both ascertaining the reasons behind Lis' dismissal and explaining why he was subsequently suspended by the outlets he had cooperated with, even though the accusations he faces have not been officially reviewed or proven (Blumsztajn 2022).

In the autumn, it was reported that Lis might return to TOK FM radio as a political commentator, but this was hampered by the journalist's subsequent stroke. Leaving aside the state of Lis' health (despite his stroke, he is active on social media, especially on Twitter), it seems that his time as Poland's most influential journalist is perhaps coming to an end, the interview analysed pre-saging this demise. The 2011 show still belongs to the era of the profoundly patriarchal public discourse, whose centre stage was taken by dominant and irreconcilable men, for whom the strategic end justified the means. This is even more evident from the perspective of the year 2022, when this sort of discourse is countenanced increasingly less often by the public.

What about the political significance of the 2011 interview? It is difficult to prove the direct impact of media interviews and political debates on citizens' electoral choices. According to some theories, John Fitzgerald Kennedy defeated Republican candidate Richard Nixon in the 1960 presidential election, because he had a "way" with television and took full account of the character of this medium before appearing in a series of televised preelection debates, which for the first time in US history preceded the vote (see e.g. McLuhan 1964).

The Polish TV debate of 1988 between Alfred Miodowicz, chairmen of the communists-dependent All-Poland Alliance of Trade Unions (OPZZ), and Lech Wałęsa, representing the Independent Self-Governing Trade Union "Solidarity", is seen by scholars not just as a symbol of the ultimate delegitimization of the communist rule in Poland, but also as one of a number of events which brought together representatives of the Polish United Workers' Party and "Solidarity" for the Round Table talks a few months later. Fast forward to 1995: Wałęsa, the sitting president running for the second term in office, offered a fierce *ad personam* argumentation in a debate with Aleksander Kwaśniewski, the candidate of the post-communist left. This performance, which was received unfavourably by the commentators and the audience alike, may have contributed to the electoral defeat of the former leader of "Solidarity" (see Budzyńska-Daca 2015, pp. 163–177).

After 2001, the gap between reality and its media representations started to grow rapidly. The 9/11 attacks put violence at the central stage of the media spectacle, and politicians all over the world gave themselves the right to ignore facts and to adopt cynical criteria for telling the truth from the lies. The watershed moment for Polish political discourse was the aforesaid Smolensk crash. This aviation accident not only altered Poland's political life, but also sanctioned the practice of replacing discussions on objective causes of unforeseen events with conspiracy theories (Czech 2015, 2019).

In this context, the social significance of the interview which the chairman of PiS granted to Lis five days before the parliamentary election is uncertain. Media outlets sympathizing with PiS announced that Kaczyński had "thrashed" Lis, while the latter argued that he managed to reveal the "true colours" of his interlocutor. On parting ways with the state-owned broadcaster a few years later, Lis pointed to this interview as one of the most important moments of his journalistic career, implying that this conversation won Donald Tusk and his Civic Platform an additional few percentage points at the ballot thanks to the votes of the previously hesitant electorate (Lis 2016). In all likelihood, the significance of this interview is overestimated by both sides. It is impossible to rule out that there were indeed some viewers whose choice at the ballot was in some way informed by this TV program. However, it appears that the majority of the audience had formed their opinions about Kaczyński and Lis – and especially about their personalities – before they tuned in to watch the interview, and this was an outcome of the increasing personalization of politics. The 3 October 2011 interview likely solidified the viewers' previously held beliefs, rather than changing them.

Methodological challenges

Methodology-wise, the chapters of the present volume share the discourse study approach, characterized by inter- and trans-disciplinary potential, while the common ground they cover topic-wise is the interview on the "Tomasz Lis na żywo" show, which may direct researchers toward the theoretically and methodologically capacious category of discourse. The obvious starting point for this discussion is the unique cognitive and social added value of discursive approaches, which may concern at least three aspects:
– reconstruction and uncovering of ostensibly obvious discourses, scholarly included (critical analyses of extremist far-right and far-left discourses, as well

as those which attempt to somewhat shift this perspective and point to the excluding nature of some elements within neoliberal or left-wing discourses),
- identification of those elements and meanings which are not explicitly articulated in discourses,
- theoretical and methodological integration of diverse research perspectives, courtesy of the multidimensionality of the very category of discourse.

These aspects may be further dissected in search for various research practices of discursive nature (cf. Nowicka-Franczak, Kumięga 2020). Following Hans-Christoph Koller (1999), we shall adopt as the ordering categories the concepts of homogeneity and heterogeneity, which may apply to both the object of study and the research process. With regard to the former, heterogeneity and homogeneity will be seen in genre, thematic, and ideological terms. The latter are about the labelling of particular discourse as e. g. extreme-right, extreme-left, or neoliberal. Meanwhile, the research process may take a specialized turn, and its value is then considered in terms of homogeneous, highly-specialized theories, methods, and tools characteristic of a particular academic field. This tendency dominates in research practice.

On the other hand, there are calls to appreciate and embrace the special significance of multi-, inter-, or even trans-disciplinary approaches. Multi-disciplinarity is the literal concurrence of theoretical and methodological perspectives. Inter-disciplinarity is a slightly more complex procedure, which stresses the dialog between these perspectives. Finally, trans-disciplinarity – being a somewhat idealistic approach which is often disfavoured on grounds of field-specific limitations – postulates a possibility of supra-genre transference and transformation of the theory and methods of one or multiple research fields from the perspective of another or multiple fields. In the present volume, we go for inter-disciplinarity and encourage the intensification of the dialog it promotes, which may open up an opportunity to cross into the most complex and cognitively compelling perspective of trans-disciplinarity.

Theo van Leeuwen identifies three models of inter-disciplinarity: centralistic, pluralistic, and integrational. The first one captures the relations between diverse and autonomous perspectives, with each assuming the central position from which it arranges its relations with the remaining disciplines. While the centralistic model is oriented to capitalizing on methods of other disciplines, the pluralistic model is focused on a research problem thought to be shared by multiple disciplines, but these are still seen as separate, independent fields. The integrational model, which served as the beacon during our workshop, recognizes that no discipline can solve research problems on its own: rather, disciplines are interconnected, and it is only under a project integrating various field-specific approaches that these problems can be successfully addressed (Van Leeuwen 2005: pp. 3 ff).

Koller (1999: 195), referring to qualitative studies, writes about two strategies of facing challenges posed by research procedures: 1) the maximalization of interpretations with a view to their critical verification and gradual reduction in the spirit of objective hermeneutics, 2) triangulation, seen as the juxtaposition of various interpretations to enable their mutual complementation. In the context of discourse studies, both approaches seem problematic because of the aforesaid interpretive reduction or the concurrence of various perspectives, which are often brought together in a cumulative and simplistic manner.

But Koller (1999) goes one step further and looks for a third, and even fourth way, which would take account of, and crucially, provide support to, the added value of interpretive variegation. He refers to linguistic theory and the concepts of Jean-François Lyotard, where discourse is treated as one whole composed of different sentences combined with each other according to specific rules, which means that particular kinds of discourses are incommensurable. This incommensurability may assume two forms: along the lines of conflict in the legal sense (Ger. *Rechtsstreit*) or along the lines of conflict in the sense of contradiction (*Widerstreit*). The latter is seen as a controversy which cannot be resolved. This controversy is particularly interesting in the context of a research process, because it activates two of the latter's dimensions, referred to as sceptical and innovative. The former consists in accepting and recognizing incommensurability in the sense of contradiction, and leaves the controversy running. This is reminiscent of the triangulation approach, where different interpretations coexist on equal footing. Meanwhile, the innovative way is about analysing the incommensurable discourses (which are seen as interpretations under a research process) in search for that which could not be expressed through them, and strives for finding an "idiom" which would enable articulating the unsaid. This approach broadens cognition and as such is more theoretically and methodologically stimulating, even if it requires adopting a panoramic and, first and foremost, thoughtful perspective.

An attempt to follow the latter approach was the "Migration and intercultural communication" conference, held in Hamburg in 1994. The participants discussed the case of a conversation between African doctoral student Kalu and German reviser Bert, which concerned Kalu's doctoral dissertation. The main idea of the conference was to study a single empirical material – a transcript of Kalu and Bert's conversation – from various theoretical and methodological perspectives. Koller (1999) offered two interpretations, in line with the aforesaid approach grounded in linguistic theory and Lyotard's discourse. The first referred to ethnomethodology and conversation analysis (Czyżewski 1996), while the other was theoretically couched in the ethnological, historical, and linguistic debate on orality and literacy (Hartung 1996). Following Lyotard, Koller juxtaposes these two interpretations and points to three options: one where they complement each other, one where they are in conflict in the sense of contradiction, and a third one, which is about identifying the interpretive moment which can be sensed in both interpretations, but was not explicitly stated. Thus, the genre homogeneity of the study object and the homogeneity of the research process may be productively enlisted in the service of identifying heterogeneity which applies to meta-reflection on the research procedure.

A similar approach was taken by "Workshops in Discourse Analysis", started by Marek Czyżewski. Their goal was to enhance cooperation between various research centres in Poland and between representatives of various disciplines which are concerned with discourse (http://analizadyskursu.pl/o-konsorcjum). A return to this model – which broadens the sociological and linguistic perspective and is additionally reinforced by the Hamburg approach – was precisely the interdisciplinary path we wanted to follow during this workshop, especially in light of the current challenges of social and political nature. We were hoping that it would see the interview in question analysed from various research perspectives and thus – in line with Koller (1999) – offer interdisciplinary insights, which would contribute to identifying at least three paths of conducting an in-depth meta-research and meta-interpretive procedure:
– the path of mutual complementation,
– the path of conflict in the sense of contradiction,
– the path of identifying the interpretation's unuttered underlying assumptions.

The workshop has clearly demonstrated the complexity of the methodological postulates put forward and thus opened up opportunities for further methodological exploration. Still, it has captured a number of essential issues, which were: meta-methodological (see the text by Marek Czyżewski), trans-disciplinary (Magdalena Nowicka-Franczak), (para-)critical (Jerzy Stachowiak), strategic-communicative (Artur Lipiński), meta-discursive (Waldemar Czachur & Marta Wójcicka), genre-rhetorical (Agnieszka Budzyńska-Daca & Marcin Kosman), metalinguistic (Magdalena Steciąg & Kaja Rostkowska-Biszczanik), constructivist-educational (Łukasz Kumięga & Przemysław Gębal), interdisciplinary (Violetta Kopińska), and multimodal (Agnieszka Kampka).

The contents of the volume

The volume opens with the text by Marek Czyżewski (Łódź), entitled "Single case as an object of analysis. In defence of a species threatened with extinction". It starts a general, meta-methodological discussion on the added value provided by single case analysis and demonstrates its potential and limitations in the field of discourse studies. This discussion takes place against the background of a broader methodological challenge arising from the primacy of the quantitative approach, and the resulting reductionism, in current scholarly discourse.

In her "The elite and their privilege to speak about themselves and others in public. Post-Foucauldian discourse analysis meets post-Marxist studies", Magdalena Nowicka-Franczak (Łódź) takes one of the directions pointed to by the workshop, which was devoted to thorough methodological reflection. It may be seen as a first step toward trans-disciplinarity. Her attempt at straddling the post-Foucauldian discourse analysis with post-Marxist research approaches results in a special interpretation of the Lis-Kaczyński interview in the context of a discussion on social and discursive divisions into the elites and the common people.

Jerzy Stachowiak's (Łódź) "Media performance. Remarks on the possibility of its analysis and critique" takes on the old but still relevant dilemmas and challenges pertaining to the suitability of a critical analysis in social studies (including in the field of discourse analysis) and to the ways in which it is performed. In the spirit of a reflective scholarly dialog, the author details and combines various contributions to this research field.

The volume's social-sciences section concludes with "Interactional strategies of journalistic neutralism and political equivocation. The case of 'Tomasz Lis na żywo' TV show" by Artur Lipiński (Poznań), who looks at various types of journalistic communicative strategies listed by Peter Bull, Steven Clayman, and John Heritage. The author's analysis demonstrates their distinctive instantiations in the Lis-Kaczyński interview.

The section focusing chiefly on the linguistic perspective opens with Waldemar Czachur (Warszawa) and Marta Wójcicka's (Lublin) "Analysis of one text from the perspective of discourse linguistics". In partial reference to Marek Czyżewski's, this text defends the single case analysis, adducing cognitive and ontic arguments. It describes discourse linguistics as an integrative research program, whose methodology covers four levels of analysis: institutional, substantive, thematic, and ideological/modal.

Invoking the rhetorical perspective, Agnieszki Budzyńska-Daca (Warszawa) and Marcin Kosman's (Warszawa) "Political interview or debate – the clash of ethoses from the perspective of rhetorical genre studies" adopts the approach of critical genre studies. Importantly, the authors take genre as the departure point for the identification of methodological aspects which structure the debate surrounding the linguistic creation of the reality of the political interview. The analysis centres on a comparison between the Lis-Kaczyński interview and the Lis-Tusk interview, which also took place in 2011.

In "*You can't speak Polish?* The disintegration of the idea of natural language in public debate (based on the material from an interview of Tomasz Lis with

Jarosław Kaczyński)", Magdalena Steciąg (Zielona Góra) and Kaja Rostkowska-Biszczanik (Zielona Góra), following the meta-reflective and – to an extent – the metalinguistic tradition, point to three ways toward a linguistic interpretation of the Lis-Kaczyński interview, invoking the notions of *lingua nativa – lingua materna – lingua fracta*. This is done with a view to identifying symptoms of communicational crisis in the course of a linguistic analysis.

In "From autonomy to inclusion. Discourse studies and constructivist teaching of Polish as a second language in the 'pretext' of Tomasz Lis's interview with Jarosław Kaczyński", Łukasz Kumięga (Gdańsk) and Przemysław Gębal (Gdańsk) look at the Lis-Kaczyński political interview in terms of its educational implications for the constructivist teaching of foreign languages, intercultural and transcultural education, and particularly the teaching of Polish as a second language. Thus, they step outside conventional cognitive models, framing the interview in a context in which it would not be normally studied.

In "The potential of interdisciplinarity in Discourse-Historical Approach. The example of the interview of Tomasz Lis with Jarosław Kaczyński in educational perspective", Violetta Kopińska (Toruń) sees the Lis-Kaczyński interview as a departure point for analyses on two levels. First – somewhat in line with Stachowiak's discussion – she adopts a moderately critical perspective on the interdisciplinary character of the variant of critical discourse analysis proposed by Ruth Wodak. Second, her analysis points to those aspects of the interview under scrutiny which address the explicitly educational perspective.

Agnieszka Kampka's (Warszawa) "The eyes, the smile, the audience – a multimodal analysis from a rhetorical perspective" deliberately serves as the volume's concluding chapter. First, it departs from the prevalent textual-centric approach to the interview and its analyses. It is an account of the verbal, paraverbal, and nonverbal context of the conversation between Lis and Kaczyński and emphasizes its multimodality from a rhetorical angle. The analysis considers the comments of online users posted under the video recording of the interview available on YouTube. The author thus offers another innovative perspective on the research object.

Conclusions and acknowledgements

To sum up, the Lis-Kaczyński interview analysed in this volume inspired at least three research perspectives, which can be characterized as follows:
- one is purely epistemic, and follows from the multiplicity of interpretations of the text of the interview and of its paraverbal and nonverbal elements; these interpretations come in abundance in each of the analyses included in this volume;

- another relates to field-specificity, since the authors, arguing from their field-specific angles (such as sociology, linguistics, political science, or teaching methodology), attempted to offer a broader analytical perspective and find interdisciplinary solutions;
- finally, a trans-disciplinary perspective was adopted, as the authors, bringing together different approaches, looked for a third interpretive way, or tried to follow paths running outside the frames traditionally imposed by the scenario of a political interview.

Finally, we would like to express our gratitude, in the first place to all those who accepted our invitation to test their research expertise against a particular product of linguistic, social, and political reality: this was a tall order, and required considerable academic courage and responsibility. We treat the contributions to this volume as the point of departure for facing similar research and methodological challenges in the future. The workshop itself and the present volume would not have materialized without necessary institutional background and support. We would like to thank Prof. Eng. Wojciech Szkliniarz, Vice-President for Students Affairs and Education of the Silesian Technical University, for the official opening of the workshop and the warm reception of strictly qualitative studies which he gave as a representative of technical sciences. We would like to extend our sincere gratitude to Prof. Eng. Arkadiusz Mężyk, President of the Silesian Technical University, dr. hab. Ewa Kusideł, Vice-Dean for Science at the Faculty of Economics and Sociology, University of Łódź, Prof. Kaja Kaźmierska, Head of the Department of Sociology of Culture, Prof. Piotr Stepnowski, President of the University of Gdańsk, and Prof. Urszula Patocka-Sigłowy, Dean of Faculty of Languages, for the financial support granted to this publication, a contribution which will be hopefully offset by this book's import, place of publication, and outreach.

Last but not least, special thanks go to the reviewer of this volume, Prof. Krzysztof Podemski (Adam Mickiewicz University, Poznań), and to the publisher's support team, represented by Ms. Marie-Carolin Vondracek. Vielen Dank!

References

arb: Dwa lata po wyroku TK ws. aborcji. Pozytywnie decyzję ocenia 8,9 proc. Polaków. 2022, available at: https://www.rp.pl/spoleczenstwo/art37276691-dwa-lata-po-wyroku-tk-ws-aborcji-pozytywnie-decyzje-ocenia-8-9-proc-polakow [5. 03. 2023].

Anioł, W.: 'On Three Modernisation Narratives in Poland after 1989', in: INTERNATIONAL JOURNAL OF SOCIAL ECONOMICS 2015/42(9), p. 777–790.

Blumsztajn, S.: Apel Towarzystwa Dziennikarskiego w sprawie Tomasza Lisa. 2022, available at: https://wyborcza.pl/7,75968,28776668,apel-towarzystwa-dziennikarskiego-w-sprawie-tomasza-lisa.html [23.08.2022].

Bobako, Monika: Demokracja wobec różnicy. Multikulturalizm i feminizm w perspektywie polityki uznania. Poznań 2010.

Buchowski, M.: 'The Specter of Orientalism in Europe: From Exotic Other to Stigmatized Brother', in: ANTHROPOLOGICAL QUARTERLY 2006/79(3), p. 463–482.

Budzyńska-Daca, Agnieszka: Retoryka debaty. Polskie wielkie debaty przedwyborcze 1995–2010. Warszawa 2015.

Czech, Franciszek: Spiskowe narracje i metanarracje. Kraków 2015.

Czech, F.: 'Saturation of the media with conspiracy narratives: content analysis of selected Polish news magazines', in: ŚRODKOWOEUROPEJSKIE STUDIA POLITYCZNE 2019/2, p. 151–171.

Czyżewski, Marek: '"Das versteh ich nich'. Grenzen der Argumentation und andere kommunikative Merkmale in der sprachlichen Beratung", in: Kokemohr, Rainer / Koller, Hans-Christoph (eds.): 'Jeder Deutsche kann das verstehen'. Probleme im interkulturellen Arbeitsgespräch. Weinheim 1996, p. 25–36.

Dziekan, Jacek: Od rytuału do konfliktu. Mediatyzacja żałoby posmoleńskiej. Gdańsk 2018.

Głowiński, Michał: Nowomowa i ciągi dalsze: Szkice dawne i nowe. Kraków 2009.

Głuchowski, P.: Nie tylko mobbing. Tajemnicze SMS-y od Lisa. 2022, available at: https://wyborcza.pl/7,75968,28665164,nie-tylko-mobbing-tajemnicze-sms-y-od-lisa.html [23.08.2022].

GUS: Społeczeństwo informacyjne w Polsce. Wyniki badań statystycznych z lat 2007–2011. Warszawa 2012.

Hartung, Marion: 'Intrakulturelle Kommunikation in einer Schriftkultur Wissen und Können', in: Kokemohr, Rainer / Koller, Hans-Christoph (eds.): 'Jeder Deutsche kann das verstehen'. Probleme im interkulturellen Arbeitsgespräch. Weinheim 1996, p. 133–174.

Jadczak, S.: "Płakałam, miałam ataki paniki". Ujawniamy zarzuty podwładnych wobec Tomasza Lisa. Dlaczego zwolniono naczelnego "Newsweeka"? 2022, available at: https://wiadomosci.wp.pl/plakalam-mialam-ataki-paniki-ujawniamy-zarzuty-podwladnych-wobec-tomasza-lisa-dlaczego-zwolniono-naczelnego-newsweeka-6783015358188512a [23.08.2022].

Jakubowska, A.: 'Język wypowiedzi publicznych Jarosława Kaczyńskiego w latach 2007–2011', in: REFLEKSJE 2011/3, p. 127–140.

Jaskułowski, Krzysztof: Wspólnota symboliczna. W stronę antropologii nacjonalizmu. Gdańsk 2012.

Jedlicki, Jerzy: Jakiej cywilizacji Polacy potrzebują. Warszawa 1988.

Kim, S.: '… Because the Homeland Cannot Be in Opposition: Analysing the Discourses of Fidesz and Law and Justice (PiS) from Opposition to Power', in: EAST EUROPEAN POLITICS 2021/37(2), p. 332–351. DOI: 10.1080/21599165.2020.1791094.

Koller, H.-Ch.: 'Lesarten. Über das Geltendmachen von Differenzen im Forschungsprozeß', in: ZEITSCHRIFT FÜR ERZIEHUNGSWISSENSCHAFT 1999/2, p. 195–209.

Krasnodębski, Zdzisław: Demokracja peryferii. Gdańsk 2003.

Krastev, Ivan / Holmes, Stephen: The Light that Failed: A Reckoning. London 2019.

Kubiak, A.: *"Bieda (z tą Polską).* Prostacy i mieszczanie: modernizacyjna naturalizacja i normalizacja peryferyjnych nierówności", in: POLITYKA I SPOŁECZEŃSTWO 2017/3 (15), p. 95–112. DOI: 10.15584/polispol.2017.3.7.

Lewandowski A. / Polakowski M: 'Elites vs. the People: Populism in the Political Thought of Law and Justice', in: ANNALES UNIVERSITATIS MARIAE CURIE-SKŁODOWSKA 2018/25(2), p. 145–163.

Lis, T.: Moje pożegnanie z TVP. 2016, available at: https://natemat.pl/blogi/tomaszlis/167 089,moje-pozegnanie-z-tvp [23.08.2022].

McLuhan, Marshall: Understanding Media. New York 1964.

Nowicka-Franczak, M. / Kumięga, Ł.: 'Od redaktorów: Analiza dyskursu a prawda o dyskursie', in: PRZEGLĄD SOCJOLOGII JAKOŚCIOWEJ 2020/16(4), p. 6–17. DOI: 10.18778/ 1733-8069.16.4.01.

Obacz, Piotr: Podział "Polska solidarna – Polska liberalna" w świetle wybranych koncepcji pluralizmu politycznego. Kraków 2018.

Orliński, W.: Mało kogo w sprawie Tomasza Lisa interesuje meritum. 2022, available at: https://wyborcza.pl/duzyformat/7,127290,28642982,orlinski-malo-kogo-interesuje-me ritum-gdy-w-gre-wchodza-znani.html [23.08.2022].

Paluchowski, W.J. / Podemski, K.: 'Mowy miesięcznicowe Jarosława Kaczyńskiego jako spektakl władzy', in: RUCH PRAWNICZY, EKONOMICZNY I SOCJOLOGICZNY 2019/ 4, p. 253–268.

Polkowska, Laura: Język prawicy. Warszawa 2015.

Popielarz, Ewa (ed.): Polska solidarna czy Polska liberalna: wyzwania dla społeczeństwa, państwa i prawa. Kraków 2011.

Raciborski, J.: Zakrzepnięcie PiS i AntyPiS. Klasa ludowa kontra średnia, minimalne przepływy – analiza Raciborskiego. 2019, available at: https://oko.press/zakrzepniecie -pis-i-antypis-klasa-ludowa-kontra-srednia-minimalne-przeplywy-analiza-raciborskie go/ [23.08.2022].

Van Leeuwen, Theo: Introducing Social Semiotics. London 2005.

Marek Czyżewski

The single case as an object of analysis: In defence of a species threatened with extinction[1]

Abstract

The text at hand has two objectives. The first of these is an attempt to substantiate and validate single case analysis – a type of analysis discredited not only in terms of quantitative research, but also in currently dominant qualitative research trends. It would seem particularly necessary, therefore, to advance a methodological argumentation in light of which it would be possible not only to demonstrate the soundness of single case analyses, but also to reveal the advantages stemming from such an approach. Addressing this aspect, I will refer to ethnomethodological conversation analysis as well as the interpretatively-oriented biographical method. The second objective is served by the presentation of a microanalysis delving into a conversation from the opening to Franz Kafka's novel, *The Trial*. This analysis will generate a conceptualization pertaining especially to the local interconnections between the sequential and categorial orders found within a single conversation. Taking any and all differences into account, it becomes apparent that similar conversational phenomena can be discerned in an interview by the journalist, Tomasz Lis with the politician, Jarosław Kaczyński. Moreover, in all probability, such phenomena can be observed in many other cases of a dialogic tug-of-war.

Keywords: single case analysis, conversation analysis, sequential order, categorial order, Franz Kafka

Introduction

The chief methodological goal of this article is hinted at in the subtitle: it is to provide arguments in support of the validity of the single case analysis, a research procedure unanimously criticized under the dominant tendencies of quantitative and qualitative models of analysis. Throughout, I will be drawing on the conversation analytic perspective. The methodological argumentation offered is

Marek Czyżewski, University of Łódź (Poland), ORCID: 0000-0001-9544-1420, marek.czyzewski@uni.lodz.pl.

1 I would like to thank Rod Watson, for our inspiring discussions on categorial and sequential order of conversation, and Fritz Schütze and Gerhard Riemann, for their insightful and helpful comments on an early draft of this article.

obviously related to an interview between Tomasz Lis, a Polish journalist, and Jarosław Kaczyński, an influential Polish politician, i. e. to the single case which is the subject of scrutiny in the present volume. Another aim of this paper is empirical in character, and its furtherance is also centered around conversation analysis and the application and – hopefully – elaboration of its underlying research apparatus. First, the focus will be on the single case analysis of the opening passage of Franz Kafka's *The Trial*. Next, relying on the same research apparatus, I will briefly refer to what I believe are the key features of the Lis-Kaczyński interview. Despite substantial differences between a literary master-piece and a product of political journalism, it is possible to posit a common denominator for both, which can be highlighted thanks to conversation analysis: in both cases, the empirical findings concern the disturbances of interactional cooperation between interlocutors, which – as proven in the course of a micro-analysis – share a number of formal features.

State of affairs and its conditions

For a vast majority of academics, there is no question that the validity of scientific findings should be determined on the basis of whether and to what extent they are grounded in quantitative analysis, that is, whether the findings which are to pass for scientific lend themselves to quantification. The prevalence of quanti-tative research methods is visible not just in natural sciences, but also in sociology and linguistics. It may appear that the quantification of social sciences follows – as in the case of linguistics – from the desire to meet the criteria of "hard" science. However, it is worth noting the non-academic sources of this tendency, which seems to be, by and large, a corollary of the interconnectedness between quantitative analyses and the governing of a population, a connection which has been steadily gaining prominence since the early modern period. The quanti-tative methodologies of social sciences grew in significance with the development of governing techniques based on normalization, rather than on normation (Foucault 2007). Normation consists in the adoption of particular behavioral patterns in the form of decisive prohibitions or specific orders, any deviations from these patterns being severely castigated. Obviously, normation is still fre-quently enforced, either by means of penalties for violating prohibitions or ad-monishments toward executing orders. But governing an increasingly complex population is more and more reliant on anticipating and avoiding risks, and as such requires normalization procedures. This is because normalization does not lay down any strict criteria in advance, but draws on an existing analysis of quantitative trends in a particular sphere of social life (e. g. it may concern the prevalence of a disease). That way, it is possible to set quantitative brackets deemed acceptable at a given juncture, and such that should alert the administrative bodies and prompt them to take preventive measures.

The relationship between social, economic, and political sciences and the governing of a population has been a subject of analyses within sociology of quantification (Espeland / Stevens 2008, Mennicken / Espeland 2019). This subdiscipline has produced classical descriptions (e. g. Alonso / Starr 1986, Desrosieres 1998), studies directly or indirectly qualifying as post-Foucauldian inspirations (e. g. Miller / Rose 2008, Beer 2016), as well as analyses focusing on robust trends percolating through the fields of quantification of social science and of social and individual life from digital technologies (e. g. Beer 2018, Mau 2019).

The sociology of quantification suggests that the connection obtaining between quantification and power relations is multifaceted. On the one hand, for decision-makers and ordinary people alike, the quantification of knowledge makes the latter more valuable than unquantified knowledge. This tendency has been well-captured in the title of one book in the field of sociology of quantification, *Making Things Valuable* (Kornberger et al 2015). It is worth noting an adverse side effect of this trend, namely, an influx of unskilled and somewhat ostensible applications of quantitative methods, whereas their meaningful employment, as well as a proper evaluation of quantitative analyses, both require professional competence. On the other hand, quantitative methods of processing data may serve to identify and shape consumer needs and political preferences. Thanks to digital technologies, which enable the collection and processing of vast amounts of data (Big Data), the perspectives of the quantification of knowledge and, consequently, of the quantification of many other spheres of social and individual life, are being constantly broadened (Beer 2018). It may be said that entirely new opportunities have opened up for governing a population by means of normalization procedures.

An important qualification shall be made at this point: a key role played by quantified knowledge in the process of governing a population does not preclude enlisting the help of qualitative analyses in the service of power relations. Quite the contrary, while quantified knowledge allows for designing and implementing political and business solutions considered valid, it is not uncommon for certain types of qualitative analyses to become the other wing of "neo-liberalization": by furnishing information about alleviating tensions in the scenario of conflict and about restoring mental balance under acute stress, they form a safety cushion neutralizing potential hotbeds of unrest. At the same time, these analyses, by promoting such personal virtues as creativity, responsibility, mindfulness, and resilience, set the standard for a model employee and citizen, who, aside from not being a strain on the system, may prove to be of political and economic utility to his or her institutional surroundings. Thus, individuals become subject to twofold flanking maneuvers: the first, quantified, flank suggests macroeconomic and macropolitical solutions seen as optimal, while the other, "humanistic", flank insures a proper level of individuals' mobilization and their sense of well-being. While Foucault only associated the "security dispositives", i. e. social mechanisms for preventing "case, risk, danger, and crisis" (Foucault 2007, p. 90), with the sphere of normalization founded on quantified knowledge, it is presently worth pointing to additional means of normalization, which are focused on the management of individual psychical life.

Single case analysis as a challenge

In the context of the omnipotent rule of quantification, the qualitative methodology of social sciences seeks validation in the form of like solutions. For examples, the advocates of the so-called grounded theory approach, a model proposed by Barney G. Glaser and Anselm L. Strauss (1967), which has been vigorously developed and widely-applicable ever since, decisively call into question the significance of analyzing single cases (e. g. a single conversation, single narrative interview, single letter, single newspaper article, etc.) and prescribe the comparison of qualitative data in order to arrive at theoretical generalizations. Thus, even if for different reasons, the modern quantitative and qualitative methodologies display a very prominent tendency to deny validity to the analyses of a single case.[2]

Therefore, it is all the more important to take account of those study approaches under which analyses of a single case (aside from analyses based on a variety of materials) have been successfully employed, such as the Chicago school, contemporary biographical method, ethnomethodology, and conversation analysis. Obviously, each of these approaches has a tradition of collecting and comparing multiple research materials in order to identify and explicate a particular social phenomenon, e. g. a type of social world, a type of biographical experience, a rule of the interpretive process, a type of a conversational sequence, etc. At the same time, all of the aforementioned approaches engage in the practice of single case analysis, which stands for studies based on an extensive examination of some isolated material. For the sake of clarity, it has to be added that single case analysis is not the same as case analysis, i. e. a study of

---

2 Some interesting inconsistencies, or perhaps evidence of certain "methodological self-misunderstanding", may be observed in empirical works by Anselm Strauss, some of which, such as *Social Organization of Medical Work* or *Mirrors and Masks*, partly rely on the single case analysis procedure (this fact was brought to my attention by Gerhard Riemann).

one complex social object, such as local community, enterprise, or family, with the use of multiple qualitative and quantitative methods (cf. Ragin / Becker 1992).

The following remarks will thus concern the single case analysis perspective. This study perspective is an alternative to the dominant quantitative or qualitative methods of analyzing multiple data. Consequently, it seems to be of particular significance to develop a methodological argumentation which will not only defend the application of single case analyses, but also demonstrate the potential advantages of this research approach. At the core of this argumentation are benefits which may arise from a qualitative sequential analysis of a single case, especially on the count of generating theoretical concepts concerning the rules of interpretive processes.

Single case analysis, though marginalized and overpowered by the prevailing quantitative and qualitative approaches based on data comparisons, is not an outlandish idea aimed at standing out against the methodological doxa, but a respectable tradition boasting serious achievements which have left their mark in the history of sociological analyses, to list just a few examples:

- in the field of the Chicago school – *The Jack-Roller: A Delinquent Boy's Own Story* (Shaw 1966 [1930]), a monograph based on the biography of a single person;
- in the field of the contemporary biographical method – *Pressure and Guilt: War Experiences of a Young German Soldier and Their Biographical Implications* (Schütze 1992), a study based on an analysis of a single narrative interview;
- in the field of ethnomethodology – *Passing and the Managed Achievement of Sex Status in an 'Intersexed' Person* (Garfinkel 1967, p. 116–185), a study based on an analysis of the transition of a single person (Agnes) who was contacted by Garfinkel over a longer time span;
- in the field of conversation analysis – *'K is Mentally Ill': The Anatomy of a Factual Account* (Smith 1978), an analysis of a single interview;
- in the field of so-called reanalyses, i. e. analyses concerning old materials but conducted with the use of new methods of qualitative analysis – *Suizidalität als Prozess* (Riemann 2007), a reanalysis of Wallace Baker's diary, originally posted and analyzed by Ruth Shonle Cavan (1928).

The theory-related paradox of single case analyses consists in the fact that such studies, while obviously concerning single cases, are supposed to be of analytical significance which extends beyond these unique examples. The following may be observed with respect to the publications listed:

- *The Jack-Roller*, an autobiographical account of one's own delinquency record, has become a valuable contribution to what was subsequently labeled

"deviant career", as well as to the discussion on how society should treat
juvenile delinquency;
- *Pressure and Guilt,* an analysis of a narrative interview with a former Wehr-
macht soldier, offers new hypotheses on the process of the formation of gaps
in collective memory;
- *Passing and the Managed Achievement of Sex Status in an 'Intersexed' Person,*
a study of a single case of transition, is still an important record of the early
stages of the sociological reflection on, and social perception of, gender
transition in American society (additionally, it seems to be of continued
relevance in the context of present-day conservative societies, such as Polish
society);
- *'K is mentally ill'* is an article which is a microcosmic account of the process
whereby we start to perceive someone who we know very well as a "mentally
ill" person;
- *Suizidalität als Prozess,* a reanalysis of the diary of a suicidal person who
eventually committed suicide, retraces an individual biographical process of a
suicidal person, and at the same time points to collective representations
exerting influence (which is often destructive) on what individuals think of,
and feel about, themselves.

Thus, analyses of single cases, thanks to their local focus, pave the way for the
formulation of theoretical hypotheses or even theoretical generalizations, or for
an overarching reflection, whereby a specific single case may serve as an illustration of a broader phenomenon. Two stances on this issue seem of particular
importance.

Fritz Schütze (2021, p. 15ff), a co-founder of the contemporary biographical
method, observes the delegitimization of single case analysis, mostly in Ger-
manophone qualitative research, and offers two arguments against this "ex-
pulsion" (Verbannung). First, a contrastive comparison of multiple data should
not be seen as the only way of arriving at theoretical generalizations. An alternative is an in-depth sequential analysis of a single processual case (e.g. a biography, autobiography, family history, text, conversation, interaction, negotiation, meeting, event, demonstration, institutional process, etc.), which allows
for identifying the formative mechanisms of social processes, and as such aids the
formation of a theory. Second, a detailed qualitative-reconstructive single case
analysis is always, almost by default, a comparative analysis, because, among
other things, a single material has to be captured in general, intersubjectively
comprehensible terms.

While Schütze's arguments bring up the question of the scope of valid generalizations enabled by single case analyses, the ethnomethodological approach
effectively sets aside the problem of representativeness. Although his prime re-

search focus is on the social organization of practical actions within laboratory science, Michael Lynch, a student and intellectual successor of Harold Garfinkel, the founder of ethnomethodology, suggests an ethnomethodological approach to conversation analysis (Lynch 2001). Under a standard model, the order of a conversation is considered in terms of conversational rules and norms which the interlocutors follow or violate. Ethnomethodological conversation analysis, just as ethnomethodology itself, turns the problem upside down (or rather puts it right side up) and deals with the reconstruction of the process of manufacturing conversational order in the course of the interlocutors' interpretive work: "The concerted production of intelligible lines of talk is both the subject and the source of such analysis" (ibid., p. 141). In particular, conversation analysis is concerned with local ways of applying conversational rules and norms which assume the form of indications exchanged by the interlocutors as to interpreting the current, singular situation as the validation, adaptation, or violation of a rule or norm: "To a larger extent, conversation analysts describe the work of replicating social technologies on singular occasions" (ibid., p. 150). It may be worth elaborating this picture by including an aspect underestimated in conversation analysis, i.e. that of the inter- and intracultural differences pertaining to conversational rules and norms. After all, the "social technologies" of holding conversations are culture-specific. Therefore, using conversational norms and rules on singular occasions may reflect culture-specific norms and rules.

Three features of the conversation analysis of a single case

Of particular interest to this article are the benefits which may arise from a focused analysis of a singular conversational material. This issue is discussed through the prism of the findings of ethnomethodological conversation analysis.

First, it is worth noting the strong validation of single case analysis offered by conversation analysis. If the radical version of conversation analysis is adopted, single case analysis proves to be a necessary research approach. Needless to say, a prerequisite of a successful quantitative analysis from the methodological perspective is the possibility to extract occurrences of a particular description, which are then to be treated as analogical, commensurable items subject to quantification regardless of their contextual specificity. The sociology of quantification would reverse this relation: it is quantification that insures commensurability of incommensurable occurrences, or, to be precise, it makes it possible to treat incommensurable phenomena as commensurable. In conversation analysis, these items should be various conversational events: single conversations, single episodes of interaction (cf. Schegloff 1987), local categorizations, or local interconnections between sequential order (i.e. the formation of interconnections between individual utterances) and categorial order (i. e. the formation of categories relating to persons directly or indirectly involved in a situation). But in each of these cases, these would be occurrences whose decontextualization would be against the rules of the research procedure under conversation analysis. Put differently, it is not certain if a qualitative analysis aimed at reconstructing the contextual placement of conversation events would even meet the preliminary and basic criteria of quantitative analysis (cf. Schegloff 1993, p. 103).

In addition, even if it was possible to sensibly extract conversation events from their local contexts (which would require meeting a basic condition that can effectively never be met, i. e. there would have to be no significant differences between these local contexts), a result of a rudimentary quantitative analysis (and at the same time the point of departure for further, more complex statistical analyses) could be the identification of a quantitative regularity of the occurrence of particular conversation events. However, ethnomethodological conversation analysis is not concerned with quantitative regularities of conversation events, but rather with ways of local interpretation of conversational rules (cf. the early formulation of this problem in Eglin 1975). In other words, conversation analysis looks for the rules of conversation "to which" conversation participants are oriented, or rules which conversation participants, in specific, singular cases, maintain, modify, combine with other aspects of conversational order, and, most importantly, such whose breaching they label as a deviation. Thus, for ethnomethodological conversation analysis, it is not important how frequently certain conversation events occur: what matters is how the local interpretation of conversational rules determines the sequential formation of conversational order, or, from a different perspective, the fact that the interlocutors, talking to each other in a particular way, express to themselves and to the others the way in which they interpret the course of the conversation. For instance, what matters is not so much the frequency of the occurrence of a pre-closing sequence before a closing sequence, as the fact of whether and in what way the lack of a pre-closing sequence (i. e. proceeding to a closing sequence by one of the interlocutors without backing it up with a pre-closing sequence first) is noticed or rectified by the participants of the conversation.

Finally, with reference to the first argument and by way of its further elaboration, it is worth pointing to a somewhat "paradigmatic" difference between the quantitative approach and comparative qualitative approach (such as grounded theory approach) on the one hand, and the qualitative analysis of a single case on the other. The quantitative approach – in the form in which it prevails in social sciences and is employed for governing a population as a whole, its parts, or the personnel of a particular company or institution – is based on the assumption that singular cases are characterized by generalization-resistant idiosyncrasies, while order may be only described on the aggregate level, once singular peculiarities have been filtered out and quantitative procedures have been applied to the extracted and commensurable features of single cases. This direction has been taken by comparative qualitative analysis, which (similarly to quantitative analysis) considers single case analyses invalid and calls for the processing ("coding") of multiple cases, seeing it as a prerequisite for drawing theoretical generalizations. A different "analytical mentality" (to use Jim Schenkein's apt formulation) is adopted by ethnomethodological conversation analysis. Emanuel Schegloff (1993, p. 117) proposes the following hypothesis on this matter: "In contrast to much of the subject matter of the social sciences - which has been taken to be fundamentally *in*determinate at the level of individual occurrences and orderly only at the aggregate statistical level – conduct in talk-in-interaction *could* then appear to be demonstrably orderly *at the level of the singular occurrence only* and, in effect, *not* orderly in any distinctive, relevant, or precisely determinable way in the aggregate".

The ethnomethodological profile of conversation analysis means that the single case analyses under this perspective stand out on another two counts (aside from the particularly strong validation): one is accountability, while the other is the methodical character of research procedure.

Accountability is a key ethnomethodological term (Garfinkel 1967, p. 1 ff) and refers to a constant process of producing verbal and non-verbal indications which the participants of a situation give to themselves and to each other to make "observable-and-reportable" how they interpret their own and others' activities. Importantly, these interpretive indications are performed in and through these very activities. That way, an ethnomethodological investigation, and consequently, ethnomethodological conversation analysis, consists in reconstructing the ways in which the participants of a situation interpret the activities they are engaged in. It is precisely in the course of and through doing conversational activities accountable that the local conversational order is gradually taking shape, in its two basic interconnected aspects of sequential order and categorial order.

It is useful to distinguish the ethnomethodological understanding of accountability (we shall label it "Accountability 1") from two further meanings of this term. "Accountability 2" refers to the commonsensical understanding – which is clearly "non-ethnomethodological" but common in social sciences – of the procedure of commenting on occurrences in which one does not participate. A single "account" is a comment (a statement or gesture) which is not part of the situation to which it refers. An analysis of "Accountability 2" is focused on the mode in which the comment refers to the events or phenomena commented upon, and consists in e.g. identifying the "accounts" in the sense of Scott and Lyman's (1968) well-known proposition (e.g. deciding if an account present in the material analyzed is a "justification" or an "excuse").

It is worth adding that the meaning of "Accountability 2" partly overlaps with dictionary definitions of the word "accountability". According to *Merriam-Webster Dictionary*, "accountability" is "the quality or state of being accountable", while "accountable" means "answerable" or "explainable". *Oxford Advanced Learner's Dictionary* takes it a step further and explains "accountable" as "responsible for your decisions or actions and expected to explain them when you are asked"[3]. Of significance, however, is the difference between the analytical term of "Accountability 2" and dictionary definitions of the word: the former refers to speech patterns which do not necessarily entail taking or enforcing responsibility, while the latter denote actual states (i.e. precisely taking or enforcing responsibility).

The meaning of the ethnomethodological notion of accountability (i.e. "Accountability 1") may now be fine-tuned: "Accountability 1" (unlike "Accountability 2") does not pertain to any particular, hand-picked means of offering (to oneself and to others) interpretations of ongoing activities, but to any and all potential verbal and nonverbal ways of doing it, and achieves this effect (as already mentioned) in and through these activities. In particular, "Accountability 1" is not limited to interpretive practices which could function as a justification or excuse. Still, just like "Accountability 2", "Accountability 1" also does not refer to an actual explication of the meaning of a particular activity, but to its interpretations, which may – "here and now", in a specific context – suffice "for all practical purposes" (in the words of Alfred Schütz).

"Accountability 3" is again a non-ethnomethodological, cultural dimension of the meanings of single statements, texts, or conversations which goes beyond the local context and refers to how a broader social reality is formed through its publicly available interpretations. A local communicational and meta-communicational activity in a given situation sometimes becomes part of a larger set of phenomena (e.g. political changes in a particular society). A case in point is Martin Luther King's famous "I have a dream" phrase, which was a fragment of a particular address delivered in specific local conditions, but at the same time became a powerful symbol of collective political mobilization.

Ethnomethodology, and ethnomethodological conversation analysis in particular, stresses a "methodical" character of its procedure. This is not in the sense of employing methods of data collection and processing which emerged in the course of the development of social sciences, such as the structured interview, survey, or grounded theory approach. The reality thus analyzed would be classified under the logic of collecting and processing data. Under a radically different ethnomethodological perspective, the job of a researcher is to reconstruct

---

3 See: https://www.merriam-webster.com/dictionary/accountable; and https://www.oxfordlearnersdictionaries.com/definition/english/accountable?q=accountable.

the interpretive methods which the actors of social life adopt while engaging in their activities. Therefore, the "methodical" character of the procedure is not imposed onto the allegedly disorderly, idiosyncrasies-riddled subject of the study. On the contrary, it is a result of a researcher's embracement of the challenge of reconstructing the interpretive methods which are part of the object of research and determine its "methodical", internally and locally ordered character. In other words, a researcher's job is to follow, step by step, the process of interpretation which unfolds in the reality analyzed, and to explicate this process. Applications of this "analytical mentality" may be observed in various texts anchored in conversation analysis, to mention just two important reference points in this respect, namely, the lectures of Harvey Sacks (1992a, 1992b), the originator of conversation analysis, and Emanuel A. Schegloff's (2007) introduction to sequential conversation analysis.

In the preliminary analysis of the single case which follows, I will be mostly referring to "Accountability 1", with only marginal remarks on "Accountability 2" and "Accountability 3". Therefore, I will focus on an attempt to reconstruct the interpretive process which determines the internally and locally ordered, "methodical" character of the material analyzed.

A single case analysis – the opening passage in *The Trial*

Unlike linguists and literary scholars, conversation analysts are chiefly concerned with naturally occurring data, i. e. conversations which are not pre-arranged by the researcher, such as colloquial conversations, conversations held in class, or as part of a radio or TV program. Moreover, they are not interested in analyzing artificial conversations, made up for research purposes, nor dialogs taken from works of literary fiction[4]. This analysis, though, concerns literary material, namely, the opening conversation of Franz Kafka's *The Trial*. This is a widely-known dialog, which has received numerous interpretations on multiple occasions. Many commentators believe that its literary gravitas arises not only from its unusual, cryptic course, but also from the fact that, just as in the case of *The Castle*, another grand novel by Kafka, the opening sequence seems to capture the symbolic meaning of the entire story in a nutshell. It is not my intention to challenge the existing interpretations of *The Trial* or its opening part, since conversation analysis does not have at its disposal the resources of in-depth literary and philosophical analyses. Actually, compared to a wide range of in-

---

4 An overview of the achievements of literary studies in the field of analyzing literary dialogs is beyond the scope of this article. Some of the relevant studies are Skwarczyńska 1932 (an early learned text only available in Polish), Hess-Lüttich 1980, Betten / Dannerer 2005.

terpretive possibilities afforded by said models, the research apparatus of conversation analysis is extremely modest, not to say limited. Still, this modest apparatus may offer notable cognitive benefits: it can help unveil a conversation's interactional scaffolding, or, in other words, retrace the gradual manufacturing of conversational order.

Most applications of conversation analysis concern the sequential order of conversation, i.e. the order of turn-taking, as the consecutive utterances of the interlocutors gradually intertwine. *A Simplest Systematics for the Organization of Turn-Taking for Conversation* (Sacks / Schegloff / Jefferson 1974) is still a classical publication in the field. A less frequently explored path under conversation analysis is Membership Categorization Analysis (MCA), where the focus is on the order of categorizations pertaining to individuals, which emerges in the course of a conversation. The latter approach was also founded by Harvey Sacks, who performed a reconstruction of categorizations relied on by suicidal persons calling a helpline and described it in one of his early articles, *The Search for Help: No One to Turn to* (Sacks 1967). A problematic feature of a bulk of the findings of conversation analysis is the fact that usually the analyses of turn-taking make no reference to categorial order, and the other way around, i.e. many categorization analyses do not attempt to reconstruct the way in which categorial order combines with sequential order.

Seminal arguments in favor of combining both strands of conversation analysis were presented by Rodney Watson (e.g. in 1997 and 2015). Under this approach, seeing as its research focus is on the interactional nature of categorial order, a misleading temptation to treat categorizations as static sets resembling cognitive maps is avoided. At the same time, a comprehensive look at conversational materials encourages not just a mere reconstruction of turn-taking, but also a thorough analysis of the interconnection between sequential order and categorial order. Taking both these aspects into account, Watson picks up and elaborates on the ideas which are included in Sacks' (1992a, 1992b) lectures and have been mostly neglected in the course of the further development of conversation analysis. Aside from those categorizations which are not entirely connected with turn-taking, such as the interlocutors' age, gender, or occupation, Watson, following Sacks, points to local "turn-generated categories" and "category-generated turns" (Sacks 1992b, p. 360ff, Watson 1997, p. 66ff)[5].

Therefore, on the one hand, Harvey Sacks points to "identities for conversation" which are determined by sequential order and, referring to opening sequences of phone calls, posits "the caller-called category pair". Emanuel Schegloff (1968), analyzing opening sequences not just in phone calls, but also in face-to-face conversations, writes about "roles" to which he attaches more gen-

---

5 Sacks' lecture of 19 April 1971.

eral labels of "summoner" and "summoned". In this and other publications, Schegloff focuses on sequential analysis and does not scrutinize the interconnections between sequential order and categorial order. Rodney Watson, in turn, notices that it was Sacks who had already paved the way for analyzing these interconnections, having made "a crucial move from *categories* toward *categorization practices* [...]. This is not only the case in relations to categorisation, but also to the situations of which such categorization practices are a part" (Watson 2015, p. 29). Recent studies in the field of Membership Categorization Analysis (Fitzgerald / Housley 2015) have also taken this direction. One of the consequences of such an approach is a suggestion to abandon the term "role", and to use such terms as "category", "categorization", and "categorization practices". At the same time, it seems reasonable to retain Schegloff's "summoner-summoned" pair, as it is more general than the notion of the "caller-called". Consequently, my suggestion is to combine the respective terminologies of the aforesaid authors and refer to "the summoner-summoned category pair".

On the other hand, Sacks notices a reverse situation, whereby interactionally-mobilized identities relating to culturally defined social statuses (pertaining to e.g. the social standing relevant to age or – in my opinion – also to the performance of an institutional role, for instance that of a teacher) translate into who stakes a claim to be in charge of local management of turn-taking, e.g. by deciding who is to ask questions and who is to see to it that they will be answered.

As the following analysis will show, the claim to control turn-taking does not have to follow from the impact of social statuses of the interlocutors, but may also arise simply from within the ongoing interaction. It is worth noting that these circumstances are an argument for a cautious treatment of differences between institutional talk and ordinary talk. In both cases, conversational order is manufactured locally, which means that institutionally rooted identities do not influence turn-taking either, unless they are in situ mobilized[6].

In order not to invite possible misleading associations with Generative Grammar, Watson (2015: 33–34) introduces, in lieu of the terms of "turn-generated categories" and "category-generated turns", those of "turn-produced categories", or "turn-formed categories", and "category-formed turns". In addition, it also seems necessary to avoid a false impression that both variants describing relations between sequential order and categorial order involve a unidirectional action (of "generating", "producing", or "forming" an outcome). For that reason, by way of another terminological modification, the following analysis will be employing, respectively, the terms of "turn-configured categories" and "category-configured turns".

---

6 Rod Watson's arguments regarding this matter are presented in Maria Wowk and Andrew Carlin (2004, p. 79 ff).

It is also worth noting that in conversation analysis, the most basic conversational sequence, which is composed of two interrelated utterances (e.g. question – answer, summon – answer, etc.), is referred to as the adjacency pair.

Reproduced below is the series of adjacency pairs which may be extracted from the opening passage of Franz Kafka's *The Trial*.[7] The transcript takes the form similar to a simplified transcription format used in conversation analysis. For the sake of clarity, each adjacency pair is given a number.

K. = K. (main character in *The Trial*)
F. = "the strange man" (in German original: der "fremde Mann")
N. = someone in the neighboring room

1. K.: [rings the bell]
    F.: [knocks at the door and enters]

2. K.: Who are you?
    F.: You rang?

3. K.: Anna should bring me the breakfast
    F.: He wants Anna to bring him his breakfast
    N.: laughter
    F.: It is not possible

4. K.: It would be the first time that's happened. I want to see who that is in the next room, and why it is that Mrs. Grubach has let me be disturbed in this way.
    F.: Don't you think you'd better stay where you are?

5. K.: I want neither to stay here nor to be spoken to by you until you've introduced yourself
    F.: It was well meant

Let me add that on two occasions, I have taken the liberty of departing from the Muirs' classical translation, a decision informed by the comparison of their version with Kafka's original. The first deviation concerns the first part of the third adjacency pair: Kafka's "Anna soll mir das Frühstück bringen" would correspond to "Anna should bring me the breakfast", rather than "Anna should have brought me my breakfast". The original wording (on the surface level, at least) conveys an expectation that something should take place, rather than irritation that what usually happens has not happened this time around. The other alteration concerns the second part of the fifth adjacency pair: German "Es

---

7 I am principally relying on Willa and Edwin Muir's classical translation of Kafka's book (1999 [1937]). In the integral text of the novel, the subsequent adjacency pairs are obviously embedded in the story's wider context. It is worth noting that the narrative's tone is mysterious and has no elements of auctorial enunciation. This tone is consistent with the indications of irritation, uncertainty, and confusion, which K.'s utterances resonate with, and which I will analyze exclusively with the use of the conversation analytic research apparatus. For the integral text of the opening passage, see: Appendix.

war gut gemeint" corresponds to "It was well meant", and not "I meant it for your own good". In this case, Mike Mitchell's new translation seems more adequate (Kafka 2009, p. 5). Finally, let us note that both German editions of *The Trial* – Max Brod's well-known version (Kafka 1983 [1925]) and the edition closely following Kafka's manuscript (Kafka 1994) – although differing from each other in a number of important aspects, are consistent in their treatment of the dialog in question (bar a slight difference in the spelling of one word).

The following remarks offer one possible way of reconstructing the interactional "scaffolding" of the conversation quoted. This "scaffolding" will prove shaky, while the interlocutors will, at the same time, rock it still further and then support it.

1. K.: [rings the bell]
    F.: [knocks at the door and enters]

The first two lines of the transcript are a two-part sequence in the form of an adjacency pair, where the first turn is a summon, and the second turn is the answer to it: K. rings a bell, F. enters the room. F.'s entering the room constitutes an interpretation of K.'s ringing as a summon. While both parts of this sequence are of non-verbal character, it is clear from how the interaction develops that it leads to a further conversational exchange, and thus serves as an opening sequence. In this local case, the interconnectedness of the sequential order and the categorial order manifests in the fact that it is the interaction-initiating summon-answer sequence, happening here and now, that "configures" the pair of situationally adequate identities which correspond to this sequence, namely, a summoner-summoned category pair. Consequently, a "turn-configured categories" pair is being produced.

2. K.: Who are you?
    F.: You rang?

The second adjacency pair begins with K.'s utterance, "Who are you?", which is a retrospective interpretation of F.'s previous conduct. With his utterance, K. indicates to F. that something expected to have happened did not, in fact, happen: on entering the room, F. did not identify himself[8]. Put differently, K. points out to F. that his previous utterance is "repairable". At the same time, K. is trying to design the further course of the conversation by suggesting self-repair, which F. could perform by introducing himself. Under conversation analytic terminology, it could be said that K. is attempting to urge F. to engage in "other-initiated self-

---

8 Cf. Harvey Sacks' remarks on how interlocutors identify and go about the fact that "something didn't happen" in a conversation (Sacks 1992a, pp. 293 ff). This issue is discussed by Michael Lynch (2001, p. 141 ff).

repair"[9]. From the perspective of the relations between sequential order and categorial order, it is worth noting that K., in his freshly established local capacity as a "summoner", stakes a claim to a "category-configured turn". In other words, K. as a "summoner" claims that F. should produce a turn K. requires form him, namely, that F. should introduce himself; or, in general, K. claims that he should be in control of the local management of turn-taking. However, K.'s proposition ends in failure, since F. not so much rejects K.'s claim as ignores it, does not identify himself, and answers with a question: his "You rang?" utterance is a retrospective interpretation of the "Who are you?" question not as a request to introduce himself (this most obvious interpretation of K.'s utterance is ignored by F.), but as K.'s apparent verbal processing of the first adjacency pair. On this occasion, F. offers a verbal answer to this initial summon and thus, in a sense, returns to the first adjacency pair and verbally complements its first part. At the same time, F. communicates to K. that what is happening is nothing out of the ordinary: he entered the room because K. rang.

3. K.: Anna should bring me the breakfast
   F.: He wants Anna to bring him his breakfast
   N.: laughter
   F.: It is not possible

The third sequence has four elements and follows the pattern of K. – [F. – N.] – F. Thus, this sequence is not a simple two-element adjacency pair, but includes an inserted expansion constructed out of an additional adjacency pair [F. – N.][10]. First, K. reasserts his claim to a "category-configured turn". This time, K. as a locally established "summoner" claims that Anna (on behalf of his landlady, Mrs. Grubach) should bring him his breakfast. In the fourth part of the sequence, F. decidedly dismisses K.'s request ("It is not possible") and thus demonstrates to him that another claim of his to a "category-configured turn" cannot be realized either. Intervening between the sequence's first and fourth elements is an insert sequence: through the half-opened door, F. is sharing an ironic comment with someone in the neighboring room, "He wants Anna to bring him his breakfast", which prompts this person to giggle. Thus, F.'s dismissal of K.'s request in the fourth part of the sequence is additionally supported: the rejection is not just consistent with F.'s stance, but also with that of another, unspecified social entity.

4. K.: It would be the first time that's happened. I want to see who that is in the next
        room, and why it is that Mrs. Grubach has let me be disturbed in this way.
   F.: Don't you think you'd better stay where you are?

---

9 Repair types in conversation are presented in Schegloff / Jefferson / Sacks (1977).
10 The types of insert expansions are discussed by Emanuel Schegloff (2007, p. 97 ff.).

The fourth sequence is another adjacency pair. Its first part, K.'s utterance, contains another one of K.'s claims ("I want to") to the control over the course of interaction. More specifically, it contains K.'s claim to two category-configured turns: K. claims the right to see who is in the neighboring room, and he also claims the right to hold Mrs. Grubach responsible for the disturbance. K.'s claims to the control over the course of interaction are an indirect admission that it is F. who is in charge of the situation. Once again, F. does not satisfy K.'s demands. F.'s utterance, the second part of the fourth adjacency pair ("Don't you think you'd better stay where you are?"), takes matters further than his utterance in the previous adjacency pair did. While this earlier utterance by F. ("It is not possible") was a direct, point-blank rejection of K.'s request, this one, though formulated hortatively (and thus formally meeting politeness criteria), contains F.'s "counter-claim" to a category-configured turn: now, it is F. who claims he should be in control of the course of the interaction.

5. K.: I want neither to stay here nor to be spoken to by you until you've introduced yourself
   F.: It was well meant

The fifth sequence is also an adjacency pair. In its first part, K. rejects F.'s "counter-claim" and repeats his claim to a category-configured turn which he already formulated within the second adjacency pair: K. claims he is allowed to require from F. that F. should introduce himself, or, in general, K. claims that he should be in control of the turn-taking. What is more, K. presents his claim as the condition for his continued presence in the room and further participation in the conversation ("until you've introduced yourself"). F.'s answer is short: "It was well meant". Yet again, F. does not grant K.'s request (he does not identify himself), while his actual utterance is a retrospective interpretation of K.'s utterance as a misplaced allegation, and a dismissal of this allegation.

It is noteworthy that K.'s utterances in the fourth and fifth sequence are longer and more elaborate than F.'s. In addition, starting in the second sequence, K. repeatedly indicates to F. that his conduct is inappropriate. Meanwhile, F.'s conduct is composed, and it indicates to K., in a polite but decisive manner, that it is K.'s conduct that is inappropriate. At the same time, a local formation of power relations in an interaction is taking place: K. is contesting the current situation and is trying, unsuccessfully, to change it, while F. remains unmoved and retains his dominant position.

In the conversation inspected, the relations between sequential order and categorial order are dynamic and tense, while the gradually emerging overall conversational order is shaky. This is particularly true for the "identities for conversation", which – as I have tried to demonstrate – are unstable. It appears that Watson's (2015) perspective of "de-reifying categories" receives additional

support, which allows for questioning reification residues already present in
Sacks' analyses. Sacks (1992b, p. 163) states the following: "A thing that called
['summoned'] can hardly ever get out from under is that they are the called ['the
summoned'] and the other is the caller ['the summoner'], and that there are all
kinds of things affiliated with that"[11]. But the conversation analyzed in this article
suggests that some alternative circumstances can be in situ produced where the
"called" (or, in the terminology proposed here, the "summoned"; in the conversation studied, it is F who is an incumbent of this category) is indeed able to
"get out from under". Such cases may happen, but they may also be marked by
the interlocutors as strange, inappropriate, disturbing, etc. This would mean – as
Watson (1997, p. 70) puts it – that the "'caller'-'called' categories ['summoner'-
'summoned' categories] are a phenomenon that telephone interlocutors [inter-
locutors in a conversation of any kind] perceive as a pervasive constraint, as
something that, for instance '... called ['summoned'] can hardly get out from
under ...'". Consequently, there is a difference between a conclusion that "the
called ['the summoned'] can hardly ever get out from under" and the *perception*
of "a pervasive constraint" on this count, where "perception" refers, as it seems,
to an interpretation of the situation as displayed in and through activities of
participants of a situation.

The analysis presented was an attempt to reconstruct "Accountability 1", i.e.
the ways in which the participants of a situation – in and through the activities
they are engaged in – interpret these very activities. To be sure, this was just a
simplified outline of the ongoing orderliness of the conversation. There are
numerous other phenomena which should be included in a more detailed
analysis. One possible way of further elaborating this analysis would consist in
taking account of a conversation analytic notion of conditional relevance. This
term refers to the relations between the first and second parts of an adjacency
pair. The first part of an adjacency pair projects a particular gamut of utterances
which may be interpreted in various ways, but always as a relevant second part of
this adjacency pair. On the other hand, the non-occurrence of such utterance
(either in the form of silence or an utterance from outside the scope of conditional relevance) is "heard" as conspicuous absence. For example, a greeting (e.g.
"Hello") creates a rather narrow spectrum of conditional relevance, which does
not embrace the other person's silence or their utterance along the lines of,
"What time is it?" It is apparent that in the suggested analysis of the opening
dialog from *The Trial*, the disturbance of the standard functioning of the turn-
taking machinery is about F.'s notorious flouting of the relevance rules, seeing as

11 The quotation comes from Harvey Sacks' first lecture in the 1970 winter semester. Cf. also Rod
    Watson's remarks (1997, p. 67 ff). Insertions in square brackets (here and in the subsequent
    quotations) are mine.

his utterances miss the relevance spectrum projected by what K. says. These violations are repeatedly indicated by K.'s utterances, which at the same time demand – to no avail – that the routine mechanism of combining both parts of adjacency pairs be restored. It is precisely in this sphere that that the process of "Accountability 1", reconstructed above, was taking place.

In his description of conditional relevance, Emanuel Schegloff (2009, p. 20) emphasizes that the non-occurrence of a relevant second pair part "is as much an event as its occurrence would have been". Schegloff's remark underlines that the process of "Accountability 1" also takes place when conditional relevance is not violated, and the conversation unfolds in a routine and undisturbed manner, as the interlocutors indicate to each other "in and through" their particular utterances. Thus, in the ethnomethodological conversation analysis, the individual turns in a conversation – aside from being capable of conveying specific meanings – are looked on as carriers of hints which serve to make the very same conversation "accountable". One of the aspects of the ongoing "Accountability 1" is establishing *in situ* whether the current conversation is routine or not, and determining which pattern of conversational routine – or of upsetting this routine – is produced by the speakers. It is worth noting that K.'s utterances suggest that in his view, the problem is not merely about the fact that the conversation is non-routine, and that F.'s statements fail to conform to conventional politeness standards: an unexpected situation cannot be captured in the available patterns which K. could rely on to determine what type of a fundamental violation of conversational routine he is looking at. On the other hand, F.'s utterances imply that he believes to be engaged in a routine conversation, and to be facing a regrettable lack of understanding on K.'s part. This mismatch on the level of defining a situation proves an additional complication to K.'s attempts to handle the situation by "pigeonholing" its sense.

In addition, in view of the wide recognizability of the conversation between K. and F. and numerous attempts to interpret its (various) symbolic meanings, account should be taken of a special culture-specific impact of the opening fragment of *The Trial*, which falls under "Accountability 3". Looking at the entire story, including the initial passages taken to be an emblematic display of the alleged message of the novel, different critics identified allegories of various ideas: from the enslavement of man in a totalitarian system, to the helplessness of the individual trapped in the absurd maze of bureaucracy, to the existential position of the individual vis-à-vis transcendence. The book's curious power of evoking allegorical readings (similar to that wielded by *The Castle*) was at one point ironically analyzed by Susan Sontag (1966), who later revisited her own early interpretation of Kafka's works (Sontag 1996). The uniqueness of Kafka's output is also worth considering from the perspective of "Accountability 2". It is striking how little it takes for critics to pigeonhole Kafka's texts, and how ready they are to replace a personal, private reading, which requires effort and open-mindedness, with some cheap cliches. It is precisely this tendency that prompted Susan Sontag to give her essay the title of *Against Interpretation* (1966). Let us add that another side effect of the hasty pigeonholing of Kafka's works is the popularity of the cliched and pseudo-intellectual expression "Kafkaesque situation".

Consequently, since it is enabled by the book's repeated interpretations aimed at extracting deeper meanings, the continued presence of *The Trial* in culture is ambivalent. On the one hand, it testifies to an extraordinary status of this book, while on the other, it implies the widespread popularity of the perfectly ordinary methods of handling this extraordinariness. An analysis of "Accountability 2" and "Accountability 3" with reference to *The Trial*, as well as of the relations between these and "Accountability 1" present in this text, is a discrete, compelling research task. However, the main focus of this article is on internal accountability, i. e. "Accountability 1". Edgar Allan Poe's (2006, p.252) observation, though formulated in an entirely different context, may serve as the grounds for the type of analysis suggested here: "Truth is not always in a well. In fact, as regards the more important knowledge, I do believe that she is invariably superficial. The depth lies in the valleys where we seek her, and not upon the mountain-tops where she is found".

A few remarks on a certain TV Interview

This volume offers different analyses of the same singular material, that is, the 3 October 2011 interview which Tomasz Lis, a popular Polish journalist, conducted with Jarosław Kaczyński, chairman of the Law and Justice party. A question thus arises as to the relations between these different analyses, together with a broader question: what can be the actual relations between different analyses of any given singular conversational material? The latter, more general, question suggests an answer pointing to a more comprehensive look at the data, following from the complementary character of individual analyses. Unfortunately, different analyses of one case usually make no references to each other, and since they sometimes adopt very different research perspectives, their interrelations are captured in perspectivist terms: perspective A leads to findings X, perspective B leads to findings Y, etc. That way, an otherwise valuable principle of mutual respect takes precedence over the much-needed discussion between proponents of distinct research perspectives, a discussion which – although likely to generate frictions and controversies – may usher in new ideas.

For the purposes of this collection of analyses, I would like to put forward another proposition. It could be encapsulated in a question as to whether and to what extent conversation analysis may furnish analytical tools allowing for a preliminary reconstruction of a material's formal features, whose multifaceted complementation could come with analyses based on other research perspectives. This question alone may be problematic under a number of different methodologies, such as those characterized by strong social involvement (e.g. the radical variants of Critical Discourse Analysis), which reject the possibility of an impartial reconstruction of the basic formal matrix of discourse material; those which emphasize the incoherence and fragmentariness of discourse (e.g. post-structuralism); and those for which an analysis of discourse materials is inextricably connected with their non-discursive surroundings (e.g. dispositive analysis). For that reason, my proposition is not intended as a manifesto, but as an invitation to open discussion.

Two issues need to be considered: one concerns any conversational materials, including the Lis-Kaczyński interview, while the other pertains to said interview in particular. In both cases, I will be referring to my earlier analysis of Franz Kafka's *The Trial*.

In early conversation analysis, the first problem was formulated as the "context free" vs. "context sensitive" issue. With reference to the turn-taking organization of conversation, a question was posed as to whether it is possible to perform an analysis which "would have the important twin features of being context-free and capable of extraordinary context-sensitivity" (Sacks / Schegloff / Jefferson 1974, p. 699). As suggested above, it is worth expanding the scope of this question to include the realm of categorial order and the relations between sequential order and categorial order. Therefore, the extended question is as follows: can the resources of conversation analysis be used to describe the basic features of the conversational order of any given conversation in such a way so as to be able to take account of possibly diverse situational realizations of conversational order? For conversation analysis, this is a question of major significance, seeing as individual conversational events under this perspective are in many respects treated as completely unique: "There is virtually nothing in talk-in-interaction which can get done unilaterally, and virtually nothing which is thoroughly pre-scripted" (Schegloff 1996, p. 22). A critical task of conversation analysis is to illustrate "how the kind of *formal* analysis of sequence organization [Schegloff does not go beyond the realm of sequential order; in line with the argumentation advanced in this text, it is worth adopting a broader perspective of a formal analysis of conversational organization] [...] – analysis which is of necessity maximally trans-situational – needs to be complemented by examination of the idiosyncratic, contextually specific details that make this *kind* of action sequence into this *singular* sequence of that kind – in *its* context, with *these* parties, at *this* point in the interaction, doing actions inflected by *these* circumstances, etc." (Schegloff 2007, p. 256).

This seems to be of key importance also in view of a somewhat reverse perspective of single case analysis. Ultimately, it is conversational single cases that the general features of conversational order (such as the principle of accountability, as well as the general rules of sequential order, categorial order, and the relations between the two) are extracted from, together with a reconstruction of their local unique instantiations. An analysis along these lines was earlier attempted in this article with reference to the dialog from *The Trial*.

The other issue touches upon a question as to the similarities and differences between the dialog from *The Trial* and the conversational features of the Lis-Kaczyński interview. Obviously, the comparison may only concern those features of conversational order whose cross-case examination is possible despite the fundamental differences between a canonical text of a literary masterpiece and the contents of a TV program from the sphere of political journalism.

The widely-accepted format of a media interview provides for the pre-allocation of turns: the journalist will be asking questions, and the guest in the studio will be giving answers. In this case, the normative and conventionally expected "identities for conversation" are the categorial pair of "interviewer-interviewee". In the terminology suggested above, a routine course of a conversation consists in the performance of particular "category-configured turns", and thus operates on the assumption that turn-taking is managed by the journalist. A striking formal feature of the Lis-Kaczyński interview is the fact that, contrary to this format, the journalist is not able to control the course of the interview at certain junctures, because the guest in the studio repeatedly stakes a claim to deciding which of the questions asked by the journalist are valid, and which response constitutes a sufficient answer to the journalist's question. The course of the interview shows that on a number of occasions, Jarosław Kaczyński challenges the pertinence of questions he is fielding, responds to them with his own questions, or says what he thinks it is that he should be asked about. Thus, through some of his utterances, Kaczyński refuses to produce contents appurtenant to the "interviewee category", i.e. he objects to a certain type of "category-configured turns". To use another term introduced by Sacks (1972), Kaczyński refuses to perform those "category-bound activities" which Lis requires from him. Instead, Kaczyński lays his own claim pertaining to what his utterances, produced in his capacity as a responsible politician, should look like, and what Lis should be saying as a responsible journalist. Thus, Kaczyński designs his very own set of "identities for conversation", which could be described (from Kaczyński's putative perspective) as the "responsible politician – responsible journalist" pair; he also designs, and partly performs, relevant "category-configured turns". Lis opposes these attempts, as he tries to recreate the routine course of the interview and force Kaczyński to answer his question – and thus make him perform the suitable "category-configured turns".

Given its course, the Lis-Kaczyński interview becomes an arena of double controversy, namely, as to who should be in charge of turn-taking, and as to what "identities for conversation" should be assumed. Both aspects of this controversy influence each other, which testifies to another locally unique interconnection between the processes of the emergence of sequential order and categorial order in a conversation, this relation being different to that observed in the dialog from *The Trial.*

The conversation analysis perspective allows for studying a number of further similarities and differences between both conversations. In both cases, conversational order is shaky. Both conversations have "critical moments", which Werner Kallmeyer (1979), in line with the conversation analysis perspective, defines as such disturbances to the course of interaction where what the interlocutors see as a problem, and thus what they direct their interpretive efforts at, is deficits of interactional cooperation.

In both conversations, the interactional advantage is gained by the party who was not expected to do so: in the dialog from *The Trial*, the host (K.) concedes ground in favor of the intruder (F.); in the Lis-Kaczyński interview, the interviewer (Lis) loses control over some of its course in favor of the interviewee (Kaczyński). In both cases, the guest (F. in *The Trial* and Kaczyński during the interview) does not fulfill a situationally relevant normative expectation: F does not introduce himself, and Kaczyński does not speak as a typical interviewee would.

Thus, it is not just a matter of disturbing the interactional cooperation of the interlocutors: this would simply result from the mutual and normatively equal claims to managing the course of the conversation and the distribution of situational identities in an interactive context which is socially defined as egalitarian. These disturbances follow from the attempts of one party to control the interaction by mobilizing the situational role of the "manager of the situation" (K. as a host, Lis as an interviewer), while the other party regularly and successfully questions the adversary's claims to wielding control over how the interaction unfolds, and issues his own counterclaims: F. ("der fremde Mann") and Kaczyński activate the situational roles of an intransigent intruder and an intractable interviewee, respectively.

Interestingly, both men observe politeness strategies – Kaczyński does it at all times, while F. only fails to do so during the insert sequence, under which he mocks K. in his presence, saying, "He wants Anna to bring him his breakfast" to N., an unknown third party in the adjacent room (see the transcript above, segment 3).

In the first case (*The Trial*), the dominated party perceives a huge deficit of interactive cooperation and expresses irritation, on top of indicating major lack of transparency in the present situation[12]. In the other case (the interview), the dominated party does not indicate major lack of transparency, merely expressing irritation at not being able to enforce his routine course of action. Both cases also differ with respect to the interactional modalities employed[13]. In the first case, both parties maintain a serious modality. K. does this as a rule, while F. only fails to maintain a serious modality in the aforementioned insert sequence, in which he is – in a sense – "fishing" for N.'s recognition by making a derisory comment about K.[14] In turn, F. receives a giggle, which proves that N. interpreted F.'s utterance as justified mockery. Let us also add that said insert sequence marks a break in the ongoing conversation between K. and F., thus functioning as a "side sequence within an ongoing sequence" (Jefferson 1972, p. 294). In the other case (the interview), the interviewer consistently sticks to serious modality, which is subject to irony on the part of the interviewee, who occasionally engages in playful modality. Interestingly, Kaczyński, just like F., is "fishing" for the appreciation of a third party, in the form of an applause of those portions of the studio audience which are on his side, although it has to be noted that Lis also receives applause from "his" sections of the crowd, as its political sympathies are divided.

In this context, it is worth noting that addressing each other, Lis and Kaczyński at the same time address the studio audience, a fact which may invite an analysis of the Lis-Kaczyński interview in the sense of Erving Goffman (1959 and 1974, among others). Such analysis would be consistent with the tradition of studies which confirm that focusing on multiple recipients is a basic element of interactional staging in political communication[15]. It has to be added that in the case of televised political journalism (which is a category to which the Lis-Kaczyński interview belongs), the speakers address not just "the other" recipient (if the audience in the studio is allowed under the program's format), but also a "third" recipient, i. e. the media audience. Then, the reactions of the studio audience are strategically important, since they may inform the reception of the original message by the media audience. In the opening dialog from *The Trial*, the situation is different: by partly opening the door and addressing N., F. makes K. the audience for his mockery of K., thus increasing his advantage in the conversation with K.

In the case of the Lis-Kaczyński interview, it would be problematic to refer to "Accountability 3", seeing as it mainly concerns grand texts of symbolic or

---

12 Cf. an analysis of literary dialogs which focuses on violations of basic interactional rules in Schütze 1980.

13 Interactional modalities are discussed by, among others, Schwitalla 2003, p. 169ff.

14 The term "fishing" is used in a different sense than in Anita Pomerantz's article, where it denotes a conversational device for indirect soliciting information from interlocutor.

15 Cf. Dieckmann 1981, Holly / Kühn / Püschel 1986, Petter-Zimmer 1990.

political culture. The Lis-Kaczyński interview, while obviously interesting, is just one of many interviews conducted by Lis, and one of many interviews granted by Kaczyński. What is more, it is not part of the collective memory of the Poles interested in politics. On the other hand, it stands out on the count of being one of two interviews between Lis and Kaczyński, and one of the last interviews which Kaczyński has since granted to a journalist of liberal media. Therefore, it is one of the most recent records of a clash between the two political visions which have for years been at the center stage of Polish (and perhaps not just Polish) public debates: the social vision, emphasizing the "primary human relations" based on trust and transparency, and the righteous vision, underscoring "the right way of doing things"[16]. Lis presents himself as a protagonist of the former vision, demanding that Kaczyński give answers to the general public, which has the right to be well-informed. Kaczyński, in turn, holds himself out as a politician who acts in the name of the vital interests of the Polish state. In this context, the Lis-Kaczyński interview as a whole could be perceived as a microscale symbolic epitome of the macroscale political dynamics.

Paradoxically, although Lis partly loses control over the course of interaction, Kaczyński, now partly in charge of the conversation, at the same time clearly implies that Lis fails to raise certain issues which deserve to be discussed in public. The symbolic dimension of this peculiar feature of this interview opens up an opportunity to interpret the latter in terms of "Accountability 3". Around the time when the interview was conducted – not to mention the subsequent years, when this tendency became apparent – the position of the left-liberal media in Poland gradually weakened in favor of the right-conservative outlets, while at the same time the latter camp (paradoxically) became even more vocal in their complaints to the effect that the mainstream – which they claimed was still liberal – was preventing the conservative right from making their voice heard. Thus, it could be said that this feature of the local, interactional framework of the Lis-Kaczyński interview may be treated as a symbol of a broader media-political situation in Poland, especially in view of the changes which were to follow. In 2011 (when the interview took place), the right-conservatives, under Kaczyński's leadership, were in the opposition. They came to power in 2015. Today (i. e. after seven years of the conservative right's rule), the Lis-Kaczyński interview – with regard to both its local, interactional aspects, and broader, symbolic implications – appears to have quietly presaged the subsequent micro- and macroscale events in the sphere of media-political communication in Poland[17].

---

16 I adapt the terminology suggested by Fantasy Theme Analysis (Bormann / Cragan / Shields 1996, p. 4).

17 It may be further considered if, and to what extent, this feature of the local, interactional framework of the Lis-Kaczyński interview, as well as its broader, symbolic implications, may be consistent with similar occurrences and tendencies in other European countries.

To an extent, a similar interpretation – looking to establish parallels between the empirically reconstructed features of a single conversation ("Accountability 1") and its broader, symbolic meaning ("Accountability 3") – may be offered in the case of the opening passage of *The Trial*. The direction which the story of Josef K. will take – and in particular his early impression and gradual realization that he has been "convicted" – become apparent during his first conversation with F. It is as early as at this point that the disturbance of the routine operation of the turn-taking machinery, as well as an unclear and cryptic character of this disturbance, i.e. occurrences taking place on the conversational microscale ("Accountability 1"), are a sign of what may happen on the biographical scale, and what may prove inevitable and at the same time imbued – in an increasingly obvious fashion – with ominous symbolism ("Accountability 3").

Concluding remarks

Three issues come to the fore in the following conclusions. First, the validity of single case analysis is problematic from the perspective of both social sciences and popular understanding, and as such requires arguments in its support, not unlike those I have tried to present here. The mistrust toward single case analysis usually comes down to trotting out the accusation of lack of objectivity and representativeness. The ability to extract from a single material the minutest of details of conversational order (in conversation analysis) or narrative order (in biographical analysis) is commendable, but may not necessarily mean according such analyses a scientific status. On the contrary, it may inspire appreciation for a researcher's exceptional observational skills and acute perspicacity, which help notice phenomena in a microscopic scale, an accomplishment also characteristic of writers in the mold of Robert Walser, who do not paint a sweeping social panorama, but sometimes provide insights into fleeting communicational events fascinating enough to warrant calling their author "a clairvoyant of the small" (Sebald 2015, p. 140, Walser 2001, p. 10). Thus, another attribute of single case analysis – provided it is to tick the boxes of a research procedure – has to be its methodical character, which implies orderliness, replicability, and openness to intersubjective verification.

Second, this possibility is being developed by research approaches specializing in the qualitative microanalysis of conversational and narrative materials. What is crucial here is, on the one hand, defining, in the course of trans-situational analysis, the basic structural components of conversational or narrative order. On the other hand, applying a basic terminological set to single case analysis must clearly demonstrate that this set is operational in this particular material and allows for explicating its contextually specific details. In this article, an attempt has been made to employ the conversation analytic research apparatus – and in particular a set of notions related to the interconnection between sequential order and categorial order of conversation – precisely in this way. The same opportunities concerning the explication of contextually specific details of a single case, and using them for the purposes of making generalizations, are offered by the research apparatus of the analysis of narrative interviews and – more broadly – biographical materials (cf. Schütze 1992, 2021). A somewhat analogous approach could be observed in Charles Tilly's (2004) late works on contentious politics in social macroscale. These studies are focused on identifying the basic social mechanisms triggering social protest, which – depending on the circumstances – may form various interrelations, rather than on discovering a uniform schematic course of social protest.

Finally, it appears that the value of single case analysis should not depend only on whether it is capable of presenting – be it in most spectacular terms – a selected but singular aspect of a given material, but also on whether the understanding of the material thus gained may be combined with other aspects of this material, which have been uncovered by means of different research approaches. To be sure, it is not possible to consolidate findings based on completely different research perspectives. In such cases, the intersection of such perspectives may be valuable in the sense of fostering conditions for scientific debate, the latter being necessary for arriving at new ideas, but at the same time increasingly less present in the age of perspectivist specialization of scholarly research.

Bibliography

Alonso, William / Starr, Paul (eds.): The Politics of Numbers. New York 1986.

Beer, David: Metric Power. London 2016.

Beer, David: The Data Gaze. Capitalism, Power and Perception. London 2018.

Betten Anne / Dannerer Monika (eds.): Dialogue Analysis IX: Dialogue in Literature and the Media, Part 1: Literature. Berlin 2005.

Bormann, E.G. / Cragan, J.F. / Shields, D.C.: 'An Expansion of the Rhetorical Vision Component of the Symbolic Convergence Theory. The Cold War Paradigm Case', COMMUNICATION MONOGRAPHS 1996/63(1), p. 1–28.

Cavan, Ruth Shonle: Suicide. New York 1965 [1928].

Desrosieres, Alain: The Politics of Large Numbers. A History of Statistical Reasoning. Cambridge 1998.

Dieckmann, Walter: '"Inszenierte Kommunikation". Zur symbolischen Funktion kommunikativer Verfahren in (politisch-)institutionellen Prozessen', in: *idem, Politische Sprache – Politische Kommunikation. Vorträge, Aufsätze, Entwürfe.* Heidelberg 1981, p. 255–279.

Eglin, P.: 'What Should Sociology Explain - Regularities, Rules or Interpretations?', PHILOSOPHY OF THE SOCIAL SCIENCES 1975/5, p. 377–391.

Espeland, W.N. / Stevens, M.L.: 'Sociology of Quantification', in: EUROPEAN JOURNAL OF SOCIOLOGY 2008/XLIX(3), p. 401–436.

Fitzgerald, Richard / Housley, William (eds.): Advances in Membership Categorisation Analysis. London 2015.

Foucault, Michel: Security, Territory, Population: Lectures at the Collège de France, 1977–78. Basingstoke 2007.

Garfinkel, Harold: Studies in Ethnomethodology. Englewood Cliffs 1967.

Glaser, Barney G. / Strauss, Anselm L.: The Discovery of *Grounded Theory*. Strategies for Qualitative Research. Chicago 1967.

Goffman, Erving: The Presentation of Self in Everyday Life. New York 1959.

Goffman, Erving: Frame Analysis. An Essay on the Organization of Experience. New York 1974.

Hess-Lüttich, Ernest W.B. (ed.): Literatur und Konversation. Sprachsoziologie und Pragmatik in der Literaturwissenschaft. Wiesbaden 1980.

Holly, Werner / Kühn, Peter / Püschel, Ulrich: Politische Fernsehdiskussionen. Zur medienspezifischen Inszenierung von Propaganda als Diskussion. Tübingen 1986.

Jefferson, Gail: 'Side Sequences', in: Sudnow, David S. (ed.): *Studies in Social Interaction*. New York 1972, p. 294–338.

Kafka, Franz: Der Prozess. Roman. Frankfurt am Main 1983 [1925].

Kafka, Franz: Der Prozess. Roman (in der Fassung der Handschrift). Frankfurt am Main 1994.

Kafka, Franz: The Trial [Der Prozess]. London 1999 [1937] (translated by Willa and Edwin Muir).

Kafka, Franz: The Trial [Der Prozess]. Oxford 2009 (translated by Mike Mitchell).

Kallmeyer, Werner: 'Kritische Momente. Zur Konversationsanalyse von Interaktionsstörungen', in: W. Frier, Wolfgang / Labroisse, Gerd (eds.): *Grundfragen der Textwissenschaft. Linguistische und literaturwissenschaftliche Aspekte*. Amsterdam 1979, p. 59–109.

Kornberger, Martin / Justesen, Lise / Mouritsen, Jan / Madsen, Anders Koed (eds.): Making Things Valuable. Oxford 2015.

Lynch, Michael: 'Ethnomethodology and the Logic of Practice', in: Schatzki, Theodore R. / Knorr-Cetina, Karin / von Savigny, Eike (eds.): *The Practice Turn in Contemporary Sociology*. London 2001, p. 131–148.

Mau, Steffen: The Metric Society. On the Quantification of the Social. Cambridge 2019.

Mennicken, A. / Espeland, W.N.: 'What's New with Numbers? Sociological Approaches to the Study of Quantification', ANNUAL REVIEW OF SOCIOLOGY 2019/45, p. 24.1-24.23.

Miller, Peter / Rose, Nikolas: Governing the Present: Administering Social and Personal Life. Cambridge 2008.

Petter-Zimmer, Yvonne: Politische Fernsehdiskussion und ihre Adressaten. Tübingen 1990.

Poe, Edgar Allan: 'The Murders in the Rue Morgue', in: Poe, Edgar Allan: *The Portable Edgar Allan Poe*. London 2006, p. 238–270 [1841].

Pomerantz, A.: 'Telling My Side: "Limited Access" as a "Fishing" Device', in: SOCIO-LOGICAL INQUIRY 1980/50(3–4), p. 186–198.

Ragin, Charles C. / Becker, Howard Saul (eds.): What is a Case? Exploring the Foundations of Social Inquiry. Cambridge 1992.

Riemann, G.: 'Suizidalität als Prozess - eine Re-Analyse des Tagebuchs von Wallace Baker in Ruth Shonle Cavans "Suicide"', in: ZEITSCHRIFT FÜR QUALITATIVE FORSCHUNG 2007/8(2), p. 287–327.

Sacks, Harvey: 'The Search for Help: No One to Turn to', in: Schneidman, Edwin S. (ed.): *Essays in Self-Destruction*. New York 1967, p. 203–223.

Sacks, Harvey: 'An Initial Investigation of the Usability of Conversational Data for Doing Sociology', in: Sudnow, David S. (ed.): *Studies in Social Interaction*. New York 1972, p. 31–74.

Sacks, Harvey: Lectures on Conversation. Vol. 1. Oxford 1992a.

Sacks, Harvey: Lectures on Conversation. Vol. 2. Oxford 1992b.

Sacks, H. / Schegloff, E.A. / Jefferson, G.: 'A Simplest Systematics for the Organization of Turn-Taking in Conversation', in: LANGUAGE 1974/50(4), p. 696–735.

Schegloff, E.A.: 'Sequencing in Conversational Openings', in: AMERICAN ANTHRO-POLOGIST 1968/70, p. 1075–1095.

Schegloff, E.A.: 'Analyzing Single Episodes of Interaction. An Exercise in Conversation Analysis', SOCIAL PSYCHOLOGY QUARTERLY 1987/50(2), p. 101–114.

Schegloff, E.A.: 'Reflections on Quantification in the Study of Conversation', in: RE-SEARCH ON LANGUAGE AND SOCIAL INTERACTION 1993/26, p. 99–128.

Schegloff, Emanuel A.: 'Issues of Relevance for Discourse Analysis: Contingency in Action, Interaction, and Co-Participant Context', in:. Hovy, Eduard H. / Scott, Donia R. (eds.): *Computational and Conversational Discourse. Burning Issues, an Interdisciplinary Account*. Berlin 1996, p. 3–35.

Schegloff, Emanuel A.: Sequence Organization in Interaction. A Primer in Conversation Analysis, Volume 1. Cambridge 2007.

Schegloff, E.A. / Jefferson, G. / Sacks, H.: 'The Preference for Self-Correction in the Organization of Repair in Conversation', in: LANGUAGE 1977/53(2), p. 361–382.

Schütze, Fritz: '*Interaktionspostulate* – Am Beispiel literarischer Texte (Dostojewski, Kafka, Handke u. a.)', in: Hess-Lüttich, Ernest W.B. (ed.): *Literatur und Konversation. Sprachsoziologie und Pragmatik in der Literaturwissenschaft*. Wiesbaden 1980, p. 72–94.

Schütze, F.: 'Pressure and Guilt: War Experiences of a Young German Soldier and Their Biographical Implications. Parts 1 and 2', INTERNATIONAL SOCIOLOGY 1992/7, p. 187–208 and 347–367.

Schütze, Fritz: 'Von der Theoriemächtigkeit einer Einzelfallstudie. Vorwort zur deutschen Ausgabe', in: Delcroix, Catherine: *Licht und Schatten der Familie Nour. Wie manche der Prekarität trotzen – Biographische Rekonstruktionen*. Opladen 2021, p. 13–33.

Schwitalla, Johannes: Gesprochenes Deutsch. Eine Einführung. Berlin 2003.

Scott, M.B. / Lyman, S.M.: 'Accounts', in: AMERICAN SOCIOLOGICAL REVIEW 1968/33(1), p. 46–62.

Sebald, Winfried Georg: A Place in the Country. New York 2015.

Shaw, Clifford: The Jack-Roller: A Delinquent Boy's Own Story. Chicago 1966 [1930].

Skwarczyńska, Stefania: 'Próba teorji rozmowy' [An Attempt at a Theory of Conversation], PAMIĘTNIK LITERACKI 1932/29(1–4), p. 1–51.

Smith, D.: '"K is Mentally Ill". The Anatomy of a Factual Account', in: SOCIOLOGY 1978/
    12, p. 23–53.
Sontag, Susan: 'Against Interpretation', in: Sontag, Susan: *Against Interpretation and Other
    Essays*. New York 1966, p. 1–14.
Sontag, S.: '30 Years Later', in: THREE PENNY REVIEW 1996/Summer https://www.th
    reepennyreview.com/samples/sontag_su96.html.
Tilly, Charles: Contention and Democracy in Europe, 1650–2000. Cambridge 2004.
Walser, Robert: Fritz Kochers Aufsätze. Frankfurt am Main 2001 [1904].
Watson, Rod: 'Some General Reflections on "Categorization" and "Sequence" in the
    Analysis of Conversation', in: Hester, Stephen / Eglin, Peter (eds.): *Culture in Action:
    Studies in Membership Categorization Analysis*. Washington 1997, p. 49–76.
Watson, Rod: 'De Reifying Categories', in: Fitzgerald, Richard / Housley, William (eds.):
    Advances in Membership Categorisation Analysis. London 2015, p. 23–49.
Wowk, Maria T. / Carlin, Andrew P.: 'Depicting a Liminal Position in Ethnomethodology,
    Conversation Analysis and Membership Categorization Analysis: The Work of Rod
    Watson', HUMAN STUDIES 2004/27(1), p. 69–89.

Appendix

The integral text of the opening passage of *The Trial* (Kafka 1983 [1925], p. 13),
without changes to the excerpted dialog (see above):

"Someone must have been telling lies about Josef K., he knew he had done nothing wrong
but, one morning, he was arrested. Every day at eight in the morning he was brought his
breakfast by Mrs. Grubach's cook – Mrs. Grubach was his landlady – but today she didn't
come. That had never happened before. K. waited a little while, looked from his pillow at the
old woman who lived opposite and who was watching him with an inquisitiveness quite
unusual for her, and finally, both hungry and disconcerted rang the bell. There was immediately a knock at the door and a man entered. He had never seen the man in this house
before. He was slim but firmly built, his clothes were black and close-fitting, with many
folds and pockets, buckles and buttons and a belt, all of which gave the impression of being
very practical but without making it very clear what they were actually for. 'Who are you?'
asked K., sitting half upright in his bed. The man, however, ignored the question as if his
arrival simply had to be accepted, and merely replied, 'You rang?' 'Anna should have
brought me my breakfast,' said K. He tried to work out who the man actually was, first in
silence, just through observation and by thinking about it, but the man didn't stay still to be
looked at for very long. Instead he went over to the door, opened it slightly, and said to
someone who was clearly standing immediately behind it, 'He wants Anna to bring him his
breakfast.' There was a little laughter in the neighbouring room, it was not clear from the
sound of it whether there were several people laughing. The strange man could not have
learned anything from it that he hadn't known already, but now he said to K., as if making
his report 'It is not possible.' 'It would be the first time that's happened,' said K., as he
jumped out of bed and quickly pulled on his trousers. 'I want to see who that is in the next
room, and why it is that Mrs. Grubach has let me be disturbed in this way.' It immediately

occurred to him that he needn't have said this out loud, and that he must to some extent have acknowledged their authority by doing so, but that didn't seem important to him at the time. That, at least, is how the stranger took it, as he said, 'Don't you think you'd better stay where you are?' 'I want neither to stay here nor to be spoken to by you until you've introduced yourself.' 'I meant it for your own good'".

Magdalena Nowicka-Franczak

The elite and their privilege to speak about themselves and others in public. Post-Foucauldian discourse analysis meets post-Marxist studies

Abstract
The paper discusses the dimensions of power that can be enforced by members of the elite who took part in the public debate. The chapter uses a political interview with Jarosław Kaczyński, one of the most prominent Polish politicians of this century, conducted by Tomasz Lis, one of the most recognizable journalists in Polish media, to address the ambiguity of the elite's discursive power: Is it the elite that defines and shapes its discourse independently, or is it the discourse itself that determines the elite's position and power resources? The analysis of the TV interview takes the approach of post-Foucauldian discourse research, which focuses on the discursive practices, strategies, and subject positioning applied in order to exclude from the public debate particular interpretations of social reality. It also adopts the post-Marxist perspective of discourse as a source of the elite's right to speak about themselves and others in public. The categories of *discursive capital* and *speaking about oneself and others* bring forth the question of the elite's power and point to the common interests and possible linkages between post-Foucauldian and post-Marxist approaches to discourse.
Keywords: elite, discursive power, discursive capital, Foucault, Marx

Introduction

The interview of 3 October 2011, when Jarosław Kaczyński, leader of the right-wing Law and Justice party (henceforth PiS), spoke to Tomasz Lis, a top liberal journalist, merits analysis for multiple reasons, most of which were listed in the introduction to this volume. In this chapter, I will focus on one of them. This interview is a special medium in which the issues of the power of the elites and their status in the public discourse combine. The elite status is not just a condition necessary for this interview to have taken place (it would be difficult to imagine a televised interview with Kaczyński conducted by a commoner or, likewise, to picture Lis speaking to an "ordinary" man in primetime), but it also

Magdalena Nowicka-Franczak, University of Łódź (Poland), ORCID: 0000-0002-4535-4246, m.nowicka_franczak@uni.lodz.pl.

determines the course of the conversation and the self-esteem of its participants. The latter aims to influence the outcome of a Polish parliamentary election that was scheduled to take place in the next few days. A TV studio is the stage of the egotistic meeting, whose participants directly and indirectly emphasize their stature and express contentment at the lines they have delivered.

But the self-satisfaction of the elites cannot prove their agency and subjectivity in the field of public discourse. In my analysis of the 2011 interview, I highlight the issue of the power of the elites in the discourse itself, exercised by discussing or refusing to discuss themselves and others in particular terms. Following on from this problem is the question of whether the elites offer a unique perception of the world or mostly use the discourse to reproduce their status. Put differently, the problem is whether the elites speak for themselves, or if this is an existing discourse that speaks through them, together with its strategies, which include ways of framing reality, telling the truth from the lies, the rhetorical disciplining of the interlocutor, and speaking about others.

The pre-election context is very significant. In 2011, no debate was held between the leaders of the two major parties, i.e., Donald Tusk and Jarosław Kaczyński. The journalist, rather than the president of the then ruling Civic Platform (henceforth PO), assumed the role of the adversary of the PiS chairman. During the election campaign, PO stoked the fears of the public by presenting PiS as a party of nationalists (which, for example, stood for the interests of the nativist circles of football hooligans), while the boogeymen which PiS used among the conservative electorate was that PO would form a coalition with the leftist Palikot Movement. The interpretation valid on either side of the conflict was that Poland was at a civilizational crossroads, and the election would decide the ideological future of the country. During the interview, both Kaczyński and Lis took on the roles of loyal spokesmen for the competing visions of Polish democracy.

Although the interview was a corollary of the immediate political context, its significance transgresses its time. It is a media afterimage of debates on Poland's civilizational character and the right way to modernize it, which have pitted different factions of Polish elites against each other since at least the late 18th century. It is also a weak offshoot of an even older "war between the robe and the tailcoat," which is a metaphor of an argument over what should be the Polish elites' benchmark of cultural, political, and moral standards: Western Europe or the mythologized domestic tradition, e.g., the Sarmatia. In addition, it is an element of the contemporary social imaginery, that is, the way in which people (in this case the elites) "imagine their social existence, how they fit together with others, how things go on between them and their fellows" (Taylor 2004, p. 23). Finally, the 2011 interview foreshadows the communication phenomena of present-day Poland. It was the last time that the PiS chairman accepted an invitation from a leading liberal journalist. What followed shortly as a result of the advancing polarization of politics and the media was a situation whereby top politicians stopped appearing in outlets that espouse a worldview opposite to theirs. The so-called identity media have grown in importance, whose actors strongly identify with a particular interpretation of Poles' collective identity and social values while brushing aside dissenting voices[1]. Lis himself (2016) considers this meeting to be one of the most satisfying episodes of his career, while Kaczyński's entourage claims that the PiS chairman emphatically won the studio battle. Rhetorical victory was clearly at stake here, but it was not crucial – and neither were the fates of Poland and the Poles, even though this was a recurrent theme of the interview. It was actually a power play to decide who would keep the status of the true Polish elite.

Elite, power, discourse

Defined in opposition to ordinary people, the elite benefit from the uneven distribution of financial capital and material and immaterial goods, including cultural competencies and social prestige. The latter two are at the core of what Pierre Bourdieu (1986, p. 243 ff) calls cultural capital, which enables social distinction and is usually acquired through inheritance and class-conditioned socialization. Privileges and resources translate into a higher standing in the social field of power. As a result, a power struggle frequently comes with calls to replace or overthrow the elites, who are seen as enjoying undeserved privileges and exploiting or manipulating people. This is also how the notion of the elite is used in populist discourses to undermine trust in political leaders and in democracy as a political system, and to give rise to or reinforce social aversion to the rulers (Wodak 2017). The anti-elitist dimension characterizes PiS's right-wing discourse. In this narrative, the liberal and leftist elites of the Third Republic do not represent the Polish people or the vital interests of the state; instead, they work to their own advantage and enlist external actors to further their vested interests.

The elite's power may be captured in Weberian terms of influencing others, for example, through institutional channels. In *The Power Elite*, Charles Wright Mills applies the eponymous category to people who, owing to their position in institutional and bureaucratic structures, "can look down upon, so to speak, and by their decisions mightily affect, the everyday worlds of ordinary men and women"

---

1 After 2010, this label was attached chiefly to conservative and right-wing media that advanced the ethnocentric and Euro-skeptical agenda. However, since 2015, this term has been used increasingly often with reference to the liberal media, whose dominant narrative is that of criticizing the PiS government and its identity politics.

(Mills 1959, p. 3). What sets the elite and officials apart is the former's reputation as people who, thanks to their resources and competencies, can influence others. Mills and other exponents of this reputation-based approach to the theory of the elites focus not merely on the fact that the elites wield power, but also on the socio-embedded roots of this power and the possibility of strategically employing its instruments. As Mills (ibid., p. 24) puts it, "Do the elite determine the roles that they enact? Or do the roles that institutions make available to them determine the power of the elite?" These questions indirectly concern the agentive subjectivity of the elite. Mills does not give definitive answers, but is inclined to accept the elite's agency within institutional structures: "They may call into question the structure, their position within it, or the way in which they are to enact that position" (ibid.).

Although Mills does not discuss journalists separately, he classifies media people as professional celebrities, and even sees high-ranking individuals in media institutions as members of the power elite (ibid., p. 74ff). Thus, both participants of the interview – Kaczyński as chairman of a major political party, and Lis as an advertisement for TV channels and press outlets – can be classified as the power elite. Their social significance materializes not just in the institutional dimension, but also in the sphere of the production of political discourse and the accompanying collective symbolism. The study question underlying this analysis is inspired by the question posed by Mills: does the elite itself define the discourse it creates and is this the source of its symbolic power, or does the symbolic power of the elite result from the role assigned to it by discourse?

In order to address the question, reference must be made to an alternative understanding of the elite and its power. One proposal was formulated by Teun van Dijk and concerns symbolic elites and the sway they hold over social communication. According to van Dijk (1993, p. 9), "the public actions of the elites are predominantly discursive", and their power afford preferential access to public discourse and such standing within its structure, which gives them opportunities to make use of the symbolic resources at their disposal. In other words, "not only do they make decisions that may affect the lives of many people, they also have significant control over the means of production of public opinion" (ibid., p. 44). Consequently, symbolic elites are groups that control the sphere of disseminating knowledge, symbols, and values (ibid., p. 46f).

By discharging their duties in public, those who qualify as symbolic elites include journalists, politicians, artists, the clergy, experts, as well as scholars and intellectuals working as media pundits[2]. They become symbolic elites when they attract audiences, their actions are admired, and what they say acquires the status

---

2 Today, this group also includes authors of opinion-forming content, such as bloggers, vloggers, or influencers.

of a point of reference in social communication, with its content not necessarily accepted: as long as it is incorporated – even critically – into an array of theoretically conceivable worldviews, the discourse of symbolic elites affects the public's perception of social reality and its actors. For van Dijk, the nature of this impact is ideological, as it shapes and solidifies people's beliefs, moral stances, and political preferences. His definition of ideology is broad, including each fixed and rather dogmatic set of beliefs and interpretations. Democracy, too, is an ideology, and symbolic elites are responsible for its dominant meaning.

One aspect of how symbolic elites function in social channels of communication is their responsiveness to social preferences and their accountability for discursive and material actions. In institutional optics, focused on political leaders, these issues are in the purview of democratic elitism (see Higley 2010, Wasilewski 2021), but discussing it here is not possible due to considerations of space. If the question concerning the scope and the dynamics of the power of the elites centres around discourse as a basic carrier of social order, then addressing it requires adopting a different perspective.

A large critical potential characterizes the post-Foucauldian approach, which attempts to apply Michel Foucault's idea of discourse to empirical studies. In this model, discourse is a carrier of the "power, control, harnessing, qualification, and disqualification" of individuals, groups, and other social actors (Foucault 2001, p. 124). A basic principle of discourse is the neutralization of various alternative outlooks on social reality and its ideological background. Such exclusion also affects the agents behind it, in that those who decide on the contents of discourse are subject to its rules and (consciously or unconsciously) formulate their statements in accordance with the applicable order of discourse (Foucault 1980). It would be problematic to suggest that someone in particular controls discourse, since elites, too, are subjected to it. For Foucault, power is impersonal and dispersed, and it concerns social processes and relations, but to different degrees. Thus, it is more warranted to posit a unique standing of the elites in discourse, which puts them at an advantage or gives them self-restraining authority exercised by means of producing discourse and adhering to its practices for strategical purposes.

In the present analysis, three relevant categories are used: *discourse subject*, *subject position*, and *speaking subject*. The first one is a theoretical category and refers to the social rules which govern the production of discourse. Said rules include the indispensability of the creator and governor of discourse, who conceals tensions between the impersonal relations of power that regulate discourse. In Foucault's model, the discourse subject is the author seen as a discourse function or "a meta-authorial figure which produces and constantly reproduces the way in which discourse that they themselves established functions" (Kobus 2021, p. 270). The subject position is a practical category that refers to discursive practices, that is, ways of regulating the production of statements that constitute discourse. Occupying the subject position comes with the power to control the content, form, and distribution of statements, but within the order of discourse, which is autonomous in relation to individual volition. The speaking subject is the empirical instantiation of the subject position, being its dimension present in social communication and interactional order. The resource at the disposal of the speaking subject is the statement (enunciation), a part of discourse that performs a particular communicative function and expresses, among others, interpretations, argumentations, or judgments (Bacchi / Bonham 2014).

In considerations on the structure of social relations of powers, it is important not to overlook their economic dimension. A consequence of measuring the constitutive processes of social order against economic criteria is the commercialization of social communication. Active participation in discourse is connected with the accumulation of symbolic resources, which may support and solidify patterns of the distribution of financial and material goods, as well as political influence. Johannes Angermuller labels these resources *discursive capital*, whose currency is subject positions in discourse, which are characterized by different degrees of focality or referentiality in a given discourse community (by which Angermuller means the group engaged in mutual communication within a particular discourse). In his words, "[f]or just like commodities, whose (exchange) value is a function of the socially necessary labor time, subject positions become valuable by absorbing the time and energy of the members of the discourse community" (Angermuller 2018, p. 418).

The varying significance of different subject positions results from the fact that discursive capital, although produced by numerous discourse participants, is in the hands of a selected few. Angermuller not only transfers the main tenets of the Marxist theory of value to discourse theory, but also (partly as a metaphor and partly as a criticism of the economic frames of discourse production) the dichotomic class division. Hence, *discourse capitalists* enhance their subject position in discourse (and typically outside it) because they serve as a topic discussed by and the point of reference for the underprivileged participants of discourse, that is, *discourse workers*. As argued by Angermuller (ibid.), "one can often observe a transfer of value from the many discourse workers (who talk only about others) to the few discourse 'capitalists' (who are talked to and about)". This criterion of distinguishing between discourse capitalists and discourse workers – the former are spoken to and about, the latter only speak about others – is overly reductionist and requires complementation. Speaking about others does not necessarily mean speaking about those high in the pecking order. It can refer to speaking in categorical terms about various others. Here, categoricalness has two meanings. First, it denotes discussing people in evaluative terms, according to the speaking subject's preference and strategic goals. Such speech appropriates the subjective position of others. Second, it refers to speaking in a declarative manner, which excludes other perspectives and is non-negotiable at a particular moment.

Speaking about oneself and others in categorical terms enhances the discourse standing of the speaking subject and diminishes the stature of those spoken about. This way of speaking may appear attractive to those audiences who look for simple and unequivocal interpretations of reality. It will also inevitably enrage others or make them adopt a critical stance. In other words, the manner in which Kaczyński and Lis spoke about each other and beyond gave the media and the audience a pretext to comment on their words, refer to their interpretations of Polish reality, and raise the issue of the way in which they decided to speak in public. Whether these were reactions of affirmation or rejection is secondary, since discourse capital is enhanced by mere public attention. In opposition to Angermuller, it would be more accurate to *classify as discourse capitalists those who speak about themselves and others in categorical terms, and to attach the label of discourse workers to those who describe the world and others using the terms suggested by discourse capitalists.* In the case of Kaczyński and Lis, *speaking about themselves and others* in categorical terms seems to be a major privilege that goes with their elitist and foundational subject position within public discourse in Poland.

Methodology: The encounter of post-Foucauldian and post-Marxist discourse studies

The aim of analysing Lis' interview of Kaczyński is to address the question concerning the power of the elites in discourse and the resources this power employs, which involve speaking and refusing to speak, and in particular in 1) *speaking about oneself and others in categorical terms* and 2) *positioning oneself and others within the discourse.* Their presence in discourse is conditional on their position in the sphere of Poland's political-symbolic power and in the structure of Polish society. Both men are members of power and symbolic elites, but on occasion, they address different classes: Lis mostly targets the middle class, while Kaczyński speaks to the lower middle class and the lower class, the so-called people's class. Their respective careers in the media and politics gained momentum in the already democratic and capitalistic Poland, are subject to market and political selection, and are sensitive to changes in audience composition.

Analysing both the properties of discourse that are responsible for forming subject position and the structural circumstances of discourse production that cause the uneven distribution of the right to speak in public requires an approach that would consider both these dimensions. The post-Foucauldian perspective draws upon Foucault's interest in the processes of exclusion, from discourse through a ban on verbalizing certain content or only giving the right to speak categorically to special discourse subjects. This aspect is expounded on in contemporary analyses of subjectification, i.e., the production in discourse of subject positions that arise from a combination of normative models of the subject with subjective self-relation (Bosančić 2019, p. 88). When assuming the role of a discourse subject, the individual exercises their right to self-identification and at the same time loses this right by getting their public self to conform to the rules of discourse.

Enjoying particular attention in the post-Foucauldian perspective is the issue of the interdependence of media discourse on the one hand, and the symbolic and institutional frames of the actions of political entities, as well as social practices (i.e., the attitudes and behaviours of individuals toward each other) on the other (e.g., Kumięga 2012, Sieber 2014, Thiele 2015). The main principle of these interdependencies is the power relations between the subjects involved in creating discourse and practical actions. This construction of subject is built upon the selection, exclusion, and subjugation of individual actions to the character of power in a particular society at a particular historical juncture. The following analysis covers one case study, and as such, aims to investigate the practices of subjects entitled to speak in public. These practices contribute to retaining the hierarchical order of discourse, as well as, indirectly, maintaining the social order.

These issues are also analysed in the post-Marxist perspective in studies on discourse. This approach is mainly associated with the Essex School of discourse analysis and names such as Ernesto Laclau, Chantal Mouffe, and David Howarth. However, it is likewise applied by many authors interested in political-economical criticism of social communication. Under this model, Marx's works are scoured for hints that foreshadowed the emergence of critical studies on discourse. In *The German Ideology, The Eighteenth Brumaire, Capital,* and the "Preface" to the *Contribution to the Critique of Political Economy,* Marx underlines the bourgeois (elitist) nature of the language prevailing in the public sphere. Language is a vehicle for ideology if used in the political and class context. Subjective action depends on the awareness and interpretation of the material world, expressed through language. It has to be transcended to make social change possible. If fetishizing the division into the material base and the symbolic-discursive superstructure is avoided, it becomes apparent that the capitalistic order of people and things is (re)produced both in discourse and beyond. Additionally, discourse, which is partly independent of the principles of economic production, has a reality-objectifying capacity, which results from the application of its semiotic and identity potential (see Fairclough / Graham 2002, Jessop / Sum 2018, Beetz / Schwab 2018).

Post-Marxist studies on discourse are sometimes referred to as *materialist discourse analysis*, since they classify as discourse those statements that have material implications, while social relations are symbolic, being articulated in discourse (Howarth 2018, p. 379 ff; pioneering works in this field were published by Stuart Hall, e. g., Hall 1973). Discourse arises in the material *conditions of production* (i. e., social mechanisms and structures pertaining to labor, economy, education, politics, and discourse production), and itself serves the purpose of reproducing the chiefly ideological *relations of production* (i. e., social relations, including class and political relations, and positions in the process of production that enable the retention or transformation of the conditions of production, see Beetz / Schwab 2018, p. 338 ff).

Unlike Marxist determinism, this approach involves studying the relationality of social forms, which receive the Foucauldian reading of discursive formations (Howarth 2018, p. 382 ff), and postulates the semi-autonomy of discourse in relation to the material structures of capitalistic production. Post-Marxist thinkers reject the Marxist notion of language and society being two related but distinct domains. They also reject the totalistic character of capitalist production which determines other social processes. Central to this perspective are all attempts to from marginalized subjectivity, which may acquire political subjectivity in the sphere of discourse. Following "controlled" heterodoxy, the terminology used under this model has adopted elements of Foucault's discourse theory. In a sense, this was triggered by Foucault himself, as he made comments on Marx's criticism of society (the most famous text concerning this issue is an essay entitled *Nietzsche, Freud, Marx*, published in 1967).

The respective post-Marxist and post-Foucauldian approaches diverge on three main scores. The first is the definition of the discourse subject. Post-Marxist theorists point to the potential of subjective agency that results from the dialectics of social processes and the gaps and contradictions that exist within the social order. Post-Foucauldian scholars refer to Foucault, claiming that power is exercised over free subjects, and that defying authority is a function of its social ubiquity. The second is the definition of truth, ideology, and the target of criticism. For post-Marxist authors, ideology, which is transmitted through discourse, refers to false consciousness and the untruth, which obscures the substantial truth. Based on this premise, it is possible to criticize ideology. For post-Foucauldian thinkers, the truth itself is a discursive construct, and subject to criticism are its prevalence or the social regime that goes with it, but not the truth as such. The third is the importance of the criticism of capitalism. For post-Marxist scholars, the criticism of capitalism and neoliberalism is the focal point, and capitalist ideology constitutes the basic logic of the (re)production of social order. In the post-Foucauldian perspective, capitalism and neoliberalism are two historically dynamic forms of controlling society. They are very influential, but somewhat incidental.

In recent years, the blending of these perspectives has been more systematic, mostly through the efforts of German scholars, its collective outcome being a 2018 publication in the "Critical Discourse Studies" series entitled *Marx and Discourse*, edited by Johannes Beetz, Benno Herzog, and Jens Maesse. Johannes Angermuller, one of the contributing authors, claims that going beyond Marxist economic determinism and the division into the base and the superstructure (the latter of which is, according to some scholars, precisely discourse), as well as noticing "a practice of valuating subject positions" in the usage of language, will reinforce the criticism of discourse as a sphere of establishing hierarchies and inequalities which are subject to quasi-economic valuation rooted in historically dynamic knowledge. As argued by Angermuller (2018, p. 417), "[y]et just like Marx, Foucault grounds knowledge in a social and historical context and asks how knowledge is mobilized in the making of social hierarchies. In many ways, Foucault extends Marx's intuitions concerning the nexus of valuation and the social order". Foucault shifted the analytical focus from material-symbolic production to the production of subjectivity. The aim of the convergence of these two perspectives is supposed to be something else, namely, a balanced analysis of material-discursive relations which arise from social dominance.

A means to that end is the de-substantiation and historicization of Marx's social theory (Howarth 2018, p. 388). This is also a reminder of Foucault's material relations of discourse (1981, p. 52, Herzog 2018, p. 403) and the uncovering of his negative normative reflection (expressed in what he saw as a question central to post-enlightenment criticism: "how not to be governed *like that*, by that, in the name of those principles, with such and such an objective in mind and by means of such procedures, not like that, not for that, not by them", Foucault 2007, p. 44). Another issue is the focus on a rather pragmatic relationship between ideology and discourse, whereby the former is a discursive practice (a collection of rules determining what is said and referring to the production of knowledge about reality; arising from these rules are linguistic, terminological, and argu-mentative structures), while the latter is a sphere of ideological labour performed employing language and symbolic means (Maesse / Nicoletta 2021, Nowicka-Franczak 2021). Since ideologies stabilize domination and exclusion, and sometimes also grief, their criticism should be of these phenomena, and not of ideological interpretations of the world (Herzog 2018, p. 403 ff), while criticism of capitalism and neoliberalism, although central to both perspectives, should not be the point of departure and the destination in discourse studies. It is "a careful and systematic *problematization* of a particular phenomenon, where the latter is related both to a particular field of academic questions, as well as the social and political issues that confront us in specific historical contexts" (ibid., p. 385), that are the starting point. Criticism that combines both approaches should pursue two goals: trace the internal logic of a given discursive phenomenon (Glynos / Howarth 2007) and ask questions about the changing reality that conditioned this phenomenon (Herzog 2018, p. 406).

The analysis of the interview

The following analysis, though foregrounding the Foucauldian approach, is where the two perspectives meet. This allows for the fine-graining of interpretations of the text studied and identifying moments when it is particularly easy to fall into the trap of literalness (i.e., of criticizing false ideologies or the dichotomic relations of the elites – the people who condition the production of public discourse) and lose track of the tension between the social status of the elite and the discursive game played in this position. The category used to investigate these material-discursive combinations is the aforesaid *discursive capital*, whose accumulation involves winning and retaining valuable subject positions in discourse, which translate into broad outreach and wide reception, and, first and foremost, in the right to *speak about oneself and others in public in categorical terms.* This is positioning others within discourse and expressing a particular *truth* about others and their circumstances. Speaking about others is a means of positioning both interactional partners and other elite members within the discourse. It is also a tool for the objectifying categorization of different non-elitist social groups and their members. In this case study, this is a discursive privilege that is a corollary of Lis' and Kaczyński's respective standings in the social structures of power. However, at the same time, this privilege is sensitive to the social reception of the discourse produced by the elites. Therefore, garnering discursive capital may, but does not necessarily have to, translate into political capital.

Research questions

The research questions are directly related to the post-Foucauldian perspective, but at the same time, are not at odds with the post-Marxist approach:
1. How was the production of the analysed statements possible? Who can speak in public, and on what conditions?
2. What overt information does the discourse contain, and what is missing? What discursive formations are the analysed statements? Do they perform an ideological function?

3. What subject positions materialize in the discourse studied?
4. In what terms does the speaking subject discuss themselves and others?
5. What kind of truth about the elites and their discourse emerges from what was said?

The attempt to address these questions incorporates elements of both approaches. The first question concerns both the practical instantiation of the right to speak, which will be discussed based on the analysis of the interview, and the material-symbolic determinants of the production of a discursive event such as a televised political interview. The conditions of production which made Lis' interview of Kaczyński in a TV studio possible are mostly connected with media production. A major TV channel – in this case, state-subsidized TVP2 – has to fill primetime with attractive content, and it has both the infrastructural and financial capacity to reach this goal. The broadcast was available to practically everybody, as long as they had the equipment necessary to receive it (Polish citizens have to pay a TV license fee, but this obligation was effectively not enforced before 2012, see Ratajczak 2019), so its value as a carrier of political-ideological content was considerable. In 2011, "Tomasz Lis na żywo" was a leading journalistic program in Polish media, and one of the indicators of being a political in-the-know was knowing "who Lis is hosting tonight". Lis and his program's institutional and symbolic stature was perhaps one of the factors that persuaded Jarosław Kaczyński – who was already cautious about appearing in liberal media – to accept the invitation.

The elite position of the interlocutors and the pre-election context ensured the interview's high audience share. The 3 October 2011 meeting was watched by around 3.2 million people, which means that 29% of the active viewers tuned in to watch TVP2. The interview of Kaczyński boasted the highest viewing figures of all pre-election installments of "Tomasz Lis na żywo" (Lisowi... 2011). Concluding whether Kaczyński's appearance in the TV studio helped him boost political capital is not the subject of the present analysis, unlike the character of the discourse capital accumulated by the interlocutors.

The structure of the program and exercising the right to speak about oneself and others

The 3 October 2011 instalment of "Tomasz Lis na żywo" had a runtime of 52 minutes and 24 seconds. It begins with a minute-long compilation of Kaczyński's public comments from the period 2005–2011, where he slams Donald Tusk and the media unfavourably reporting on PiS. This is done to promote the image of Kaczyński as a political and social demagog who incites conflicts. In the interview proper, there are seven thematic segments. They are summarized in Table 1 (p. 70–75), along with the different instantiations of *speaking about oneself and others.*

Prevailing in the interview are discursive practices pertaining to the elites *speaking about themselves and about other elites.* They are mostly used by Kaczyński, who presents the achievements and program of his party, discredits his political opponents, and questions Lis' credentials as a professional journalist. By granting himself the right to speak and not speak about certain issues that the interviewer asks about (for example, naming the minister of economy in a potential PiS government), Kaczyński tries to come across as the moderator of the discourse content. Meanwhile, by lecturing Lis on what questions he should be asking, he appears to aspire to the position of discourse guardian, deciding which contents and discursive practices pertain to the *truth* about Poland and which ones do not. His ability to garner discourse capital is curbed by Lis, who focuses on proving that Kaczyński is speaking in bad faith. What Lis says serves as an obstacle to Kaczyński's intention to accumulate discursive capital and helps Lis build up his own capital as an impartial journalist who is on a quest to lay bare the verbal manipulations of his interlocutor. The disputed issue is Kaczyński's attitude to other members of the elites (e.g., Prime Minister Tusk, President Komorowski, or members of Kaczyński's political camp), which means that *discourse capitalists* are mostly speaking about other *discourse capitalists.* The Polish people and their problems are only discussed to a very limited extent. The few issues concerning non-elitist social groups (e.g., the poor, nurses, football hooligans, or mothers of very small children) can only materialize in this interview as a property that arises from the subject position of the person who is speaking about these groups and is capable of affecting them in material reality.

The analysis of the discursive practice of speaking about oneself

Demonstrating how *the right to speak about oneself and others in public* is instantiated as a *discursive practice* (see above) requires finer analytical tools than a reconstruction of the thematic sequence. The following analysis of excerpts from the interview is focused on the relations between the speaking subject, the subject discussed, and the knowledge serving to validate a statement as referring to a particular truth about the world. Two fragments include direct references to other social groups and are a distraction from what otherwise is an egotist discourse of the elites speaking about themselves. As a contrast, the third fragment concerns the way in which Kaczyński speaks about Donald Tusk, which Lis takes issue with. This is an example of the elites talking about the elites, which is part of the elitist power play, with a high standing in their own discourse at stake.

Table 1. The structure of the program against the right to speak about oneself and others

No.	Issues tackled	Speaking about oneself	Speaking about the interlocutor and the elites	Speaking about other social groups
1.	Economic crisis, the new minister of economy should PiS win the election, evaluating economic, social, and fiscal policies during the PiS government of 2005–2007	Kaczyński about himself as PiS chairman, mostly as a collective subject ("we", "during our tenure"), rarely as an individual subject ("I contest these calculations") Lis about himself as an impartial journalist (e.g., "I don't use adjectives, I provide numbers")	Lis about Kaczyński: he accuses him of falling short of European political standards by refusing to reveal the name of the potential minister of economy Kaczyński about Lis: he questions his knowledge and credentials as a journalist (e.g., "You are underestimating the wisdom of the Poles", "You know full well that I can't answer such questions", "You seem not to know how certain fees are collected, so I'm trying to explain this to you") Both speak about former ministers of economy; Kaczyński refuses to speak about the minister in the potential PiS government	Lis asks questions about the "poor people in Poland" Kaczyński speaks about "financial transfers" to the most impoverished groups and calls the nurses' strike an original "enterprise"
2.	PiS's coalitional potential and the composition of a potential government	Kaczyński about himself as PiS chairman, mostly as a collective subject (we want a coalition for a new Poland), rarely as an individual subject (e.g., "The closer the election day, the less I speak")	Kaczyński about Lis (and himself): emphasizes differences in outlooks, parries his questions (e.g., "There's no use discussing this"), and accuses him of failing to notice the problem of post-communist elites	Kaczyński about his electorate: "Polish patriots" Lis about the costs of decommunization promoted by Kaczyński: "out of the taxpayers' pockets"

Table 1 (*Continued*)

No.	Issues tackled	Speaking about oneself	Speaking about the interlocutor and the elites	Speaking about other social groups
		Lis about himself: only in the role of an impartial journalist (e. g., "I'm asking", "the viewers are not interested in my opinion")	Lis about Kaczyński: emphasizes his political ambitions, recalls his words from the past to trick him into discussing the composition of the shadow cabinet	Lis makes an unsuccessful attempt to pacify the spectators in the studio who are cheering Kaczyński (they were participants named by PiS)
			Both speak about controversial candidacies for cabinet members, i. e., Antoni Macierewicz and Zbigniew Ziobro, and about postcommunist elites	
3.	Kaczyński's attitude to Angela Merkel, Germany, the European Union, and Civic Platform, and the issue of Poland's position in Europe	Kaczyński about himself as a political subject ("I was fully aware of what I was doing", "I don't want to be the prime minister of a large but client state [...], but of one that is sovereign and independent") Lis about himself as a journalist, he also indirectly positions Kaczyński (e.g., "I just wanted to verify this", "maybe I'm hearing things, but I believe that it's you, not me, who wants to be prime minister", "our viewers [...], without a shadow of a doubt, are	Kaczyński about Lis: says he does not qualify as a journalist acting in Poland's interests (e. g., "a Polish journalist should display a serious attitude toward their own nation", "you belong to a certain formation, which is, unfortunately, very popular in Poland, and is harmful to us") Kaczyński about Tusk, and indirectly himself as prime minister: "taking orders from a foreign capital [...] does not behove the prime minister"; about political opponents (e.g., "Poland is hurt	In this segment, nobody speaks about social groups other than the elites.

Table 1 *(Continued)*

No.	Issues tackled	Speaking about oneself	Speaking about the interlocutor and the elites	Speaking about other social groups
		interested in your beliefs, not mine")	by those who are so terrified of those in Berlin [...], in Moscow") Lis about Kaczyński: disqualifies him as prime minister of Poland, ironically: "a seasoned politician who has been present on our political stage for more than 20 years and wants to be prime minister of a 40-million country in the middle of Europe – I have to take your words seriously", "The tenor of insinuation does not behave a man who wants to be prime minister of Poland", "The election day is still to come, and you're already dividing us"	
4.	Kaczyński's attitude to Donald Tusk and various social groups, and his refusal to take part in a pre-election debate with Tusk	Kaczyński about himself as a self-determining political and speaking subject who denies controversial statements ascribed to him (e.g., "There was no stick to beat me with", "I speak as I see fit") Lis about himself as a self-determining speaking subject: "And I ask as I see fit")	Kaczyński about Lis: dismisses his journalistic interruptions (e.g., "Where's your sense of humour?", "No, you won't be moderating my way of speaking about Donald Tusk", "I'd gladly take a question concerning issues vital to Poland") Kaczyński about Tusk: discredit-	Kaczyński lists the derogatory labels used by Tusk and PO to describe society, especially the PiS voters (e.g., "mohair berets", "mob", "cemetery hyenas"): "For the last six years, there has simply taken place an unprecedented campaign of defamation, or insult, against a large part of the society")

Table 1 (*Continued*)

No.	Issues tackled	Speaking about oneself	Speaking about the interlocutor and the elites	Speaking about other social groups
			ing Tusk as a politician and interactional partner (e.g., "I'm not into debates shrouded in absurdity", "If someone's lying, it's difficult to have a discussion with them", "It is this man that compromises the principles of democracy")	Lis counters him, saying that he offends the Silesians; he also returns to the subject of a debate with Tusk, claiming that "from the perspective of millions of voters, a pre-election debate is one of the principles of democracy"
			Lis about Kaczyński: he recalls an anecdote which tells of how the latter once carried a loaded gun to a meeting with Tusk; accuses Kaczyński of compromising European standards of political communication (his refusal to have a debate with Tusk), lectures him on the proper way to refer to the prime minister	
5.	The attitude of Kaczyński and PiS to the nationalist circles of football hooligans	Kaczyński about himself as a political subject: he speaks about political decisions he would make as prime minister regarding violence in football stadiums, answers Lis' question about his own participation in football games	Kaczyński about Lis: accuses him of double standards (he claims that he is not outraged when PiS is attacked) He criticizes the government, emphasizing that PO only took the football hooligans on when	Both speak about Piotr Staruchowicz, alias Staruch, a controversial leader of Legia Warsaw's hooligans. Lis calls him a "thug". Kaczyński distances himself from such labels and calls football hooligans for what they are

Table 1 (Continued)

No.	Issues tackled	Speaking about oneself	Speaking about the interlocutor and the elites	Speaking about other social groups
		In this segment, Lis does not speak about himself.	they started to express right-wing political slogans Lis about Kaczyński: he accuses him and PiS of countenancing violence in stadiums and radicalism for the sake of political expediency	Lis speaks about PiS's attitude toward football hooligans: "You keep saying that these hooded figures, who mothers with baby strollers give a wide berth, are the essence of patriotism"
6.	Kaczyński's cooperation with president Bronisław Komorowski	Kaczyński about himself as prime minister who should cooperate with the incumbent president: "I will respect the constitution and other laws" Lis about himself as an *impartial* journalist: "My opinion does not matter, Mr. Chairman"	Lis about Kaczyński: accuses him of insinuations directed at president Komorowski and submissiveness to father Tadeusz Rydzyk[a] Kaczyński discredits Komorowski, recalling his derogatory comments about Lech Kaczyński, and tests Lis' impartiality ("Do you think that someone like this could still be an active politician in a democratic country?"), he contrasts the president's comments with those Rydzyk made about Lech Kaczyński and his wife, Maria (e.g., "different quality of different cases")	Kaczyński speaks about people manipulated by Komorowski's words, who on this strength, tarnish the memory of Lech Kaczyński

Table 1 (*Continued*)

No.	Issues tackled	Speaking about oneself	Speaking about the interlocutor and the elites	Speaking about other social groups
7.	Women running for parliament with the backing of PiS	In this segment, neither Kaczyński nor Lis speaks openly about themselves, but they define their positions, speaking about each other	Lis tests Kaczyński's knowledge of the seven women that PiS backs who are running for parliament and who are photographed together on billboards endorsing the party. He asks him about their names and their places on the ballot lists	Lis about the female candidates from the election billboard: "Beautiful, attractive, and smart women". To Kaczyński: "You deem them worthy of appearing on your billboard, but not worthy of a first or second place on a list, and standing any chance at all to be voted into office".
			Kaczyński agrees to be tested and points out Lis' mistake (he is wrong about the ballot list and a candidate's place on said list): "You failed to do your homework prior to this program"	Kaczyński gives the names and surnames of the candidates (one name is supplied to him by the audience)
				Lis ends the program with a call for a high voter turnout: "In six days, it will be up to us to decide whether Poland does indeed deserve more"

ª A Polish clergyman, founder of Catholic mass media, including the popular Radio Maryja and Telewizja Trwam. He has come in for criticism for financial malfeasance, close ties to the right-wing ruling camp, and countenancing hate speech in the media he controls. In 2007, he made derogatory comments about Maria Kaczyńska, the then First Lady, who spoke against plans to tighten the abortion law.

Fragment 1, 2:06–3:58 mins[3]

TL: Good evening, Mr. Chairman [1], thank you for accepting the invitation.

JK: Good evening.

TL: Mr. Chairman, Europe, and elsewhere too, are plunged into the most severe economic crisis in the last 90 years [2a]. Could you reveal who, in your government, if you win the election [2b], would be responsible for the economy?

JK: Sir, I have repeatedly stated that it would be a grave mistake on my part [3a] if at this point, just before the election, we all know that the ballot is only a few days away, I were to set in motion all sorts of discussions about names [3b]. This will definitely be a tried-and-tested person with great acumen, one who can handle things. But we won't be naming names right now [3c].

TL: But don't you think, given the gravity of the situation, that millions of Poles [4a] should be given certainty, clarity who this person is going to be? Like in countries such as France or the US, which are seasoned democracies, where the leader of a party that aspires to rule says, 'in our administration, this-and-this will be responsible for the economy' [5a].

JK: Sir, different things happen in different countries, and additionally, you are underestimating the wisdom of the Poles [4b]. The Poles make educated guesses, and that is enough [4c].

TL: Is professor…

JK: They will vote for Law and Justice; well, those who will, will at the same time vote in favour of particular economic and personal solutions [4d].

TL: And when you don't name names, don't you think you're making Poles buy a pig in a poke [5b]?

JK: No, no, I'm not, precisely because they are intelligent people. Please, have some more appreciation for Poles, sir [6]. (applause in the audience) [**numbers by the author**]

The interview opens with conventional greeting formulas, but what immediately becomes apparent is the strategy of positioning Kaczyński as a particular political subject, i.e., chairman of the party [1], and not a former prime minister. Kaczyński agrees to such a convention. Lis posits the existence of a major economic crisis in Europe [2a], which enhances the significance of the question about who will be the minister of economy in a potential PiS government [2b]. Kaczyński refuses to answer, invoking political ramifications of his decision to reveal the name [3a and 3b]. His refusal is categorical [3c] and is linked to the right not to speak about problematic issues. As a result, Lis takes on the role of a concerned member of the elites who insists that Poles are entitled to know PiS's political plans [4a]. The reference point here is Western "seasoned democracies" [5a], and not the actual problems of the Polish people. Lis' position is not about activating a

---

3 The timespans correspond to the program available on the TVP website: https://www.tvp.pl /publicystyka/polityka/tomasz-lis-na-zywo/wideo/jaroslaw-kaczynski-03102011/5286585 [30.11.2021].

social perspective, but reproducing the order of things whereby it is the elite that announces to the people who will be governing them and in what way. Kaczyński rejects the parallels with Western standards and challenges this order. Poles are intelligent and do not require being apprised by the elites [4b] – and still, this "common" knowledge cannot be directly verbalized. Kaczyński refuses to reveal this information and terminates the topic, again exercising the right not to speak [4c]. However, he qualifies this by saying that he does not mean all Poles, but the PiS electorate, who is aware of what economic solutions they are voting in favour of [4d]. Lis is adamant and again insists that the elites inform the people about the details surrounding the appointment of a new minister of economy and professes his concern for the wellbeing of the Poles [5b]. Kaczyński refuses to budge, once again citing the wisdom of the Polish people. The accusation that Lis does not appreciate this wisdom casts doubts not just on his position as an impartial journalist acting as an intermediary between the elites and the people, but also on the interpretation of the world invoked by the discourse of liberal elites [6].

Fragment 2, 9:25–10:29 mins

> TL: Mr. Chairman, you speak about the poor people in Poland, which is indeed a very numerous group, but you, when you were prime minister, you mostly took care of the rich Poles [1].
>
> JK: So this is what you say [2]?
>
> TL: This is what the facts and figures indicate [3a].
>
> JK: Then I would advise you to take a closer look at various social transfers, financial transfers [3b], which greatly, and I mean, greatly…
>
> TL: And what are these transfers exactly, Mr. Chairman [3c]?
>
> JK: Well, all these transfers which related to the countryside, the increasing of numerous social benefits, increasing the minimum wage…
>
> TL: Mr. Chairman…
>
> JK: … increasing, restoring the revalorization of pensions, increasing the salaries of… [3d]
>
> TL: But sir, the taxes were… [4]
>
> JK: Why don't you let me finish [5a]?
>
> TL: Yes, please [5b].
>
> JK: Increasing the salaries of healthcare professionals; they are mostly people who earn little money. I'm not talking about doctors, although back then doctors, too, often earned very little [6a].
>
> TL: And nurses [6b].
>
> JK: Yes, nurses, a third… [6c].
>
> TL: But when did that happen? After the strike, after nurses protested outside the prime minister's offices [7a].
>
> JK: No, sir, that, as a matter of fact, happened earlier. A strange thing about this strike

was that it took place after the biggest pay rise in the history of the Polish healthcare system. This was precisely what made for the originality of that enterprise [7b].

The interviewer starts talking about the lower class, calling these people "poor" (thus using a traditional label that refers to differences in material status). But it is not the poor people that are the theme of this statement, but Kaczyński's alleged hypocrisy (he is talking about "the poor," but he looks after "the rich") [1]. Kaczyński deflects this accusation and reduces its status to that of Lis' opinion [2]. At this point, references to "the poor people" cease to be the interlocutors' argumentative resource. Lis mentions statistics [3a], and Kaczyński adopts an impersonal way of discussing social and wage policies, referring to social and financial "transfers" [3b]. Lis expects greater precision [3c], and this is what he gets, as Kaczyński is now given an opportunity to speak about the successful policies of the former PiS government [3d]. Discussing the accomplishments of PiS is out of keeping with Lis' strategy in this program (see below), so he tries to change the subject and talk about fiscal policies [4]. Kaczyński will not be distracted from discussing an issue that is to his political advantage [5a and 5b]. He starts to speak about healthcare professionals as people who earn little [6a]. At this point, people once again briefly become an argumentative resource in the dispute between the two members of the elites. Lis mentions the nursing profession [6b], and Kaczyński attempts to add the increased salaries of this group to the list of PiS achievements [6c]. Lis interrupts him, recalling the nurses' strike of summer 2007[4] [7a]. Kaczyński will not discuss its provenance but emphasizes that it took place following "the biggest pay rise in the history of the Polish healthcare system", thus invalidating the logic behind the protest [7b]. In the following part, not covered by the transcript, Lis does not oppose it, abandoning the subject of the nurses, and reintroducing the issue of fiscal policies, this time successfully.

Fragment 3, 34:59–35:39 mins

JK: You are saying that my refusal to speak to a person who uses absurd argumentation and with whom it is simply impossible to speak in a normal manner means that I'm compromising the principles of democracy [1]. My answer is this: no, it is this man that compromises the principles of democracy, this man compromises the principles of democracy [2a]...

---

4 Nurses went on strike between 19 June and 15 July 2007, demanding higher salaries and the reorganization of the healthcare system in which they worked. It was labeled "the white village", a reference to the color of nurses' uniforms and the tents set up outside the Office of the Prime Minister in Warsaw. The then incumbent was Jarosław Kaczyński. Although it was the largest such protest, no agreement was reached.

TL: Do you think…

JK: It's this man that is responsible for…

TL: Why do you keep saying, "this man", and not "the prime minister"? [3a]

JK: … the fact that the police storm the apartment of some blogger at six in the morning [2b].

TL: Again, why do you keep referring to Donald Tusk as "this man"? [3b]

JK: I speak as I see fit [4a].

TL: And I ask as I see fit [4b].

JK: Well, then you have the right to ask, and my answer is that this is what I see fit, and that is that [4c].

The third fragment is the climax of part 4 (see Table 1), which concerns Kaczyński's attitude to Donald Tusk, the incumbent prime minister. Kaczyński summarizes Lis' accusation that his refusal to take part in a pre-election debate with Tusk is out of line with democratic standards. He also denies Tusk the ability to participate in a debate in a rational manner [1]. He deflects criticism and directs it at Tusk ("it is this man that compromises the principles of democracy") [2a]. He further discredits him by referring to when the Internal Security Agency searched the apartment of a blogger suspected of slandering president Komorowski [2b]. Lis interrupts him twice [3a and 3b]. His question regarding the form in which Kaczyński addresses the prime minister ("this man") is an attempt to position the PiS chairman as a political anti-subject, someone who not only fails to observe politeness strategies, but also disrespects the principles of politics. Kaczyński's response indicates different discourse positioning, which results from his self-knowledge and identifying the right to speak with political subjectivity [4a]. Lis responds with the same discursive structure [4b]. Kaczyński sanctions Lis' words, but, first and foremost, his own. He terminates the subject in yet another attempt at exercising the right not to speak about a particular issue [4c].

A comparison of discursive formations and their ideological functions

Based on a critical reading of what transpired in the excerpts analysed, both differences and similarities can be spotted in the discursive practices governing the respective statements of Kaczyński and Lis. The former appears to more consistently exercise and define his right to speak, also enforcing his right not to speak about particular subjects. However, his categorical manner of speaking about himself and others is a response to what Lis does to exercise his right to speak in the face of his interlocutor's objection to expressing judgments about a given topic or in a particular fashion. Speaking about oneself and others becomes the practice of rationing the contents discussed in public and formulating an implicit message as to the veracity of one's own statements and the falsehood of what others say. This selective transmission is made coherent by the internal logic of discourse and strategic goals.

The properties that help discriminate between the respective performances of Lis and Kaczyński at the level of what is being said, but at the same time equalizing them regarding selected meta-discursive aspects, can be distinguished by invoking the category of *discursive formation*, i.e., a collection of qualitative rules that shapes statements and combines them into a given discourse (Foucault 1972, p. 31 ff). Andrea D. Bührmann (2006), who operationalizes this category for empirical studies, recognizes, after Foucault, four dimensions of discursive formation: 1) *Object/area of knowledge* – a common theme of an utterance and its anchoring in knowledge, 2) *Expression modality* – a way of validating the content communicated, also through the speaking subject's stance toward what is being said, 3) *Concept construction* – a coherent structure of terms and classifications that appear in statements, 4) *Strategic choice* – the strategic goal that the statement serves. Aside from these, the following comparative analysis takes account of the implicit message about what is true and what is false, as well as the *points of incompatibility, points of equivalence,* and *points of compatibility* of discursive formations (cf. Foucault 1972, p. 65 ff), which are used here as the comparative categories for different discursive formations that Kaczyński and Lis' statements belong to. The final addition is the aspect of the *ideological function* of these formations, which is related to the strengthening of a particular discourse position at the expense of others and, consequently, to the exclusion of certain interpretations of reality.

Table 2. A comparison of discursive formations presented by Lis and Kaczyński

	Tomasz Lis	Jarosław Kaczyński
Object/area of knowledge	The topics discussed are mostly Jarosław Kaczyński as a political anti-subject, as well as the state of democracy, the economy, and the public sphere Lis refers to numerical data and macroeconomic knowledge without giving sources (he presents common knowledge about economy)	The topics discussed are mostly Kaczyński himself and his party's policies, but also Donald Tusk as a political anti-subject and Poles as the PiS electorate Kaczyński refers to implicit knowledge as a valid source of his interpretation of reality that he shares with "his" Poles
Expression modality	High confidence expressed regarding the veracity of his statements; directly stated conviction that his stance is anchored in verifiable knowledge	High confidence expressed as to the veracity and validity of his own statements; directly stated conviction that it is not necessary to explain and justify his own discursive actions

Table 2 *(Continued)*

	Tomasz Lis	Jarosław Kaczyński
	Negative attitude toward Kaczyński's words and mostly reactive attempts at self-determination in the discourse	Attempts at relativizing and subjectifying Lis' stance and mostly active attempts at self-determination in the discourse
Concept construction	Terms and classifications related to the economy and liberal democracy, e.g., PiS vs. "seasoned democracies" – PiS is not up to the standards of Western democracies; "economic crisis", "the economy" as a politically crucial domain; "poor people", but then "numbers", "figures", "facts", "transfers" – poverty as a statistical rather than social problem	Terms and classifications related to the division of Poles into his own electorate and others, e.g., "Poles are intelligent, make educated guesses" – creating opposition: mature Poles vs. seasoned Western democracies; "social transfers", "financial transfers", "increased wages", "revalorization of pensions" – an impersonal vision of being concerned for the people; a "strike" as an "enterprise" – protesting as a deliberate action
Strategic choice	Revealing contradictions in Kaczyński's statements and discrediting his discursive formation	Positioning himself within discourse as the leader of the state and Poles (but not all of them), and discrediting the opposing discursive formation
Implicit message about what is true/false	Laying bare the deceit of another discourse subject, positioning Kaczyński as an insincere politician, and self-positioning as the one who exposes the lie. Lis' words suggest that Kaczyński's discursive practice is to conceal data, names, motivations, etc. Lis pretends to be merely asking questions, but he effectively challenges the stance of his interlocutor	Self-positioning as an instance of truth and a subject who reveals the truth about others (e.g., Tusk's deceit) Contesting Lis' right to formulate particular types of statements, invalidating selected questions, treating Lis' voice as a subjective and partial voice that deliberately misrepresents politics
Points of incompatibility	According to Lis, Western democracies are a model for Poland, and Donald Tusk, as prime minister, is a guarantor of Western standards. Kaczyński questions both points of reference: the former is relativized, and the latter is rejected. Taking their place is Kaczyński's proposal where he is the guarantor of the Polish state's sovereignty in relation to the West	
Points of equivalence	In both formations, what regulates the political conflict is the concern (motivated by vested interests) about Poles' political knowledge. The sources of this knowledge differ, though: for Lis, it is the elites who communicate with the people, while for Kaczyński, it is the people who share his worldview	

Table 2 *(Continued)*

	Tomasz Lis	Jarosław Kaczyński
Points of compatibility	Both formations have a similar modality and depict lower classes in similar objectifying, non-subjective terms	
Ideological function	Both formations fulfil the ideological function, contributing to public discourse being dominated by the elitist perspective, which marginalizes or takes advantage of the perspectives of other social classes. These formations generate competing and mutually exclusive visions of Poland. For Lis, this is not a country for Euro-sceptics, and for Kaczyński, it is not for those who submit to the West	

During the interview, neither Kaczyński nor Lis instantiates discursive formations that are fully *proprietary*. They follow, respectively, the pro-Western paternalistic liberal discourse, or the equally paternalistic discourse that is sceptical of the West. What they say is shaped by their attitudes toward each other and a high degree of confidence that they communicate the *truth* about the world. The similarities between the formations also arise from their strategies of positioning themselves in discourse as the governors of what can be publicly said about themselves and others, as the guardians of truth, and those who lay bare the ingenuity of their political opponents.

Speaking about others and the truth about discourse

The excerpts analysed should again be referred to the entirety of the interview, and, by means of abductive reasoning, it is also possible to draw some conclusions about the elites' public discourse as such. First, both Lis and Kaczyński can validly say as much as another subject vested with the right to speak lets them, and as much as can be accommodated by the ideological frames of political discourse. Conversational conventions may be transgressed for the purpose of achieving strategic goals. Being allowed to speak are those who embed their statements in knowledge, and the knowledge is legitimized through the focality of the speaking subject.

Second, this interview conceals more than it reveals, but overtly present is the animosity between the political extremes. What is implicit is the similarities between the formations to which Kaczyński's and Lis' statements belong, and in particular, their ideological function. Essentially, the interview does not tackle issues other than those that relate to economic, social, and international policies, which may be indicative of the commercialization of political discourse and its focus on the image of the state or the image of the speakers.

Third, the subject positions instantiated in the interview are by definition competing. Although they do enjoy a certain degree of agency in the institutional and practical spheres, their subjectivity in public discourse is a function of the conflict relation between Kaczyński and Lis, which holds in the discourse and beyond it. What they have in common is the practice of enforcing categoricalness and non-negotiability of their own outlook on things. Yet, this outlook is not completely their own; rather, it is consistent with the patterns of public discourse (including the personalization of conflict, discreditation, the reduction of social structure to its economic dimension, among others).

Fourth, in an attempt to step outside of this interview's context and toward the nature of the public discourse of the elites, it can be concluded that what typifies this discourse is a way of speaking about others that is, in essence, speaking about oneself, one's own beliefs, and modes of operating in accordance with a preferred ideology and the pertinent discourse practices. This categorization of others is in line with one's own discursive formation. When the focus of discourse is the elites' concern for people, we are looking at a manner of *speaking on behalf of others* that is not sanctioned by them. This is also projecting their own vision of the *truth* about the world and their own knowledge onto what others make of reality and their situation. What is important is that the other participants of the discourse take this *truth* to be a binding reference point in the public debate because it is espoused by a member of the elites and a central subject of public discourse.

Fifth, what emerges from the analysed statements is a certain truth about the elites, whose members produced them. They are interested in society to the extent to which this collective non-subject shares their worldview, especially the interpretation of political goals. However, although they subscribe to these patterns of perceiving political reality, the people do not become the subject of the elites' public discourse; they are merely one of the themes it is concerned with.

Summary

The self-satisfaction of Kaczyński and Lis at taking part in the 2011 interview is partly justified. Both enhanced their discursive capital. Competing for meaningful subject positions, i.e., that are central, order knowledge, and categorize others, they reasserted the positions held thus far and, indirectly, the social status of the elite. They instantiated the practice of speaking about themselves and others mostly through positioning within the discourse of their interactional partners as the spokespersons of deceit and destroyers of the order of knowledge, while they themselves were the ones to expose the lie, serving as defenders of truth and guardians of the preferred order of knowledge. One of the instruments employed to that end was the objectifying categorization of non-elite social groups.

Thanks to Lis and Kaczyński's standing in the structures of political and symbolic power, the broad reach of the program in which they participated, and their skilful exercise of the right to speak in public, the interview sparked numerous comments that went beyond this context and referred to the entirety of their public activity. Their *discursive capital* was undoubtedly enhanced. However, it is not a resource that can be simply abstracted from discourse and employed in other spheres of social activity (e.g., to win an election). Its value is guaranteed by discourse and is estimated therein. Public discourse is, in turn, sensitive to material and symbolic social and political processes. The principles of statement production are regulated by both the conventional discourse order at a particular historical juncture and social dynamics. The elites' response to the precariousness of their social position is the accumulation of *discursive capital*, mostly through reproducing their position of advantage in discourse. This is what the elites' power in discourse results from. They use the discourse of the elites, because it is a carrier of their social dominance. But it may let them down sometimes. The subsequent careers of Kaczyński and Lis (see the Introduction) appear to testify to this.

References

Angermuller, J.: 'Accumulating Discursive Capital, Valuating Subject Positions: From Marx to Foucault', in: CRITICAL DISCOURSE STUDIES 2018/15(4), p. 414–425.

Bacchi, C. / Bonham, J.: 'Reclaiming Discursive Practices as an Analytic Focus: Political Implications', in: FOUCAULT STUDIES 2014/17, p. 173–192.

Bosančić, S.: 'Interpretive Subjectivation Analysis – A Critical Perspective On The Discursive Situatedness Of Human Subjectivities', in SOCIETY REGISTER 2019/3(1), p. 87–104.

Beetz, J. / Schwab, V.: 'Conditions and Relations of (Re)Production in Marxism and Discourse Studies', in: CRITICAL DISCOURSE STUDIES 2018/15(4), p. 338–350.

Bourdieu, Pierre: 'The Forms of Capital', in: Richardson, John G. (eds.): *Handbook of Theory and Research for Sociology of Education*. New York 1986, p. 241–258.

Bührmann, A.D.: 'The Emerging of the Enterprising Self and Its Contemporary Hegemonic Status: Some Fundamental Observations for an Analysis of the (Trans-) Formational Process of Modern Forms of Subjectivation', in: FORUM: QUALITATIVE SOCIAL RESEARCH 2006/6(1), Art. 16, available at: http://nbn-resolving.de/urn:nbn:de:0114-f qs0501165 [12.11.2021].

Fairclough, N. / Graham, P.: 'Marx as a Critical Discourse Analyst: The Genesis of a Critical Method and its Relevance to the Critique of Global Capital', in: ESTUDIOS DE SOCI-OLINGÜÍSTICA, 2002/3, p. 185–229.

Foucault, Michel: The Archeology of Knowledge and the Discourse of Language. New York 1972.

Foucault, Michel: 'The Order of Discourse', in: Young, Robert (eds.): *Untying the Text: A Post-Structuralist Reader*. Boston-London-Henley 1980, p. 51–78.

Foucault, Michel: 'Le discours ne doit pas être pris comme…' in Foucault, Michel: *Dits et écrits II. 1976–1988*. Paris 2001 [1976], p. 123–124.

Foucault, Michel: 'What is Critique?', in: Lotringen, Sylvère (ed.): *The Politics of Truth*. Los Angeles 2007, p. 41–81.

Glynos, Jason / Howarth, David: Logics of Critical Explanation in Social and Political Theory. Abingdon 2007.

Głowiński, Michał: Nowomowa i ciągi dalsze: Szkice dawne i nowe. Krakow 2009.

Hall, Stuart: Encoding and Decoding in the Television Discourse. Birmingham 1973.

Herzog, B. 'Marx's Critique of Ideology for Discourse Analysis: From Analysis of Ideologies to Social Critique', in: CRITICAL DISCOURSE STUDIES 2018/15(4), p. 402–413.

Higley, John: 'Elites' Illusions About Democracy', in: Best Heinrich / Higley John, (eds.): *Democratic Elitism: New Theoretical and Comparative Perspectives*. Leiden 2010, p. 79–94.

Howarth, D. 'Marx, Discourse Theory and Political Analysis: Negotiating an Ambiguous Legacy', in: CRITICAL DISCOURSE STUDIES 2018/15(4), p. 377–389.

Hunter, Floyd: Community Power Structure. Chapel Hill 1953.

Jessop B. / Ngai-Ling S. 'Language and Critique: Some Anticipations of Critical Discourse Studies in Marx', in: CRITICAL DISCOURSE STUDIES 2018/15(4), p. 325–337.

Keller, Suzanne: Beyond the Ruling Class. Strategic Elites in Modern Society. New York 1963.

Kobus, Aldona: Autorstwo. Urynkowienie literatury i fantazmat podmiotu autorskiego. Toruń 2021.

Kumięga, Łukasz: 'Medien im Spannungsfeld zwischen Diskurs und Dispositiv', in: Dreesen, Philipp / Kumięga, Łukasz / Spieß Constanze (eds.): *Mediendiskursanalyse. Diskurse-Dispositive-Medien-Macht*. Wiesbaden 2012, p. 25–45.

'Lisowi pomógł Kaczyński…'. 2011, available at: https://film.interia.pl/telewizja/news-liso wi-pomogl-kaczynski,nId,1800672 [14.11.2021].

Polkowska, Laura: Język prawicy. Warsaw 2015.

Pallus, P.: '2,9 mln widzów TVP2 pożegnało Tomasza Lisa. Czas na Onet.pl'. 2016, available at: https://www.wirtualnemedia.pl/artykul/2-9-mln-widzow-tvp2-pozegnalo-tomasza-lisa-czas-na-onet-pl [9.10.2021].

Ratajczak, M.: 'Abonament RTV może zaskoczyć. Poczta Polska i KRRiT złapały 9,5 tys. telepajęczarzy'. 2019, available at: https://www.money.pl/gospodarka/abonament-rtv-moze-zaskoczyc-poczta-polska-i-krrit-zlapaly-95-tys-telepajeczarzy-642969646782220 9a.html [14.11.2021].

Sieber, Samuel: Macht und Medien. Zur Diskursanalyse des Politischen. Bielefeld 2014.

Thiele, Matthias: 'Vom Medien-Dispositiv zum Dispositiv-Netze-Ansatz', in: Othmer, Julius, / Weich, Andreas (eds.): *Medien – Bildung – Dispositive. Beiträge zu einer interdisziplinären Medienbildungsforschung*. Wiesbaden 2015, p. 87–108.

Van Dijk, Teun. Elite Discourse and Racism. Newbury Park 1993.

Wodak, Ruth: 'The 'Establishment', the 'Élites', and the 'People': Who's who?', in: JOURNAL OF LANGUAGE AND POLITICS, October 2017, p. 2–14.

Mills, Charles Wright: The Power Elite. New York 1959.

Wasilewski, J.: 'Demokratyczny elityzm: Zmiana ustroju i relacje elita – masy', in: STUDIA SOCJOLOGICZNE 2021/240(1), p. 7–41.

Jerzy Stachowiak

Media performance. Remarks on the possibility of its analysis and critique

Abstract
Tomasz Lis' talk with Jarosław Kaczyński is a particular kind of media performance. Its basic formal arrangement comprises at least four aspects: (a) specific temporal structure, (b) discursive pattern of speaking about speaking, (c) highly limited set of conventional interactional moves, (d) mutual presentation of interlocutors as not being conversation partners for each other. These aspects are also indicative of the circumstances media performance sets up for and before the public. As such media performance can be both an object of discourse analysis and criticism. However, the notion of the media performance as offered in this chapter is an outcome, not a prerequisite, of the empirical examination reported below. This means that at the beginning of the study criticism was theoretically allowed but methodologically hold back until the conceptual result of research takes its shape. This chapter argues for the possibility and potential benefits of deferring criticism in discourse studies.
Keywords: performance, critique, discourse analysis, discursive psychology

Introduction

The present text has two aims. The first is to consider a situation whereby discourse studies are somewhat forced to take sides, and either to refrain, by default, from a critical analysis of discursive phenomena, or to accept discourse criticism as the ultimate obligation of research. This aim will be pursued under introductory remarks. The second goal is to analyse Tomasz Lis' talk with Jarosław Kaczyński in order to expose what would allow to recognize it as a media performance. This will be done by determining the basic formal structure of the media performance, which makes it possible to reconstruct the circumstances in which the interview embeds its audience.

Jerzy Stachowiak, University of Łódź (Poland), ORCID: 0000-0002-7727-1082, jerzy.stachowiak@uni.lodz.pl.

These goals are interconnected. To waive the right to criticize seems equally unsatisfactory as being obliged to criticism at all costs. In the following remarks efforts are made to defend the critical and socially engaged potential of the inquiry but at the same time to provide arguments for the benefits of deferring criticism. The basic meaning of media performance adopted in this text was not taken from other studies. Rather, this study aimed at the possibility of its own findings and deriving the formal structure of the talk between Tomasz Lis and Jarosław Kaczyński from an empirical work which might eventually, but not necessarily, lead do criticism towards the problem captured in the final theoretical category. There is yet another, more general, questions these two interconnected goals relate to. How extensive or how limited are the empirical prerogatives of discourse studies as a source of criticism? How far-reaching can this criticism be if discourse analysts were to stay within their professional competences? These questions cannot be fully answered here and can only remain in the background of the main discussion.

The attempt to reach both goals is preparatory. This means that the following remarks can be treated at least twofold: either as an exercise in public discourse studies, or a procedure of the taking of evidence conducted so that the public can judge the circumstances which the media performance offers it. In both cases, the criticism of media performance is a specific kind of criticism, since it relies on the empirical work done on talk and text in the first place.

On deferring criticism

Among the many taxonomies present in discourse studies, there is one that introduces a particularly sharp distinction. Situated on one extreme are studies professing full commitment to academic purposes defined as a pursuit to observe social reality, rather than change it. The other extreme sees studies promoting the idea of research unconditionally devoted to striving for certain social goals. This dichotomy is well-known and continually valid. It offers a choice which – at its most radical – is between treating participation in social conflicts as a privilege worth waiving, and using the research apparatus towards morally-driven involvement in changing the reality studied. Thus, self-limitation to expertise deriving from professional training is pitted against espousing particular non-academic goals.

There have been numerous attempts to resolve this antinomy by means of settling somewhere between the two extremes. Conversational analysis, to the extent that it adheres to the principle of ethnomethodological indifference and to Harvey Sacks' original aspirations, sets itself strictly academic goals: making sociology a natural observational science (Sacks 1984, p. 21). However, the definitional approach to social problems, proposed back in the 1960s by John Kitsuse and Malcolm Spector, introduces a clear distinction between what one can validly say as a member of society, and what one says in their capacity as analyst. Kitsuse and Spector do not deny scholars the right to moral judgment and to determine some aspects of social reality as social problems, but indicate that "this practice must be clearly separated from a *theoretical* mandate to do so" (Spector / Kitsuse 1987, p. 63; original emphasis). Similarly, in discursive psychology, analyst can and generally should get involved in problems of society, but this very involvement (participation in public definitional processes) means that analyst is no longer doing analysis but "provides further materials for analysis" (Edwards 1997, p. 16). Consequently, keeping these two spheres separate is seen as a value in its own right.

But in other approaches, such definition of the role of a researcher is either considered impossible or futile, or it stops just short of fulfilling the proper vocation of intellectual and academic life. In critical discourse analysis – much as this umbrella term fails to do justice to its internal complexity and tensions between scholars invoking this name in their works – aspiring to influence the reality studied is taken to be constitutive of a legitimate inquiry. "Criticism" is interpreted in various ways: less radically, as uncovering ideology, hegemony, and injustice in power relations (Duszak / Fairclough 2008, p. 10), and more radically, as a means of anti-discriminatory policy, which first highlights manifestations of oppression and xenophobia, and then stands up to them within the political institutions of deliberative democracy (Reisigl 2010, p. 57, Reisigl / Wodak 2001, p. 266). Edward Said, who has also inspired discourse analysis outside the postcolonial studies, writes that attempting to comment on issues within one's professional purview only is "the perennial escape mechanism". This is, on the one hand, a criticism of shirking responsibility for dealing with more global matters, which sees one "block the larger and [...] the more intellectually serious perspective" (Said 2003, p. 14), and disapproval of deliberately settling for a description of the world, without commenting on its condition, on the other.

Despite the diversity of works developed under the labels of "discourse psychology" or "conversational analysis", their basic evolution trajectory and research demand are relatively stable: studies under either approach stop short of criticism, do not tend toward it, and do without announcing it in public. On the other hand, in critical discourse analysis, in studies indebted to Said, but also in a bulk of post-Foucauldian studies, research in a sense begins once the decision to engage in criticism has already been made. In this line of inquiry, the need for criticism is pre-established and as such it subsequently determines the purport of research activity. There are valid grounds for both options, and it is precisely for that reason that any attempts to advocate either are typically directed at abolishing the persisting antinomy. However, they run the risk of yielding utterly unsatisfactory results. This is because revoking this dichotomy by rejecting one of its constituents would be too big a loss to incur, while their synthesis would have internally contradictory outcomes. Additionally, either scenario is as inadequate as concluding that the competing options make up an ostensible dichotomy, and that their strengths and weaknesses could be eventually balanced and reconciled into a perfect whole. Rather, this opposition is not unlike other social value conflicts, which "are not merely apparent and cannot be overcome by sage moderation" (Kołakowski 1963, p. 206), instead requiring acceptance precisely in this form.

The problem gets complicated still further, as this antinomy is followed by another. In discourse studies (and elsewhere), there are two general directions of conceptual work which are analytically distinct, but occasionally partly concurrent. One consists in confirming the validity of concepts. It entails research subjugated to the concepts which inspired it in the first place; they are adopted in order for the research to confirm the significance of the original motivation. The other direction consists of deriving concepts. It reflects the aspiration to extract problems which may be conceptually unspecified at a particular moment. It is a step toward what is still unknown. This division of labour between confirmation and derivation marks two directions of thought, and as such does not overlap with a division into particular strands of research or schools in discourse studies. The direction of thought has nothing to do with this or that research tradition. For this reason, post-Foucauldian studies span works venturing into the unknown, moving from issues identified by Foucault towards issues formulated independently (e. g., Bröckling 2015), but also those that take as their starting point certain Foucauldian notions, such as power-knowledge or subjectification, to eventually conclude that particular aspects of social reality "proves" to be an instance of power-knowledge or a method of subjectification (Fejes / Nicoll 2008). Thus, it is crucial what is taken as a study's departure point, and what is this study's destination. In other words, the difference is that between confirming the validity of notions already available and, consequently, of established types of criticism on the one hand, and arriving at new concepts and types of criticism in the course of the current research on the other.

More promising prospects of resolving the issues which arise from these antinomies could follow from not being forced to choose between its constituents. There is a possibility which posits "the refusal, once and for all, to make a choice for all future time between two mutually exclusive values" (Kołakowski 1963, p. 204). The inconsistency suggested by Kołakowski is tactical and not strategic: it stands for the unwillingness to renounce cherished values which, at the same time, are at odds with each other (ibid.), and for the commitment to considering each situation on individual basis. To follow this type of inconsistency means that making forced decisions in favour of one methodological options would be as insufficient as taking no action when faced with an antinomy.

It is only against this backdrop that the fundamental problem arises, which can be formulated as follows: "Discursive psychologists aim to avoid coming to conclusions that analysis can reveal people's true beliefs and attitudes. We avoid coming to such conclusions not because it is wrong to do so, but as a matter of methodological principle. Furthermore, we avoid this practice in relation to every topic [...] Yet once this methodological move is made, it turns out to be not so much an avoidance of the real issues, of dealing with 'actual' prejudice, attitudes, memories, causal explanations, and so on. Rather, it becomes a re-definition of what prejudice, etc., is" (Edwards 2003, p. 32)[1]. Any effort toward grasping the methodological sense of this radical principle allows for figuring out that it underlies not just a basic research approach in discursive psychology, but also one of the reasons why this field has not seen a transition from analysis to an open discussion on its condition on the part of publicly engaged analysts. Meanwhile, in certain other approaches to discourse, such as critical discourse analysis, various types of social oppression are highlighted. In this research tradition, the problem of re-definition is not an issue, it is not in demand. Importantly, critical discourse analysis aspires to exploit the notion of criticism comprehensively: its goal is to retain the scientific significance of distinctions it introduces, as well as to be morally involved in the public demystification of social injustice and domination. Pointing to the differences between these research approaches is neither to undermine nor defend them on grounds of decided superiority of any one of them. The point is quite different: to the proponents of socio-political involvement of discourse studies, the radicalism of the issue of re-definition may be utterly futile and amount to a failure to pursue the supreme goal of research.

However, there might be another option. Perhaps the very same thing that prevents discursive psychology from progressing from analysis to public significance could serve to pave this way. What is consistent with the proposition "to approach discursive phenomena as discursive ones without trying to see through, or see past, to some other reality behind or beneath" (ibid.) can bring about criticism in a different form than suggested by the common-sense understanding of the relations between the discursive sphere as overt (but mystified) and non-discursive sphere as covert (though undeniable). It is precisely not treating discourse solely as a verbal screen or a distortion of reality that opens up an opportunity to consider various discursive phenomena – from prejudice (in the sense of discursive psychology), to media performances, to their numerous in-

---

1 On a side note, *Analyzing Race Talk* is another publication presenting methodologically diverse analyses of the same material (research interview).

terdependencies – as problematic in their overtness: not because they conceal "actual" problems, but because they create problems themselves due to their own character. A criticism that makes no attempt to see through, or see past is not a way to transform discursive psychology. Discursive psychology has its own merits and respectable aspirations and does not require any transformation postulated from without. Rather the point is to build upon the research on talk and texts as medium for action and try to find out if the analysis of discursive action could be a sufficient condition for criticism. In order to do so one would have to allow the possibility that the non-discursive sphere does not have to be an irrevocable starting point for criticism of discourse phenomena. This type of criticism would distance itself from the classic Marxist notion of ideology as deceptive ornamentation of facts, an idea which frequently permeates into discourse studies. It would also be unbound to follow the notion of social representations, which often entails the necessity to postulate (and equally often the inability to demonstrate) access to non-discursively transmitted knowledge of what is socially represented. In addition, it would not have to rely on the idea of social consciousness as a set of notions or beliefs, since consciousness, just like prejudices or attitudes, is precisely that which is subject to re-definition. It would offer a chance to examine what the scrutinized phenomena do in the sphere of discourse and what they do with it. As such it could be of use in the ability to defer the decision on whether the object of analysis should be subject to criticism.

The present chapter is not planed as an interpretation of a particular school of discourse analysis. It acknowledges the importance of these schools, but makes no attempt to elaborate on their theoretical and methodological capabilities, just as it does not stake a claim to doing it better than their founders, distinguished representatives, and numerous advocates. Rather, it processes influences and inspirations deriving from the varieties of research procedure which constitute the aforesaid antinomies. Among these varieties is a methodological instruction from the field of conversation analysis: "to begin with some observations, then find the problem for which those observations could serve as (elements of) the solution" (Schegloff 1995: xlviii). This advice is understood in line with what it was originally intended to be, namely, an encouragement to engage in independent research. This formulation does not express anything by means of established theoretical notions, and certainly does nothing to indicate which observations qualify for criticism. Although originally this instruction was not connected with the demand for criticism, such wording alone does not rule it out. More importantly, discourse (or text) "is, analytically, what we have got, what we start with" (Edwards 1997, p. 272), and the problem emerging in the course of analysis may also become the object of criticism of "what we have got". If that happens, then this problem also has a chance to become analytically demonstrable. The significance of this point of departure lies in the following: instead of expediting the fulfilment of critical aspirations by having the object of criticism in a conceptually established form, it would see a delay in the realization of said aspirations. In that case, the selection of the object of criticism is postponed until it takes shape in the course of research, which will itself rise to the expected status of a procedure of sanctioning the validity of criticism.

This means that the conduct of inquiry is more than the professional harnessing of the primary drive to moral struggle, and that methodological and theoretical preparation for research is just a conscious or unconscious means of professional expression or promotion of partisan social interests. Adopting such chronology (first identifying the social interest worthy of scientific support and then conducting this scientific supporting procedure) is very frequent. Subject to debate are also the validity of this approach, its moral value, and its sustainability. Similar considerations are by all means useful. However, they are not the same as resigning oneself to the ostensibly inevitable reduction of research to the level of scientific legitimization of correcting injustice. Likewise, they do not mean accepting that new studies on discourse will only be sanctioned as long as they rubber-stamp the conceptual handiness of the tried-and-tested terms which direct scholarly attention toward the criticism of what has repeatedly come in for it in the past. A premature promotion of an intention of criticism can potentially devalue observations, turning them into a mere confirmation of what is already known and requires condemnation in its apparent unequivocalness. This creates an impression of setting out on a journey whose destination has been already reached on departure. Said prematurity frequently leads to validating ways of criticism which have already proved their usefulness (on multiple occasions), and, in the empirical investigation, gives primacy to extracting from the study material that which directs one to the well-trodden path of critical thought. Finally, it introduces an imbalance between two ways of understanding criticism: it exalts criticism as a practice of a theoretical exposition of negatives, at the same time diminishing the significance of criticism as a practice of making provable distinctions.

Hypothesis and analysis

The following part of the chapter is devoted to analytical remarks on Tomasz Lis' talk with Jarosław Kaczyński[2]. In line with the working hypothesis, the exchange is built on the requirement of the permanent ignorance of the audience, rather

---

2 An account of the situation in Polish political and media life before the 2011 elections as well as comments on the main characters who contributed to this situation can be found in the introduction to this volume.

than the latter's readiness to be educated. Assuming the ignorance of the public is a characteristic feature of this talk and, by extension, of the culture of public communication to which it contributes and thus solidifies. If this is a conversation set up as a debate (which, moreover, substitutes for an election debate between Kaczyński and Donald Tusk), then, in principle, it gives the public a chance to buy into one of the stances presented. Although this talk does not require political or civic acumen on the part of the public, it revolves around the idea of influencing them. The show could see the public stick to their preferences or flip sides. If a conversation were to make people withdraw their support for "their" debater and shift it to the other party, the audience would have to fall for what goes down in the course of the exchange (e. g., for what the opponent says and how they do it). Only it is precisely what takes place during a conversation that assumes said permanent ignorance of the public and thrives on it. Then, in order to keep supporting "their" debater, the public would have to entrench themselves in their ignorance still further, and brush aside that their debater has a hand in promoting this sort of conversations at all. "This sort" stands for media performances characterized by four features: (1) specific temporal structure of the conversation, (2) such organization that makes a conversation an act of speaking about speaking, (3) schematism that limits a conversation to four interactional moves, (4) schematic and mutual indication to the public that the interlocutors are not partners to each other. These four characteristics are interconnected, complementary, and mutually pervasive, and it is precisely in this form that they constitute the basic characteristics of the circumstances set up for and before the public.

Both the concept of media performance and its main features is a result of an analysis which initially covered the full transcript of the talk. It was only in the course of the emergence of the research problem and on the basis of a sequential breakdown of the entire discussion that the extracts quoted below were abstracted to serve as an exemplification of the aforesaid features. Therefore, the selection of extracts is informed by the criterion of theoretical substantiality (Edwards 1994, p. 221) for a research problem which gradually takes shape as the study progresses. The hypothesis indicates the phenomenon reconstructed as a result of analysis. But a discussion of the hypothesis will not centre on reporting the methodology of arriving at the hypothesis, instead being an empirically concrete expression of what supports it.

Temporal structure

A media performance is a temporal phenomenon, and two global aspects of its temporal structure can be indicated. First, the program is an example of a media-transmitted conversation *which has to continue*, regardless of whether there is anything of substance that the interlocutors have to say to each other. The show takes place as a scheduled conversation which has a fixed runtime, is broadcast live, and cannot be interrupted at a given moment and without a very sound reason. In media-political culture, observing this rule is a normative pledge which the interlocutors take into account and agree to honour. It is this conscientious fulfilment of that obligation that makes the few and thus unique examples of disrespecting it newsworthy. In this culture, it is precisely the rarity of interrupting a program or of one party prematurely leaving the studio that highlights the binding principle of continuity. Put differently, this is a conversation which continues despite all else: the interlocutors can do what they do, because they might assume it is highly unlikely that something will break the interaction. The continuation of a conversation is at odds with the accumulation of discourse practices employed by both parties, which in extra-medial contexts could potentially see the interaction disintegrate. It is because these practices are continually employed, a threat that the conversation should end abruptly is not weighing on this program. The actual improbability of the dissolution of the interaction and the concurrent amassment of activities hinting at its substantial futility is one of the factors in the conversation's change into a performance.

Second, a conversation which has to continue is at the same time – though for different reasons – one *that has to conclude*. Saying one thing prevents another from being said: it is, strictly speaking, stealing the time that could be taken up by other statements. When timeslots for having a say are fixed in advance, speaking is directly connected with the temporal irrevocability of interaction. Both parties take this aspect of a conversation into account and, at particular junctures of the program, accelerate or decelerate the conversation, depending on their judgment of the situation in which they find themselves. Sometimes, participation in a media performance set up as a debate will rely on the strategies that allow for seeing it out (as in the case of a boxer who has recourse to a clinch or escapes to a corner to merely survive the round rather than win the fight in its course), while on other occasions, it will employ methods for hurried intensification of the conversation. For that reason, the temporal structure of a conversation is related to its rhetorical dynamics: each statement can be potentially presented by one of the participants as squandering the elapsing time or as making use of it in a productive manner. The interlocutors may promote different ideas of productivity and erect the conversation's rhetorical edifice on them. That the media transmission of a conversation is at the same time its institutional management is one thing: another is that strictly speaking talking is spending time.

Consequently, a media performance is a corollary of the conversation being made accessible to the public, but the fundamental meaning of this performance lies precisely in what is conditioned by its temporal organization. A performance owes its basic characteristics to its temporal structure. Involvement in a performance is, first and foremost, being involved *for the duration* of this performance. Media performance is episodic in the same sense as numerous non-media interactions are (Goffman 1959), especially those that are institutionally organised and performed in repetitive patterns subject to formal rules (e.g., school teaching). Traditional media broadcasting standards with their fragmentation of airtime and the rhythmic succession of thematic content and advertising blocks seem to be a transformation of this basic episodic nature of interactional patterns. Hence, there is something rather obvious in calling this talk media performance. Obviously two people (and the spectators in the studio) present themselves to the public and do what they can to influence it. But the concept of media performance as adopted here is not about the methods of making an impression but about the circumstances created for the public and before it. The question is what offer is given to the public and what type of public this offer assumes.

The talk that is set up as a media debate has to fit to these standards regardless of the consequences. Therefore media performance will be deemed complete if the participants meet the expectation of speaking long enough in the presence of each other and in front of the public. But while the performance takes the form of a conversation which *has to continue* and *has to conclude*, any other expectations about it (with regard to its substance, quality, or content) are secondary: they may be voiced directly or indirectly, but there is nothing that could force their fulfilment. Thus, the performance will not be adversely affected if it is executed in a way whereby a guest refuses to answer questions and thus avoids giving information, or "explains" to the public that the host asks irrelevant questions and that way is personally responsible for rendering the conversation useless. It is precisely this sort of performance that the interlocutors mount in front of the public and for its sake. The anticipation of witnessing precisely this sort of performance is thus an indirect indication of assuming certain expectations that the audiences have of the performers.

Speaking about speaking

The conversation between Tomasz Lis and Jarosław Kaczyński is an example of speaking about speaking, and an argument about statements, quotations, comparisons, texts, interviews, or words credited to either of the participants. This specific characteristic of the talk does not raise any doubts of the participants and none of them formulates any objections to it. It could be assumed that according to a common definition, a "meaningful" conversation is *about* something: it has its topic, which is discussed by means of words, but is not words itself. In current understanding, conversation is substantial if words play an auxiliary role, they are in the service of something else. Likewise, in certain academic fields which specialize in deliberating on words and their application (e. g., in literary or translation studies), conversations exclusively devoted to words are frequently treated as devoid of meaningful substance. Common understanding of conversations between prominent figures of power and symbolic elites (Van Dijk 1993, Czyżewski / Franczak / Nowicka / Stachowiak 2014) often share similar characteristics: considering a conversation as an argument over words is effectively accusing it of verbosity. Making words the topic of speech usually has negative connotations and is thought of as not being grounded in so-called hard facts or heart of the matter. Under such a model of conversation, defining its basic property as speaking about speaking would amount to pointing out its vice, whose implications would be felt the more acutely the more sheer verbiage would detract from the substance.

However, more important than pointing to the disproportions between arguing over words and the reality of extraverbal facts is seeing the criticism of speaking about speaking as a critique of discourse. It is the interlocutors themselves that organize their conversation along the lines of speaking about speaking, and this is precisely what the public is offered. Words are the theme here, and the content of one statement is the expected topic of another. That way, the conversation becomes a discussion of words: one's own or someone else's, uttered in the course of past talks or in the course of the present conversation, or quoted from books or informal statements. Conducting a conversation in the mode of speaking about speaking frequently takes the form of talking about lack of statements on particular topics, attempts to abort discussing certain issues, or being coy on a given subject. Therefore, speaking about speaking also encompasses practices of discussing reasons, sources, risks, or ramifications of the absence of words: it is speaking about not-speaking.

Based on the thematic criterion, it is possible to extract the following ten sequences from the entire talk: (1) economy, (2) public finances, (3) government coalition, (4) composition of the government (Antoni Macierewicz),

(5) Germany, (6) debating with Donald Tusk, (7) football hooligans, (8) relations with the president, (9) Fr. Tadeusz Rydzyk, (10) women in the Law and Justice party. Seven of these (4–10) are almost exclusively devoted to speaking about speaking. The other three (1–3) partly follow this pattern (speaking about words alternates with speaking about other issues). Thus, a unique feature of the media performance mounted for the public is that speaking about speaking takes up most of the time, although to those who look for the meaningfulness of a conversation in the interlocutors' transgressing words toward what is called facts (or the state of affairs), speaking about speaking will be devoid of substance. Even if the focus on speaking about speaking is not an ideal model of "real conversation" about "real problems" for either interlocutor, this is the path they tenaciously follow throughout their performance, but at the same time, they publicly announce that their preference is to have a conversation on concrete issues (Tomasz Lis), or request questions relating to important Polish matters (Jarosław Kaczyński). The ability to make use of the contrast between concrete and potentially abstract issues, and between important matters and some unimportant ones, is a practical locutionary skill, which for the speakers is pragmatically aligned, rather than logically inconsistent, with maintaining a conversation whose character is that of speaking about speaking. The structure of the media performance thus includes a certain assumption about the public, which accept this ostensible consistence and move on.

The following transcript covers the beginning of sequence 5[3]. Tomasz Lis (TL) opens it by quoting a passage from a book by Jarosław Kaczyński (JK), which is read out by a narrator (N). During this part of the conversation, the applause of the spectators (S)[4] can also be heard.

---

3 The transcription method is inspired by conversation analysis, although it uses a simplified set of symbols. The transcript convention is explained in the appendix.
4 For the sake of the analysis, a distinction has to be introduced between the public and the spectators (S), i. e., the people present in the studio and co-creating the media performance for the public.

Extract 1

```
1   TL:   e: mister chairman ┌you wrote a book    ┐ you wrote a book
2   S:                       └((scattered applause))┘
3         the Poland of our dreams let's listen to a fragment of what you wrote
4         about German chancellor Angela Merkel
5   N:    I don't believe that Angela Merkel's chancellorship was a result of
6         sheer coincidence but I will not elaborate on this belief
7         I leave it to political scholars and historians
8   TL:   mister chairman what did you want to say about Angela Merkel
9   JK:   you can't speak Polish? ((smiles))
10  S:    ((applause))
11  TL:   ┌what did you want┐ to say?=
12  JK:   └(well I guess)   ┘         =it was very clearly ┌said      ┐
13  TL:                                                    │not very  │
14                                                         └not clearly┘
15  JK:   well ┌in your/    ┐
16  TL:        └I will not┘ elaborate on the rest I leave it to political
17         scholars and historians it was not a result of sheer coincidence what
18         did you want ┌to say              ┐
19  JK:                 └well because clearly┘ it was not a result of sheer
20         coincidence it was a result of broadly speaking the fact that
21         two parts of Germany were united which led to all
22         sorts of tensions and at one point they needed someone from the
23         eastern part of Germany to all ┌sorts of consequences┐
24  TL:                                   └so why didn't you/    ┘
25  JK:   and the
26  JK:   and the rest please leave it ┌to historians and political scholars┐ I would kindly
27  TL:                                └I am not saying/                     ┘
28  JK:   ask you to do it=
29  TL:                   =mister chairman I can't leave the rest to historians
30         because out of respect to you a seasoned politician who has been in
31         domestic politics for more than twenty years who aspires to be the
32         leader of a forty-million-strong country in central Europe I have to
33         take your words seriously
```

In lines 1–8, TL directs the conversation toward discussing a selected part of JK's book, that is, toward speaking about what JK wrote. Despite interactional hurdles which JK plants in front of the host, the latter, throughout this extract, is speaking about speaking and intends to discuss "what did you want to say". JK joins him in speaking about speaking: even the aforesaid obstacles refer to what was 'said' and to the (in)ability to understand it. In lines 19–27, JK makes a yet another move and offers a response different to what he said during his first turn. His answer is formally relevant to the question: formally, he is saying (now) what he wanted to say (back then, in his book). At the same time, such formulation of the answer relates to JK's demanding that what he "did want to say" be no longer discussed. JK's changed approach does not see either interlocutor cease to speak about speaking. After JK requests that the issue be settled, TL (in lines 28–32) explains why this is not an option. Thus, the extract begins with an attempt to speak about JK's words included in his book, and concludes with speaking about ceasing to speak about this subject.

Speaking about speaking may be introduced by the party initiating a topic (that is, encouraging to take up the topic suggested), but also by the party who decides what to do with this invitation. This is the difference between reducing a

conversation to speaking about speaking in the first move (raising a topic) and
doing so in the second move (reaction to raising a topic). The extract quoted
below comes immediately after a fragment of another talk with JK is played in the
studio, during which JK reacts to the journalist's questions about whether
Zbigniew Ziobro and Antoni Macierewicz will be offered positions in a potential
government. Using a recording of another conversation involving JK helps TL
introduce a new topic and a new sequence, (4). That way, TL makes the conversation about Antoni Macierewicz, one of the most controversial figures in
Polish politics.

Extract 2

```
1    TL:   so mister Ziobro as we heard will certainly be offered a position and
2          you think mister Macierewicz will too right
3    JK:   your tone is accusatory ((smiles))
4          and ⌜what is wrong with that what is wrong with that⌝
5    TL:      ⌞I am asking I am asking mister chairman          ⌟
6    TL:   I am asking
7    JK:   sir
8    TL:   and can you can you confirm or deny mister chairman
9    JK:   if I said it then I said it
10   TL:   so you think mister Macierewicz will be in the government will will
11         in your opinion
12   JK:   well I think it is pointless if we keep
13         discuss⌜ing this it was                 ⌝
14   TL:        ⌞because it is inconvenient⌟ to you
15   JK:   it was on the second it was the second of September and it's already
16         October the situation is excellent
17   TL:   the closer to the election ⌜the less you know about the makeup of⌝
18                                     ⌊the cabinet                          ⌋
19   JK:                              ⌊te/ m:                                 ⌋
20         no I know more but I speak less about it ⌜((smiling))     ⌝
21   S:                                            ⌊((applause))     ⌋
22   TL:                                           ⌊mhm      y::⌟ do you
23         think that this possibility was raised in what you said do you think
24         that Antoni Macierewicz sitting on the cabinet is a good idea
25   JK:   sir I suggest that we agree on something
26         we hold different beliefs and I read your periodical and a-a-as a
27         result I think it is pointless to consider this issue=
28   TL:                                                         =no mister
29         chairman ⌜this is not pointless we want to know⌝ who wi/ who wants
30   JK:           ⌊I mean this is                       ⌟
31   TL:   to govern Poland and we the citizens have the right to know it and you
32         ⌜aspire⌝ to I'm sorry mister chairman you aspire
33   JK:   ⌊I/    ⌟
34   TL:   to rule a central European country populated by forty million people
```

In this case (lines 1–2), TL plans the beginning of a new sequence so that the next
turn includes a confirmation of JK's words which could be heard in the recording. The attempt to elicit an answer consistent with the format of the
question is not yet speaking about speaking, which only occurs in a second move,
that is, when the topic suggested by TL is rejected. What JK says in lines 3–4 is
designed in a way that could potentially shift the focus to discussing the manner
in which TL is speaking (the accusatory tone of his voice). TL tries to prevent this

shift, again forcing a situation where JK could say what the host expects him to say. It is noteworthy that the raising of the topic (lines 1–2) and its resumption (in line 8), although relating to the same subject matter, draw different reactions from JK. While in the first case JK responds as if TL's raising the subject could be quipped about, he subsequently responds as if he was cornered and coerced into giving an answer he has no intention of giving. JK is thus on the point of openly rejecting the topic suggested at the beginning and again reducing the conversation to speaking about speaking.

While the conversation consists in speaking about speaking up to line 13, from this line onward it revolves around speaking about not-speaking. This means that in the second part of this extract the participants topicalize what already happened between them in the first part, and to that extent part two is a meta-communicational exchange about how the interaction has been unfolding so far. In this sense, the second part of the excerpt does overtly what was implicit earlier anyway. When in line 22 TL again tries to persuade JK to discuss Antoni Macierewicz, JK again speaks about the pointlessness of any such discussion. The arguments he adduces to support his stance (e. g., different beliefs espoused by the interlocutors) are one thing, but what is also important is the protracted passages – which irreversibly consume the fixed timespan of the media performance – of speaking about reasons behind not-speaking (this is what JK does) and of arguments in favour of speaking (TL).

Sequential organization of interactional moves

The examples quoted above allow for excerpting one more property of this conversation, namely, the constant availability of a set of interactional moves whose systematic and mutual application constitutes a specific pattern. This set is extremely limited and comprises a handful of moves recreating the schematism of a conversation acted out in public. Turns revolve around a system of four moves.

– Move A: opening. This move is made by TL and it expresses an intention of starting a conversation on a new topic. The ten-part sequential structure of the program would suggest that TL is ready to discuss as many main topics. However, as a result of reacting to JK's interactional moves, he raises additional subtopics, which JK sometimes tries to use as an opportunity to change the subject. Opening is a basic act which TL is entitled to in his capacity as the host of the interview. As a result, opening typically takes the form of a journalistic question. If move A is not realized as a question, it is formulated as a statement which engages TL in an open confrontation. Consequently, the way in which this move is made potentially situates TL inside the formal journalistic purview, or outside it, that is, in a context in which he participates in a political confrontation.

- Move B: evasion. This move is made by JK. He performs his part of a talk participant to the extent that he accepts switching between the roles of the hearer and speaker, but thanks to evasions he excludes himself as a party supplying information sought by the show's host. This move is typically instantiated as parrying a question (ignoring the opening), a derisive and derogatory retort, or engaging in an open verbal scuffle.
- Move C: closure. This move is made by JK. It takes the form of efforts toward ending a discussion on the topic suggested by TL. This move is a major encroachment on TL's role of the program's host. Closure is sometimes formulated as a demand, and sometimes as a request, but on each occasion JK is in a position of power, as he decides on the thematic structure of questions asked in a show to which he has been invited as an interviewee.
- Move D: opposition (TL). This move is made by TL. It is a direct reaction to JK's attempts to end the subject which he is supposed to speak about. JK does not usually demonstrate his understanding of this move as questioning the substance of what he says, but as an action introducing a new topic which becomes a new point of reference for move B or C. Opposition is effected by means similar to those employed on opening: using statements which take the form of a journalistic question and engaging in an open confrontation. Two main differences between opposition and opening are their respective positions in the sequence of turns (opposition is a reaction to move C) and TL's various forms of invoking the ideal model of political culture based on the public accessibility of information about the authorities. Thus, opposition realizes as statements formulated in such fashion so as to highlight those aspects of JK's words which are at odds with the ideal of power transparency in a democratic state. TL's role as a journalist allows him to both oppose JK's dismissing the topics suggested and to reserve the right to start new subjects.

These moves are interconnected in a specific way, which shapes the trajectory of the majority of conversational sequences, especially those which constitute a media performance based on speaking about speaking. Thus, specific dynamics of the entire program becomes apparent.

The basic pattern of moves is ABCD. It begins with opening (A), followed by evasion (B) and an attempt at closure (C), which faces opposition (D). But this basic order usually comes in a more complex form, which could be labeled $(AB)^nCD$. The first two moves, A and B, occur a few times, one after the other (n times), and how many times each of them is going to be performed is determined by the ending move C. A direct response to C is move D.

As regards move D, it can be interpreted precisely as opposition (this scenario is labelled below as D) or as the opening of a new subject, that is, as move A (this case is labelled below as D>A). This is one way in which JK gets an opportunity to influence theme selection, which is ultimately a prerogative of the show's host. The alternativity of the interpretation of move D enables a new progression of all four moves and means that the entire schema of sequential organization of moves assumes the form of $(AB)^nC(D/D>A)$. This alternativity is indicated with a slash in the second bracket.

Move D (opposition) is always directed at the final part of the preceding turn: it refers to an attempt at closing a topic, but on all occasions lends itself to an interpretation under which TL actually makes move A (opening). Likewise, because of the direction which the conversation takes following move C (closure), the latter can be always interpreted as move B (evasion). It has to be noted that move B (evasion) does not invariably trigger move C (closure).

This basic schema of interactional moves is independent of the thematic structure. The interlocutors adhere to it even if they change the subject (a thematic sequence changes) or make temporary changes to the subject within a thematic sequence. However, this schema is not a principle which governs the conversation: it is more of a structure both available to the participants and co-created by them, being the focus of the actions they perform in front of the public and thus construct a media performance. This means that the $(AB)^nC(D/D>A)$ schema allows the interlocutors to synchronize their statements under a 50-minute progression of actions and reactions. It is the "loose algorithm" of this interaction: it is an "algorithm", since it points to a finite and sequentially ordered set of subsequent moves, and it is "loose", because rather than serving as a rigid frame of the interaction, it is a repertoire of moves on which both parties focus and with which they align their statements.

The following transcript is the very beginning of the show.

Extract 3

```
 1   S:    ((applause))
 2   TL:   good evening mister chairman thank you for accepting
 3         ⌐the invitation⌐
 4   JK:   ⌊good evening ⌋ ((smiling))
 5   TL:   mister chairman Europe and elsewhere too is plunged in the most
 6         severe economic crisis in the last 90 years could you reveal who in
 7         your government if you win the election would be responsible for the
 8         economy.
 9   JK:   sir I have repeatedly stated that it would be a grave mistake
10         on my part if at this point just before the election we all know that
11         the ballot is only a few days away I were to set in motion all sorts
12         of discussions about names this will definitely be a tried and tested
13         person with great acumen one who can handle things but
14         we won't be naming names right now.
15   TL:   but don't you think given the gravity of the situation that millions
16         of Poles should be given certainty (.) clarity who this person is going
17         to be like in countries such as France or the US which are seasoned
18         democracies where the leader of a party that aspires to rule says in our
19         administration this and this will be responsible for the economy.
20   JK:   sir different things happen in different countries
21         and additionally ((smiling)) you are underestimating the wisdom of
22         the Poles the Poles make educated guesses and that is enough
```

The sequence of moves in extract 3 is fairly straightforward[5]:

[1] A   (5–8)
[2] B   (9–13)
[3] C   (13–14)
[4] D>A (15–19)
[5] B   (20–22)
[6] C   (22)

In lines 5–8, TL does what under the circumstances could be expected from the party performing the role of a journalist: he introduces a new topic (the first one). That way, move A is made. JK's statement which follows is focused on with-holding the information demanded by the host of the show. This means that, reacting to TL's seeking information, JK employs move B (evasion). In the opening part of the program, JK makes moves B and C in the same turn, but they are clearly distinguishable from each other. The transition is marked: in line 13, the word "but" – which is stressed and is an audible separation of two actions – ends move B and is the beginning of move C. The closure is much shorter than the evasion, a pattern which also characterizes the subsequent attempts at per-forming the sequence of B and C (cf. lines 20–22).

The formulation of JK's closure suggests that he is ending the discussion about "names" (line 14). Meanwhile, TL makes his own move, D, thus opposing move C. Where JK is in favour of not-speaking, TL presses for speaking, and for this speaking to be of a particular quality. Referring to "millions of Poles" should

---

5 The numbers in square brackets refer to interactional moves, while those in round brackets indicate the lines in the transcript.

be given "<u>certainty</u> (.) <u>clarity</u>" and to "seasoned democracies" is a means of opposition and hints at the uncertainty facing the Poles and, consequently, at the incompetence of JK's prospective government. JK uses this opposition as an opportunity to change the subject. Line 19 concludes one ABCD sequence of moves and simultaneously triggers another. Coming in lieu of discussing the theme of "different countries" (line 20) is speaking about what JK considers TL's earlier original question (concerning the "names", lines 13–14). That way JK reacts to TL's opposition in move [4] as if it was the opening of a new topic (D>A).

What follows (line 21) is a sequence of moves which reproduces that in JK's previous turn: JK openly ("additionally") makes move B, this time through a derisive and ironic retort, before he proceeds – again openly – to move C. As was the case in the previous turn, JK marks closure as a complementary move, but one distinct from evasion. The words "and that is enough" are ambiguous: they may refer both to JK's words "the Poles make educated guesses" (if it is guessing that suffices, then there is no need to announce to the Poles the names which TL asks about), but they could also mean that what JK has already told TL is "enough", so JK is not going to further elaborate. But this ambiguity is of little relevance: move C is on this occasion made in the same way as in [3], namely, as an abrupt *cut* which marks the point of no return to discussing the previous topic. In both turns, closure is distinct from evasion: the words "<u>but</u>" (13) and "and" (22) make it a separate part of interaction.

In extract 2 (transcript above), the sequence of turns is as follows:

[1]	A	(1–2)
[2]	B	(3–4)
[3]	A	(5–6)
[4]	B	(7)
[5]	A	(8)
[6]	B	(9)
[7]	A	(10–11)
[8]	C	(12–13)
[9]	D>A	(14)
[10]	B	(15–16)
[11]	D>A	(17)
[12]	B	(18–20)
[13]	A	(21–23)
[14]	C	(24–26)
[15]	D	(27–33)

In this case, too, the conversation unfolds according to the sequential order of interactional moves, and not the order of gathering information. The beginning of this exchange covers TL's four attempts to receive an answer to the question about whether Antoni Macierewicz will be part of a future government. The sequence of moves A and B concludes only a fourth turn of JK, when he makes move C as he tries to end the subject suggested by TL. TL opposes, but he refers to the ideal of democratic transparency indirectly, that is, not by highlighting its importance to the people, but by suggesting that acting against it is JK's intention. With this kind of opposition, TL does not directly stand up for this ideal, but provokes a verbal scuffle. Still, TL formulates his statement as asking for information, that is, opening a new topic. The result is that TL formally still performs the role of a journalist, but at the same time it is JK that decides whether to provide the information sought, in line with the asking party's formally voiced request, or to interpret opposition as opening (D>A), which can be followed by evasion again. Eventually, opposition in the form of opening a new topic is treated by JK as a cue to make move B.

While topic-wise the statements in lines 14–20 appear interjective, on the score of interactional moves they are twice filled with the sequence of D>AB. This means that although the topic of the conversation changes, the interlocutors adhere to a sequence of moves licensed by the basic schema. When the thematic interjection ends, that is, when the spectators' laughing and applause tell the public that the scuffle has been lost by the party who provoked it, TL decides against further squabbles, revisits the topic from before the interjection, and again asks about Antoni Macierewicz. That way, TL returns to move [7] from lines 10–11, and JK acts accordingly, as he reproduces move C, which he made in lines 12–13. The schema indicates that a direct corollary of move C is opposing it. No matter what argumentative-rhetoric strategies are adopted in extract 2 considered as a part media performance, they are employed as part of the $(AB)^nC(D/D>A)$ schema. This does not diminish the importance of said strategies, but suggests that they should be embedded in a broader context in which they are pursued[6].

Two models of the public sphere

The interlocutors constantly imply they are not conversation partners for each other, and this is how the conversation proceeds (regardless). This could be another paradox of debating in public, if only it was not another aspect of the media performance. Both parties hint that the problem is to talk to this particular person, in no small part due to how this person talks. The nature of this problem is that TL works to create the impression that a conversation with this guest is substantially counterproductive, while JK implies that speaking to the host of the show is substantially pointless. At the same time, neither party suggests that the

6 In the conversation analyzed, there are much more examples of the $(AB)^nC(D/D>A)$ schema. Another two can be found in the appendix.

very act of having a discussion is problematic. What is counterproductive on the one hand and pointless on the other is what takes place under these particular circumstances and in the company of this particular interlocutor. What is said during the program is somewhat based on this original premise, which at the beginning of the conversation is its unsaid but overt aspect. TL and JK bring in two different models of public sphere. This means that the public is to face a situation characterized by four properties:

a) The public is cast as witnesses to something that is being set up for them as an interview. But while JK agrees to be questioned, which follows from the show's format, he objects to be quizzed, which follows from the fashion in which the conversation is handled by the host. TL presents himself as an entity which can hold the authorities accountable, while JK poses as an authority which is independent.

b) The questions asked by TL are "reasonable", but only in the context of the liberal approach to the public sphere, under which journalists oversee political power. The show's guest does not espouse this view and uses the conversation to demonstrate his personal sovereignty, that is, standing outside the valid system and being able to repeal its rules. Under such a model of personal sovereignty, which is consistent with the rightist notion of legal-political sovereignty going back at least to Carl Schmitt (1986, p. 7), what becomes crucial is the difference between discussion and decision, that is, between submission to the principle of the public transparency of political authority on the one hand, and the primacy of a political decision over its verbal validation on the other. To the extent that decision overrides discussion, JK has no obligations toward an opposition journalist. Therefore, continual demonstration of incommensurable models of the public sphere is a part of the media performance.

c) The differences in terms of models of the public sphere translate into differences in ideas about who might be considered partner in a meaningful conversation. TL takes part in the conversation, assuming it can take place because of the likely differences between the interlocutors, whereas JK participates in it and at the same time says explicitly (cf. excerpt 2, lines 25–27) that a meaningful conversation can only be held between parties whose beliefs are compatible with each other from the very beginning. Under the interlocutors' respective stances, there are no such discrepancies between the interlocutors that could be worked out.

d) TL manages his participation in the conversation as if he was trying to gather information that will incriminate his guest in the eyes of the public. To accomplish this goal, he needs minimal cooperation from JK. But JK paints TL as a person who incriminates himself precisely because of these attempts. This has certain implications. JK is not a randomly selected guest: he is a representative of a right-wing conservative party, which competes with the Civic Platform, a party supported by TL, which in the 2011 election also aspired to rule the country. If JK's potentially relinquishing control of the conversation to a liberal journalist could be seen as a form of cooperation with a political competitor, then lack of cooperation is a device of political rivalry.

To the extent that news audience is primary recipients of the talk (Heritage / Greatbatch, 1991, p. 107) in journalistic interviews, underlying the entire conversation is an assumption that the audience has to be given a conversation structured precisely in this manner. The interlocutors do not pretend that they are having a private conversation, but take account of the absent parties, that is, the audience outside the studio. Assuming the presence of other recipients "must be managed in and through the design of the talk" (ibid.), as "you should, as much as possible, design whatever you're telling about [...] with an orientation to the other" (Sacks 1995, p. 540). If the audience is watching the debate because it is these particular persons that have it, then the character of the conversation is instructive of the "recipient design" it adopts (ibid.). What is spoken and how it is spoken is adjusted to the idea of what the public is.

It is precisely for the sake of the public – for example in extract 1, where the topic discussed is Antoni Macierewicz's inclusion in the cabinet – that TL makes efforts toward maintaining formal journalistic impartiality (Heritage / Greatbatch 1991, p. 107, Ciołkiewicz 2014, p. 146–172). Its main aspect is avoiding statements which could be interpreted as a personal opinion of the journalist or their employer (in this case a TV outlet) about what the party questioned says. Asking questions is a basic prerogative of the journalist, and its conscientious fulfilment is often said to guarantee that they take part in a conversation precisely in their capacity as a journalist, and not as an opponent or rival of the person invited (Ciołkiewicz 2014, p. 149 ff). Formal neutrality prevents the journalist from engaging in open confrontation and launching an outspoken attack, and it is in this form that it is part of the media performance, since there is no indication that neutrality (without a formal status) is of any use to TL in his talk with JK. What he needs is formal neutrality as a method of constructing a sphere of journalistic safety (Heritage / Greatbatch 1991, p. 121). But while formal journalistic neutrality can be simply interpreted as a token of occupational professionalism, it can be also associated with the notion of liberal professionalism. The format of asking questions where the host comes over as a person who steers clear of partisan judgments and aspires to impartiality, and where the interviewer is cast in the role of an intermediary between the interviewee and the public, is not only responsible for the perceived contrast between TL and JK, but also validates, so to speak, his liberal philosophy of journalism.

In extract 1, the opening of the subject (1–8) is not just the first move in a sequence, but also a basic means of observing formal journalistic neutrality. Invoking a book authored by JK and handing over to the narrator who reads out a passage from it indicates that rather than mounting an attack, TL impartially refers to a hard fact. Therefore, of importance is not just beginning (again) to speak about speaking, but also an invitation to speak on a particular subject. The specificity of this invitation is that it could be interpreted in many different and often mutually exclusive ways. First, TL asks this question ("mister chairman what did you want to say about Angela Merkel", line 8) in such a way as if it concerned an intention which was not directly verbalized. Second, it could be seen as a demand that JK justify his own words. Third, it could be heard as an accusation of resorting to insinuations. Fourth, what TL does could be interpreted as encouraging to reveal something that has been made secret. Fifth, a reaction to TL's question could retain the incongruence present in the opening, namely, that the passage quoted concerns the "chancellorship" (5), as in "office", while TL's question (8) implies that something was not said about Angela Merkel the person.

Each of these options means taking the conversation in a different direction, and each could be defended on grounds of the format of the journalistic interview, where a journalist tries to acquire information. The common denominator of all these alternatives is that TL formulates his turn as if JK's words hinted at something unknown which should become known. The unknown is implied to be the opposite to "sheer coincidence", which in turn suggests that Angela Merkel's chancellorship was a result of someone's deliberate intervention. TL causes the change of the speaker, as a result of which JK should explain his own words quoted in the previous turn, but presented as unfounded, in the absence of overt validation. That way, TL embroils JK in a confrontation, where JK cannot give any "correct" answer.

This is because underlying the question ("mister chairman what did you want to say about Angela Merkel") is an assumption that a "correct" answer (revealing what was to remain secret or conceding that there is nothing between the lines, which means that JK is guilty of insinuating) would show JK in a bad light. Such formulation of the subject contains two mutually exclusive aspects: on the one hand, it is an invitation, that is, an act which by definition requires the interlocutor's cooperation in their next turn, and on the other it negates JK as a partner in conversation by setting a task which he cannot undertake to complete. JK cannot publicly challenge his own words, all the more under pressure from TL. That way, the opening of a subject is an offensive action, provoking the interlocutor to accept an impossible mission and presenting him as a person to whom asking such questions is acceptable. JK, in his turn, does not respond to the insolubility of the challenge, but to its confrontational nature, and himself makes it known to the public who he thinks he is dealing with.

Encouraging a discussion of a new topic is both giving voice to the interlocutor and leaving it up to them to decide (a) how to respond to the invitation (accept or decline it) and (b) what to do with the invitation itself. Invitation as an action indicates one's readiness to cooperate with their interlocutor, but at the same time the change of a speaker amounts to one's interactional exposure to the unpredictability of the next move. JK (a) declines to speak on the topic suggested and (b) uses an opportunity to attack which presents itself when TL stops speaking. JK takes his turn by making an ironic and absurd joke devised as if its purpose was to challenge the host's basic cultural competences. As a result, and in tune with the pattern of interactional moves, line 9 is evasion, but it's an evasion which presents the resulting degradation of the interlocutor as amusing. JK may hope that the spectators will show the public what his words were, and what is their preferred reception (cf. JK's smile in line 9 and the applause of the spectators in line 10). Thus, JK is not duty-bound to either respond to TL's question in a way that would suggest to the audience that answering questions from *this* journalist is a serious matter, or to actually address his direct interlocutor. JK's smile which caps this statement and the applause which immediately follows indicate that the steps taken are not just in all respects successful in terms of rejecting the invitation, but also prompt the public as to how to "correctly" respond to what it is witnessing. The audience is supposed to reward and applaud actions which are built as an indication of hostility toward the interlocutor.

Rejecting the invitation comes without delay and is not qualified or additionally explained. Such rejection is a "dispreferred format response", which, unless complemented with those caveats, may be easily construed as "hostile or rude". (Heritage 1984, p. 268–280; Antaki 2012, p. 532). In addition, dispreferred format responses are disaffiliative and destructive of social solidarity (Heritage 1984, p. 268, Etelämäki / Heinemann / Vatanen 2021). Irony further reinforces this effect by adding a derisive dimension. Preference organisation is one of the means through which "persons manage courses of action that either promote or undermine social solidarity" (Heritage / Raymond 2005, p. 16). The interlocutors agree on the character of preferred and dispreferred responses. It results from the format of the journalistic interview and from the public significance of a conversation between these particular individuals. As a result, the destruction of social solidarity is the destruction of the other party as a conversation partner.

But what makes it possible to hear JK's reaction as "hostile" or "rude" also characterizes TL's question. This question is not accompanied by any explanation of the rationale behind discussing these particular words, and there is nothing to indicate that the TL distances himself from the question. Formulating a question in this way may be construed as condescending or arbitrary, or as an attempt to call the interlocutor to account. To that extent, this is a dispreferred format question. Therefore, the character of the dispreferred format response (second move) is potentially justifiable through the character of the dispreferred format question (first move). If JK were to be accused of not responding "correctly", he could claim that he merely responds in kind, which would be in line with the strategy which he adopts throughout the talk[7]. TL capitalizes on his right to invoke the just-asking trope, that is, essentially doing what he should do in his capacity as a journalist, and what his interlocutor should not oppose if the talk is to continue as a journalistic interview. That way, the sphere of journalistic safety covers not just asking questions, but also the ability to take a conversation in the direction of speaking about speaking (in this case, this speaking about a particular way of asking questions).

Closing remarks

The analysis performed points to four properties of the conversation under scrutiny: its temporal structure, which makes it a conversation which has to continue and which has to conclude; its focus on speaking about speaking; the schematism of four basic interactional moves which the interlocutors rely on; showing the audience that neither interlocutor considers the other a partner for a conversation, but they will converse nevertheless. Together, these properties constitute basic aspects of the media performance, founded on the assumption of the permanent ignorance of the public for which this performance is mounted.

This article lends itself to at least two-fold interpretation. (1) It can be treated as an exercise in studies on public discourse. In this case, it would serve as an introductory analysis of the issue captured in the hypothesis, and could be taken in at least two directions: that of an independent criticism of the media performance following from a detailed empirical analysis, or that of a criticism which can work in the context of other forms of critical studies, e. g., looking on the media performance as a phenomenon whose complementary part is "staged and manipulative publicity" (Habermas 1989, p. 231–232) "of the public sphere which takes on feudal features" (ibid., p. 195–196). The public sphere undergoing

---

7   This is JK's recurrent strategy, which consists in defending the way of speaking criticized by TL on grounds that someone else has spoken in similar fashion about JK or his circle: in sequence 5, TL tells JK that the language which JK uses reinforces social divisions, and the guest responds, "forgive me but am I getting it wrong or did someone actually speak about us in a certain way?"; in sequence 8, TL quotes JK's words about keeping up appearances of cooperating with president Komorowski and asks, "is this going to be easy cooperation in the wake of what's been said?", and JK replies, "sir and do you think it was easy for my late brother to cooperate after remarks along the lines of like the assassin like the assassination?".

refeudalization again becomes a domain which entails the presence of representatives of political and symbolic power, so that they can assert their authority and vie for "plebiscitarily defined acclamation" (ibid., p. 201). This authority demands approval, "but it 'addresses' its citizens like consumers" (ibid., p. 195–196). However, the notion of the media performance is not grounded in the notion of refeudalization, just as the latter does not require the former. But the microanalysis of the media performance could go hand in hand with the macroanalysis of the public sphere.

(2) This analysis can be also treated as the taking of evidence, i.e., the procedure conducted before the comprehension of the very same audience for whose sake the media performance has been staged. In this case, too, the empirical work would be essentially preparatory. The right to judge is subsequently exercised by those who under the requirements of the media performance are *just* the public, and, under the requirements of politics based on media performances, *just* the electorate. The analytical demonstrability of the media performance makes possible the fulfilment of the majority of the criteria of the procedural directness principle: the jury has an opportunity to examine the evidence directly, without a third-party intermediary. Seeing as the basic material for analysis is not hidden but available in the form of a recording and transcript (of the entire material or its relevant extracts), the publicness of the evidence has the potential to make the "trial" itself public as well. But said trial – as long as an effort is made to judge in the first place – would be unique in that the evidence collected in the process would not serve to reveal something that the jury has not been able to access so far, but to expose that which may have been unnoticed in the proceedings, but which cannot be neglected for the sake of the fairness of the judgment. Thus, it would amount to sketching the figure (in the sense of gestalt psychology) where there has been a plain background. This does not mean, however, that an analysis has to conclude with indictment (for it is not her obligation), but equally, it does not mean waiving the right to bring it.

Nothing prevents reconciling these two options. Together, they could be conducive to reflexive criticism (in the sense of Boltanski and Chiapello, 1999, p. 81 f) directed at examining the public activity of power and symbolic elites (Van Dijk 1993, Czyżewski / Franczak / Nowicka / Stachowiak 2014). On the one hand, starting with the observation of a conversation and making it a basis for postulating the requirement of the permanent ignorance of the audience enlivens this reflexive criticism. To that extent, observation can serve to make reality unacceptable (Boltanski 2008). On the other hand, "critique can bring into relief the impositions and demands made on people [...] but it cannot show people how to escape" (Bröckling 2016, s. 199). The effort to find out how to escape is a task that requires preparatory work, but at the same time goes beyond it.

Appendix

Transcription symbols

<u>but</u>	emphasis
m:	prolonged vowel or consonant
/	interrupted speech
[ ]	the start and end of overlapping speech
= =	no hearable gap between the words
(.)	micropause
(well I guess)	best possible hearing
((applause))	transcriber's descriptions
TL	Tomasz Lis
JK	Jarosław Kaczyński
S	spectators in the studio
N	narrator

In extract 1, whose transcript has been provided, the sequence of moves is as follows:

[1] A (1–8)
[2] B (9)
[3] A (11)
[4] B (12)
[5] A (13–18)
[6] B (19–23)
[7] C (25, 27)
[8] D (28–32)

Sequences of interactional moves can also be found in other parts of the talk, e. g., in the extract 4 in which a debate between JK and Donald Tusk which never materialized is discussed.

Extract 4

```
1   JK:   it's this man who is responsible
2          ┌for the fact that the police sto/ storm                      ┐
3   TL:   └why do you keep saying this man and not the prime minister?┘
4   JK:   the apartment of some blogger ┌at six in the morning          ┐
5   TL:                                 └again why do you keep referring┘ to
6          Donald Tusk ┌as this man┐
7   JK:               └I speak as ┘ I see fit
8   S:    ((murmurs))
9   TL:   and I ask as I see fit
10  S:    ((scattered applause))
11  JK:   w/ well then you have the right to ask and my answer is that this is
12         ┌what I see fit and that is that sir there is no point/      ┐
13  TL:   └don't you think/ mister mister chairman you aspire to rule┘ a forty
14         million strong country ┌we are being watched┐ by a few million people
15  JK:                          └ye:s of course      ┘
16  TL:   you have just said that your party is disrespected don't you
17         think that you now have a perfect perfect opportunity
18         to show the true political culture the end of the Polish-Polish
19         war so don't say mister Tusk this man but prime minister Donald Tusk
20         the way you then expect to be addressed
21  JK:   whe/ ┌when            ┐ civic platform abandons this
22  S:         └((applause))┘
23  JK:   social engineering which it keeps using just renounce it I'm not even
24         saying ┌apologize┐ and apologize it should but as soon as it renounces it
25  TL:          └aha     ┘
26  JK:   then this will obviously happen but as things stand I won't have you
27         moderate how I should refer to mister e Donald Tusk
```

In extract 4 the sequence of moves is as follows:

[1] A   (3)
[2] B   (4)
[3] A   (5–6)
[4] B   (7)
[5] A   (9)
[6] C   (11–12)
[7] D>A (13–20)
[8] B   (21–26)
[9] C   (26–27)

References

Antaki, Ch.: 'Affiliative and disaffiliative candidate understandings'. DISCOURSE STUDIES 2012/14(5), p. 531–547.

Boltanski, Luc: Rendre la réalité inacceptable. À propos de "La production de l'idéologie dominante". Paris 2008.

Bröckling, Ulrich: The Entrepreneurial Self. Fabricating a New Type of Subject. London 2016.

Ciołkiewicz, Paweł: 'Instrumentalizacja wiedzy eksperckiej w dyskursie publicznym. Przypadek telewizyjnej rozmowy o stenogramach', in: Czyżewski, Marek / Franczak, Karol / Nowicka, Magdalena / Stachowiak, Jerzy (eds.): Dyskurs elit symbolicznych. Próba diagnozy. Warszawa 2014, p. 146–172.

Czyżewski, Marek / Franczak, Karol / Nowicka, Magdalena / Stachowiak, Jerzy (eds.): Dyskurs elit symbolicznych. Próba diagnozy. Warszawa 2014.

Duszak, Anna / Fairclough, Norman (eds.): Krytyczna Analiza Dyskursu, Interdyscyplinarne podejście do komunikacji społecznej. Kraków 2008.

Edwards, D.: 'Script formulations: An analysis of event descriptions in conversation', in: JOURNAL OF LANGUAGE AND SOCIAL PSYCHOLOGY 1994/13, p. 211–247.

Edwards, Derek: 'Analyzing racial discourse: the discursive psychology of mind–world relationships', in: van den Berg, Harry / Wetherell, Margaret / Houtkoop-Steenstra, Hanneke (eds.): *Analyzing Race Talk. Multidisciplinary Perspectives on the Research Interview.* Cambridge 2003, p. 31–48.

Edwards, Derek: Discourse and Cognition. London, Thousand Oaks, New Delhi 1997.

Etelämäki, M. / Heinemann, T. / Vatanen, A.: 'On affiliation and alignment: Non-cooperative uses of anticipatory completions in the context of tellings', in: DISCOURSE STUDIES 2021/23(6), p. 726–758.

Fejes, Andreas / Nicoll, Katherine (eds.): Foucault and Lifelong Learning. Governing the subject. London and New York 2008.

Erving, Goffman: Presentation of Self in Everyday Life. Doubleday Anchor Books, New York 1959.

Habermas, Jürgen: The Structural Transformation of the Public Sphere. Cambridge 1989.

Heritage, John / Greatbatch, David: 'On the institutional character of institutional talk: The case of news interviews', in: Boden, Deirdre / Zimmerman, Don. H. (eds.): *Talk and Social Structure. Studies in Ethnometodology and Conversation Analysis.* Cambridge 1991, s. 93–137.

Heritage, John, Garfinkel and Ethnomethodology. Cambridge 1984.

Heritage, J./ Geoffrey, R.: 'The terms of agreement: Indexing epistemic authority and subordination in talk-in-interaction', in: SOCIAL PSYCHOLOGY QUARTERLY 2005/ 68(1), p. 15–38.

Kołakowski L.: 'In praise of inconsistency', in: DISSENT 1963/10(1), p. 201–209.

Reisigl, M.: 'Dyskryminacja w dyskursach', in: TEKST I DYSKURS – TEXT UND DISKURS 2010/3, p. 27–61.

Reisigl, Martin / Wodak, Ruth: Discourse and Discrimination: Rhetorics of Racism and Antisemitism. London and New York 2001.

Sacks, Harvey, 'Notes on methodology', in: Atkinson, John Maxwell / Heritage, John (eds.): *Structures of Social Action. Studies in Conversation Analysis.* Cambridge 1984, p. 21–27.

Sacks, Harvey: Lectures On Conversation, Volume II. Oxford 1995.

Said, Edward W: Orientalism. London 2003.

Schegloff, Emanuel A.: 'Introduction', in: Sacks, Harvey: *Lectures On Conversation. Volume I.* Oxford 1995, p. ix–lii.

Schmitt, Carl: Political Theology. Four Chapters on the Concept of Sovereignty. Cambridge 1986.

Spector, Malcolm / Kitsuse, John I.: Constructing Social Problems. New York 1987.

Van Dijk, Teun: Elite Discourse and Racism. Newbury Park London New Delhi 1993.

Artur Lipiński

Interactional strategies of journalistic neutralism and political equivocation. The case of "Tomasz Lis na żywo" TV show

Abstract

The TV show "Tomasz Lis na żywo" broadcasted six days before the electoral day provides very convenient entry point allowing to understand the strategies employed by J. Kaczyński and T. Lis in the context of communicative conflict. The paper is based on the assumption that regardless of the individual actor's belief journalistic neutralism is the result of specific procedures employed to create such stance. Similarly, the equivocation can be manifested through the number of interactional strategies employed by the interviewed politician in a situation of communicative conflict when all the replies would put politician's face in jeopardy but nevertheless the reply is still expected. The paper highlights several conversational strategies of T. Lis, including footing, asking hostile questions, references to third party opinions or rhetoric of numbers. Regarding J. Kaczyński, it examines politician's reaction to adversarial claims of the interviewer by highlighting their lack of validity on the basis of truthfulness, appropriateness and sincerity, challenging the macrovalidity of the debate or its specific issues or producing responses formulated as questions.

Keywords: communicative strategies, political interview, equivocation, neutralism, footing

Introduction

An important part of the campaign before the 2011 parliamentary elections were the "debates about debates". Donald Tusk, the then Prime Minister and the leader of conservative liberal Civic Platform (hereafter: PO), invited Jarosław Kaczyński, the President of the populist right wing Law and Justice party (hereafter PiS) twice to a debate not only to reveal Kaczyński's lack of knowledge and competence to govern the country but also his aggressive and antagonistic style of doing politics. However, Kaczyński remembered very well his defeat in the debate with Tusk in 2007, which contributed to the defeat of his party in the parliamentary elections that year. For this reason, he decided not to participate in a debate with the Prime Minister, instead proposing a series of debates on selected

Artur Lipiński, Adam Mickiewicz University in Poznań (Poland), ORCID: 0000-0003-3904-0598, artlip@amu.edu.pl.

specific policies with other ministers. Additionally, Kaczyński introduced some terms and conditions of these debates which were either unacceptable or for-mulated at such general level that it was not possible to react to them. For example, Kaczyński announced that he would debate when the Prime Minister "takes down the white flag towards the mighty in Poland, but also towards the mighty outside Poland" (Grochal 2011). Such an expression contained the hostile implication that Tusk's government was unable to defend Polish interests.

Given this background, the interview by Tomasz Lis with Jarosław Kaczyński in "Tomasz Lis na żywo" TV show broadcast by public television on 3 October 2011 might be conceived as a proxy electoral debate organized to uncover the antagonistic face of Kaczyński, who, for the electoral purposes, decided to adopt a decisively more moderate style of campaigning. As Lis recalled in his book, "Kaczyński has once again, in another campaign, funded Poland with a great masquerade. He pretended to be gentle and moderate, willing to cooperate with the opposition and ready to make compromises. [...] I had no doubts that this man was extremely dangerous for Polish democracy. [...] If it had been possible to tear the mask of meekness off Kaczyński's face within an hour, it would have cost him several percentage points on election day" (Lis 2018, p. 341f). Ka-czyński's decision to appear in one of the most popular political TV shows hosted by the journalist well known for his vehement criticism of PiS was dictated by the moderate line PiS adopted before the elections and their willingness to convince at least part of the 2 million viewers of the show. The goal of this paper is to analyse interactional strategies used by Lis and Kaczyński during the TV show "Tomasz Lis na żywo" broadcast six days before the electoral day to achieve their respective professional and political aims, given the complexity of the commu-nicative situation and professional and political requirements of the roles of these two actors.

The media and political background of the TV show

In order to understand the stakes, one has to highlight the specific characteristics of the Polish media system and the political situation before 2011 parliamentary elections. The interview took place in a specific context of extremely politicized media system. According to Bogusława Dobek-Ostrowska, the Polish public broadcasting system can be described as the "politics of the broadcasting system" (Dobek-Ostrowska 2012, p. 43) where the public media are controlled by the politicians, the news agenda is governed by the political requirements not the newsworthiness of specific events, journalism is dominated by interpretation and commentaries, media content is dominated by the advocacy style and journalist display partisan viewpoints and they are "convinced that their civic responsibility requires them to promote what they personally consider to be the best political course for the country" (Dobek-Ostrowska 2012, p. 43). Consequently, such a media system contributes to the strong political polarization and encourages journalists to employ an adversarial and confrontational style. In the context of other types of media systems, the interviewer, in order to keep their high professional status and advance the career, should maintain balance between posing relevant questions and preserving neutrality. In the model of polarized pluralism in Poland (cf. Hallin / Mancini 2004), the balance is shifted towards the political engagement of the journalist who usually concentrates on the sharp criticism of a politician from the opposite political camp. On the other, neutralism is still seen as a desired professional standard in journalism which forces journalists to navigate between contradictory positions. Additionally, there are requirements of interview genre itself which impose own discursive norms on the strategies employed by the journalists. The following excerpt from Lis memoirs related to interview with Kaczyński aptly reflects this: "I could not speak my mind or argue. At best, I could ask questions. So it was necessary to tear off Kaczyński's mask without abandoning the convention of a conversation, an interview" (Lis 2018, p. 342).

The situation was no less difficult for the leader of PiS. Initially he did not want to appear in Lis' show but the potential benefits of reaching the large audience ultimately outweighted the risks. Moreover, his decision to participate was in line with the electoral strategy adopted by PiS on the eve of the 2011 electoral campaign. By employing moderate rhetoric and conciliatory style of campaigning, PiS sought to shed its public image of an aggressive and radical party it earned during in the 2005–2007 period, when the party strived to implement a project of revolutionary changes known as the Fourth Republic. The incumbent Civic Platform was using this image to dissuade the voters from supporting PiS and present itself as a party "best placed to prevent the Law and Justice returning to power" (Szczerbiak 2013, p. 485). Striving to attenuate its agenda, PiS backgrounded its traditional points, such as dealing with the communist past or fighting crimes and corruption, and emphasized economic issues in an attempt to position itself as a mainstream party focused on modernizing Poland (Kalukin 2015). Further, in an attempt to warm up its image, PiS decided to display on billboards and elections posters its young and attractive female candidates running for the parliamentary seats. It was supposed to attract the support from the youngest strata of the electorate, as the places on the electoral lists from which these young women started gave them no chance to win in the elections. Moreover, PiS decided to background its most controversial politicians, including Antoni Macierewicz (former deputy minister of defence and head of the Military Counterintelligence Service) or Anna Fotyga (former foreign policy minister), known of their antagonistic style and polarizing or failed policy decisions during PiS incumbency between 2005 and 2007.

All these steps were met with the public distrust as Kaczyński had adopted such consensual strategies already before the snap presidential elections of 2010 following the Smolensk catastrophe in an attempt to reach out centrist voters. Immediately after the defeat in presidential elections, Kaczyński moved back to the old aggressive rhetoric and boycotted the inauguration of the new president. In the forthcoming months PiS focused on the issue of Smolensk air crash as the main point of its agenda, accusing the PO government of bearing moral and political responsibility for the tragedy and spreading many conspiracy theories, such as the alleged conspiracy of Tusk against Lech Kaczyński, the former President who tragically died in the catastrophe. Unsurprisingly, silencing antagonistic stance on the eve of the parliamentary elections of 2011 provoked the media comments emphasizing cynicism of PiS and the two-faced strategy of Kaczyński. The discourse on insincerity and the discursive measures drawn from the semantic field of mask, un-masking, wearing the mask, double-faced PiS, etc., was widespread in the liberal media, traditionally critical towards Kaczyński and PiS. For example, Janina Paradowska, the then leading journalist of liberal weekly "Polityka", when inquiring an expert about the sources of PiS's popularity asked the following question: "Mr. Professor, not so long time ago, the prevailing opinion was that the chairman of the Law and Justice party, after dropping the mask from the presidential campaign, would not fool anyone into pretending to be gentle again in the future. Have we been fooled a second time?" (Paradowska 2011). Another article employed similar rhetorical tropes: "The thing is, Kaczyński doesn't have to do many things, because he has others to do it for him. He can be a quiet gentleman himself, and the useful [aggresive – AL] content will still find its way into public sphere. This election circus is therefore unmasking itself, but that doesn't deter the audience" (Janicki / Władyka 2011). These media accusations were even reinforced by a few passages from Kaczyński's book published in the last days of campaign where he was undiplomatically insinuating that there was a conspiracy behind the then German Chancellor Angela Merkel's political position and that she was trying to rebuild German hegemony (Kaczyński 2011). Such messages, together with support given by some of the PiS's prominent politicians to the millieu of anti-government football hooligans, undermined the coherence of the party's conciliatory image and made it difficult to defeat the Civic Platform. Ultimately, inconsistencies in PiS electoral strategies negatively affected its electoral result and the party got the second place in the parliamentary elections held on 9 October 2011.

Theoretical approach and research problems

According to Anita Fetzer and Peter Bull, political interviews provide an opportunity to translate politics into text and talk, transfer macro-domain politics into micro-domain, and personify political agenda (Fetzer / Bull 2013, p. 84). They are public which means that they are oriented to the audience as a "ratified overhearer of the talk in progress", enabling ordinary people to encounter politics (Clayman 2015, p. 5). Even more importantly, political interviews are one of the most important components of the public sphere through which journalists can hold politicians accountable for their actions (Montgomery 2008, p. 262). During an interview, politicians are not only information givers but are obliged to clarify and justify their views to a critical and inquisitive journalist. In this way, the public is given the underlying reasoning of the policy agendas and negotiation of meaning (Andone 2013, p. 37).

The literature points at a number of features characteristic to broadcast interviews. Although interviews are to some degree unscripted and unpredictable, its highly institutionalized discourse is governed by the set of tacit social conventions. The agendas of interviews are predetermined and the interviews themselves take the form of a dispute. Although they assume a dialogical form of exchange between public figures, they are also targeting "overhearing audiences". Furthermore, interviewer and interviewee are attributed with unequal interactional rights and obligations. The asymmetry of roles stems from the power of a journalist to determine when the participants may talk and control the agenda of the interview (Brito 2017, p. 564). Importantly, interviews can be characterized by their high level of tolerance for an equivocal tone (Kampf / Daskal 2011, p. 178).

The ideal type structure of the interview consists of a number of defining features. First, it is defined by the clear-cut tasks and purposes, which can be narrowed down to asking questions to elicit information and giving answer to provide the information. Secondly, clear-cut division of roles between the journalist as interviewer and politicians as an interviewee. Thirdly, the use of a non-emotional, neutral language (Fetzer / Bull 2013, p. 85). All these elements impose restrictions on the interactional behaviour of the parties involved in an interview. The actual interviews, however, deviate from this ideal and take a much more complex shape as interviewers and interviewees manoeuvre or even stretch the institutional rules. It results, to large extent, from the role of a journalist as the representative of the public striving to elicit the information from the political elites, confront them with the opinions of their opponents, highlight the contradictions between past and present statements or emphasize inconsistencies between their declarations and actual political decisions. It is also the outcome of the commercialization of the media production and tabloidization of the media content including spectacularization, dramatization, emotionalization and negativity (Lengauer / Esser / Berganza 2012). Accordingly, it is expected that a journalist should adopt an adversarial mode but at the same time stick to the institutionalized norms of an ideal interview where objectivity and neutralism are considered supreme professional values.

The strategic manoeuvres of journalists balancing between confrontational behaviour and neutralism are accompanied by the growing evasiveness of the interviewed politicians, a process observed by scholars analysing media interviews (Kampf / Daskal 2011). Although in an interview the major aim of the politicians is to promote their own programs and achievements and criticize the political opponents, they frequently resort to equivocation when pressured by confrontational interviewers. Their equivocation is defined as the intentional use of evasive, obscure or ambiguous language which takes place in the context of "communicative conflict" or situation characterized by "avoidance-avoidance" (Bull / Simon-Vanderbergen 2019, p. 249, 251). According to the Situational Theory of Communicative Conflict developed in the field of experimental social psychology (see Bavelas et. al. 1990), people equivocate when they are challenged with a question "to which all of the possible replies have potentially negative consequences, but where nevertheless a reply is still expected" (Bull / Simon-Vanderbergen 2014, p. 3).

The theory was subsequently reconceptualized in Erving Goffman's definition of "face" – loosely understood as prestige, reputation or successful presentation of actor's identity (Goffman 2012, p. 5f). All communicative actions are driven not only by the need to exchange information but also to exchange information in relation to face-related needs. Accordingly, the linguistic strategies of the social actors are rational in their pursuit to minimize threats to their positive face defined as "the want of every member that his wants be desirable to at least some others" or negative face understood as "the want of every 'competent adult member' that his actions be unimpeded by others" (Brown / Lewinson 1987, p. 62, quote after: Bull / Fetzer 2010, p. 157). Regarding the latter, politicians will avoid the communicative actions which may limit or hamper their future courses of action. Consequently, the elected politicians are particularly sensitive to face-threatening acts as they might seriously affect their position in the party and chances for electoral success. Given this context, politicians tend to equivocate when "the least face-threatening option for an interviewee is either a non-reply or an incomplete reply" (Bull / Simon-Vanderbergen 2019, p. 251). These theoretical assumptions are strongly confirmed by the empirical research showing that politicians are more likely to be asked face-threatening questions in comparison to non-political interviewees and that equivocation is their typical reaction. For example, the analysis of thirty three television interviews with British politicians between 1987 and 1992 revealed that intermediate replies and non-replies constituted fourteen and forty-three percent of all the answers, respectively (Bull 2003, p. 112).

Importantly, the face should be perceived as a dynamic and context-dependent phenomenon of two parties involved in the interview, constantly deconstructed and re-constructed during the interactional processes. Although political interviews are typically based on the unequal distribution of power between interviewees and interviewers, the former, particularly the high profile figures with a significant symbolic capital, are able to threaten the face of journalists as well. The academic literature on interviews provides numerous typologies of journalistic questions and responses from politicians used to promote their positive face, avoid limitations imposed on the negative face, prevent face-threatening acts or minimize the results of such acts. For example, a journalist may interactionally manoeuvre between professional norms of neutralism and commercial requirements of adversarialism through the references to the third party or to the people, and the use of prefaced questions, questions with presuppositions, or various mechanisms of setting an agenda (Clayman / Heritage 2002). Regarding the answers of politicians, Bull developed the extensive typology of mechanisms of intermediate replies and non-replies when the interviewees equivocate in order to protect their face from threatening questions. Thirty-three different types of equivocations were distinguished which were organized into twelve superordinate categories: ignore the question; acknowledge the question without answering it; question the question; attack the question; attack the interviewer; decline to answer; make a political point; give an incomplete reply; repeat the answer to a previous question; state or imply that the question has already been answered; and apologise or interpret the question literally where it was clearly not intended as such (Bull 2003, p. 114f).

This paper applies typologies developed by Steven Clayman, John Heritage and Peter Bull to analyse the strategies adopted by Lis and Kaczyński in "Tomasz Lis na żywo" TV show to reconcile the contradictory forces inherent to the specific context of that interview. Given the political and media context of the interview, the stakes were complex for both actors. At the most general level, the aim of the journalist was to create a media event which will attract and keep the attention of the largest possible audience by unmasking and discrediting Kaczyński's strategy of self-presentation as a centrist politician. More specifically, Lis wanted to affect the positive face of Kaczyński by making him look radical and dangerous, and influence his negative face through limiting his freedom of future actions due to the moderation strategies he adopted during the electoral campaign. At the same time, Lis strived to promote his own positive face as an inquisitive but not aggressive or biased journalist concerned with the public interest rather than political interests.

On the other hand, Kaczyński's general goal was to maintain his image of a moderate politician to convince the undecided segments of the electorate. Bearing in mind the popularity of "Tomasz Lis na żywo" at that time, Kaczyński calculated that a successful interview might bring him additional votes necessary to secure an electoral victory. The accompanying goal was to reveal the aggressive stance of Lis as a non-neutral, unprofessional journalist driven by political interests rather than the willingness to elicit information. The following sections of the chapter shall focus only on the journalistic strategies of manoeuvring between neutralism and adversarialism employed by Lis and equivocal responses of Kaczyński striving to defend his moderate image and attempting to expose the bias of the interviewer.

Adopting the neutralistic stance – the strategies used by Tomasz Lis

As Clayman notes, there is a widespread professional role expectation that journalists should "not allow their personal opinions to enter into the interviewing process; to the best of their ability, they are supposed to remain neutral as they interact with public figures" (Clayman 1992, p. 163). Furthermore, he underlines that expressive moderation is particularly important in the television news interviews. Here the journalistic practices are broadcast "live" and as such they are open "to the immediate scrutiny of fellow journalists, government officials, social scientists, and a mass audience with diverse interests and ideological sympathies" (ibid., p. 164). Consequently, in order to keep the neutral, impartial and unbiased status, interviewers should avoid to express their personal opinions and affiliate or disaffiliate with the opinions of their interviewees (Clayman/ Heritage 2002, p. 126). In practice, the issue of neutrality is not related to the actual intents, attitudes or motivations of the journalists but the professional practice of employing discursive procedures which allow to construct a neutralistic stance. Moreover, neutralism is an interactional achievement, therefore the relevant, cooperative reactions of the interviewee are important, contributing factors (Garcia 2013, p. 269). The willingness to play "the interview game" by the interviewee, despite the frequently adversarial character of the questions, might manifest itself, for example, through repeating the frames imposed by the questions, withholding from answering the prefatory statements of the journalist preceding his question or by considering journalists presuppositions contained in questions as mistakes rather than expressions of journalist's opinions (Clayman / Heritage 2002, p. 127).

The neutralistic stance is maintained by the turn taking structure of the interview itself with its format of questions-answers considered by the parties involved as a normative system. When challenged by the politicians, journalists can defend themselves by claiming that their role is just to "ask questions" (ibid., p. 131). Lis resorted to this strategy when asking about the personal composition of the future PiS government.

Excerpt 1

TL: So Mr. Ziobro, as we heard, will certainly be offered a position (in a new government – AL) and you think Mr. Macierewicz will (be offered the position – AL) too, right?
JK: =your tone is accusatory. [↑And what is wrong with that, what is wrong with that/]
TL: [I am asking, I am asking, Mr. Chairman].

In this example, Lis begins with a reference to the interview Kaczyński gave to another TV station a few weeks before ("as we heard") where he declared that Zbigniew Ziobro would be offered a ministerial position. As Ziobro and Macierewicz were widely considered as highly controversial politicians, the question could have been considered very adversarial. Accordingly, Kaczyński challenged the tone of the interviewer in order to protect his positive face as a moderate politician considering all possible personal options. The immediate repetition of the very name of the speech act ("I am asking, I am asking") was used by Lis to defend and strengthen his legitimacy as a journalist only fulfilling his professional duties.

The explicit references to numbers and objective language used by Lis provided additional measures to construct himself as an impartial and unbiased journalist. As numbers possess "quasi factual authority" (Wodak 2018, p. 72), they are considered as self-explanatory data which is objective, unloaded and neutral representations and as such do not need any interpretation. Consequently, the use of numbers in the questions allow journalists to position themselves as detached and objective observers. The avoidance of adjectives "considered 'pollutant' of subjectivism" serves similar purposes (Muñoz-Torres 2007, 231).

Excerpt 2

TL: =Mr. Chairman, indeed, at that time (.) we had an economic growth. Let me remind you of 2006 – 6.2%, 2007 – 6.8%, but the global economic situation (.) helped everyone, and some neighbouring countries had a much higher growth. You know that, don't you?
JK: = Well, not much bigger, a little bit bigger. [The Czech Republic had actually]
TL: [Lithuania/]
JK: A little bit bigger.

TL: >Lithuania 7.8%–8.9%, Slovakia 8.5%–10.5%, Ukraine 7.3%–7.9%<. ↑And besides that, you have to admit, Mr. Chairman, that (.) that is largely due to your predecessor. (.)

[…]

JK: You want to convince us by all means that, back then it was bad. No, it was very good. >One million and three hundred thousand new jobs< this is a really great result.

TL: [I don't use adjectives/] I don't use adjectives, I provide numbers. Mr. Chairman (.), you say in interviews that you would like (.) to reduce the deficit. How?

Excerpt 3

TL: =Mr. Chairman, you speak about (…) the poor people in Poland, >which is indeed a very numerous group<, but you (…), when you were prime minister, you mostly took care of the rich Poles.

JK: (.) So thus us that what you say↑?

TL: =That is what (.) the facts and figures indicate.

In the excerpt 2, Lis criticizes the results of PiS government during its first term (2005–2007) for not being able to provide a high economic growth by referring to comparisons with other Central and Eastern European countries. The last turn of Lis, in reaction to the adversarial strategy of Kaczyński, was to resort to the rhetoric of numbers as contrasted with the usage adjectives. The repetition enhanced the implication of objectivity and detachment from the evaluative stance. In fact, numbers were strategically deployed to show the allegedly poor economic policy results of PiS and affect the positive face of Kaczyński and his party. In excerpt 3, the references to numbers serve to deflect the implied accusation that Lis simply expressed his own personal opinion.

Another way of defending oneself against accusations of asking hostile questions is to use footing shift which allows to produce and at the same time distance oneself from the produced statement. Goffman distinguished between various "production formats": the animator, author and principal. The animator only utters the sequence of words, the author composes the specific words in which position is encoded and the principal is the person whose viewpoint is "now expressed in and through the spoken words" (Clayman 1992, p. 165). The usefulness of footings stems from the fact that it allows journalist to be interactionally adversarial while "remaining officially neutral" (ibid., p. 196). Specifically, the shifts in footing enhance journalistic validity, credibility and legitimacy and they might be achieved in a number of ways. First, it might be manifested by attributing expressed point of view to some third party: an individual, a group or anonymous collectivity. Actually, the third party might be even not named but referred to by using an attributive verb in the passive voice with the agent deleted (Clayman / Heritage 2002, p. 153). Secondly, an important way to strengthen the validity or credibility of the claim is to attribute it to the experts supporting promoted worldview. The authoritativeness and inter-subjective validity of the claim might be further enhanced by the scope of experts and elaborated characterization of their professional credentials, experience etc. Thirdly, the legitimacy of the claim might be bolstered by shifting to the position of the "tribune of the people" (Clayman 2002). Moreover, references to the audience legitimize not only the specific viewpoints, but also the very question itself. They make it more difficult for the politician to evade such questions, as such an act may be considered as offensive not merely to the interviewer, but to the larger audience as well. In the analysed interview, Lis resorted to footing shift many times, referring not only to experts, but also ordinary people and official documents used to challenge the interviewee.

Excerpt 4

> TL: [Mr. Chairman] Everything you have said does not add up to 70 or 100 billion zlotys, because (.) that is (.) the amount of your election promises, if you were to imple-ment it.
> JK: =Sir (.) These are the calculations of the specialists on 300 billion, such as >Mr. Rostowski<. He really is a man of great numbers.
> TL: =No, [Mr. Rostowski speaks about]
> JK: [Please, do not/]
> TL: About one hundred billion, Mr. Balcerowicz says seventy billion. Do you question the first calculation, the second, all of them?

In the excerpt 4, Lis attempts to display Kaczyński's electoral promises as based on miscalculations or being silent about the real costs of these promises. Lin-guistically, it takes the form of an assertion rather than a question. In turn, in a pre-emptive step, Kaczyński reveals and ridicules the then Minister of Finance Jacek Rostowski ("a man of great numbers") as the potential source of in-formation for Lis. The reference to the third party, well known Polish neoliberal economist Leszek Balcerowicz allows not only to strengthen the validity of the claim on miscalculated electoral promises of PiS but also to construct unin-terested, positive face of the journalist and at the same time portray Kaczyński as an antagonistic, quarellsome and unreasonable politician. The positive face of an impartial journalist was also constructed through the adoption of the "tribune of the people" stance.

Excerpt 5

TL: Do you think that (.) this possibility was raised in what you said do you think that
Antoni Macierewicz sitting on the cabinet is a good idea?

JK: =Sir (.), I suggest that we agree something. We hold different beliefs and I read your
periodical and as a result (.) I think (.) it is pointless to consider this issue.

TL: No, Mr. Chairman, this is not pointless. [We want to know]

JK: [I mean this is/]

TL: who wi[ll], who wants to govern Poland, and we, the citizens, have the right (.) to
know it, and you (.) aspire to [that/].

Excerpt 6

TL: [Mr. Chairman, will you cooperate with President Komorowski?]

JK: And at the same time./ But maybe you will let me finish?

TL: =But this is a very important, vitally important issue for the citizens.

Both excerpts provide apt evidence for the scholarly claim that interviewers
employ such a stance during highly adversarial lines of questioning (Clayman /
Heritage 2002, p. 172). In both cases, one can notice disagreements, interruptions
and efforts to control the agenda of the interview by both parties involved. The
extract 5 commences with the journalist turn asking yes-no question which meets
the evasive answer of the interviewee and his attempt to change the agenda. Lis
expresses open disagreement with such a step ("No, Mr. Chairman (…) we want
to know") and shifts to the collective pronoun "we" represented as collectivity
simply interested in the answer ("want to know"). The second sentence is even
stronger, with its references to the politician's obligations towards citizens. The
collective "we" refers specifically to citizens and the question is legitimized
through the language of rights, not simply the will to know. In other words, the
rationale behind the question is framed not as resulting from mere curiosity, but
an important civic right necessary to make an informed electoral decision. A
similar strategy was employed in excerpt 6 when footing shift and emphasis on
the significance of the issue justifies the journalistic interruption of the politician's answer.

The construction of a neutralistic stance is also achieved by the reference to
official documents. In the following example, Lis refers to the police record of
Piotr Staruchowicz, nicknamed "Staruch", a leader of hooligan followers of the
Legia Warsaw football team. He became well known as one of the most vocal
adversaries of Tusk's government after PO- controlled parliament passed the law
against football hooliganism. Importantly, in an attempt to secure potential
political support, PiS decided to exploit these contentious, anti-governmental

moods. One example of that was a surety granted by a PiS parliamentarian, Beata Kempa, to Piotr Staruchowicz, who at that time was arrested and accused of robbery.

Excerpt 7

> TL: [From the police record] of Mr. Staruch: >2008 stadium ban after the match with Odra Wodzisław, 2011 – stadium ban after the match Legia-Ruch, shouts after the death of Jan Wejchert. 2011 – infringement of physical integrity, striking a foot-baller in the face. 2011 – running onto the pitch, Bydgoszcz, 2011 – robbery, events on 1 August, four independent witnesses<. Is he a thug or not?
> JK: =Sir, well, but there were no convictions in this case, and I/
> TL: That's why I don't say he's a criminal, I only say he's a thug [in our Polish language].

The excerpt above was directly preceded with the yes-no question of Lis, asking whether Kaczyński was ashamed with the support granted to football hooligan by PiS parliamentarian. The aim of the interviewer was to compromise the positive face of Kaczyński and validate the accusation of his party as treating law and justice issues instrumentally, despite its very name. Lis shifts to the format of an author merely juxtaposing facts from documentary data casually treated as self-evident. He cast himself as disinterested journalist merely invoking objective information, factuality of which is guaranteed by the character of the source. Moreover, shocking information from the police records followed by the yes-no question ("Is he a thug or not?") constitutes an adversarial line of questioning which leaves the interviewee very little room for manoeuvre. However, the very fact of quoting documents plays an important role of legitimizing such line and protects the journalist against the charges of non-neutrality.

Equivocation strategies used by Jarosław Kaczyński

According to the research, interviewees, striving to avoid damage to their positive and negative face, frequently resort to evasive answers, particularly in the context of adversarial political interviews. However, evasiveness itself might affect the face of the politicians in a number of ways. First, interviewers might highlight acts of sidestepping, comment on these acts and ask follow up questions, thus putting the politicians in an even more difficult position. Secondly, refusal to answer a question or offering only partial answers after repeated requests from a jour-nalists might become the subject of the subsequent news stories and political commentaries. Thirdly, the audience might interpret these acts of evasion as the manifestation of hidden motives (ibid., p. 239f). These contradictory pressures are dealt with in a variety of ways depending on the specific micro-context of the questions asked by the journalists, the status of the interviewer and interviewee, the broader context of the interview itself, and macro-context of the social and political situation.

By taking part in the TV show run by a journalist representing opposite political views a week ahead the parliamentary elections, Kaczyński, a leader of a highly centralized major oppositional party, had to defend not only his personal political face but also the party's face. The adversarial character of the interview, strengthened by the political parallelism of the Polish media system, led to a significant number of various types of equivocation. As Kaczyński strived to portray himself and his party as moderate, he reacted to the adversarial claims of the interviewer by highlighting their lack of validity. An interviewee can declare that an interviewer's claims have no validity in the three ways: "by saying the claim is not true (reference to the objective world), not appropriate (reference to the social world), or not sincere (reference to the subjective world)" (Simon-Vandenbergen 2008, p. 352). One can recognize all the types of challenging reactions in the interview analysed in this paper.

Excerpt 8

> TL: [You keep saying], you keep saying that these hooded figures, who mothers with baby strollers give a wide berth, are the essence of patriotism, because they carry the Polish tradition.
> JK: No, when did I say something like that?
> TL: Many times, it was Ms. Kempa in this studio, sitting in this chair.
> JK: =When did I say something like that?

Excerpt 9

> TL: [Will Professor] Will Professor Zyta Gilowska join your governmental team?
> JK: =Sir, you know I can't answer [such questions] at the moment.
> TL: [But why?]
> JK: Well, simply because there are certain rules here and please ask Professor Zyta Gilowska about it.

Both excerpts contain equivocations of a politician employed to avoid potentially negative consequences for the positive and negative face. In the first case, the stake is the positive face of PiS as Lis attempts to align the party with football hooligans ("these hooded figures") and detaches the party from the ordinary, innocent people ("mothers withbaby strollers"). Moreover, excerpt 8 provides an example of attacking the question based on an implication that the journalist's claim is not true. By using the grammatical form of the question Kaczyński moderates the assertion that the journalist is lying and, by repeating the question, pushes the interviewer to admit himself that the question is unfounded. In the excerpt 9, Lis asks to confirm whether Zyta Gilowska, former deputy prime minister and minister of finance in the PiS government between 2006 and 2007 will be nominated as a minister after the potential victory of PiS in parliamentary elections. Although media at the time reported talks between Kaczyński and Gilowska, the latter one did not confirm the desire to take up a governmental post. A full reply to the question of the interviewer would affect Kaczyński positive face and show him as an indiscrete person. Moreover, it could also seriously inhibit the room for negotiations with Gilowska, thus affecting the politician's negative face. Importantly, a refusal to answer the question was framed by the impersonal rule of appropriateness ("I can't answer", "the are certain rules"), not some idiosyncratic motives. Also, the reaction of Kaczyński suggested the insincerity of Lis, who pressured the interviewee to break the social principles of trust, confidentiality and not speaking on behalf of someone else (Bull 2003, p. 118).

Kaczyński also challenged the macrovalidity of the entire debate and explicitly requested to change the agenda. The following excerpts illustrate the instances of overt attacks on the question or the journalist by claiming that the questions do not pertain to the issues important to the general audience and public interest.

Excerpt 10

JK: =Don't, don't try this method any further, because I repeat (.) – this whole discussion leads to absurdity. Well, you (.) are simply discussing [in such a way as/].

Excerpt 11

JK: However, all I can tell you (…) is that I would really like to ask you for some (…) questions concerning issues vital to Poland, because you are constantly (…) trying to (.)

One can also discern more subtle and implicit attempts to change the agenda when Kaczyński acknowledges that the interviewer has asked a question but then fails to provide an answer and follows his own agenda instead.

Excerpt 12

> TL: She is the first/ >She is the first place candidate on the Law and Justice electoral list. Are you not taking responsibility for her?
>
> JK: Let me answer the question (.) We proposed a bill to the Sejm [lower chamber of Polish parliament – AL], which would have tightened the fight against this kind of phenomena, and it was rejected. And the second (.) proof of – let's say – a peculiar kind of involvement of those in power today in the fight (.) against hooliganism is (.) the permission for (.) alcohol in stadiums. Well, nobody will convince me that alcohol in stadiums will serve [order.]

The excerpt commences with the journalist's adversarial negative question related to Kempa's support for the football hooligan. Reacting to the situation of communicative conflict Kaczyński decided to equivocate. Accordingly, his initial declaration ("let me answer the question") serves only to obscure the subsequent positive presentation of his party as the only one actually interested in combating football hooliganism. Further, he makes two political points to defend the positive face of his party and attack the political opponents (Bull 2003, p. 118). The positive face is constructed through the information about PiS's legislative activity, irrelevant to the question asked by the journalist. Moreover, positive self-presentation is accompanied by negative other-presentation, namely the criticism of the policy of the incumbent PO.

The adversarial lines of questioning were also challenged by the interviewee on the procedural grounds. The following extract displays the significance of the normative character of the interview structure.

Excerpt 13

> JK: And there is a party that is still in power today (.) that has rejected them. And once again I repeat that the same party at the moment wants to introduce alcohol (.) [To the stadiums].
>
> TL: [Mr. Chairman, will you cooperate with President Komorowski?]
>
> JK: And at the same time./ But maybe you will let me finish?

In extract 13, the interviewee overtly reacts to the interruption by Lis. However, the breach of the normative rules of conducting an interview by the journalist is corrected by Kaczyński in a soft fashion by using a question with an adverb "maybe". Such reaction is employed despite the adversarial nature of the question implying that the politician as the potential future Prime Minister will not cooperate with the highest office in Poland.

Another type of reaction of Kaczyński to the situation of a communicative conflict is the production of a response formulated as a question. Again, it is an attempt of the politician to challenge the journalist's assertion but also not escalate the adversarial character of the exchange as it would affect moderation strategy of the party. Consequently, by answering the question with a question rather than overt disagreement Kaczyński opts for the less threatening act.

Excerpt 14

TL: "A certain formation". You're going to the old language, Mr. Chairman. Why? (.) It wasn't supposed to be like that.

JK: =And, excuse me, hasn't someone said various words about us, that I don't even want to quote here? Isn't it the case that Donald Tusk constantly, and by the way he is coming back to it now, says (.) something that constantly refers to those [famous mohair berets?][1]

The extract starts with a reference to the divisive language Kaczyński used in the previous turns by ambiguously distinguishing "certain formation" that is harming Poland. These words were used by Lis as an opportunity to unmask the old antagonistic essence of a politician hidden behind the mask of a moderate. The reply in the form of a question offered by Kaczyński can be perceived as an attempt to change the agenda and position his party as a victim of the aggressive rhetoric from political opponents. Victimization is strengthened by the meta-discursive passage pertaining to the words of PiS's political opponents, represented as so aggressive and unjust that they do not deserve to be quoted. The last sentence with the specific agent named (Donald Tusk) and specific expression ("mohair berets") exemplifies the agentless and general accusation of the previous sentence. The reply in the form of question might be also interpreted as conveying the implicit accusation of Lis of forgetting about aggressive words directed against PiS. As such, it implies non-neutrality and bias of the journalist. Therefore, the analysed strategy would contain attack on journalist as another strategy of equivocation.

The next strategy escapes clear cut types of equivocation distinguished by Bull (2003, p. 121). On the one hand, it is closest to an unwillingness to answer, and on the other, it bears some traces of a statement or implication that the question has already been answered.

---

1 Mohair berets – pejorative expression depicting the people holding conservative and national Catholic views. This expression originated from the characteristic headgear worn by the stereotypical listeners of the Radio Maryja and supporters of its founder Fr. Tadeusz Rydzyk (Zimny, Nowak 2009, p. 154). As the support given to PiS by Rydzyk contributed to the strong political position of PiS, the term is used more widely to describe the voters of this party.

Excerpt 15

> TL: Mr. Chairman, what did you want to say about Angela Merkel?
> JK: (1.0) ↑You can't speak Polish?
> TL: What did you want to say?
> JK: =Well, I guess it was very clearly [said].
> TK: [Not very clearly]
> JK: [Well, in your/]
> TL: ["I will not elaborate on the rest, I leave it to the political scholars and historians. (.)
> It was not (.) the result of sheer coincidence"]. What were you want to say?
> JK: =well, because clearly it was not the result of sheer coincidence. It was the result of
> broadly speaking the fact that two parts of Germany were united which led to all
> sorts of tensions and at one point they needed someone from the eastern part of
> Germany […]
> TL: [So why didn't you/]
> JK: And the rest please leave it to historians and political scholars, I would kindly ask
> you to do it.

The exchange above was directly preceded by the following quotation from
Kaczyński's book, read by a narrator: "I don't believe that Angela Merkel's
chancellorship was a result of sheer coincidence but I will not elaborate on this
belief. I leave it to political scholars and historians". The aim of Lis was to provide
another example of insinuative and divisive discourse used by Kaczyński which
could have had negative consequences for the Polish-German relations if he had
become the Prime Minister. The interviewee employs several types of resistance
to the adversarial line of the journalist which allows him to maintain his moderate image. In his first turn, the politician implicitly avoids to answer the
question by formulating his answer as a question which challenges the sincerity
of the journalist ("You can't speak Polish"). In his next turn, Kaczyński employs
another equivocation suggesting that the answer had already been given. Words
"well, I guess" introduces modality which mitigates the adversarial character of
his non-reply. In the third turn, being under pressure from the journalist, the
interviewee simply pretends to answer the question by using the word "well,
because" and provides pseudo-explanation of his words by invoking very general, uncontroversial, well-known historical facts. Ultimately, facing the confrontational line of Lis, the interviewee overtly asks him twice to change the
agenda. Moreover, the expression from the book to leave the issue to "historians
and political scholars", repeated by Kaczyński, served to legitimize the request by
representing the issue as requiring wider historical perspective and inappropriate
for a journalistic debate.

The moderating strategy of PiS did not preclude the attacks on the journalist's
positive face to unmask his non-neutral stance, non-professional behaviour and
portray him as detached from the national community and unconcerned with the

national interests. A particularly interesting line of attack is the latter one, presumably used to index the right-wing integrity of Kaczyński which was necessary to maintain the support of the conservative part of the electorate. In general, however, the attacks were either implied, as in the aforementioned examples, or adopted in the context of the adversarial line of questioning.

Excerpt 16

JK: =Look for that symmetry! [Look for that symmetry. More confidence in yourself, sir!]
TL: [Mr. Chairman, I remember/]
JK: More Polish self-confidence!

Extract 16 refers to the questions pertaining to Kaczyński's opinion on Merkel. The interviewer insinuates that there is an alleged asymmetry between Polish and German journalists. German journalists would not, according to the leader of PiS, be as concerned with the words of a German politician about Poles as Polish journalists are by Kaczyński's words about Merkel. The first turn provides an example of a ridiculing strategy as the lack of confidence is framed in personal turns. The next turn converts the previous expression ("more confidence in yourself") by adding an apparently redundant adjective "Polish" into a more serious attack on the integrity of Lis' national identity.

Conclusions

The paper was based on the assumption that regardless of the individual actor's belief journalistic neutralism is the result of specific procedures employed to create such stance. Similarly, the equivocation can be manifested through the number of interactional strategies employed by the interviewed politician in a situation of communicative conflict when all the replies would put politician's face in jeopardy but nevertheless the reply is still expected. The aim of the paper was to reconstruct the strategies of manoeuvre between neutralism and adversarialism adopted by the journalist and equivocation strategies of the politician. Given the complexity and often contradictory character of stakes Lis and Kaczyński had before 2011 parliamentary election "Tomasz Lis na żywo" TV show provided very convenient entry point allowing to understand the strategies used by two actors involved. As a journalist, Lis had to manoeuvre between neutrality and objectivism as important aspects of journalistic role expectation and antagonistic stance. The latter one resulted not only from the personal goal of the journalist but also commercial pressure of the genre. On the other hand, Ka-czyński striving to present moderate image of himself and his party resorted to various types of equivocation strategies to avoid answering adversarial questions. However, his interactional strategies were also driven by the motivation to por-tray Lis as biased, non-neutral journalist.

The analysis found that among many strategies employed by Lis footing featured most prominently. In order to defend oneself against accusations of asking hostile questions he used third-party opinions, including experts and ordinary people as well as official documents. Moreover, he referred a number of times to turn taking structure of the interview to present his assertions as question resulting from the division of roles in the interview. Finally, references to numbers and neutral language were invoked to keep his image a neutral journalist.

Regarding Kaczyński, he reacted to the adversarial claims of the interviewer by highlighting their lack of validity on the basis of truthfulness, appropriateness and sincerity. Moreover, he challenged the macrovalidity of the entire debate and explicitly requested to change the agenda, justifying these steps by claiming that the questions are not related to issues of public importance. He also challenged the journalist by claiming that the question The analysis allowed to reveal some covert interactional practices as well. For example, in order to challenge the adversarial character of the question, but at the same time to avoid the escalation of the adversarial exchange Kaczyński produced responses formulated as questions. In another part of the interview he attempted to change the agenda by announcing to answer the question without actually doing so.

Finally, the communication strategies were occasionally "thicker" than types originally developed by Bull (2003), Clayman and Heritage (2003). Many types of the strategies of equivocation discerned in the interview at the same time realized other strategies. For example, one of the replies formulated as a question con-tains victimization and, at the implicit level, attack on journalist strategy. It would be important line of future investigations to study the polyvalence potential of the strategies employed in political interviews. It would be also interesting to study how these universal strategies are articulated together with the local meanings of journalistic and political culture.

References

Andone, Corina: Argumentation in Political Interviews: Analyzing and Evaluating Re-sponses to Accusations of Inconsistency. Amsterdam 2013.

Bavelas, Janet Beavin / Black, Alex / Chovil, Nicole / Mullett, Jennifer: Equivocal Com-munication. Newbury Park 1990.

Brito, E.P.: '"I love homosexuals like I love gangsters": epistemics and evidentiality in a Brazilian hybrid television news interview', in: TEXT & TALK 2017/37(5), p. 561–585.

Bull, Peter: The Microanalysis of Political Communication: Claptrap and Ambiguity. London 2003.

Bull, P. / Fetzer, A.: 'Face, Facework and Political Discourse', REVUE INTERNATIONALE DE PSYCHOLOGIE SOCIALE 2010/2(23), p. 155–185.

Bull, P. / Simon-Vandenbergen, A.-M.: 'Equivocation and doublespeak in far right-wing discourse: an analysis of Nick Griffin's performance on BBC's Question Time', in: TEXT & TALK 2014/34(1), p. 1–22.

Bull, Peter / Simon-Vanderbergen, Anne-Marie: 'Conflict in political discourse: conflict as congenital to political discourse', in: Evans, Matthew / Jeffries, Lesley / O'Driscoll, Jim (eds.): The Routledge Handbook of Language in Conflict. London and New York 2019, p. 246–270.

Clayman, Steven: 'Broadcast news interviews', in: Tracy, Karen / Ilie, Cornelia/ Sandel, Todd L. (eds.): The International Encyclopedia of Language and Social Interaction. New York 2015, p. 1–19.

Clayman, Steven: 'Footing in the achievement of neutrality: the case of news-interview discourse', in: Drew, Paul / Heritage, John (eds.): Talk at Work: Interaction in Institutional Settings. Cambridge 1992, p. 163–198.

Clayman, S.: 'Tribune of the people: Maintaining the legitimacy of aggressive journalism', in: MEDIA, CULTURE & SOCIETY 2002/24(2), p. 191–210.

Clayman, Steven / Heritage, John: The News Interview: Journalists and Public Figures on the Air. Cambridge 2002.

Dobek-Ostrowska, Bogusława: 'Italianization (or Mediterraneanization) of the Polish Media System? Reality and Perspective', in: Hallin, Daniel C. / Mancini Paolo (eds.): Comparing Media Systems Beyond the Western World. Cambridge 2012, p. 26–50.

Fetzer, Anita / Bull, Peter: 'Political interviews in context', in: Cap, Piotr / Okulska, Urszula (eds): Analyzing Genres in Political Communication: Theory and Practice. Amsterdam 2013, p. 73–99.

Garcia, Angela Cora: An Introduction to Interaction. Understanding Talk in Formal and Informal Settings. London, New Dehli, New York, Sydney 2013.

Goffman, Erving: Rytuał interakcyjny. Warszawa 2012.

Grochal, R.: 'Warunki Kaczyńskiego, czyli prezes PiS widzi białą flagę', in: GAZETA WYBORCZA 4.09.2011, available at: https://classic.wyborcza.pl/archiwumGW/7467123/Warunki-Kaczynskiego–czyli-prezes-PiS-widzi-biala, accessed: 12.01.2022.

Janicki M. / Władyka W.: '2007, 2010, 2011. Nowe kampanie, stare chwyty', in: POLITYKA 27.09.2011, available at: https://www.polityka.pl/tygodnikpolityka/kraj/1519916,1,2007-2010-2011-nowe-kampanie-stare-chwyty.read, accessed: 12.01.2022.

Kaczyński, Jarosław: Polska naszych marzeń. Warszawa 2011.

Kalukin, R.: 'Nowa droga do IV RP', in: NEWSWEEK 5.07.2015, available at: https://www.newsweek.pl/jakie-panstwo-chce-stworzyc-jaroslaw-kaczynski/4s3g6by [20.01.2022].

Kampf, Zohar / Daskal, Efrat: 'When the watchdog bites. Insulting politicians on air', in: Ekström, Mats / Patrona Marianna (eds.): Talking Politics in Broadcast Media: Cross-cultural Perspectives on Political Interviewing, Journalism and Accountability. Amsterdam 2011, p. 177–197.

Lengauer, G. / Esser, F. / Berganza, R.: 'Negativity in political news: A review of concepts, operationalizations and key findings', in: JOURNALISM 2012/13(2), p. 179–202.

Lis, Tomasz: Historia prywatna. Warszawa 2018.

Montgomery, M.: 'The discourse of the broadcast news interview', in: JOURNALISM STUDIES 2008/9(2), p. 260–277.

Muñoz-Torres, Juan Ramon: 'Underlying epistemological conceptions in journalism', in: JOURNALISM STUDIES 2007/8(2), p. 224–247.

Paradowska, J.: 'Sądy i sondaże', in: POLITYKA 4.10.2011, available at: https://www.poli tyka.pl/tygodnikpolityka/kraj/1520076,1,sady-i-sondaze.read, accessed 12.01.2022.

Simon-Vandenbergen, A.-M.: '"Those are only slogans": A linguistic analysis of argumentation in debates with extremist political speakers', in: JOURNAL OF LANGUAGE AND SOCIAL PSYCHOLOGY 2008/27(4), p. 345–358.

Szczerbiak, A.: 'Poland (Mainly) Chooses stability and continuity: The October 2011 Polish parliamentary election', in: PERSPECTIVES ON EUROPEAN POLITICS AND SOCIETY 2013/14(4), p. 480–504.

Wodak Ruth: 'Revival of numbers and lists in radical right politics', in: RES RHETORICA 2018/5(4), p. 69–75.

Wroński, P.: 'Kto stoi za Merkel?', in: GAZETA WYBORCZA 10.03.2011, available at: https://wyborcza.pl/7,76842,10403197,kto-stoi-za-merkel.html, accessed: 20.01.2022.

Zimny, Rafał / Nowak, Paweł: Słownik polszczyzny politycznej po roku 1989. Warszawa 2009.

Appendix 1

Transcription conventions

(.)   pause of half a second or less
(1.5)   pause timed in seconds
[beginning of overlapping stretch of speech
[ ]   overlapping talk
=   introduces latched turn

Waldemar Czachur / Marta Wójcicka

Analysis of one text from the perspective of discourse linguistics

Abstract

The aim of this paper is to answer two questions – whether a single text chosen by discourse researchers can constitute the basis for discourse analysis and what research tools and methods discourse linguistics can offer for the discoursological study of one text. Assuming that the methodological foundation of discourse linguistics is the principle of design and integrationism, we assume that the analysis of a single text can be the basis for discourse analysis, because we define a text as a serially organized, subjectively-shaped and discursively conditioned communicative event that produces, records and visualizes collectively shared meanings/knowledge. In this context, the key criterion for selecting a single text is the discourse researchers' knowledge about the specificity of discourse, its actors and the texts that are key to this discourse, and which determine the discourse dynamics. The principle of integrationism is expressed in the way of designing a discourse as a subject of research, that is, in integrating its heterogenous aspects, and in the way of designing a multi-level research procedure that integrates various linguistic methods for specific research questions.

Keywords: text, discourse, discourse linguistics, text analysis, integrationism

Context

Discourse is a communicative and social phenomenon that is omnipresent, and influences holistically the way we think, speak and act. At the same time, discourse as a subject of research, in this case, of discourse linguistics, unlike a word, sentence or text, is an intangible object, and so difficult to grasp. Therefore, it must be designed by the researcher, taking into account the cognitive and ontic perspective (Czachur 2020).

Waldemar Czachur, University of Warsaw (Poland), ORCID: 0000-0002-8343-4765, waldemar.czachur@uw.edu.pl.
Marta Wójcicka, University of Maria Curie-Skłodowska in Lublin (Poland), ORCID: 0000-0002-9846-9776, marta.wojcicka@poczta.onet.pl.

The aim of the article is an attempt to answer two questions: whether a single text, selected by discourse researchers, can constitute the basis for a discourse analysis, and what research tools and methods can discourse linguistics offer for the discoursological study of one text. The issue is important to us because, so far, discourse linguistics, based on the methodological assumptions of corpus linguistics, postulated the need to build larger textual corpora, guided by the principle of representativeness in qualitative (which texts and genres are included in the corpus) and quantitative (how many texts are included in the corpus) terms. In this article, we ask to what extent can one text, in this case an interview of the journalist Tomasz Lis with the politician, chairman of the Law and Justice party, Jarosław Kaczynski, be the subject of discourse analysis and what levels of the text should be explored so that it is possible to talk about discourse analysis. For this purpose, a proposal developed on the grounds of discourse linguistics will be used, which designs discourse on its four ontic levels: institutional, substantive, thematic and modal/ideological.

Discourse and text from the perspective of discourse linguistics

The focus of discourse linguistics is the use of language and the belief systems it produces, which are manifested in meanings specific to particular discourses. We assume that, because it reflects on the shaping of the relationship between language use, collective belief systems and knowledge selection processes, discourse linguistics seeks an answer to the question of how the perspectival uses of language in discourse create meanings shared by society, and thus model specific images of reality/the world. When asking about the discursively conditioned processes of meaning creation, it is also interesting to explore the rules that co-decide what can be said in the discourse and what cannot (Czachur 2020, p. 217, also Spitzmüller / Warnke 2011, Czachur 2016).

The methodological foundation of discourse linguistics is the design and integrationism principle. The design principle says that it is the discourse researcher who designs discourse as the subject of research (its corpus and research procedure), guided by an adopted (conscious) cognitive perspective and a specific (thematic, institutional, substance or modal/ideological) ontic perspective of the discourse. The principle of integrationism is expressed in the way of designing a discourse as a subject of research, that is, in integrating its heterogenous aspects, and in the way of designing a multi-level research procedure that integrates various linguistic methods for specific research questions.

The main methodological inspirations for discourse linguistics come primarily from Michael Foucault's reflections on discourse (Angermuller 2014, Kumięga 2013, Nowicka 2016, Nowicka-Franczak 2017). In his concept of discourse, three issues play a constitutive role: knowledge, power and the subject. The relations between them can be summarized as follows: *Knowledge,* as understood by the French philosopher, is a collective and linguistically created system of beliefs; the way in which we interpret (using language) the reality that surrounds us, each time subjectively, i. e., within perspective, taking into account a specific point of view and the interests of specific entities operating within the discourses. As Foucault says, "knowledge is also the space in which the subject may take up a position and speak of the objects with which he deals in his discourse" (Foucault 1972, p. 182) and "the field of coordination and subordination of statements in which concepts appear and are defined, applied and transformed" (ibid., p. 182–183). The fact that subjects occupy certain positions in the discourse in accordance with the represented beliefs/knowledge is motivated by the pursuit of power. *Power* is thus expressed in the fact that *subjects* impose and control (also through the use of institutions), in particular societies, a linguistically produced vision of reality, as well as legitimize and sanction this vision. Power and knowledge, thus understood, remain in a conditioning relationship insofar as it is power that can make a group of collective beliefs "real" and ideologize knowledge. Knowledge resources circulating in discourses and through discourses, initiated, activated, distributed and stabilized by individual (competing) social groups at the same time co-shape the identities of these entities, establishing their positions in the discourse and their mutual relations. "Discourse is not simply that which translates struggles or systems of domination but is the thing for which and by which there is struggle, discourse is the power which is to be seized" (Foucault 1981, p. 52–53). Discourse becomes then "the set of enforced and coercive meanings that permeate social relations" (Foucault 2003, p. 164).

We define discourse as a set of habitual communication practices carried out by various actors in the form of serial statements (texts), which, through interactions, shape specific view of the world according to accepted cultural rules (Czachur 2020, p. 144). Therefore, we perceive discourse as a linguistic category in so far as it is viewed in terms of interactive linguistic acts and texts, as their forms of manifestation and social impact, as well as a broad socio-cultural context which determines the creation of meanings, which subsequently influence the visions of reality.

However, we do not see discourse linguistics as a methodology or as a research perspective but, rather, as a transdisciplinary research program that draws on the broadly defined changes in the humanities[1]. Discourse linguistics studies the

---

1 It is worth pointing out the differences between the interdisciplinary approach on one hand, and the transdisciplinary and integrative approach on the other. We understand interdisciplinarity as the use of methods typical of various scientific disciplines to work on one

discursively shaped relations between the use of language, collective belief systems, knowledge selection processes and culture, and it also asks how linguistic perspectivising creates socially shared meanings, thus modelling specific images of reality. Thus, discourse linguistics becomes an integrative and designing discipline. It integrates different theoretical, methodological and methodical perspectives in designing its research subject, cognitive objective and research procedure (Czachur, 2020).

In the context of these assumptions, it is no longer sufficient to state that a text is an independent (semantically and formally integrated) communicative macrosign that has its subject and recipient as well as a recognizable intention immersed in a specific speech genre (Bartmiński / Niebrzegowska-Bartmińska 2009, p. 36). Discourse linguistics very clearly emphasizes that a text is both a communicative product and a means of action; a form constituting knowledge and a means of its distribution (Labocha 2011, Dijk 2014, Antos 2020). This perception of a text is based on the assumption that a text is reproducible. Only what is repeated becomes a sensible sign, and thus becomes a collectively shared good/ resource. The principle of reproducibility of texts is thus expressed in their genre, intertextuality and discursiveness (Warnke 2002). This means that each text becomes not so much an individual and unique communication event, but a part of a series. We perceive the seriality of the occurrence of texts in a certain arrangement to be evidence of the discursive nature of the texts which is revealed in their immersion in a genre and in the network of intertextual references. Foucault also drew attention to this phenomenon, writing about statements: "there is no statement in general, no free, neutral, independent statement; but a statement always belongs to a series or a whole, always plays a role among other statements, deriving support from them and distinguishing itself from them: it is always part of a network of statements, in which it has a role, however minimal it may be, to play" (Foucault 1972, p. 99). He also says: "There is no statement that does not presuppose others: there is no statement that is not surrounded by a field of coexistences, effects of series and succession, a distribution of functions and roles" (ibid.). Thus, we look at a text as a serially organized, subjectively/

---

research problem – it is then viewed from different angles, usually within an interdisciplinary research team, in which each of the researchers analyzes a given problem using methods and categories typical of their discipline. Integrationism is a method that goes a step further, i.e. it combines/integrates various theoretical, methodological and methodological perspectives in the area of designing a research subject, e.g. discourse. On the other hand, we understand transdisciplinarity – following Anna Duszak and Norman Fairclough – as a relationship between disciplines that not only enables the recontextualization of categories and methods of one discipline in another but also the transformation of categories and methods existing in a given discipline as a result of creating their coherent relationship with categories and methods which have been recontextualized (Duszak / Fairclough 2008, 13).

prospectively shaped and discursively conditioned communication event that produces, records and reveals collectively shared meanings/knowledge.

Discourse analysis and the corpus

From the perspective of discourse linguistics, also inspired by the achievements of corpus linguistics, a researcher of discourse designs it based on serial, dispersed texts which are selected in the process of creating a research corpus. A corpus is not a discourse, but only its substrate, a model; it is "a collection of (1) machine-readable (2) authentic texts (including transcripts of spoken data) which is (3) sampled to be (4) representative of a particular language or language variety" (McEnery / Xiao / Tono 2006, p. 5). The principles developed by corpus linguistics explain the process of creating and analysing corpora (Stefanowitsch 2020). It is assumed that a corpus should be representative of the studied discourse, i. e., balanced in terms of speech genres, language variants and subjects/voices relevant to the examined discourse. In this area, discourse linguistics has developed many models of corpus analysis (Bubenhofer 2018).

Discourse-based corpus analysis or corpus-based discourse analysis starts from the premise that corpora provide examples of language in use. For this reason, it is interested in the analysis of the linguistic surface. The analyses will be, alternately, data-driven, hypothesis-generating ('corpus driven') and/or hypothesis-driven ('corpus-based'), in each case based on large text sets. By analyzing the frequency of specific lexical units, their collocations and concordances, n-grams, keywords, topic models, as well as specific grammatical constructions, the repetition of certain patterns of use, as well as their discursive relevance (network of intertextual references), are determined. Therefore, corpus analysis guarantees the verifiability of theses based on a set of texts (their number depends on the research question or researchers' capabilities), as well as a combination of quantitative and qualitative methods.

We intend to reflect on the discoursological analysis of one text or, in other words, on the one-text analysis of discourse. We are interested in the criteria for selecting the one text that could represent a studied discourse, i. e., the one that researchers want to make the subject of their research. We also want to enquire into the method of its analysis.

If we look at the definition of discourse as proposed by Busse and Teubert (1994, p. 14) who say that discourse includes all texts that are related to a specific topic, linked by intertextual and semantic references and/or a common communicative and functional context, and fall within the framework defined by a specific time range, area of influence and belonging to a genre (cf. Busse / Teubert 1994, p. 14), then there is nothing to prevent one text from being considered representative of the analysed discourse. This is because in the analysed text we can find all intertextual relations as well as those formations of knowledge that are constitutive of the discourse under study. However, the question is, on the basis of what criteria should we choose the key text for discourse and how should we study it?

In this case, there are two possible approaches. On the one hand, a discourse researcher may identify the key text that meets the requirements of representativeness using the tools of corpus linguistics. It includes using criteria such as, for example, citation. On the other hand, it is possible to choose the text guided by the knowledge of the discourse and the discourse function of the given text which researchers consider to be crucial for the specific discourse (Fix 2021, p. 411). We recognize the key character of texts by their function in the discourse, by their syntagmatic and paradigmatic (semantic, intertextual) density, in which we recognize the features of discursive seriality. We assume that a researcher who aims to analyse a discourse has an understanding of the specificity of this discourse, as well as the factors, including texts, that co-shape it.

When selecting the text for the discourse (discursological) analysis, the researcher finds important, as Czachur (2020) points out, two perspectives: the cognitive one (what the researcher finds interesting in discourse) and the ontic one (how discourse is revealed to the researcher). We understand the cognitive perspective as a way to design discourse as a subject of research which derives from the researcher's cognitive interest and from the fact that research is placed in a dynamic epistemological context of discourse linguistics in relation to media linguistics, cultural linguistics, stylistics, text linguistics, etc. The ontic perspective is understood as the way in which discourse is revealed to the researcher to become the subject- matter of analysis from a specific cognitive perspective. Based on how discourse has been defined and modelled in empirical research, we distinguish four dominant dimensions: institutional, substantive, thematic and modal/ideological, all of which require the researcher to undertake nuanced and reflexive action when designing the research procedure, which we perceive as a "user manual" for the discourse under study, corresponding mainly with the cognitive objectives and the methods that exist in linguistics. The research procedure should also imply the design of the research corpus and the methods used to analyse it (Czachur 2020, p. 222–249).

We also assume that these four perspectives are important for text analysis which is conducted as a part of discourse analysis. In the further part of this article, we will try to show what research methods may be applied to the discursological analysis of a text on the four above-mentioned levels: institutional, substantive, thematic and ideological/modal. The subject of the analysis will be an interview conducted by the Polish journalist Tomasz Lis with the Chairman of the Law and Justice Party, Jarosław Kaczyński on the TV program "Tomasz Lis na żywo" [Tomasz Lis live] on 3 October 2011.

Case study

As stated above, the aim of this paper is, on the one hand, to reflect on the criteria for selecting a single text as representative of a specific discourse and, on the other hand, on the criteria of its analysis If we assume that discourse is a set of communication practices implemented by various actors in the form of serial statements (texts) which, through interactions, shape a specific way of seeing the world in accordance with the adopted cultural rules, then the task of discourse analysis/discoursological analysis of one text, will be to capture these linguistic/communicative practices that co-create socially shared meanings and those rules/discursive conditions that significantly co-decide what can be said, and thus shape specific images of the world. In the following analysis four ontological levels will be applied.

The institutional level allows to analyse a single text (case) as part of the social discourse, in the case of our example – to present it in the context of media and political discourses, as an exemplification of these discourses. Another reason why the institutional level is important to us is because it enables us to grasp the (culturally conditioned) rules of expression, i.e., those rules that significantly contribute to what can and what cannot be said.

In this context, a single text (Tomasz Lis' interview with Jarosław Kaczyński) can be analysed:

1) In the synchronic approach – in relation to the media and political discourse at the time of this interview, i.e., in 2011 and in the years immediately preceding the interview. Let us recall that the Law and Justice Party, the party that describes itself as guided by the idea of social and national conservatism, solidarity, and Christian democracy, and is described by the opposition as a populist and Eurosceptic group, was in power in the years 2005–2007. The interview was conducted on public television TVP2, by the journalist who is credited with liberal views, as part of the program "Tomasz Lis na żywo" which was broadcast on TVP2 from February 25, 2008 to January 25, 2016.

2) In the diachronic approach, that is in the longer perspective, the following facts are important: In 2014, the party won the local government elections, and in 2015 – the presidential and parliamentary elections. Since then, the party has been in power to this day (2023). Conversational strategies clearly outlined in this interview (e.g., the us-them opposition) – we know this in retrospect – are continued by The Law and Justice Party to this day. In the

diachronic view, i. e. in the longer-term perspective, the following facts are important:

The analysed interview is a representative example of the narrative used by the party in the following years. This, in a way, announces the ways of building a national narrative and the party's construction of social moods.

At the institutional level, the analysis asks questions about social actors, communication strategies and the speech types typical of a given institution, in this case television. In the analysed interview there should be noted:

1) transmitting-receiving relations constituting the frame for a specific meeting, and resulting from the distinguishing features of the television interview genre. We place the Lis–Kaczyński interview in the context of roles inscribed in a given genre: the journalist-host, the politician-guest. In accordance with the genre's premises, the journalist asks questions that introduce new local topics, while the politician provides answers. The subject of the analysis is the question of the constancy of these roles: are the questions asked only by the journalist? how does the transmitting-receiving situation change and go beyond the framework imposed on the actors by the genre? (e. g., JK to TL: "So this is what you say?"), what communication roles do both parties take?

2) In addition to these two main social actors, the interview features the audience – a mute participant in the act of communication. The audience in the studio – divided as it is – applauds some of the statements of one or the other of the actors, and this also becomes one of the threads of the analysed conversation. For example, TL says to the audience: "I only have one request to you, the several dozen people who came with the chairman, to reward him with an applause, but maybe not while he's speaking, because then you're making it difficult for Mr. Chairman to speak".

3) The institutional convention also includes the audience in front of TV sets, which is also taken into account here *expressis verbis:* TL: "But I need to look after not only your interests, but also those of the viewers".

4) The TV interview is a hybrid, mixed genre which contains both elements of oral communication (along with extensive non-verbal communication which can also become the topic of the conversation), and elements of other mixed messages – the previously mentioned TV interviews or quoted fragments of oral or written statements of the guest (in this case, from a book by Kaczyński) (Loewe 2018, Gianmarco 2019).

The substantive level "refers to the discourse carrier that models forms of communication and does not influence the created content" (Czachur 2020, p. 227). In this case, we are dealing with a television discourse (Loewe 2018) characterized by multimodality and a sense-creating function in the mediasphere (Lorenzo-Dus 2008).

In the analysis at this level, we consider the following aspects:

– the specificity of television as the medium in which the analysed interview was broadcast. We mean both the television discourse as such, as well as the public television discourse in Poland at that time, and the status of TVP2. The interview was carried out on TVP 2 which, at that time, was not referred to as the "Law and Justice tube", "regime television", "on the pitch" of Tomasz Lis – the host of the program "Tomasz Lis na żywo" broadcast on TVP2 from February 25, 2008 to January 25, 2016.

– in the diachronic perspective, we take into account the fact that this interview is present on the internet today, and so we analyse it in relation to the Internet discourse (with the possibility of posting comments which we can also, from the perspective of time, take up today and analyse). The presence of the interview on the Internet has transferred it into new consitulations which added new meanings to the conversation, imposed on it in the processes of reception at specific moments following the broadcast.

– because of the multimodal nature of the medium, we analyse communication not only at the verbal level, but we are also interested in elements of non-verbal communication (kinestics, ophthalmology, proxemics, etc.). Both participants in the interview are sitting opposite each other, taking confrontational positions. Throughout the interview, Kaczyński is looking directly into the eyes of the interviewer, he smiles – especially when he uses such speech acts as: rhetorical questions: "Is this what you think?", "You can't speak Polish?", "How do you know that?" [as he would write in the book – MW]; assertions-comments to the interviewer's behaviour: "Your tone is accusatory" or "You too had such ambitions" [to rule Poland – MW], "But I understand that you are from a different formation, that you wouldn't want that [if offending Poles in Germany were treated the same way as offending the French or Jews – ed. MW], that you are too shy"; requests: "And the rest please leave it to the historians and political scholars"; assertions expressing regret and pity: "But you obviously are so frightened of them [outsiders]. I really feel sorry for you. I do feel very sorry for you. You belong to a certain formation, unfortunately very common in Poland which is harmful to us"; advice: "Let us free ourselves from Polish history. You too liberate yourself from it"; wishes and encouragement: "But I would also very much like Polish publicists and journalists to be bolder. And I encourage you to do so with all my might".

Kaczyński seems to be relaxed, he gesticulates little, and reacts freely to Lis' questions and behaviour. The latter, in turn, at the beginning does not make eye contact with the guest, he is distracted by sheets of notes, he seems tense, anxious, and very serious.

At this level of analysis, we also take into account the relationship between the verbal and non-verbal parts – which are also the subject of the conversation, as the guest points out when he says: "And you are looking at me with your face so tense and you do not want to be convinced".

The subject of the analysis are also genres of speech constitutive for television (and the internet), in this case an interview, one part of which is a pre-prepared element, included in the scenario, to which Lis reaches and which in this case seems to be limiting. The other part is a prepared, but spontaneous and immersed in the "here and now" communication. On the one hand (Lis) we are dealing with a secondarily spoken text (written questions), on the other (Kaczyński) – with a spoken text. The first one seems to be limiting, influencing the phatic function of the interview. In this part of the analysis, we also take into account fragments of Kaczyński's earlier texts/statements (hybridization) cited in the interview, which constitute a reference point for the conversation. Lis is trying to verify them: "So Mr. Ziobro, as we heard, will certainly be offered a position. And you think that Mr. Macierewicz will too, right? JK: Your tone is accusatory. And what is wrong with that?" Or [about an excerpt from a book about Angela Merkel: "What did you want to say about Angela Merkel? Because, if it was that what you just said, you would have written it in your book in exactly this way".

On the thematic level the subject of the analysis are the local issues (e.g., names of people who will join the Law and Justice government, economy, possible coalitions, Angela Merkel, a debate with Donald Tusk, The Civic Platform, Law and Justice support for fans, limits of the freedom of speech, JK's relations with President Komorowski, JK's relations with Father Rydzyk, women on the Law and Justice election posters) raised or imposed by actors participating in the interview. We thus consider local topics and their cultural/historical and political contexts. For example, Tomasz Lis says: "The viewers are not interested in my opinion. It is you who wants to rule Poland. I'm asking you the question", to which Kaczyński responds: "You too had such ambitions", recalling the context of Lis removal from TVN[2]. Due to speculations about the possibility of his

2 Let us recall that on January 26, 2004, the "Newsweek Polska" weekly published a poll conducted by the PBS research company which showed that Lis had a good chance to win the upcoming presidential election. The PBS survey showed that: 43% of Poles would consider voting for the journalist and, if he were to compete with Lech Kaczyński in the second round, he would have beaten him with the result of 64% to 36%, and if with Andrzej Lepper, he would have won with an advantage of 80:20; in the ranking, he was losing only to Jolanta Kwaśniewska, the wife of the still incumbent president, by a ratio of 43% to 57% (however, Kwaśniewska herself announced that she would not run in the elections).

running in the presidential election and unclear declarations of the journalist himself (after three years, in an interview with Michał Iwanowski from *Gazeta Lubuska*, Lis explained his resignation from running in the elections on personal grounds), Lis was suspended from editorial duties by the station's authorities. Then on February 10, 2004, he was dismissed on suspicion of failing to meet the terms of his contract. Lis announced that he would sue the station for the layoff, but in the end, they agreed on a settlement. Similarly, the historical context is recalled during the conversation with reference to Kaczyński's reluctance to debate with Donald Tusk. Such a debate took place four years earlier. After losing the meeting to Tusk, Kaczyński admitted: "I made a fatal mistake by agreeing to a television discussion with Tusk, which I lost". He spoke about the debate on October 12, 2007. "I was tired and sick at that time. I should have declined, or taken a week off, to see what form Tusk was in in his debate with Aleksander Kwaśniewski" said the former Prime Minister in an interview with Jerzy Sadecki, the author of the interview collection entitled *Thirteen. Prime Ministers of independent Poland*, published in 2009.[3]

At this level, we also define the communicative roles of the actors constituting the discourse. The analysis shows that despite the fact that it is Lis who asks questions, it is Kaczyński who controls the course of the conversation, responds and speaks as he wants and what he wants (TL: "Why do you keep referring to Donald Tusk as 'this man'? JK: I speak as I see fit. TL: And I ask as I see fit. JK: Well, then you have the right to ask, and my answer is that this is what I see fit, and that is that."); he instructs the journalist: "Do not worry about it, because there was something else written there. Let's not go back to it, because at this point you are reaching the level of really terrible disgrace. Because, to refer to such newspapers, really, really, sir" [he's shaking his head]. Often it is Lis who behaves as if he was attacked ("Are you accusing me of a frivolous attitude? Good. It's your right, Mr. Chairman") and, when questioned, he explains himself: "I am not appealing. It was your people who reported this to the prosecutor's office", he is trying to redirect the attention towards his interlocutor: "Our viewers are certainly not interested in my views. They are interested in your views", and he defends his communicative role: "I am only asking". Many times, JK "bounces the ball", answering a question with a question, e. g., TL: "Mr. Chairman, are you not ashamed of the support – de facto support – of Mrs. Kempa for the thug Staruch? JK: Sir, was there any court verdict in this case?" Or, TL: "Do you think it will be easy for you to cooperate with Komorowski after these statements? JK: And do you think that it was easy for my late brother after such statements: like sniper, like attack".

3　See more on: https://www.wirtualnemedia.pl/artykul/debata-jaroslaw-kaczynski-donald-tusk
　-historia.

There are also clashes (an interview may be described as a series of clashes between the interlocutors, it can be broken down into sequences – rhetorical and communication round, which in this case will not coincide with local topics), in which it is Lis who instructs the guest: "You have a fantastic opportunity to show what real political culture looks like. The end of the Polish-Polish war. Not to say: Mr. Tusk, this gentleman, but rather: Prime Minister Donald Tusk, just as you would like to be addressed in a near future". Kaczyński sets conditions: "When the Civic Platform resigns from this social engineering technique, which it uses constantly – it will simply quit, I'm not saying that it will ever apologize, because it should apologize, but only that it will resign – it will certainly be like that. And now you will not dictate the way I am to talk about Mr. Tusk" – he shows the journalist his role – a person asking question, not instructing the guests. Kaczyński evaluates the journalist's work several times, suggesting that the latter is asking irrelevant questions ("I would really like to ask you for some questions relating to issues vital to Poland") lor directly assessing and criticizing the interlocutor: "You are really completely unprepared for today's broadcast. I'm sorry. I'm really sorry. Really sorry".

At the final, ideological level of analysis, we analyse the ways of conducting the liberal discourse (by Lis, the liberal journalist involved in public media) and conservative discourse (by Kaczyński, politician, head of the conservative Law and Justice party). Noteworthy is the creation of the interlocutor as an opponent, also ideologically, mainly by Kaczyński, who says: "You belong to a certain formation, which is, unfortunately, very popular in Poland, and is harmful to us. TL: Harmful to you? And who is this 'you'?" Both interlocutors use at some point the personal pronoun "you", clearly indicating to the recipients that they are antagonists (despite Lis assurances, that he is "only asking"). For example, JK: "you keep referring to court sentences that one cannot say that someone is a criminal. A thug is a heavy criminal. And here you're saying about someone that he is a thug. [...] TL: You keep saying, you keep saying that these hooded figures, who mothers with baby strollers give a wide berth, are the essence of patriotism".

The analysis of one text at an ideological level shows:
1) the instability/variability of transmitting and receiving roles. The journalist is trying here to play the role of:
   a) an assistant who asks additional questions, e.g., "Mr. Chairman, you say in interviews that you would like to reduce the deficit. How?" He tries to steer the interlocutor's line of argument by asking questions, e.g., "Could you reveal who, in your government, if you win the election, would be responsible for the economy?" He formulates the conclusions: "Mr. Chairman, you speak about the poor people in Poland, which is indeed a

very numerous group, but you, when you were prime minister, you mostly took care of the rich Poles".

b) a representative of the public opinion, when speaking on behalf of a community or referring to common judgements: "But don't you think, given the gravity of the situation, that millions of Poles should be given certainty, clarity who this person is going to be? Like in countries such as France or the US, which are seasoned democracies, where the leader of a party that aspires to rule says, 'in our administration, this-and-this will be responsible for the economy'", and: "We want to know who wants to govern Poland, and we, the citizens have the right to know it. And you aspire, I'm sorry, Mr. Chairman, you aspire to rule a central European country populated by forty million people" (see Wojtak 2004: 239);

c) an interpreter: TL: "Because you, the party leader, when you are saying, 'you are in our way',, then I am thinking, the election day is still to come, and you're already dividing us";

d) an expert – engages in a polemic with the interlocutor: JK: "Most importantly, the poor benefited. TL: No, this is not true".

e) a moralizer: TL: "But Mr. Chairman, I just wanted to verify this. Can you elaborate on your thought? Because it is a matter of responsibility for words, which should be proper to people who want to lead great nations", and: "Because you know, there is an insinuating tone in this sentence, which is not befitting a person who wants to be the Prime Minister of Poland".

Initially, it is the journalist who tries to set the tone for the meeting. As an interviewer, he is in a privileged position within the framework/genre situation typical for media discourse. And yet, in the course of the interview, there is a clearly visible change in this relationship; it is the guest politician who takes control of the course of the conversation, imposes its tone, draws the boundaries (when asked about the name of the Minister of Economy, he replies: "But we won't be naming names right now"). He uses linguistic means of avoidance ("certain option", "Poles make educated guesses"), he advises, instructs, and even asks: "Do you think so?" Or "Sir, do you know a country where the Prime Minister says about large social groups that they are mohair berets? In which they say that grandmothers – and now they are talking about young people – that things have to be taken away from them, their ID cards stolen? When people are referred to as 'cattle'? It is said by a well-known politician... or 'cemetery hyenas'?"

The guest, using an eristic trick ("the one I teach becomes a pupil"), pushes the journalist into the role of a pupil who – according to the interviewer – is poorly informed about the topic of the conversation (JK: "Sir, different things happen in different countries, and additionally, you are underestimating the wisdom of the Poles. The Poles make educated guesses, and that is enough" [Lis is trying to ask a question] "They will vote for Law and Justice; well, those who will, will at the same time vote in favour of particular economic and personal solutions" or: "Sir, it is so that if someone has 20,000, then indeed some mechanisms that take place here are different than in the case of 2,000, and these are the laws of arithmetic. You seem not to know how certain fees are collected, so I'm trying to explain this to you". Finally, from the position of authority, he assesses the journalist, saying that the latter in unprepared.

2) The material is also interesting in terms of eristic techniques used by both actors:
   a) Lis uses, for example the inclusion (inclusive) strategy: I (the journalist) as a part of the community (I=Poles), Kaczyński: the exclusion (exclusive) strategy ("you are underestimating the wisdom of the Poles" = YOU≠-Poles, thus suggesting that he – the party leader is close to voters, that he knows and appreciates them. This strategy, following Marek Kochan, can be described as a technique that works directly on the audience, winning over the viewers through the soft-version "camera" technique, i.e., Kaczyński mentions the viewers, but does not address them directly (Kochan, 2007, p. 138). By excluding Lis from the community, placing him outside the community, Kaczyński deprives him of the role of an intermediary and of being the voice of people while, at the same time, complimenting Poles, and winning them over.
   b) Kaczyński, when he says: "You want to convince us by all means that, back then [under the previous Law and Justice rule – MW] it was bad. No, it was very good. One million and three hundred thousand new jobs – this is a really great result", is using the technique described as "sticking labels, that is, the hateful category of concepts", which consists in "classifying the views or behaviour of the interlocutor into a category that will make negative associations in the viewer and thus will result in the rejection of this interlocutor's views, and the debater who is using the label will be released from the need to deal with an uncomfortable issue" (ibid., p. 161), and, at the same time, it challenges the impartiality of Lis as a journalist and shows his role as an opponent. The fact that Lis feels attacked is evidenced by his answer: "I don't use adjectives, I provide numbers", trying to unmask Kaczyński's superlative strategy, while defending himself with the meaning of numbers – objective data. Kaczyński uses the same strategy several times, suggesting that Tomasz Lis is fearful and shy.

c) A splinter in the eye (ibid., p. 92) is the technique of "counterattacking and pointing out to the interlocutor their mistakes or vices, the existence of which invalidate the just noticed mistakes or vices of the speaker" (ibid., p. 92). It is used by Kaczyński when there come uncomfortable questions, e.g., about the relationship between the Law and Justice and football fans: JK: "You keep referring to court verdicts [...] And you say that someone is a thug; TL: Hooked noses, sir, is this freedom of speech too? Is Widzew-Żydzew also included in this freedom of speech? JK: There were incidents... TL: These are the fans who support you. On mutual terms, unfortunately. JK: There are examples of such behaviours which exceed the scope of freedom of speech. We have such cases very often when it comes to the attitude towards our political formation. I haven't noticed much outrage on your side in response to this".

d) The "examiner, or query tactic" technique is used by both interlocutors, and while its use by the journalist seems justified by his role and results from the conventions of the interview genre, its use by the visitor is an attempt to change the balance of power. The questioning-examining, and thus also assessing the work of the journalist politician creates his image as someone stronger and more important, and the questioned, criticized, and judged journalist is treated as a "test taker", i.e., a "weaker, lower-ranking person, who must justify and prove himself with appropriate knowledge" (ibid., p. 200), e.g., TL: "Mr. Chairman, you raised taxes... that is, you lowered... JK: So which one is it: lowered or raised? Make up your mind. Because you are getting carried away, sir".

e) "Dilution, or generalization" or, more precisely, "defensive dilution", that is, an escape into generalities (ibid., p. 68) is used by Kaczyński in the following examples of clashes: TL: "Will you cooperate with the president or just keep up appearances? JK: I will respect the constitution and other laws. That's all".

f) "It has happened before" is a strategy of changing the topic. In the analysed interview it was used by Kaczyński when he answered the question about the Silesian identity (as a camouflaged German option: "Well, sir, I did not write it. It was an editorial mistake. And that is all. This matter has been long settled. And besides, there are words such as 'cattle', 'cemetery hyenas': they have not been uttered, and you should direct these complaints in the right direction. For six years there has simply taken place an unprecedented disinformation campaign of defamation, or insult, which is offensive towards a large part of the society. There is something going on that should end, and it can only end in such a way that we win the elections".

g) Both actors perform different speech acts. It follows from the definitions of an interview and its generic conventions that speech acts are assigned to conversational roles: the journalist – asks, but also undermines, verifies, and even attacks, the guest – replies. Meanwhile, in the analysed interview, speech acts are not assigned to these roles. Kaczyński breaks interview conventions, and he seems to be doing it consciously and on purpose. He also uses questions, mainly rhetorical, diverting attention away from himself and redirecting it onto the journalist who emphasizes several times: "Mr. Chairman, [...] I have the impression that it is you yourself who wants to be the Prime Minister, not me or I don't think you should be wasting your time reviewing the weeklies. The viewers are not interested in my opinion. It is you who wants to rule Poland. I'm asking you the question". Kaczyński, by asking Lis a question, or commenting on his statements or behaviour, suggests that the journalist is biased. What speech acts are used by both actors?

Tomasz Lis, mainly:
- Assertions presenting the context of a question as well as questions (closed or asking for a resolution): "Do you think that Macierewicz in the government is a good idea? You are returning to the old language. Why? It wasn't supposed to be like this".

Expressives in the form of a compliment used for eristic purposes: "Mr. Chairman, I can't leave the rest to historians [about Angela Merkel] because out of respect to you a seasoned politician who has been in domestic politics for more than twenty years, who aspires to be the leader of a forty-million-strong country in central Europe I have to take your words seriously". Jarosław Kaczyński uses:
- Assertives: "But I will take care of myself; It is me who tells you that standing to attention in front of any capital city other than Warsaw like, for example, Berlin, is really not befitting the Polish Prime Minister".
- Directives in the form of advice: "Free yourself from it"; "You should, sir, however, take a look at all sorts of social flows; I believe this thread is not worth pursuing"; Look for that symmetry! Look for that symmetry! More confidence in yourself!"; in the form of an order: "Lowered or raised? Make up your mind"; or in the form of an apparent request: "If we win this elections, which I am convinced we will, please do not worry about us"; "Please, have some more appreciation for Poles, sir"; "Please, do not mislead our viewers, please, do not compare the increases in Lithuania and Poland, because these economies are of completely different sizes. We can be compared to large countries".
- Expressives: "I am very glad that you know this is what is going to happen [we will win the election]"; "We hope that our constituents will give us a chance'; "I

feel sorry for you, sir"; "You are saying it with a type of irony which, I must admit, I do not appreciate very much. Because a truly Polish journalist should display a serious attitude toward their own nation".

- Commissives: "Sir, I suggest that we agree on something we hold different beliefs and I read your periodical and as a result I think it is pointless to consider this issue".

Discussion on the results of the analysis of a single text

When analysing the discourse and, in particular, linguistic/communication practices, the researcher asks about the culturally and socially conditioned systems of enunciability and, consequently, about the images of the world produced by the participants and distributed in the media. In this case, the worlds of liberal and conservative values, clash. The analysis of the four levels also showed how both actors create images of themselves (self-presentation) and the opponent, as well as the values and traits that both sides of the interview (or communication dispute) attribute to each other.

Jarosław Kaczyński characterizes Tomasz Lis directly, describes him as a representative of a different faction, one that is harmful to Poland, fearing those from the outside, i.e., Germans and Russians, and also as an "unprepared journalist". In this way, he presents him as a journalist who lacks in neutrality or objectivity, and serves the political faction stigmatized by the politician promoting conservative values.

In contrast, Jarosław Kaczyński presents himself as a person confident in his righteousness. Kaczyński equates "we" (Law and Justice and its voters) and Poland, and builds an opposition "we" (=Poland) vs "you". We are brave, you are "shy", and "afraid" (implicitly: cowards). We want to strengthen the position of Poland – and you "make them ignore us completely"; "those who fear Poland becoming a big, strong nation". The second opposition, clearly visible in Kaczyński's statements, is them (the Civic Platform) vs us (our political formation): "they use social engineering to rule, tell fairy tales about us, and use an incredible desinformation campaign against us, which means, they offend a large part of the society, use the terms 'mohair berets', 'cemetery hyenas', and 'cattle'"; "they fear Poland becoming a big, strong nation"; their Prime Minister "departs from the principles of democracy, he uses absurd arguments, conducts discussions in the fumes of the absurd, and lies"; while "we" do not need this social engineering, our people behave properly: "one of my friends did what is prescribed by law"; "Antoni Macierewicz has a great historical merit. He could achieve a lot in terms of cleaning Poland of various remnants of the old system, which was a very bad system, although you may have a different opinion on this matter, one that depends on the foreign power. It is a very good legitimacy, to be in the government. For Polish patriots".

The party represented by Jarosław Kaczyński – in his opinion – wants Poland that is strong, independent of foreign, external powers, to raise from its knees while, according to the guest, it has been bending in front of others as a result of the politics pursued so far. Such behaviour is harmful to Poland. According to the journalist – although it is not verbalized *expressis verbis* the way Kaczyński's views are – Poland is harmed by non-diplomatic behaviour, sentences which imply another bottom of other people's actions. The journalist accuses the party represented by the visitor of hate speech, of waging Polish-Polish war, disrespecting current rulers, supporting and using the so-called football fans, and succumbing to the influence of Father Rydzyk. These are the two visions of Poland – confrontational and one based on dialogue.

In the analysed interview, we also observe: the reversal of roles which seem to be established by institutional representation of certain types of discourses (Lis – media, Kaczyński – political), playing with genre conventions on the part of Kaczyński, his verbal and non-verbal advantage, and the multiplicity and variety of speech acts and eristic techniques used by the visitor. The analysed example goes far beyond conventions of the interview genre. In fact, it is a clash of two visions of Poland, a clash of political opponents, although not rivals in power. Both Tomasz Lis and Jarosław Kaczyński are representatives of the symbolic elites (journalist/politician). Their conversation consists of questions from a journalist with political ambitions intended to provoke/evoke the politician's response, and thus to create a media framework for the interlocutor to express his views. These actions, however, are accompanied by a polemical goal, and this, in turn, shifts the analysed example towards a new discursive effect, consisting of a worldview clash that remains "under the control" of the journalist, but with the visitor's active "spoiling" of this effect (which is confirmed by the conversational roles mentioned above).

Conclusions

The aim of this paper was to answer two questions – whether a single text chosen by discourse researchers can constitute the basis for discourse analysis and what research tools and methods discourse linguistics can offer for the discoursological study of one text. The latter question also implies levels of viewing the text as the subject of analysis.

Assuming that the methodological foundation of discourse linguistics is the principle of design and integrationism, we decided that the analysis of a single text can be the basis for discourse analysis, because we define a text as a serially organized, subjectively-shaped and discursively conditioned communicative event that produces, records and visualizes collectively shared meanings/ knowledge. In this context, the key criterion for selecting a single text is the discourse researchers' knowledge about the specificity of discourse, its actors and the texts that are key to this discourse, and which determine the discourse dynamics.

The cognitive goal of discourse analysis, even if its subject is a single text, does not change. It is about capturing perspective giving uses of language, and certain communication practices that significantly create meanings shared by society, and thus model specific the worldview. There is also an important question about the culturally conditioned rules that co-decide what can be said in the discourse. These rules are conditioned by, among others: the situation of the TV talk show with the inherent in the genre dramatization which serves spectacularity, the then strongly felt labile position of Tomasz Lis situated between journalism and politics, as well as political interests of Jarosław Kaczyński who took part in the program mainly with the intention to ideologically strengthen his electorate, rather than answer the questions of the program host.

The exemplary analysis of a single text throws light on the political tension between the conservative discourse (in the ideological dimension) which, at that time, was once again in opposition and striving to take over power in Poland, and the liberal discourse represented both by the journalist and the public television itself at the time.

Also, the choice of four levels of viewing the text made it possible to design a multifaceted model of discourse analysis. These four ontical levels of discourse have been consciously treated on an equal footing. Which of the levels plays a role in shaping the research procedure depends on the formulated research goals. This is where the designing character of discourse linguistics is expressed. Its integrating character is manifested, as we have also shown in the analysis of the interview, in the selection of the texts determined by the analysed corpus of texts. In the spirit of methodological eclecticism, linguistic methods are integrated on all four levels, even if they come from different research trends. In this way, the qualitative criteria for linguistic research are also guaranteed.

References

Angermuller, Johannes: Poststructuralist Discourse Analysis. Subjectivity in Enunciative Pragmatics. Basingstoke 2014.
Antos, Gerd: Wissenskommunikation. Gesammelte Aufsätze. Berlin 2020.
Bartmiński, Jerzy: Aspects of Cognitive Ethnolinguistics. London 2009.

Bubenhofer, Noah: 'Diskurslinguistik und Korpora', in: Warnke, Ingo H. (ed.): *Handbuch Diskurs*. Berlin, Boston 2018, p. 208–241.

Busse, Dietrich / Teubert, Wolfgang: 'Ist Diskurs ein sprachwissenschaftliches Objekt? Zur Methodenfrage der historischen Semantik', in: Busse, Dietrich / Hermanns, Franz & Teubert, Wolfgang (eds.): *Begriffsgeschichte und Diskursgeschichte. Methodenfragen und Forschungsergebnisse der historischen Semantik*. Opladen 2014, p. 10–29.

Czachur, W.: 'Discourse linguistics and the discursive worldview', in: EXPLORATIONS: A JOURNAL OF LANGUAGE AND LITERATURE 2016/4, p. 16–32.

Czachur, Waldemar: Lingwistyka dyskursu jako integrujący program badawczy. Wrocław 2020.

Dijk, Teun A. van: 'Language, discourse and knowledge', in: Dijk, Teun A. van (ed.): *Discourse and Knowledge: A Sociocognitive Approach*. Cambridge 2014, p. 222–309.

Duszak, Anna / Fairclough, Norman (eds.): Krytyczna analiza dyskursu. Interdyscyplinarne podejście do komunikacji społecznej. Kraków 2008.

Fairclough, N.: 'Discourse and Text: Linguistic and Intertextual Analysis within Discourse Analysis', in: DISCOURSE & SOCIETY 1992/3, p. 193–217.

Fix, Ulla: 'Die EIN-Text-Diskursanalyse. Unter welchen Umständen kann ein einzelner Text Gegenstand einer diskurslinguistischen Untersuchung sein?', in: Fix, Ulla (ed.): Fix, Ulla: *Stil – Denkstil – Text – Diskurs*. Berlin 2021, p. 407–427.

Foucault, Michel: 'Gespräch mit Michel Foucault', in: Defert, Daniel / Francois, Ewald (eds.): *Michel Foucault. Schriften in vier Bänden. Band 3: 1976–1979*. Frankfurt am Main 2003, p. 186–212.

Foucault, Michel: 'The order of discourse', in: Young, Robert (ed.): *Untying the text: A poststructuralist reader*. London 1981, p. 48–78.

Foucault, Michel: The archaeology of knowledge. Translated from the French by A. M. Sheridan Smith. New York 1971.

Gianmarco, Vignozzi: Assessing the language of TV political interviews. A corpus-assisted perspective. Newcastle upon Tyne 2019.

Kochan, Marek: Pojedynek na słowa. Techniki erystyczne w publicznych sporach. Kraków 2007.

Kumięga, Łukasz: 'Warum Diskurs? Zum Potenzial der postfoucaultschen Diskursforschung', in: STUDIA GERMANICA GEDANENSIA, 2013/29, p. 173–185.

Labocha, J.: 'The object of study of text linguistics (Textology)', in: STUDIA LINGUISTICA UNIVERSITATIS IAGELLONICAE CRACOVIENSIS 2011/128, p. 59–68.

Loewe, Iwona: Dyskurs telewizyjny w świetle lingwistyki mediów. Katowice 2018.

Lorenzo-Dus, Nuria: Television discourse: analysing language in the media. Basingstoke 2008.

McEnery, Tony, Richard, Xiao, & Tono, Yukio: Corpus-Based Language Studies. An Advanced Resource Book. London / New York 2006.

Nowicka Magdalena: 'Postfoucaultowska analiza dyskursu – problemy i szanse dydaktyczne', in: Czachur, Waldemar / Kulczyńska, Agnieszka / Kumięga, Łukasz (Eds.): *Jak analizować dyskurs? Perspektywy dydaktyczne*. Kraków 2016, p. 159–181.

Nowicka-Franczak, M.: 'Postfoucauldian Analysis of the Discourse on Education. Workshop remarks', in: KULTURA-SPOŁECZEŃSTWO-EDUKACJA 2017/2(12), p. 171–198.

Spitzmüller, J. / Warnke, I.H.: 'Discourse as a 'linguistic object': methodical and methodological delimitations', in: CRITICAL DISCOURSE STUDIES 2011/8:2, p. 75–94.

Stefanowitsch, Anatol: Corpus linguistics: A guide to the methodology. Berlin 2020.

Warnke, Ingo H.: 'Text adieu – Diskurs bienvenue? Über Sinn und Zweck einer post-strukturalistischen Entgrenzung des Textbegriffs', in: Fix, Ulla / Adamzik, Kirsten / Antos, Gerd / Klemm, Michael (Eds.): *Brauchen wir einen neuen Textbegriff? Antworten auf eine Preisfrage.* Frankfurt am Main 2002, p. 125–141.

Wójcicka, Marta: Collective Memory and Oral Text. Translated by Przemysław Łozowski. Berlin 2020.

Agnieszka Budzyńska-Daca / Marcin Kosman

Political interview or debate – the clash of ethoses from the perspective of rhetorical genre studies

Abstract

The study is predominantly grounded in genre criticism and rhetorical analysis. This triangulation of methods allowed for a thorough investigation of an unorthodox artifact. The interview was treated as a hybrid genre, i.e. as a modification of an already existing genre in the face of a new rhetorical situation (Jamieson 1982, Fetzer / Bull 2013). Ethos was perceived as the credibility of the speaker and how he or she exposes his or her positive traits such as intelligence or morality (Aristotle 2007). The analysis of Lis and Kaczyński's ethos was conducted on three levels – competence, morality, and identification with the audience (Budzyńska-Daca 2015). An interview with Tusk that Lis conducted in a similar time period (5 October 2011) served as a reference point. The findings suggest that while portrayed himself as a common man, emphasizing his bond with the audience; Kaczyński, on the other hand, highlighted his morality and patriotism.

Keywords: debate, ethos, genre, rhetoric, political interview

Introduction

In the present paper, a critical rhetoric perspective on genres was adopted. This perspective assumes that the investigation of the generic properties of an artifact will facilitate the understanding of the message formulated by communication participants. The choice of genre imposes certain behaviour conventions on the actors involved in communication (Miller 1984, p. 162 f). Therefore, in order to answer the question about the relationship between a journalist and a politician in this particular artifact, it is necessary to start with the interpretation of the genre. Furthermore, the rhetorical ethos of the participants of the meeting will be discussed.

Agnieszka Budzyńska-Daca, University of Warsaw (Poland), ORCID: 0000-0003-1002-7197, a.budzynska@uw.edu.pl.
Marcin Kosman, University of Economics and Human Sciences in Warsaw (Poland), ORCID: 0000-0003-1811-9723, m.kosman@vizja.pl.

Rhetorical ethos is perceived as the speaker's credibility based on the three pillars of persuasion: *arete, phronesis,* and *eunoia* (Aristotle 2007). While analysing the behaviour of the participants of the event in question, these three categories should be interpreted as: the qualities of the character (personal qualities of the speaker), the way of presenting competence (knowledge, experience, skills), and identification with the audience (the ability win over the audience and indicating a benevolent attitude towards them), respectively (Budzyńska-Daca 2015).

Why is determining the generic profile of the discussed event significant for its interpretation? Communication is realised through genres (Bakhtin 2014), and genres are indicators of communication, signposts of sense interpretation (Bazerman 1997). What is more, according to Fairclough (1995, p. 14), "genres are socially ratified ways of using language in connection with a particular type of social activity". Furthermore, Jamieson (1973, p. 163) suggests that in unprecedented situations, hybrid genres are formed. Hybrid genres may take the form of a conglomerate of already existing genres. If new genres become stable and repeated over time, they may become standardised. Genres are therefore constantly evolving and dynamic phenomena (Jamieson / Stromer-Galley 2001).

The participants of communication enter into it by bringing the original intentions of the genre into their communicative practices. These intentions may change under the influence of interaction and cooperation with the communication partner, who may interpret participation in the act of communication differently from the interlocutor partner. Then, if the partners of the dialogue want to cooperate, they adjust the previously assumed communication intentions, so that the conversation goes on uninterrupted, and the previously assumed message can flow to the audience.

In order to understand why the meeting between Lis and Kaczyński garnered so much media attention, it is worth considering the generic attitude of the participants of the meeting. This is the key to understanding their behaviour and their rhetorical ethos, which can be analysed further. Generic awareness belongs to the communicative competence of those engaged in political discourse (Duszak 1998, Fras 2005). While this awareness may be low among the recipients of political discourse, Fras (2005, p. 65) argues that in order to construct political statements, professionals (e. g., politicians) need to exhibit a high level of it. Therefore, in the case of the discussed event, there is a need to outline the manifestations of this awareness.

Further, as Halliday (1978, p. 33) suggests, people adjust their discourse depending on what is being discussed (field), the relationship between the participants of a given communicative event (tenor), and the channel of communication which is being used (mode). Therefore, the investigation of the discussed event should take into account not only the linguistic means but also its broader context. Further, the target audience should also be considered as argumentative strategies of both interviewers and interviewees depend on the audience the interview is aimed at (Fetzer / Weizman 2006, p. 144). This is of particular significance since the conversation between Lis and Kaczyński took place right before the 2011 Polish parliamentary elections. Thus, one could argue that the target audience of the episode consisted of all Poles who had the right to vote.

Generic interpretation of the conversation between Kaczyński and Lis

Jarosław Kaczynski appeared on Tomasz Lis' program on 3 October 2011, six days before the elections. Earlier, he refused to take part in a debate, which Lis had organised on 5 September 2011, and which was hailed as "Leaders' Debate". Along with Kaczyński, Donald Tusk (Civic Platform), Grzegorz Napieralski (Democratic Left Alliance), and Waldemar Pawlak (Polish People's Party) were supposed to take part in it. Only Tusk appeared in Lis' program. Thus, instead of a debate, the program was in essence a conversation between a politician and a journalist.

With regard to its generic interpretation, the event was described by the media in various ways. For example, the daily journal "Polska Times" (2011) called it "a quasi-debate"[1]. Interia.pl (2011), one of the biggest Polish Internet media, wrote that "Tusk debated with Lis. Others didn't come". In "Gazeta Wyborcza", Poland's biggest daily journal, one could read the following sentence:

> On Monday evening, Tomasz Lis explained why there was only one guest on his program, and why the viewers would watch an interview instead of a debate (Kondzińska 2011b)

Similarly, "Wprost" (2011b), a centre-left weekly, described the event as "an interview" and "a program".

It is worth mentioning that the meeting between Lis and Tusk garnered considerably less media attention than the meeting between Lis and Kaczyński. The names used by journalists indicate that it was necessary to change the genre because of the lack of participants for the debate. It may be assumed that Lis was put in a problematic situation, since the invited guests did not turn up, and he had to propose a different generic formula, having only one candidate in the studio, so that the program could be realised. In the press comments, one can see an attempt to explain this situation and treat the change as a natural necessity in the face of a force majeure – the lack of candidates willing to debate.

---

1 The translations from Polish into English were provided by the authors.

With regard to the Lis-Kaczyński meeting, the situation was different, because the conversation with Kaczyński was not marketed as "Leaders' Debate". It had been known before that only one politician would take part in the program. The media coverage of this episode was considerably bigger than in the case of the conversation with Tusk. Moreover, the episode with Kaczyński was watched by 2.951.627 people, whereas the one featuring Donald Tusk was seen by 2.102.903 viewers (film.interia.pl 2011). This suggests that the conversation with Kaczyński garnered more attention not only from the media but also from regular viewers. Thus, it was perceived as a more relevant event.

While discussing the conversation between Lis and Kaczyński, the media used different terms, some of which were negatively valenced. The conservative website wPolityce.pl wrote that:

> It was neither an interview nor a debate (although Lis definitely took the place that Donald Tusk will not be given in the near future). The term "interrogation" is probably the closest to the truth (wpolityce.pl (a) 2011).

> It did not look like an interview with Jarosław Kaczyński but like a debate between politicians (wpolityce.pl (b) 2011).

> Since it was impossible to start a debate with Donald Tusk, they thought, let Kaczyński be shot down by the Überjournalist (wpolityce.pl (a) 2011).

In the centre-right daily "Rzeczpospolita" a sports metaphor was used:

> The boxing match between Tomasz Lis and Jarosław Kaczyński will go down in media history. The star of pro-government media was preparing to beat the leader of Law and Justice. There are many echoes of the duel between Tomasz Lis and Jarosław Kaczyński (Zawadzki 2011).

The centre-right "Dziennik" similarly referred to "Lis' program", calling it a "duel". Press.pl wrote about "a conversation" and "a program" in which "Tomasz Lis [...] lost in a battle of words, but also of arguments, and further on that the journalist and the politician had a boxing match" (dziennik.pl 2011).

Radio Tok FM, although also used a neutral term "program", organised a poll: "Who fared better: Lis or Kaczyński?" (tokfm.pl 2011), which suggests that their interpretation of the event was slanted towards a political confrontation inherent in a debate. "Gazeta Wyborcza" and "Wprost" both suggested neutral terms such as "meeting", "conversation", and "a program" (Kondzińska 2011a; wprost.pl 2011a).

Overall, one might notice that three main terms were used: the neutral name "program", as well as two generic names: "interview" and "debate". Also, metaphorical terms such as: "clash", "duel", "boxing match" were observed. In addition, the event was also described by verbs: "spank", "defeat", "box". Interestingly, the conversation between Lis and Kaczyński was most commonly described as a debate and with the use of sports/war metaphors by right-wing oriented media (wPolityce.pl, "Rzeczpospolita", "Dziennik"), whereas centre-left and left-wing media ("Gazeta Wyborcza", "Wprost", TOK FM) generally preferred to discussed the event using relatively neutral terms. This might suggest that right-wing media tried to portray Lis as a political agitator, masquerading as a journalist, whose goal was to discredit the leader of the opposition. On the other hand, liberal-left media attempted to maintain the image of Lis as a journalist.

The preliminary data regarding the generic interpretation of this particular episode of Lis' program suggests that it would be difficult to estimate the extent to which generic modifications influenced its overall character. Therefore, we will establish how "Tomasz Lis na żywo" was generically classified as a series aired from 2008 to 2016, and estimate what distinguishes the particular episode from others.

The series "Tomasz Lis na żywo", which was aired on TVP2 (Poland's public mainstream TV channel) during prime time, was defined on the VOD channel as "a current affairs program" and "Lis' own program". From the point of view of media studies, these terms are relatively vague, and may refer to multiple genres (cf. Furman / Kaliszewski / Wolny-Zmorzyński 2000). Wikipedia characterises the series as a current affairs program and as a talk show. Similar names appear in the literature as well as articles in the press and on the Internet. Thus, Lis created a broad generic formula, as in his program he conducted interviews and discussions pertaining to politics and social issues[2]. The fact that this particular episode was called a debate was certainly influenced by the importance of the meeting, but also by the fact that it was treated as an equivalent of a pre-election debate between the leaders of political parties, which should have taken place at that time, as it had been the case in Poland (cf. Budzyńska-Daca 2015).

In order to investigate the event, it is not enough to label a media event with a generic term. Rather, it should be investigated what generic intentions guided its participants. The rhetorical perspective implemented in the study requires the introduction of the category of rhetorical ethos into the analysis. The rhetorical ethos of a debate participant is based on different generic premises than the rhetorical ethos of an interview participant. This applies to the roles of both the politician and the journalist. Thus, the question of the basis of the credibility of the speakers (Lis and Kaczyński) will be discussed. Further, the addition of the

---

2 One of the most popular episodes (as of November 2021 it was watched almost 2.5 million times) featured Janusz Korwin-Mikke, a controversial right-wing politician and former MEP (see Chwedczuk-Szulc / Zaremba 2015), Karolina Korwin-Piotrowska, a film critic and TV personality, Krzysztof Cegielski, a former speedway rider and pundit, and Jan Mela, a disabled explorer who was the first teenager to have conquered the North and the South Pole in the same year. In that episode, the participants discussed the overall status of disabled sportsmen and whether the Paralympic Games should be aired on TV.

category of rhetorical ethos to the analysis is crucial in determining the generic properties of the artifact. The category of dispute is different in a political interview and a debate. If we show that the interviewer (Lis) or the interviewee (Kaczyński) focused on creating their own respective ethos and/or destroying the opponent's ethos, it will be a clear signal that they the discussed variant should be perceived as a hybrid of the above-mentioned genres.

Debate – the rhetorical ethos of the participants

The predominant feature of a debate is grounded in its adversarial character: two speakers with different views present them to persuade the audience. In pre-election debates, speakers are politicians running for important state offices. When considering the rhetorical ethos of the participants of a pre-election debate, one should pay attention to the standard communication situation and the goals of the participants of the genre. Usually, a representative of the government intends to remain in power whereas a politician representing the opposition wants to obtain the legitimacy that would grant them an opportunity to become an authoritative entity in future political actions (Cabrejas-Peñuelas / Díez-Prados 2014, p. 161).

The pre-election debate of leaders differs from other debates (parliamentary, academic, television) in that the issue organizing the interaction is the question "Which candidate is better, X or Y?". In order to highlight its specific character, Cabrejas-Peñuelas (2015, p. 516) makes a distinction between van Dijk's (2005) definition of parliamentary debates and her understanding of pre-election debate. Regarding the former, they are perceived as *local manifestations of the global political acts of legislation, governing, and control of government* (van Dijk 2005, p. 67) in pre-election debates the aspect of wanting to perform these acts is highlighted. Such debates take place shortly before the elections and politicians who present their vision also market themselves as candidates for office. The participants of the dispute become at the same time the subject of it:

> Hence, capturing the goodwill of the audience (*captatio benevolentiae*) is interwoven with invoking their dislike of the rival. Thus, the speaker presents his or her own ethos in confrontation with the ethos of the competitor and co-operates with the audience [...] (Budzyńska-Daca 2015, p. 145).

Moreover, given that pre-election debates are televised[3], their participants address not only their rivals but also a larger audience (Komlósi / Tarrósy 2010,

---

3 In Poland, the first televised pre-election debate took place in 1995 (Hinton / Budzyńska-Daca 2019, p. 5). Since then, they have been a vital part of Polish election discourse.

p. 959). Also, this fact presupposes the presence of a journalist. Regarding their role in a pre-election debate, if we consider the model version of the genre, the journalist/media representative acts as a spokesman for the voters and his task is to be the moderator of the debate. The moderator's task is to make sure that the politicians participating in the debate have an equal chance of presenting their arguments. This is achieved by observing the rules of the debate: equal time for speaking, appropriate questions which would neither discriminate nor privilege any of the participants.

The audience of the debate are voters who are to decide for whom to cast their vote. The analysis of Polish pre-election debates (Budzyńska-Daca 2015) shows that the roles of journalists in a pre-election debate can be described as a coordinator (guardian of the format rules), as an intermediary between the speakers and the audience, and as a creator of discourse. Moderators either give the field to politicians limiting themselves only to ensuring the proper course of the debate or take the role of polemicists wanting to extract the information that politicians do not want to give, which effectively makes them co-creators of discourse.

It is worth mentioning that such a debate is usually induced in the pre-election discourse both by the media and politicians themselves. Whether it actually takes place depends on the marketing calculations of politicians and their staff. During the 2011 elections, the leaders' debate did not take place at all. Instead, there were thematic debates (Kochan 2016). The meetings with Tusk and Kaczyński organised by Lis in his program took place one month apart from each other and one could expect them to have a similar formula – as two interviews instead of one debate.

Political interview – the rhetorical ethos of the participants

It goes without saying that interview is one of the key genres in media studies. Given that it is beyond the scope of the present paper to discuss its all (sub)genres, attention will be paid mostly to the genre of political interview. Not only is this relevant to the artifact analysed in the present paper but it also relates to the fact that the genre has received the most attention out of main sub-genres of news interview (see Blum-Kulka 1983, Clayman / Heritage 2002, Fetzer 2002; Lauerbach 2006, Hutchby 2022).

Despite difficulties with coming up with a well-defined typology (Fairclough 2009, p. 295), there have been attempts at proposing the definition of the prototypical political interview. For example, Hutchby (2017, p. 103–104) discusses the conventional, adversarial, hybrid, and reflexive types. Fetzer and Bull (2013, p. 85) suggest three distinctive features of the genre. Firstly, there are clearly defined tasks and purposes, i.e., hosts ask their guests questions, who are in turn obliged to give specific answers. In other words, hosts elicit relevant information from their guests. Secondly, not only are tasks and purposes clear-cut, but so are discursive roles. Namely, journalists function as interviewers, and politicians are interviewees. Lastly, there are strict rules as regards the use of language: it should be neutral and not emotionally laden. Still, Fetzer and Bull (2013, p. 88) state that the political interview is a genre with fuzzy boundaries, generically heteroge-neous, and hybridised, given that it rarely adheres to its prototypical form. Ra-dulović and Jovanović (2020, p. 591) enumerate possible instances when political interviews fall out of their standard form. Namely, a lack of agreement between the participants, attempts at a positive self-presentation, the type of questions asked as well as the fact that in many cases neither questions nor answers can be completely neutral. Also, Chilton (2004, p. 76–80) states that in many cases both interviewers and interviewees tend to delegitimise one another, especially when they disagree in principle as regards the issue being discussed. Moreover, Bull and Fetzer (2010, p. 163–164) point out that while it may seem that the question-response format of such interviews helps allows journalists to maintain neu-trality, there are a number of techniques in which they may challenge, criticise or even delegitimise the politician. Among them are equivocation, footing, or the strategic use of forms of address (Bull / Fetzer 2006).

The roles of journalists in an interview are categorised in the Polish literature in various ways. According to Stępień (1993), the journalist may be the admirer, partner, adversary. On the other hand, Bauer (2008, p. 341) argues that they could be the intermediary, intermediary-helper, partner-student, partner-expert, or partner-representative of public opinion. Also, Worsowicz (2006, p. 50) suggests they may take the role of the student, petitioner, mirror, admirer, prosecutor, expert, partner. Regarding the international literature on the subject, in their seminal book Bell and van Leeuwen (1994, p. 22) discuss the roles of the inter-pellator, student, social researcher, parent or teacher, and interrogator. The in-terpellator role would refer to interviews with politicians.

When it comes to more contemporary perspectives, researchers distinguish between the journalist as the interactional manager (their role is to allow all the participants to clearly express their standpoints), critical political journalist (they act as the representative of given social groups and/or the institution of jour-nalism as w whole), and television producer (they act on behalf of the media organisation they work for; thus, their main goal is to attract audiences and grab their attention, which affects the way interviews are conducted). Oftentimes, the journalist has to manoeuvre between these three roles at the same time (De Smedt and Vandenbrande 2011, p. 76–78). Similarly, de Beus (2011, p. 26) considers the journalist to be a figure that has to swing between sense-making, fact-finding, and fun-making. Moreover, Baym (2013, p. 489–490) states that political inter-views have progressively gravitated towards hybridity and infotainment. Journalistic genres are, therefore, constantly changing and it is difficult to pinpoint to any prototypical forms. Thus, referring to the rhetorical ethos of interview participants, it is impossible to unambiguously and normatively determine what the basis of the three basic rhetorical areas (character, competence, and identification with the audience) of their ethos should be. Rather, it depends on the decision of its creators and initiators (media publishers and journalists themselves).

Compared to a pre-election debate, which has proper rules of interaction to ensure equal treatment of participants and is a genre with clearly defined social functions in a democratic state, the rules of a political interview may not be defined as clearly. In accordance with the notion that genres represent a specific type of discourse (Miller 1984, Fairclough 1995, Grzmil-Tylutki 2007), one may suppose that a political interview conducted in the pre-election period will differ from other types of political interviews, just as a pre-election debate differs from other debates, as it is a specific representation of pre-election discourse, aimed at influencing voters' decisions.

The interpretations of commentators from both sides of the political scene are best summed up by Lis' own statement, in which he spoke directly about his intentions accompanying the conversation with Kaczyński. As he states, his goal was to prevent a politician from the opposite camp from winning the elections Thus, he placed himself in a political position and acted not as a journalist – an intermediary between politicians and voters – but as a creator of political discourse.

A selection of crucial quotes by Lis is outlined below:

> I was afraid of it, I had a sense of responsibility. Kaczyński didn't agree to a debate with Tusk, I thought to myself: 'Well, it can be different, if I'm knocked out fair and square, it may cost us (sic!) a few points'.
> The idea was to show the real Kaczyński. Let him hit me above the belt, or preferably below the belt, let him hit me hard, let him get more and more excited. The more we see the real Kaczyński, the better.
> I left that studio with a very far-reaching sense of optimism that he would not win the elections. And when next morning he said in response to Jakub Sobieniowski, my friend from TVN, he said: "It's good to be a Polish journalist, isn't it?", I thought to myself: "It's already settled. We're taking a breath, there's a good chance that Poland will get another four years of normality" (wirtualnemedia.pl 2018).

Furthermore, numerous press studies suggest that "Wprost", whose editor-in-chief at the time was Tomasz Lis, in 2011, portrayed Law and Justice and politicians associated with the party negatively, while showing a positive assessment of Civic Platform and its candidates. For example, Szwed (2013) observed that certain articles in "Wprost" presented Kaczyński as an unpredictable and mentally unstable politician. Further, Civic Platform, the ruling party at that time, was said to be afraid of the dangers connected with Kaczyński's rise to power. On the other hand, the newspaper portrayed prominent politicians of Civic Platform, Bartosz Arłukowicz and Joanna Kluzik-Rostkowska, not only as efficient and professional politicians, but also as empathetic human beings who care about others.

Moreover, Gmerek (2012) analysed daily journals and opinion weeklies with regard to their portrayal of the 2011 Polish parliamentary campaign during its final two weeks. Out of four opinion weeklies which were analysed ("Wprost", "News-week", "Polityka", "Gość Niedzielny"), "Wprost" portrayed Law and Justice and its candidates in a negative light in eight texts (the highest number of all the journals) while not once portraying them positively. Also, Panicz (2011) suggested that "Wprost" would repeatedly describe Kaczyński using military metaphors, trying to paint him as an authoritarian figure. Therefore, it seems that there is ample evidence to suggest that Lis has not been able to maintain a neutral attitude towards Kaczyński and his party. Rather, he has been one of their staunchest critics, oftentimes not acting in accordance with the ethos of a journalist. Moreover, more recent research concerning "Newsweek Poland" (Lis has been its editor-in-chief since 2012) suggests that Lis has been fairly consistent in criticizing Law and Justice, as the majority of his articles has been devoted to that topic (Śliwa 2016).

On the whole, given the literature and Lis' own statements, our research hypothesis claims that the episode with Kaczyński is a hybrid of a political interview and a pre-election debate since he combined two roles of a journalist and a politician. We suggest that Lis placed himself in the role of a spokesman of Tusk's political camp and as a political opponent of Kaczyński. Given the fact that there was not a separate debate between leaders, as it had been the case in previous years, we argue that such a debate was somehow expected by voters. Thus, steering the conversation with Kaczyński towards a pre-election debate by Lis might have been an attempt at fulfilling these expectations.

A clash of ethoses – a critical analysis

Lis' statement about the conversation with Kaczyński is particularly relevant for its generic interpretation. The intentions of the journalist expressed in 2018 did not necessarily have to correspond with his intentions in 2011. One should also take into consideration the possibility that the perception of the situation could have changed for the journalist due to later evaluations about it, which defined him as a loser in the debate with Kaczyński. Thus, Lis' answer could have been a subjective diagnosis of the situation: "I provoked attacks on myself and I did it for our cause", that is, to prevent PiS from winning. Without exploring the journalist's actual intentions (consciously or unintentionally allowing and attacking the interlocutor) we analyse the transcript of the conversation as it took place.

In assessing the behaviour of the participants of the program "Tomasz Lis na żywo" in terms of the realization of generic assumptions, we will rely on the method of studying the clash of ethos in pre-election debates, where it is assumed that each candidate constructs his ethos in three aspects: moral character (*arete*), experience, knowledge, competence (*phronesis*) and identification with the audience (*eunoia*), simultaneously destroying the ethos of his opponent by referring to the same areas. (Budzyńska-Daca 2015). The table below shows an extended overview of the analysis of politicians' statements taking into account the three temporal aspects.

Table 1. Patterns of constructing one's own ethos and destroying the ethos of the opponent.

	Own ethos			The opponent's ethos		
Temporal perspective - - - - - - - Type of ethos	Past	Present	Future	Past	Present	Future
Ethos – Moral character	I did X / I voted for X / I cared for X	I am responsible for X / I am prepared to hold office X / I know how to be a good leader	I will reform X / I will take care of X / I will govern fairly	They made mistakes / They voted wrongly on X / They neglected X / They did not do X	They do not know how to deal with X / They are wrong / Their judgement is wrong / They are unprepared for role X	They will not be a good leader
Ethos – Experience, knowledge, self-confidence	On X, my position was as follows	On X, I propose such and such a solution	On X, I will take the following measures	On X, they had a different opinion from me / They used to have a different opinion on X than they do now	On X, they have a worse proposal than I do	On X, they will not fulfil their promises / Their decisions will have negative consequences
Ethos – Audience identification	I cared about your interests	I am at your disposal	I will take care of you	They will not care about your interests	They instil fear in you	They will not fulfil their promises

Source: Budzyńska-Daca 2015, p. 147.

In the case of an interview, the variants of possible behaviours of the participants in the interaction are more complex. One important issue is dominance in the interaction, i.e., authorship of the interview (Szylko-Kwas 2013, p. 41). The journalist determines the topic, constructs the questions, and is responsible for its proper course. The interlocutor, on the other hand, is the one whose views the audience wants to know and it is the one who creates the conversation with their answers. The authorship of the interview can therefore be a contentious issue, when both participants have the need to dominate the interaction.

Therefore, the pattern of possible ethos constructions in the interview cannot be unequivocally determined, as it was in the case of the pre-election debate, where the focus is on the dispute and its object is clearly defined. However, it is possible, by inferring from the analysis of the rhetorical situation, to reconstruct the way in which the ethos of the speakers was constructed in this particular interview, and to check whether it contained elements of destroying the ethos of the opponent.

Having divided the components of ethos into character, competence, and identification with the audience, we will determine how each of the interlocutors, in creating their ethos, related to the opponent, taking into account the division into the above-mentioned three spheres of ethos. We will juxtapose two interviews: Lis-Tusk and Lis-Kaczyński, in order to identify the differences in creating and destroying the ethos of the politician and that of the journalist. As the conversations were not debates between candidates for office *per se*, it would be inappropriate to apply the full research method with the temporal aspects that politicians usually refer to, as shown in Table 1. In this case, the research method will be reduced to characterizing the ethos of the speakers and the conflict between the interlocutors. Thus, the study will answer the following research questions:

1a) How did the journalist (Lis) construct his ethos? Did the journalist as the moderator of the interaction destroy the ethos of the politician (Kaczyński)? If so, how?
1b) How did the politician (Kaczyński) construct his ethos? Did the politician as the interlocutor destroy the journalist's ethos? If so, how?
2a) How did the journalist (Lis) construct his ethos? Did the journalist as the moderator of the interaction, destroy the ethos of the politician (Tusk)? If so, how?
2b) How did the politician (Tusk) construct his ethos? Did the politician as the interlocutor destroy the journalist's ethos? If so, how?

We will also examine whether and how the two politicians spoke about each other in conversation with List. Are there any traces of destroying the ethos of the political opponent in their statements? We will base our investigation of the interviews on the following research questions:

3a) Did the politician (Kaczyński) destroy the ethos of his rival (Tusk) during his interview with the journalist (Lis)? If so, how?
3b) Did the politician (Tusk) destroy the ethos of his rival (Kaczyński) during his interview with the journalist (Lis)? If so, how?

1a)   Lis on Kaczyński

Lis addresses his interlocutor as "Mr. Chairman". Not once did he use the form 'Mr. Prime Minister', which is often used by journalists towards former state leaders (Kostro / Wróblewska-Pawlak 2016) as Kaczyński was Prime Minister in the 2006-2007 period. Thus, one might see that Lis does not adhere to the standard practice in the media, which lowers the prestige of Kaczyński in the eyes of the audience.

Lis begins the conversation with a question about Kaczyński's potential government. This question is stretched into a series of follow-up questions. Kaczyński's answers are accompanied by comments in which he strongly disagrees with his opinions and interpretations, thus entering the role of an opponent. Further, Lis repeatedly uses comparison based arguments in which Kaczyński comes off worse, e.g.,: in seasoned democracies the composition of the cabinet is known before the elections – in the case of the Law and Justice leader it is not; in European countries debates are held – the leader of Law and Justice did not agree to a debate (only Russia and Belarus have similar standards); four years ago we knew the composition of the government – now we do not; neighbouring countries had a much bigger economic growth than Poland under Kaczyński's rule – conclusion: they were better managed.

Pointing out Kaczyński's shortcomings in terms of competence and character also builds Lis' journalist's position. There is a crucial phrase, which Lis repeats several times: "You aspire to rule a central European country populated by forty million people".

The phrase makes the viewers doubt whether the politician's ambitions are right. At the same time, it helps to build Lis' image as the spokesman of the audience. By using the pronoun "we" in his questions (e.g., "We, the citizens have the right to know it") he attempts to speak on behalf of voters. Also, he justifies his questions by emphasizing that he cares about his audience who deserve to obtain meaningful responses:

> The viewers are not interested in my opinion. It is you who wants to rule Poland.
> Our viewers, and now we are being watched by a few million people, are certainly not
> interested in my views. They are interested in your views.

The repetition of such phrases throughout the interview is quite telling. They sound like an accusation of incompetence towards Kaczyński – a lack of satisfactory answers to the questions asked is highlighted.

Lis points out the features which disqualify a politician as a statesman, e.g., pettiness (Kaczyński's reaction to a satirical picture of the Kaczyński brothers in the German press; refusal to cooperate with President Komorowski due to Kaczyński's old grudges), lack of honour (no reaction to Father Rydzyk's words about his sister-in-law, Maria Kaczyńska), compromising behaviour, timidity (affair with a gun), lack of respect for people (Kaczyński's remark that he refers to Tusk as "this gentleman" and not as Prime Minister. Lis tries to evoke a sense of shame in Kaczyński (his people support "hoodlums"), diminishes his position in relation to his brother suggesting that the late Lech Kaczyński was a better politician than his twin brother. Further, Lis reprimands Kaczyński, saying that his behaviour is inappropriate. He accuses him of wanting to appoint the wrong politicians as ministers, insinuating about Angela Merkel, and tolerating stadium hooliganism in exchange for support for his party.

At the end of the conversation, Lis discusses young female candidates on the lists of Law and Justice. This is a seemingly irrelevant topic as none of them could be classified as a prominent politician of the party. However, Lis mentions them because he tries to paint Kaczyński as a calculated politician who treats others as pawns. Also, Lis tries to show that the leader of Law and Justice does know the young candidates, which would prove that their presence on the list is solely for marketing reasons. Thus, Lis starts questioning Kaczyński about their names and positions on the list. During that part of the conversation Lis makes a mistake regarding the constituency of Ilona Klejnowska: she represented Płock, not Bydgoszcz, as Lis was trying to suggest. This rather desperate attempt at showing Kaczyński's supposed instrumental treatment of his party's members proves that Lis was determined to paint Kaczyński in a negative light; as demonstrated above, to the detriment of his own ethos of the journalist. Similarly, when Kaczyński accuses Tusk of disrespecting others, Lis resorts to a *tu quoque* argument: "but you insulted the Silesians". A *tu quoque* fallacy involves criticizing the opponent for the same behaviour or actions that he or she condemns the interlocutor for (Ferreira 1983). In other words, this is an attempt to expose Kaczyński's hypocrisy, even though Lis' remark does not appear to be relevant to their conversation.

The statements of Lis, in which he refers to personal qualities, competence and attitude towards voters, undermine Kaczyński's ethos. The journalist utters them from the position of someone who has a sense of his own superior competence in the subject of the dispute. He clearly points out the shortcomings of the politician to the voters. The table below depicts the most important elements of the destruction of Kaczyński's ethos.

Table 2. A summary of rhetorical strategies of Tomasz Lis regarding Jarosław Kaczyński.

	Own ethos	**The opponent's ethos**
Ethos – Moral character	Inquisitive and courageous.	Small-minded, fearful, without a sense of honour. A hypocrite.
Ethos – Experience, knowledge, self-confidence	Competent, experienced, and well prepared for the conversation.	Does not respect democratic standards. Mismanaged Poland when he was Prime Minister. Holds grudges, non-cooperative.
Ethos – Audience identification	Speaks on behalf of voters, looks after their interests and their right to be informed.	Does not want to tell Poles the truth about his government. Sexist and cynical.

1b)   Kaczyński on Lis

When referring to Lis' ethos of the journalist, Kaczyński clearly suggests that Lis is an opponent of his. Kaczyński states that he reads Lis' newspaper and as a result he knows Lis' views, which run counter to values such as patriotism and conservatism. Therefore, the leader of Law and Justice positions Lis as a spokesman of the opposite camp. In doing so, Kaczyński criticises Lis' moral stance:

> You are obviously so terribly afraid of them [foreign politicians]. I really feel sorry for you. I do feel very sorry for you. You belong to a certain formation, unfortunately very popular in Poland, which is harmful to us.

The theme of cowardice is continued in several statements of Kaczyński. He accuses Lis of being afraid of the opinion of Western countries and advises him to free himself from this fear. He addresses him mockingly and disparagingly:

> But I understand that you are from a different formation. I understand that you would not like this, that you are too shy. Maybe your children or grandchildren will be bolder. Look for the symmetry, look for the symmetry. More confidence in yourself, sir, more Polish self-confidence.
> Really? Are you that fearful?

Oftentimes, Kaczyński's remarks are not justified and the audience has to take them for granted. His statements as regards Lis' incompetence are absolute and not subject to further discussion.

When it comes to Lis' morals, Kaczyński accuses him of not taking Poles seriously, undermining his identification with the audience. Namely, Kaczyński argues that Lis knows that Poland is not "some small country that has to succumb to everyone", but his political agenda involves acting to the detriment of Poland. Namely, Kaczyński claims that Lis uses double standards with regard to Polish and Western politicians. According to Kaczyński, Lis does not have the courage to criticise Erika Steinbach, the then president of the German Federation of Expellees, who "would have been kicked out of German politics had she said such things about the French or Jews". Thus, Kaczyński attacks Lis' ethos of the journalist by saying that he did not do enough to condemn Steinbach for her remarks which Kaczyński considers to be offensive. Also, the leader of Law and Justice claims that Lis is considerably more eager to attack his formation than foreign politicians who criticise Poland.

Furthermore, the leader of Law and Justice accused Lis of supporting "the old system" (communism). When discussing his potential government, Kaczyński uses Lis as a point of reference, claiming that politicians of his party cherish the values that are not respected by Lis. Finally, Kaczyński reminds Lis and the audience the fact that Lis considered running for president in 2005, pointing out that both of them used to have similar ambitions. Therefore, throughout the conversation Kaczyński portrays Lis as an active politician rather than an objective journalist.

On the whole, Kaczyński attacks undermine not only Lis' morals, but also his competence. Throughout the whole conversation Kaczyński attempts to prove that Lis is not prepared for it:

> At this point you are reaching the level of really terrible disgrace.
> Don't, don't try this method any further, because, I repeat, this whole discussion leads to absurdity. Well, you are simply discussing in such a way.
> Well, you are simply not telling the truth.
> Then please check it out. You are really completely unprepared for today's episode. I'm sorry. I'm really sorry. Really sorry.

Also, Kaczyński points out that he, not Lis, should be perceived as a spokesman of the audience. In the discussed episode, there were numerous instances where Kaczyński referred to the audience so that he could, firstly, present himself in a positive light, secondly, accuse Lis of not disrespecting the viewers. Namely, Kaczyński urged Lis to "have some more appreciation for Poles [because they are intelligent]" and not to "mislead our viewers". He also added that Lis should not "want to convince us by all means that, back then it was bad [during Kaczyński's term as Prime Minister]. No, it was very good". Therefore, Kaczyński attempts to portray himself as close to common people and, at the same time, discredit Lis as a representative of the cosmopolitan elite that considers itself superior. This stark contrast between the elite (cosmopolitan, left-wing, liberal, laic) and the nation (patriotic, right-wing, conservative, catholic) is one of the most common tropes in Kaczyński's rhetoric (Kim 2021).

Table 3. A summary of rhetorical strategies of Jarosław Kaczyński regarding Tomasz Lis.

	Own ethos	The opponent's ethos
Ethos – Moral character	Sincere, honest, courageous.	Cowardly, lacks patriotism, submits to foreign powers. A proponent of the old system.
Ethos – Experience, knowledge, self-confidence	Knows the economy. An experienced politician. A patriot who believes that Poland should be a force to be reckoned with.	An ally of Donald Tusk. Has political ambitions. Untrustworthy as a journalist. Cannot take a joke.
Ethos – Audience identification	Cares about those who are disrespected by the elite.	Acts to the detriment of Poland. Deliberately misleads Poles.

The above juxtapositions prove that both the journalist and the politician were engaged in an argument based on destroying the ethos of the interlocutor. The discussed statements prove that the conversation resembled a dispute, which is characteristic for the debate genre. In an interview, even a political interview, such intensity of mutual criticism may lead to communication breakdown, distorting the standards of a political interview. In the case of a debate-like setting, the participants are aware of the fact that they are entering a genre with eristic features (Walton 1999, p. 190, Budzyńska-Daca 2015, p. 140–158).

2a) Lis on Tusk

In his interview with Donald Tusk, Tomasz Lis creates his ethos as an inquisitive journalist who asks about issues "concerning millions of Poles" on behalf of voters who "are supposed to give the Prime Minister a collective assessment". Thus, he presents himself as their spokesman and somebody who appears genuinely concerned about Poland. Both Lis and Tusk express their regret that other leaders did not turn up.

The questions directed at Tusk concern unfulfilled election promises. Having read out the promises from the election program of Civic Platform, Lis asks about their execution (e. g., the situation of young people, healthcare, infrastructure, a reform of the social security system) and about the financial state of Poland. Since these questions concern relevant issues, they should be regarded as *ad rem* questions. Lis concludes his series of accusations by uttering the following sentence: "My impression is that what seemed like wishful thinking now looks like a set of unfulfilled promises".

It is worth noting that Lis gives Tusk space to present his answers. Tusk's statements are not interrupted. The then Prime Minister has enough time to respond to all points that Lis makes. Thus, in comparison to the Lis-Kaczyński meeting, the conversation with Tusk has a considerably more organised structure.

Only in a few cases does Lis refer to Tusk's character and personality. In Lis' statements there are sometimes *ad hominem* remarks, particularly when he reproaches Tusk for unfulfilled promises: "however, you said, you made specific promises, and these were not supposed to be smoke and mirrors, but on the 'we will do it' principle". The accusation against the Prime Minister is clear: his promise was not kept and millions of Poles will have to decide whether they want to trust him again.

Also, Lis puts in doubt Tusk's attempts to portray himself as one of many common people. For example, he asks him the following question: "Have you ever been to the Maria Skłodowska-Curie Institute of Oncology, have you seen that shorter queue of people you have been talking about?"

Still, when Tusk says that he does know how it is to have a family member who needs chemotherapy and even though he is Prime Minister he also has to wait for his turn, Lis does not question his statement and switches the topic of the conversation.

Overall, in his interview with Tusk, Lis mainly criticises his government, his remarks are not aimed predominantly at Tusk's character. Thus, Lis positions himself as a competent journalist who holds a politician accountable.

Table 4. A summary of rhetorical strategies of Tomasz Lis regarding Donald Tusk.

	Own ethos	The opponent's ethos
Ethos – Moral character	–	Does not keep his words.
Ethos – Experience, knowledge, self-confidence	Knowledgeable, prepared to review government actions.	Not as effective as promised.
Ethos – Audience identification	Speaks on behalf of the unprivileged and common people.	Does not know everyday problems of Poles.

2b)   Tusk on Lis

During their conversation, Lis and Tusk exchange relevant arguments. Their criticism towards each other is rational and while there are multiple disagreements between them, it appears it is rational and just. While responding to Lis' arguments, Tusk does not attack him personally and focuses on giving factual information. In comparison to Kaczyński, Tusk does not try to attack Lis nor does he question his morals and competences. Therefore, Tusk does not see Lis as a political opponent. Overall, Tusk's ethos in his interview with Lis is based on building a positive impression about his character and personal virtues. Tusk portrays himself as a fighter (he was not afraid of a debate with other leaders and was the only one to show up). To highlight this analogy, Tusk makes a reference to a boxing match, which is particularly relevant given the Adamek vs. Klitschko bout which was to take place shortly after the episode.

Moreover, Tusk presents himself as an efficient Prime Minister, knowledgeable in matters of state management. He explains he could not fully keep his promises due to the difficult political situation in Poland (lack of consent of the majority in parliament) and the economic situation (world crisis). Also, he brings up *Doing Business* rankings (a series of reports done by the World Bank from 2003 to 2021), saying that they could be regarded as "objective data". Therefore, in order to challenge Lis' arguments, Tusk refers to concrete data and facts rather than emotions. One might thus conclude that Tusk respects Lis as a journalist. The leader of Civic Platform answers his questions and does not undermine his right to ask them (which is a stark contrast to Kaczyński, who constantly questions Lis' morality and competences). On the whole, both interlocutors fulfil their roles as a journalist and a politician. Moreover, the politician did not destroy the ethos of the journalist.

Table 5. A summary of rhetorical strategies of Donald Tusk regarding Tomasz Lis.

	Own ethos	**The opponent's ethos**
Ethos – Moral character	Courageous, magnanimous, and determined. Able to own up to his mistakes.	–
Ethos – Experience, knowledge, self-confidence	Presents objective data to support his claims. Knows how to solve problems, efficient as a politician.	–
Ethos – Audience identification	Presents himself as a common man, understands Poles.	–

In the following subsections it will be verified how the politicians spoke about each other during their respective conversations with Lis.

3a)   Kaczyński on Tusk

In the course of the episode, Kaczyński repeatedly refers to Tusk (both as a person and a politician). When asked a question as to why he did not want to debate with Tusk, Kaczyński asks a series of accusations that were supposed to diminish his rival's moral attitude. For example, there is a claim that Tusk humiliates people (although it refers mostly to Kaczyński's electorate) by referring to them as "cattle", "cemetery hyenas", "mohair berets"[4]. Regarding the phrase "mohair berets", even though Tusk has since apologised for using that expression, Kaczyński comes back to his gaffe, trying to portray him as a politician representing the elite who considers himself superior to common people.

Kaczyński accuses Tusk of urging people to "hide IDs from grandmothers" to prevent them from voting. This a reference to a campaign from 2007 when many people in Poland would receive SMS messages in which hiding IDs was compared to "saving the country". While Tusk and Civic Party had no direct connections to the campaign, Kaczyński attributes it to Tusk, attempting to prove that he does not respect Kaczyński's electorate and Tusk considers himself superior to older people[5].

Kaczyński refers to Tusk as "this gentleman" (instead of Prime Minister or simply using Tusk's name), to which Lis reacts by criticizing this behaviour and reprimanding Kaczyński for it. Still, throughout the whole episode the leader of Law and Justice was consistent in using that form. By not addressing Tusk using his formal credentials, Kaczyński diminished his role and position, suggesting that Tusk was not the right person to govern Poland.

What is more, Kaczyński considers Lis's remarks a personal attack directed at him. The leader of Law and Justice does not feel that he needs to explain his position, arguing that he addresses Tusk as he pleases and any further discussion as regards his lexical choices is futile, disregarding Lis' suggestions. This is

---

4 The term "mohair berets" is a derogative expression that refers to the type of headgear worn by elderly people (mostly women) who are listeners of Radio Maryja, a catholic and right-wing oriented radio station owned by Father Tadeusz Rydzyk. As Law and Justice is disproportionately supported by older people, the term is often used to disparage the electorate of the party. While it was not Tusk who coined the phrase, in 2005 he used the term "mohair coalition" to describe a parliamentary coalition which consisted of Law and Justice, the League of Polish Families, and Self-Defence.

5 It is worth mentioning that even though the organisers of the action were not members of Civic Platform, they did support the party (Jakubowski 2012, p. 103).

consistent with Kaczyński's strategies of undermining Lis' competences and morality. The leader of Law and Justice speaks from the position of authority and he does not need to clarify his statements to both his interlocutors and the audience. Also, when Lis remarks that he should agree to the debate because he would crush Tusk and take 10% of the votes, Kaczyński agrees that he would probably crush Tusk, but he is merciful. While this is clearly a tongue-in-cheek comment, Kaczyński emphasises his superiority with regard to Tusk, positioning himself as a more skilled politician.

Furthermore, Kaczyński undermines Tusk's ethos by suggesting he and his party use a special strategy aimed at Law and Justice. Kaczyński describes it as "a smear campaign", claiming that Tusk insults large groups of people and Civic Platform "has to tell lies about our government". In contrast, Kaczyński highlights that he and his party do not need such strategies. Using Tusk as a point of reference, Kaczyński construes his own ethos. One might observe that the leader of Law and Justice relies on the same rhetoric with regard to both Lis and Tusk – having presented them in a negative light, he proceeds to discuss his own virtues.

Table 6. A summary of rhetorical strategies of Jarosław Kaczyński regarding Donald Tusk.

	Own ethos	The opponent's ethos
Ethos – Moral character	Self-confident and determined. Honest, serious, with a sense of humour.	Dishonest and not serious.
Ethos – Experience, knowledge, self-confidence	A serious politician who would win a debate with Tusk.	Unable to have a serious conversation with. Incompetent as Prime Minister. Acts to the detriment of Poland, depends on Russia and Germany.
Ethos – Audience identification	Cares about those who have been disrespected by Tusk and his camp.	Divides people into good and bad, despises certain groups.

3b) Tusk on Kaczyński

In his interview with Tusk, Lis mentions Kaczyński expecting a reference to his words and behaviour: refusal to take part in their debate, comments that Tusk put up a white flag, that he puts Tusk in a corner. The journalist provokes Tusk to comment on Kaczyński. However, Tusk is rather moderate in this regard. He speaks allusively, although he is critical of his rival, e.g., regarding the debate: "when you agree to a duel, you go for it and don't pretend that your mother is calling you for dinner".

Thus, Tusk undermines Kaczyński's courage, accusing him of cowardice. Further, Tusk argues that Kaczyński let down voters as they were expecting a debate which never materialised due to his unwillingness to confront his views with Tusk. Clearly, Tusk considers his Kaczyński's excuses insufficient and not credible. To strengthen this line of argument, Tusk brings up Tomasz Adamek, who was to be interviewed by Lis after him, saying that a true political leader should "have the it-factor", just like a boxing champion. The implication here is clear: it is only Tusk who can be considered a true leader and Kaczyński is the one who did not rise up to the challenge.

The lexis used by Tusk in the aforementioned sentence is particularly interesting as it helps create the impression that the leader of Civic Party is closer to people as not only is he the only politician who answered their expectations (by taking part in what was supposed to be a debate between leaders) but also Tusk uses informal language, which signifies that he is not that different from common people.

Afterwards, Tusk voices his criticism not only towards Kaczyński, but aims it at Law and Justice as a whole. He mentions that Kaczyński and his party insisted on buying vaccines for swine flu in 2009 despite the fact that they had not been properly tested. During the conversation with Lis, Tusk asks a rhetorical question ("Where were you then and what arguments did you use?"), portraying Kaczyński and his party as irresponsible.

Moreover, Tusk presents himself as conciliatory and ready to rise above political differences for the good of Poland. He highlights that he is not in politics for "seeking revenge". Further, Tusk strengthens his political ethos by refraining from overstepping his competence as he says that it is the prosecution that decides whether politicians of Law and Justice should be held criminally liable.

In addition, Tusk highlights the inclusivity of his party, saying that he is willing to cooperate with politicians of Law and Justice (provided they did not breach the law). Thus, he presents himself as somebody whose main interest is not to exacerbate already existing political tensions ("politics is not the art of inflicting pain on people"); rather, he intends to ease them by presenting his own "positive program". In a way, Tusk's favourable self-presentation is created in opposition to Kaczyński and his party. There is a clear implication that only Tusk and Civic party want to implement this positive strategy, whereas Law and Justice clearly deviates from it.

It is worth mentioning that Tusk never shifts the conversation to discuss Kaczyński. Rather, he is provoked to do that by Lis as Tusk brings up his rival only in response to Lis' questions and comments. This observation further strengthens the assumption that it is Lis who is interested in discrediting Kaczyński as Tusk only responds to Lis' statements about the leader of Law and Justice.

Table 7. A summary of rhetorical strategies of Donald Tusk regarding Jarosław Kaczyński.

	Own ethos	The opponent's ethos
Ethos – Moral character	Cooperative, courageous, and magnanimous.	Cowardly and irresponsible.
Ethos – Experience, knowledge, self-confidence	Skilful politician who takes a realistic view of politics.	Unable to make difficult decisions.
Ethos – Audience identification	Presents himself as one of many. Cares for fellow citizens.	Let Poles down by not participating in a debate.

A comparison of the data from the two interviews brings out the differences in the attitudes of the interlocutors towards one another. The Lis-Kaczyński meeting was abundant in eristic attempts to destroy the opponent's ethos. This is true for both the politician and the journalist.

Although the formal structure of the conversation resembled that of an interview, the attitude of the interlocutors was marked by strong tensions between them. The journalist asked questions and in the course of answering them, the politician interrupted him with comments undermining his credibility. The politician tried to expose the journalist's true intentions as Kaczyński painted Lis as a spokesman of Civic Platform, not the audience. Also, Kaczyński's main strategy centred around ascribing negative qualities of Tusk to Lis as he considered both to be representatives of a rival political party.

With regard to Lis' questions, their point is often to undermine Kaczyński's character and morality. This strategy seems typical for election debates, but does not seem to be fully compatible with the structure of a political interview whose aim is to provide the audience with relevant answers of an interlocutor, not discredit them. Also, Lis resorted to *ad hominem* arguments, oftentimes at the expense of his own journalistic credibility as the information he claimed to be true in some cases turned out to be incorrect. This proves that Lis' main goal was to demean Kaczyński rather than to elicit important information from him.

At a quantitative level, one could compare the type of questions asked by Lis to both politicians. As regards the conversation with Tusk, Lis asked 48 questions (including interjections and appositions). On the other hand, Kaczyński was asked 177 questions. Even adjusting for time constraints (the episode with Tusk lasted for 34 minutes, with Kaczyński – 49), it appears that Lis directed considerably more questions at the leader of Law and Justice.

Furthermore, there was a significant difference in the way the interaction was managed and main questions and follow-up questions were asked. In the episode with Kaczyński, Lis asked 29 questions which pertained to the personal credibility of the interviewee, whereas in the conversation with Tusk, Lis asked 9 such questions and four of these were in fact directed at Kaczyński since they concerned the Leader of Law and Justice rather than Tusk himself. Thus, the conclusion that Lis undermines Kaczyński's ethos in a more direct way than when it comes to Tusk can be observed also at a quantitative level.

A juxtaposition of the data from Tables 2, 3, 4, and 5 shows the differences between the Lis-Tusk and Lis-Kaczyński interactions in the way the ethos of their respective opponents was destroyed. It shows the contentious nature of the meeting between Lis and Kaczynski with and a non-confrontational character of the conversation between Lis and Tusk.

With regard to Kaczyński and Tusk's strategies, the politicians obviously were not able to talk to each other directly, but there were many instances when each of them referred to their absent rival.

Kaczyński's main strategy is to attack Tusk's morals. In his criticism, Kaczyński attempts to persuade the audience that Tusk is dependent on foreign governments, which disqualifies him as Prime Minister of an independent country. Kaczyński also emphasises Tusk's alleged lack of respect towards the electorate of Law and Justice. It is worth noting that Kaczyński implements similar strategies with regard to Tomasz Lis. Thus, morals and audience identification appear to be the main target of Kaczyński's attack, and this is relevant for both undermining Tusk's ethos of the politician and Lis' ethos of the journalist. Kaczyński uses them as a point of reference as he presents himself as a statesman who is concerned about every Polish citizen, regardless of their political preferences. He also highlights his courage and determination – the two qualities that neither Tusk, nor Lis have. It thus appears that Kaczyński's attacks on Lis are in fact aimed at Tusk since in Kaczyński's narrative they both represent the same formation.

In comparison to Kaczyński, Tusk does not make his political rival the main point of reference. He discusses him only after being asked to by Lis. Even when he does mention Kaczyński, Tusk uses allusions and implications. It helps him create his image of a reasonable politician who does not intend to take revenge on his political opponents. The only fragments where Kaczyński is clearly used as a benchmark occur when Tusk mentions his courage and readiness to continue his mission as Prime Minister. Thus, the indirect dispute between the two politicians is centred around the traits of courage and morality.

Conclusions

The comparison of the clash of ethoses in both episodes shows that the politicians interpreted their participation in Lis' program differently: Kaczyński as a debate, Tusk as an interview. For the Leader of Law and Justice, his participation in the program allowed him to voice his criticism against the then Prime Minister, which was a critical point of his election campaign as he was the leader of opposition running for Prime Minister. Thus, as there was not any debate between the candidates, Kaczyński used the program as a substitute for a debate.

On the other hand, Tusk perceived the episode as a political interview and did not question Lis' position as a journalist. His attacks on Kaczyński were sporadic as Tusk's fundamental goal was to present himself as a trustworthy leader and refute the journalist's objections regarding his term. Thus, Tusk stuck to the formula of a political interview and did not try to steer it into a debate with an absent rival.

Since the host of the program was in charge of the interaction in both cases, he played an important role in the behaviour of the two leaders. Lis' criticism of Kaczyński and Tusk was disproportionate: he was destroying Kaczyński's ethos in all aspects throughout the whole episode. Also, the attempt to discredit Kaczyński might have been his main goal as he resorted to personal attacks and quoting incorrect information (which was not observed in the episode with Tusk).

Conversely, Lis allowed Tusk to create his ethos without criticizing his character traits, competence and identification with the audience. Simultaneously, his questions were relevant and inquisitive as they concerned issues pertaining to the program of Civic Platform and Tusk's term as Prime Minister, not his morality or character.

We therefore conclude that voters were able to observe two different genres of pre-election discourse: a non-adversarial political interview (the episode with Donald Tusk) and a hybrid of a political interview and a debate (the episode with Jarosław Kaczyński).

References

Aristotle: On Rhetoric: a Theory of Civic Discourse, transl. G. Kennedy. New York. 2007.
Bakhtin, Mikhail: 'The Problem of Speech Genres', in: Ruff, David (ed.): Modern Genre Theory. London 2014, p. 82–97.
Bauer, Zbigniew: Wywiad prasowy. Gatunek i metoda, in: Bauer, Zbigniew / Chudziński, Edward (eds.): *Dziennikarstwo i świat mediów*. Kraków 2008, p. 186–196.

Baym, G.: 'Political Media as Discursive Modes: A Comparative Analysis of Interviews with Ron Paul from *Meet the Press, Tonight, The Daily Show,* and *Hannity*', in INTERNATIONAL JOURNAL OF COMMUNICATION 2013/7, p. 489–507.

Bazerman, Charles: The life of genre, the life in the classroom, in: Bishop, Wendy / Ostrom, Hans (eds.): *Genre and Writing: Issues, Arguments, Alternatives.* Portsmouth 1997, p. 19–26.

Blum-Kulka, S.: 'The Dynamics of Political Interviews', in: TEXT 1983/3(2), p. 131–153.

Budzyńska-Daca, Agnieszka: Retoryka debaty. Polskie wielkie debaty przedwyborcze 1995–2010. Warszawa 2015.

Bull, P. / Fetzer, A.: 'Who are *we* and who are *you?* The strategic use of forms of address in political interviews', in TEXT AND TALK 2006/17(1), p. 3–37.

Bull, P. / Fetzer, A.: 'Face, facework and political discourse', in REVUE INTERNATIONALE DE PSYCHOLOGIE SOCIALE 2010/23(2), p. 155–185.

Cabrejas-Peñuelas, A.B.: 'Manipulation in Spanish and American pre-election political debates: The Rajoy–Rubalcaba vs. Obama–McCain debates', in INTERCULTURAL PRAGMATICS 2015/12(4), p. 515–546.

Cabrejas-Peñuelas, A. B. / Díez-Prados, M.: 'Positive self-evaluation versus negative other-evaluation in the political genre of pre-election debates', in DISCOURSE & SOCIETY 2015/25(2), p. 159–185.

Chilton, Paul: Analysing Political Discourse: Theory and Practice. London and New York 2004.

Chwedczuk-Szulc, K. / Zaremba, M.: 'Janusz Korwin-Mikke and the rest: the Polish eurosceptic right wing', in: THE POLISH QUARTERLY OF INTERNATIONAL AFFAIRS 2015/2, p. 121–134.

Clayman, Stephen / Heritage, John: The News Interview: journalists and public figures on the air. Cambridge 2002.

de Beus, Jos: 'Audience Democracy: An Emerging Pattern in Postmodern Political Communication', in Brants, Kees / Voltmer, Katrin (eds.).: *Political Communication in Postmodern Democracy: Challenging the Primacy of Politics.* Basingstoke 2011, p. 19–38.

De Smedt, Eva / Vandenbrande, Kristel: 'Political television formats as strategic resources in achieving journalists' roles', in: Ekström, Mats / Patrona, Marianna (eds.): *Talking politics in broadcast media: Cross-cultural perspectives on political interviewing, journalism and accountability.* Amsterdam/Philadelphia 2011, p. 75–92.

Duszak, Anna: Tekst, dyskurs, komunikacja międzykulturowa. Warszawa 1998.

dziennik.pl: 'Poseł partii rządzącej o pojedynku w TVP: Mamut zgniótł lisa', 04. 10. 2011, available at: https://wiadomosci.dziennik.pl/wybory/psl/artykuly/359498,posel-psl-lis-probowal-stac-sie-namiastka-tuska.html [28. 11. 2021].

Fairclough, Norman: Critical Discourse Analysis: The Critical Study of Language. London 1995.

Fairclough, N.: 'Genres in Political Discourse', in Mey, Jacob (ed.).: *Concise Encyclopedia of Pragmatics. Second Edition.* Oxford, p. 293–298.

Ferreira, J.M.: 'A Common defense of theistic belief: Some critical considerations', in: INTERNATIONAL JOURNAL FOR PHILOSOPHY OF RELIGION 1983/14(3), p. 129–141.

Fetzer, Anita: '"Put Bluntly, You Have Something of a Credibility Problem": sincerity and credibility in political interviews', in: Chilton, Paul / Schäffner, Christina (eds.): *Politics as Text and Talk*. Amsterdam, p. 173–201.

Fetzer, Anita / Bull, Peter: 'Political interviews in context', in: Okulska, Urszula / Cap, Piotr (eds.): *Analyzing Genres in Political Communication: Theory and Practice*. Amsterdam/ Philadelphia 2013, p. 73–99.

Fetzer, A. / Wiezman, E.: 'Political discourse as mediated and public discourse', in: JOURNAL OF PRAGMATICS 2006/38, p. 143–153.

film.interia.pl: 'Lisowi pomógł… Kaczyński', 05.10.2011, available at: https://film.interi a.pl/telewizja/news-lisowi-pomogl-kaczynski,nId,1800672 [28.11.2021].

Fras, Janina: Komunikacja polityczna. Wybrane zagadnienia gatunków i języka wypowiedzi. Wrocław 2005.

Furman, Wojciech / Kaliszewski, Andrzej / Wolny-Zmorzyński, Kazimierz: Gatunki dziennikarskie. Specyfika ich tworzenia i redagowania. Rzeszów 2000.

Gmerek, Maria: 'Parlamentarna kampania wyborcza 2011 roku w prasie drukowanej', in: Turska-Kawa, Agnieszka / Wojtasik, Waldemar (eds.): *Wybory parlamentarne 2011*. Katowice 2012, p. 221–236.

Halliday, M.A.K.: Language as Social Semiotic. The Social Interpretation of Language and Meaning. London 1978.

Hinton, M. / Budzyńska-Daca, A.: 'A Comparative Study of Political Communication in Televised Pre-Election Debates in Poland and the United States of America', in: RESEARCH IN LANGUAGE 2019/17(1), p. 1–19.

Hutchby, I.: 'Hybridisation, personalisation and tribuneship in the political interview', in JOURNALISM 2017/18(1), p. 101–118.

Hutchby, Ian: 'Neutrality, Non-neutrality, and Hybridity in Political Interviews', in: Feldman, Ofer (ed.): *Adversarial Political Interviewing. Worldwide Perspectives During Polarized Times*, Singapore 2022, p. 25–42.

Jakubowski, P.: 'Reklama wyborcza w kampanii parlamentarnej 2007 w Polsce', in: ROCZNIK SAMORZĄDOWY 2012/1, p. 95–107.

Jamieson, Kathleen M. Hall / Stromer-Galley, Jennifer: 'Hybrid Genres', in: Sloane, Thomas O. (ed.), *Encyclopedia of Rhetoric*. New York 2001, p. 361–363.

Jamieson, K.M.H.: 'Generic constraints and the rhetorical situation', in: PHILOSOPHY AND RHETORIC 1973/6(3), p. 162–170.

Kim, S.: '…Because the homeland cannot be in opposition: analysing the discourses of Fidesz and Law and Justice (PiS) from opposition to power', in: EAST EUROPEAN POLITICS 2021/37(2), p. 332–351.

Kochan, Marek: 'Od święta demokracji do teleturnieju. Przemiany konwencji debat telewizyjnych w Polsce', in: Budzyńska-Daca, Agnieszka (ed.): *20 lat polskich telewizyjnych debat przedwyborczych*. Warszawa 2016, p. 15–89.

Komlósi, L. I. / Tarrósy, I.: 'Presumptive arguments turned into a fallacy of presumptuousness: Pre-election debates in a democracy of promises', in JOURNAL OF PRAGMATICS 2010/42(4), p. 957–972.

Kondzińska, A. (a): 'Kaczyński do Lisa: Pan patrzy na mnie z jakąś napiętą miną', 04.10.2011, available at: https://wyborcza.pl/7,75398,10403361,kaczynski-do-lisa-pan-patrzy-na-mnie-z-jakas-napieta-mina.html [28.11.2021].

Kondzińska, A. (b): 'Lis zorganizował debatę. Przyszedł tylko Tusk', 05.09.2011, available at: https://wyborcza.pl/7,75398,10236582,lis-zorganizowal-debate-przyszedl-tylko-tus k.html [28.11.2021].

Kostro, Monika / Wróblewska-Pawlak, Krystyna: Panie Prezydencie, Monsieur le Président... Formy adresatywne w polskim i francuskim dyskursie polityczno-medialnym. Warszawa 2016.

Lauerbach, G.: 'Pragmatic Aspects of Political Discourse in the Media', in JOURNAL OF PRAGMATICS 2006/38(2), p. 196–215.

Miller, C. R.: 'Genre as social action', in: QUARTERLY JOURNAL OF SPEECH 1984/70(2), p. 151–167.

Panicz, U.: 'Kreowanie dyskursu publicznego w Polsce – rola mediów krytycznych wobec Prawa i Sprawiedliwości', in: REFLEKSJE. PISMO NAUKOWE STUDENTÓW I DOK-TORANTÓW WNPID UAM 2011/3, p. 141–156.

PolskaTimes.pl: 'Tusk jest, Kaczyńskiego nie ma: quasi-debata w programie Tomasza Lisa', 05.09.2011, available at: https://polskatimes.pl/tusk-jest-kaczynskiego-nie-ma-quaside bata-w-programie-tomasza-lisa/ar/447161 [28.11.2021].

Radulović, M. / Jovanović, V.Ž.: 'The pragmeme of disagreement and its allopracts in English and Serbian political interview discourse', in: PRAGMATICS 2020/30(4), p. 386–413.

Stępień, Tomasz. 'Wywiad', in. Pytasz, Marek (ed.): *Leksykon szkolny. Gatunki paraliter-ackie, publicystyczne i użytkowe*. Gorzów Wielkopolski 1993, p. 203–221.

Szwed, Anna: 'Prywatność w mediach – obraz polityka w tygodniku opinii "Wprost"', in: POLITEJA: PISMO WYDZIAŁU STUDIÓW MIĘDZYNARODOWYCH I POLITYCZ-NYCH UNIWERSYTETU JAGIELLOŃSKIEGO 2013/10(25), p. 569–584.

Szylko-Kwas, Joanna: Wywiad telewizyjny – cechy twórcze a norma gatunkowa. Warszawa 2013.

Śliwa, Agnieszka: 'Publicystyka Tomasza Lisa na łamach "Newsweek Polska" w 2015 roku', in: Dajnowicz, Małgorzata / Miodowski, Adam (eds.): *Polityka i politycy w prasie XX i XXI wieku*. Białystok 2016, p. 91–102.

tokfm.pl: 'Kto wypadł lepiej: Lis czy Kaczyński? Wyniki naszego sondażu', 04.10.2011, available at: https://www.tokfm.pl/Tokfm/7,103087,10403714,kto-wypadl-lepiej-lis-cz y-kaczynski-wyniki-naszego-sondazu.html [28.11.2021].

van Dijk, T.: 'War rhetoric of a little ally: Political implicatures and Aznar's legitimatization of the war in Iraq', in JOURNAL OF LANGUAGE AND POLITICS 2005/4(1), p. 65–91.

Walton, Douglas: Appeal to Expert Opinion: Arguments from Authority. Pennsylvania 1999.

wirtualnemedia.pl: 'Tomasz Lis: gdybym przegrał w wywiadzie z Kaczyńskim, kosztowa-łoby to nas w wyborach kilka pkt (wideo)', 09.03.2018, available at: https://www.wi rtualnemedia.pl/artykul/tomasz-lis-gdybym-przegral-w-wywiadzie-z-kaczynskim-kos ztowaloby-to-nas-w-wyborach-kilka-pkt-wideo [28.11.2021].

Worsowicz, Monika: Gatunki prasowe. Łódź 2006.

wPolityce.pl (a): 'Donald Lis kontra Jarosław Kaczyński. Gdy dziennikarz próbuje być politykiem...', 04.10.2011, available at: https://wpolityce.pl/polityka/119636-donald-li s-kontra-jaroslaw-kaczynski-gdy-dziennikarz-probuje-byc-politykiem [28.11.2021].

wPolityce.pl (b): 'Tomaszowi Lisowi puściły nerwy. To nie wyglądało jak wywiad z Jar-osławem Kaczyńskim, a jak debata polityków', 04.10.2011, available at: https://wpoli

tyce.pl/polityka/119647-tomaszowi-lisowi-puscily-nerwy-to-nie-wygladalo-jak-wywi
ad-z-jaroslawem-kaczynskim-a-jak-debata-politykow [28.11.2021].

wprost.pl (a): 'Kaczyński u Lisa: skład mojego rządu? Wiem więcej, mniej mówię', 04.10.
2011, available at: https://www.wprost.pl/kraj/264276/kaczynski-u-lisa-sklad-mojego-r
zadu-wiem-wiecej-mniej-mowie.html [28.11.2021].

wprost.pl: 'Tusk u Lisa: Kaczyński przed Trybunał? To cuchnie na kilometr', 05.09.2011,
available at: https://www.wprost.pl/kraj/260489/tusk-u-lisa-kaczynski-przed-trybunal-
to-cuchnie-na-kilometr.html [28.11.2021].

Zawadzki, Adam: 'Tomasz Lis na deskach. Gorące komentarze po debacie z Jarosławem
Kaczyńskim', 04.10.2011, available at: https://www.rp.pl/publicystyka/art14210671-to
masz-lis-na-deskach-gorace-komentarze-po-debacie-z-jaroslawem-kaczynskim [28.
11.2021].

Magdalena Steciąg / Kaja Rostkowska-Biszczanik

"You can't speak Polish?" The disintegration of the idea of natural language in public debate (based on the material from an interview of Tomasz Lis with Jarosław Kaczyński)

Abstract

The following analysis of the conversation between Tomasz Lis and Jarosław Kaczyński is qualitative in nature and aimed at maximizing interpretation. The assumption of the analysis is that in the background of the entire interview, various conceptualization of language are being evoked. The research procedure involves triangulation. Conceptualizing natural language will be presented through the prism of the three concepts: lingua nativa as colloquial language relating to the 'world of things' and everyday experiences; lingua materna as native language that is absorbed 'with one's mother's milk' – and therefore based on ethnicity; lingua fracta as conventional language in which communicative behaviour is subjected to the rigors of mediatized public debate. As a result of the analysis, three colloquial expressions referring in various ways to the situation of speaking were recognized as unspoken 'idioms' framing the pragmatically asymmetric and discursively disproportional conversation between Tomasz Lis and Jarosław Kaczyński.

Keywords: folk linguistics, semantics of understanding, lingua nativa, lingua materna, lingua fracta

Introduction

Although the idea of natural language has very ancient roots, over the millennia it has been dealt with in many different ways. In Plato's *Kratylos*, considered to be the oldest linguistic treatise in the European tradition, it is associated with a dispute among philosophers as to whether language can be a tool for learning about reality, and if so, to what extent its relationship with the outside world is natural (*physei*), and to what extent it is conventional (*thesei*). The answer was to be provided by etymology, understood not as explaining one word through

Magdalena Steciąg, University of Zielona Góra (Poland), ORCID: 0000-0002-6360-2987, m.steciag@ifp.uz.zgora.pl.

Kaja Rostkowska-Biszczanik, University of Zielona Góra (Poland), ORCID: 0000-0001-7997-4649, kaja.rostkowska@gmail.com.

another – older or foreign, but through its supposed truth relation to the reality being marked (Heinz 1978, p. 29 f, Partee 1972).

Binary thinking within the nature-culture opposition also gave rise to discussions about language as the essence of humanity, dominated by linguistic essentialism based on the belief that language is a species distinguishing feature of *Homo sapiens* in the world of higher-order living creatures. From this tendency, two opposing positions emerged: monism and dualism (Wąsik 2007, p. 217). In monism, which perceives man as a psychosomatic unity, language is treated as an effect of evolution that could arise when, as a result of man's adaptation to the natural and social environment, appropriate anatomical, physiological and psychological properties were developed in their body. Dualism, in turn, recognizes that the word is for human beings consisting of soul and flesh an expression of their mental depth, and only through the word is it possible to reach their consciousness.

The often stereotypical or even 'mythical' opinions so deeply engraved in tradition and culture concerning language as a tool of understanding reality proper to a human being are revealed not only in statements devoted strictly to language, they basically exist in the background of communication as obviousness. In folk linguistics, these common opinions about language are treated as an important element of community knowledge relating to typical experiences, beliefs and ideas about the surrounding reality, conventional behaviours and well-established scenarios in interpersonal relationships in specific situations. They are considered as an emanation of linguistic culture, produced in communities connected by language, which consists of: "collective ideas, values, beliefs, attitudes, prejudices, myths, religious structures, and all other cultural 'baggage' that speakers bring to their dealings with language from their culture" (Schiffman 2006, p. 112).

From this perspective, casual remarks on the language made by ordinary speakers (as opposed to experts or language professionals) can serve as valuable material to discover the ideological background of communication – not only at the micro level, i. e., in relation to the individual attitudes of participants in a specific interaction, but also at the macro level:

> Folk linguistic commentary is more than just linguistically interesting: it gives expression to the cultures, workings and ideologies of a community as they relate to language. As with any language ideology research, folk linguistic talk may be valuable to a much broader range of social science endeavours (Albury 2014, p. 90).

The perspective of folk linguistics will be adopted in this article to trace the symptoms of the communication crisis in public debate in Poland based on an interview of Tomasz Lis (TL) with Jarosław Kaczyński (JK) through the prism of three widespread language conceptualizations (Steciąg 2019):

- *lingua nativa* as colloquial language of the 'world of things' and everyday experiences;
- *lingua materna* as native language that is absorbed 'with one's mother's milk' – and therefore based on ethnicity;
- *lingua fracta* as conventional language in which linguistic behaviour is subject to the constraints of mediatized public debate[1].

The aforementioned interview was a widely commented media event in Poland in 2011 and still remains the research matter of great analytical, interpretative and methodological potential. The assumption of this analysis is that behind the side-threads taken up in the interview, and casual remarks about language or the way it is used, there are opinions about the standards of public communication and the nature of its instruments, deeply rooted in culture, worldview or thinking patterns. In search of what is unspoken and assumed in communication between the participants of the conversation, the deductive order is assumed, which means that the conceptualization itself has priority, and more broadly – the interpretive frame – that motivates the understanding of natural language in a specific context.

In Charles Fillmore's semantics of understanding, the interpretive frame is considered to be the 'conceptual scaffold' modelling 'knowledge' as an interrelated epistemological grid (knowledge becomes intelligible if it refers to a schema, and not a formless set). On the other hand, "the motivating context is some body of understandings, some pattern of practices, or some history of social institutions, against which we find intelligible the creation of particular category in the history of language community" (Fillmore 1982, p. 119). It should also be remembered that the frame is regulative in nature, as it triggers certain expectations due to the fact that in order to understand one element, one must know the entire structure in which it is located.

Analysing the interview at a deeper level will explore the language from a cognitive perspective, and more precisely within the interpretive framework apparatus. This approach is intended to reconstruct the supposedly obvious discourses concerning language in the course of critical revision and gradual reduction in the spirit of hermeneutics (Koller 1999, p. 195). The advantage of this analysis method is that it goes beyond the content of the conversation, allowing us to see the implications of the functioning of the message in discourse

---

1 The concept of *lingua fracta* goes along with genres theory, which are defined as indicators of communication, signpost of sense interpretation or socially ratified ways of using language in connection with a particular type of social activity. Generic analysis of the conversation between Jarosław Kaczyński and Tomasz Lis is included in: A. Budzyńska-Daca, M. Kosman, 'Political interview or debate – the clash of ethoses from the perspective of rhetorical genre studies' (this volume).

and culture. Still, there are also disadvantages as "researchers run the risk of finding frames they are consciously or unconsciously looking for" (Matthes / Kohring 2008, p. 259). The presented analysis is also exposed to this risk as it concerns a problem not expressed directly in the research material and a topic that did not appear in the analysed conversation as a separate thread.

Lingua nativa

According to the intuitive understanding, *lingua nativa* appears as a certain potential available to all language users: "It is like air: imperceptible, most often used without reflection, but at the same time indispensable for any deeper contact between people, as well as for the inner life and human development" (Grzegorczykowa 2007, p. 12 [translation by the authors]). The repertoire of essential features of natural language includes, first of all:
- conventionality (meanings are based on social usability, and therefore require knowledge of conventions) and interchangeability (alternate code adopted by users interactively);
- phonicity (sequences of sounds produced by the organs of speech) and two-stage (diacritics creating significant sequences);
- bi-class and productivity (lexicon – limited lexical resource, grammar – rules enabling the creation of an infinite number of word combinations, sentences, texts);
- abstractness and remoteness – the ability to talk about phenomena that are absent and yet considered, occurring not only here and now, but distant in time and space;
- polysemicity and creativity (the possibility of creating new names with the use of mental mechanisms based on similarity);
- universality (the ability to talk about everything that a person can think of) and abuse (the ability to use lies);
- self-reflexivity (the possibility of getting informed about oneself, i.e., about the language).

Additionally, it sees the language of everyday experience acquired early in life as 'something natural', the language of the 'world of things', which is highly effective in most everyday situations. In the postmodern instability, it can be a 'lesson in sober realism', drawn from one's own linguistic practice and the interactivity of communication, as even if it is a social construct produced and sustained in cultural practices, it creates a convincing illusion of everyday life.

In the analysed interview, Lis seems to be an advocate for such language. More than once in self-reflexive statements he emphasizes that it is supposed to express the truth about reality. Mere 'speaking' may attest to the truthfulness of things, e.g.,:

TL: Can you confirm or deny, Mr. Chairman?
JK: If I said it then I said it

JK: Is that what you are saying?
TL: Yes, I'm saying so.

TL: I have to take your words seriously.

Therefore – in order to maintain the connection of language with reality – one should speak 'clearly', first in the articulation sense. During the conversation, the interviewer shows his impatience with the sloppiness of his interlocutor's speech, e.g.,:

TL: What did you want to say?… I must have misheard it…
JK: Well, I guess it was very clearly said…
TL: Not very clearly…

Sloppy articulation becomes the source of misunderstanding, for example when the host is not sure what phrase Jarosław Kaczyński uses to address him ('sir' or 'doctor' [Polish words: *doktor* and *redaktor* may sound similar when pronounced sloppily]). Tomasz Lis emphasizes this feature of his adversary's speech, signalling its negative assessment.

Speaking 'clearly' in this conceptualization, however, is primarily of referential significance – 'to the point', precisely, accurately and unambiguously. Lis often criticizes the "insinuating tone" of his interlocutor. He points out that participants in public life are 'responsible for the word' – also when expressing opinions (he himself declares twice: "I don't use adjectives"). He tries to separate the conclusions from the hypotheses or statements cancelling the assertion in the guest's statement, for example when he asks for the use of conditional instead of declarative: "The conditional, Mr. Chairman, the conditional sentence." He often asks him for clarification of the meanings of particular statements and words, for example "What did you want to say …" This provokes the interviewed politician to a meaningful reaction: "You can't speak Polish?" followed by applause from the audience gathered in the TV studio.

Kaczyński's approach to language is different. Both interlocutors seem to be adopting an interpretive framework based on dualism, i.e., the belief that language is the expression of the spirit inherent in the Romantic tradition. Still, Lis clearly adheres to the postulate of 'speech fidelity' in an adequate description of reality, expressed in the well-known quotation all too familiar to Poles from their school education "To give each thing – a proper name" as expressed by Polish Romantic poet Cyprian Kamil Norwid (transl. Mikoś 2002, p. 134). Meanwhile, Jarosław Kaczyński is more concerned with the creative power of language, following the words of another Polish bard from the Romantic period – Juliusz Słowacki: "My point is, may the flexible tongue/ Phrase everything the head will think of" (transl. Mikoś 2002, p. 86).

Subordinating language to 'one's own thoughts', treating it as a tool for shaping reality is revealed in the statements of Kaczyński primarily in the tendency to precede assertions with modalisers that strengthen its truthfulness. It is about frequently repeated phrases expressing (1) belief, (2) repetition, (3) assertion such as:

(1) I am (deeply) convinced that...
(2) as I say...; I repeat once again that...; I have said many times that...
(3) I assure you that... it is for sure that...

As cognitivists note, such formulas create a certain anchoring background, i. e., they establish the perceptual relationship between the subject and the conceptualization object (Langacker 1995, p. 96). A characteristic feature of anchor prediction in the mentioned grammatical-lexical schemas is that the contents that follow cannot be expressed objectively, because the object itself does not exist outside the subject in this perceptual system. Both strong modality, revealing the belief in the truthfulness of one's own statement, and an anchoring prediction, situating all contents within one's own vision – are conceptual structures that serve to naturalize ideology in the discourse (Stecią̇g 2009). At the other extreme, there are deviations from this worldview that will be conceptualized as untruths and fabrications. In the analysed conversation, Kaczyński mentions various examples of deviations from the description of reality he promotes, which are described as follows: "type of irony", "to daydream in the haze of the absurd", "hysteria", "telling fairy tales", because of which "it is impossible to speak". In a nutshell: when there are different visions of reality, no common language can be found.

The conviction of the politician about the creative power of language is also reflected in the introduction into public circulation of expressions that have not existed or been used so far. An example from the analysed media meeting is "diffamation social engineering" – a hermetic, stylized scientific term that replaces the more familiar in contemporary Polish public debates language cluster (conceptual amalgam) with the same meaning: "the industry of contempt". If one were to apply the two-stage qualification procedure in terms of truthfulness to assess this neologism – including firstly the verification of the reference field, secondly, discursive affiliation on a scale from extensional, mimetic to intensional, imaginary discourses – it turns out that from the point of view of 'order' of natural language, the expression seems to be a semantic phantom, i. e., an extensively apparent name (Kiklewicz 2017, p. 77).

Another strategy is answering the interviewer's questions indirectly, which is signalled again with the help of speech verbs, but this time with prohibitive markers, e. g., "you can say that..., let's say... let's agree..." indicating different possibilities of using language in relation to reality. In structures of this type, pragmatic factors prevail over denotation, which determines the relationship between a thing / concept and a name. This gives rise to epistemological tensions known for a long time: in a cognitive situation, each language user is, on the one hand, connected with the object they are talking about, and, on the other hand, with the community within which they speak, and their utterance simultaneously performs a representative and communicative function. The 'truth' about an object, in the sense of all materiality, is thus agreed in communication and 'naturalized' in discourse. It can then be concluded that *lingua nativa* for Kaczyński, is not so much the language of the 'world of things' as of 'an imagined community'.

Lingua materna

The concept of *lingua materna* is – similarly to that of *lingua nativa* – deeply rooted in the community's knowledge of language, and thus serves as an interpretive framework for understanding it in the perspective of common perceptions. The historical source of this conceptualization are the Enlightenment ideals of language and the connection of the concept of the nation with the linguistic community. According to Eric Hobsbawm (1990, p. 37f), tracking the sources of European nationalism, in the nineteenth century a common language in the Herderian meaning of the speech of the nation (Volk) was a significant complement to the notions of nation and state, and even earlier it was one of the basic elements of constructing national cohesion in the three phases of implementation set out by Benedict Anderson in *Imagined Communities* (2006):

1) Language creates a community of communicating elites, becoming a 'pilot project' for the 'nation', or – to use Ernest Gellner's (2006) terminology – transforms 'wild cultures' that arise and recreate spontaneously into more complex 'garden cultures' maintained by qualified personnel in a bureaucratic, written system.
2) Language binds the elite together as a 'permanent' and 'eternal' community factor. The 'uniform language' effect is achieved at this stage mainly due to the popularization of printing and the standardizing role of publishers in creating autonomous literary cultures in national languages.
3) The language of the elite and those in power functions as an official language thanks to its dissemination through public education and state administration. Linguistic nationalism activates the legitimizing power of language,

making it 'an instrument of symbolic power' (Bourdieu 1991). Paradoxically, authoritarian standardization of it in this phase is not conducive to unification, but to hierarchical diversification and, consequently, social tensions.

As a consequence, under the pressure of nationalist ideologies in Europe in the first half of the 20th century, monolingualism became a natural state in the life of the community, linking language with kinship relations in the interpretive framework. *Muttersprache*'s gender-loaded and emotionally-heavy concept is at the centre of a new paradigm where monolingualism is the norm and multilingualism is a threat to individual integrity and community cohesion. In this paradigm, the homogeneity of languages is assumed, the boundaries between them are obvious and insurmountable, based on the lack of the possibility of mutual understanding between users of different ethnolinguistic backgrounds (Gal 2006, p. 14). Each language is also credited with exclusive access to numerous common values:

> What is called 'mother tongue' combines within it a number of ways of relating to and through language, be it familial inheritance, social embeddedness, emotional attachment, personal identification, or linguistic competence (Yildiz 2012, p. 205).

From this perspective, Lis's conversation with Kaczyński seems to be a test of Polishness of some kind. The interrogatively expressed doubt: "You can't speak Polish?" express not only the inability to communicate within different visions of reality, but is also the litmus test of one's belonging to the national community. The interlocutors attempt to outdo each other in respecting the standards of the correctness of the Polish language and discussing the principles of etiquette. However, they do it in an overbearing manner, inconsistent with the rules of linguistic politeness applicable in the Polish community (Marcjanik 2001, p. 31 f). The host in the studio constantly corrects his guest, not only when the latter – intentionally or not – confuses facts, but also when, for example, he pronounces certain words unclearly or incorrectly, for example, the name of Angela Merkel (Kaczyński pronounces it the English way rather than stick to its German pronunciation); while the guest – by imposing on the host what is 'correct and appropriate' in his speech – clearly expresses his opposition to the standards of common Polish language, to which the host refers, for example when Lis asks for the use of an appropriate phrase to refer to the acting Prime Minister, Donald Tusk, i.e., "Mr. Prime Minister":

> JK: And now you will not dictate the way I am to talk about Mr. Tusk.

Linguistic politeness also opens up the issue of intergenerational relations and leaves some space for stereotyping in this regard. This becomes especially apparent when the topic of a politician owning a gun emerges – which is supposed to be the interviewer's turning point. The interviewer resorts to the trick of making the guest read his own statement from years before and catch him telling the untruth. However, the interlocutor cannot see the letters and so the younger interviewer must read it for him. He assumes the servant role as his senior interlocutor cannot read the text without glasses. Additionally, exploiting the contrast between older and younger, Kaczyński ascribes to Lis the stereotypical features of a young person, i. e.,: lack of knowledge (1), lack of mature perception (2), chaotic reasoning (3), lack of courage (4). At the same time, he relies on overbearing speech acts that often occur in hierarchical parent-child or teacher-student communication, but are non-standard (non-normative) in communication among equal partners, e. g.,: pointing out ignorance and reprimanding (1), pointing out the lack of preparedness and assessment (2), admonition (3), pointing out the defect and encouraging improvement (4).

(1) JK: You seem not to know how certain fees are collected, so I'm trying to explain this to you
    TL: Yea...
    JK: Well, these fees are paid by people who earn well from a part of their salary...

(2) JK: You are really completely unprepared for today's broadcast. I'm sorry. I'm really sorry. Really sorry.

(3) TL: Mr. Chairman, you raised taxes... that is, you lowered...
    JK: So which one is it: lowered or raised? Make up your mind. Because you are getting carried away, sir.

(4) JK: You are shy [...] More confidence in yourself, sir.

The communication behaviours of interviewees reveal other attitudes towards the mother tongue. While Lis is characterized by perfectionism, i. e., striving for the ideal, which is precise, correct and clear language, Kaczyński is characterized by a certain disinvolution towards the rules of language use. He expresses this attitude directly in the interview: "I speak as I see fit". This is not a one-off incident, but rather an expression of a more persistent tendency to abuse symbolic power. When, during one of the parliamentary debates, opposition deputies pointed a mispronunciation out to him (saying: 'włanczać' instead of 'włączać'), he replied in a similar fashion: "I will speak as I speak". This would confirm that he puts himself above the standards of the Polish language. At the emotional level, however, one can notice Kaczyński's attachment to his native tongue, which is not revealed *expressis verbis* in the analysed conversation, in some declarations (although they were also uttered by both interlocutors), yet avoiding any foreign-language interjections. This is characteristic of purism, or nationalist purism, based on the belief that the mother tongue needs protection from outside interference in order to remain 'pure' (Markowski 2006, p.126ff). A different attitude to the native language is presented in this regard by Lis, who eagerly refers to the common roots of European culture, for example by quoting Latin sentences in the original (*Pacta sunt servanda*). He also follows the pronunciation rules of foreign languages, not 'Polonising' foreign names and paying attention to their correct articulation (as in the case of the aforementioned name of Angela Merkel). Such linguistic behaviour can be considered as manifestation of selective cosmopolitanism (Yildiz 2012, p. 209).

Lingua fracta

The concept of *lingua fracta* is not as widespread as the previous two. It emerged in the field of research on Media Ecology, which is derived from the Technological Determinism Theory of Marshall McLuhan. The framework of this concept is, however, the well-known conceptualizations considered in this analysis – *lingua nativa* and *lingua franca* (Brooke 2009, p. XIV–XV). The difference between the natural language used in direct interpersonal communication and the media code enabling not only data transmission, but also the organization of cultural content and the exchange of experiences, is considered in environmental terms: "Our mother tongues are like environments in which we immerse ourselves completely. They change our perception. So, if we were to speak Chinese, we would have different senses of hearing, smell and touch" (McLuhan 1995 [1969], p. 245f). Subsequently media are considered 'languages', which – by creating their own communication conventions and new rules of communication – play a decisive role in shaping social bonds, creating complete 'media environments'. The boundary between the 'natural' or immediate linguistic environment and the 'artificial' or indirect media environment is blurred, and these environments remain closely related to each other, with McLuhan reluctantly giving priority to natural language, arguing that the media change human sensitivity and transform the mental structures of perception to such an extent, that their status as a tool of knowing reality is unique. This intersemiotic relationship is rendered in the concept of *lingua fracta* as a fracture (Latin *fractare*) the supremacy of the verbal code in the processes of social communication in favour of multimodal message, which is related to the gradual 'dispersion' of natural language with its veritable reference to reality.

Conversely, from the perspective of Media Ecology *lingua franca* of modernity is not only global English, but also – and perhaps most of all – media technology that weaves people around the world, making it a global village. One of the paradoxes of media transmission based on specific communication conventions is that apart from the community dimension it creates divisions into fractions (from Latin *fractare*):

At the same time that technology connects us to one another in various ways, it also encourages different axes of separation. [...] We may appreciate our 'up-to-the-minute coverage' of events around the world, but these events are still mediated for us, albeit in a fashion that often tropes on immediacy. Listserv discussions may transcend temporal and geographic boundaries, but the cost is often misunderstanding, and sometimes, outright flame wars (Brooke 2009, p. XV).

The conversation between Lis, one of the most famous TV presenters, and Kaczyński, the leader of the right-wing party during the media campaign before the parliamentary elections, takes place in the studio of the publicly accessible TVP2, Polish state television. Its participants recognize the applicable media conventions well, which does not mean that they necessarily comply with them. The program "Tomasz Lis na żywo" [Tomasz Lis live] adheres to the format of a talk show, that is, a television interview with the participation of an audience. The conversation is a concrete realization of the genre as part of a broader public debate. Its content is public affairs: mainly political, but also economic and social issues. The participants of the meeting are representatives of the symbolic elite "[...] exercising direct control over publicly available knowledge, publicly valid beliefs, over the shape and content of public discourse [own translation]" (Czyżewski / Kowalski / Piotrowski 1997, p. 17).

Interview as a media convention follows a specific pattern, which consists of higher and lower level units. The higher-order unit is the interview phases/sequences, the basic unit – adjacent pair/dialogue replica. In this case, the phases are schematic: there is an opening sequence, a phase of presenting themes and sequences that expand them, and a closing phase. The opening and final parts contain courtesy formulas such as greeting and introducing, and closing the conversation and saying goodbye – all in accordance with the norms of public communication and the genre convention. At the level of sub-units, the situation becomes more dynamic.

Asymmetry is typical in an interview – the journalist's task is to ask questions, the role of the guest is to provide answers; the journalist speaks less, and their interlocutor has the right to make longer, digressive or anecdotal statements, as long as the host does not interrupt them. In the analysed TV conversation, however, there is a striving for symmetry. In many sequences, replicas are dynamized, resembling a polemic in which interlocutors have the same rights to express themselves and can force themselves to shift roles, fluctuating between the speaker and the listener. Interestingly, it is not the interviewer, but the interviewed politician who creates the conditions for symmetry, giving the host the opportunity to comment, encouraging expressing opinions. The host, in turn, tries to stick to the convention and rejects the symmetrical system that inevitably leads to conflict, stressing several times that millions of viewers are not interested in his opinion, but in the opinion of the politician – the leader of the largest opposition party that is getting ready to take power in Poland:

> TL: The viewers are not interested in my opinion. It is you who wants to rule Poland. I am asking you the question.

> TL: Mr. Chairman, with all due respect, our viewers – and now we are being watched by a few million people, are certainly not interested in my views. They are interested in your views.

> TL: My opinion does not matter, Mr. Chairman.

Dialogue replicas of a confrontational nature dominate the mid sequences of the interview, but other, not based on a conflict, also coexist. It is worth emphasizing that it is the interviewer who tries to conciliate participation in the conversation. Although in adjacent pairs numerous interruptions can be found, still it is the interviewer stops the questions in favour of his interlocutor. It also allows him to finish when – despite his intervention – the politician does not stop speaking. Kaczyński, on the other hand, consistently puts the interviewer in the role of an opponent – an opponent in the ideological dispute ("your formation", "we simply disagree"). Finally, Lis reacts directly, reminding the politician of the 'language of divisions' / 'fractional' language:

> TL: The election day is still to come, and you are already dividing us. You are getting in the way … You are returning to the old language, Mr. Chairman. Why?

The structure of the television conversation also includes many non-verbal elements influencing the nature and order of interaction as well as its shape. It is primarily about integrating the previous recordings and the applause of the audience, which is rhetorical in the case of an interview, as these elements may weaken or strengthen the message of the interlocutors. The recordings are presented four times as separate audio materials, prepared for broadcast at the time planned by the host. They contain quotes and statements uncomfortable for the visitor, which are then commented on by the interviewed politician. On the other hand, the participation of the audience, even if planned, disrupts the course of the conversation. The applause drowns out the statements, forcing the interviewer to stop and repeat questions. In such situations, Lis repeats the addressing formula many times ("Mr. Chairman"), and then admonishes Kaczyński's followers located in the studio behind his back, to reward him with applause *after* the statements:

> TL: […] not while he's speaking, because then you're making it difficult for Mr. Chairman to speak.
> JK: I can handle it, sir.

Tomasz Lis, directing his speech towards the audience in the studio, gives high rank to that applause which functions as a weapon to fight hegemony in the conversation, inspire to act or take away the confidence of the interlocutors. The viewers in the studio evaluate the accuracy of the responses and the suitability of the joke; they score interlocutors on a regular basis. It is not a random group, but selected in accordance with the *talk show* format requirements – it becomes one of the thematic threads of the interview (which proves that not only natural language has the feature of self-reflexivity). The interviewees argue whether the right number of people was allowed in the studio and how they had been selected:

JK: There is [on the election bill] Mrs. Ilona, whom you did not let in here…
[laughter and applause]
TL: We agreed on 30 people. Pacta sunt servanda, you know…

These unplanned elements confirm that the program is broadcast in real time, i.e., within the 'live' formula that mimics spontaneous direct communication, giving authenticity to the media event (mimetic discourse). The parallel plan shows the veritative value of the content of the conversation. It is worth noting that the next group of reactions by Lis, which determines the specificity of this media meeting, are negative statements. Negating means denying the truthfulness of the judgment expressed by the interlocutor, although this judgment cannot be directly equated with falsehood. The linguistic exponent of negation can be the particle 'no', pronouns 'nobody, nothing, never' or pronouns such as 'none, more than one'. Negation can be strengthened by the appropriate use of the genitive or lexically intensified by adding: almost, nearly, barely, hardly, hard, not at all. These exponents often appear in the conversation, e.g.,:

JK: Reductions, but also reductions in pension contributions, and everyone benefited from it, especially the poor…
TL: No, that's not true.

TL: This is not pointless.

TL: I don't use adjectives, I provide numbers.

Additionally, Lis repeats the same questions over and over again in the course of the interview. In most cases, he does not get specific answers, often the answers are very short and concise in content; he even meets with refusal to be granted an answer:

JK: Don't ask me about it, please.
TL: Why not?
JK: There are rules, you know, […]

JK: I think that this thread is not worth continuing.
TL: Because it is inconvenient for you, right?

TL: The closer to the elections, the less you know about the composition of the government?

JK: The more I know, the less I speak, though...

/Applause/

JK: I suggest that we agree on something we hold different beliefs and I read your periodical and as a result I think it is pointless to consider this issue.

TL: No, Mr. Chairman, this is not pointless.

JK: I'd gladly take a question concerning issues vital to Poland.

Dialogue replicas of this type are the opposite of an open journalistic conversation; rather, they embrace the 'grabbed interview' pattern (Boyd 2001 [1988], p. 108), in which the protagonist does not want to answer the questions asked, disturbs the free course of the conversation, resists the selection of threads, etc. The medium is of great importance here: "The grabbed interview usually works best on camera, where, even if the subject says nothing, he or she can be watched by the audience and his or her reactions noted" (Boyd 2001 [1988], p. 109). The audience of the show can observe the mimic and gestural reactions of the interlocutor who avoids answering the question: narrowing of the eyes, ironic smile, immobilization of the hand, prolonged eye contact ('looking at each other' as a demonstration of strength).

The interviewer tries to stay calm and control the communication standstill, but on the basis of articulation there is a reluctance to talk and to the interlocutor. Lis 'pushes words through his teeth', slowing down the pace of speech while flattening the articulation of sounds as a result of limited mobility of the speech apparatus (especially with vowels requiring a wider opening of the mouth). This is noticed by the interlocutor, who then comments: "And you are looking at me with your face so tense..." For both sides, it is an unpleasant meeting, continued mainly due to the durability of the convention, which seems to be the only brake against breaking contact. At this stage, it is worth adding that it has never been repeated so far – Lis has never again hosting Kaczyński at the studio.

Conclusions

The symptoms of the communication crisis presented in the interview by Tomasz Lis with Jarosław Kaczyński show the disintegration of the idea of natural language in three versions: *lingua nativa, lingua materna* and *lingua fracta*. As it turns out, the language of the 'world of things', the native language and the language spoken in non-mediated interpersonal communication – although they are widespread conceptualizations – may be the field of contact for various ways of understanding language, its functions and meanings. At the points of this contact, numerous tensions arise, resulting in ineffective communication. Interestingly, the gradual disintegration is accompanied by the unwavering involvement of interlocutors in maintaining the continuity of contact. The interlocutors are ready for the interview and focused on achieving the goals: the interviewer has prepared audiovisual materials and numerous notes (questions, statements, arguments), during the interview the guest expresses the judgments proving that the journalist's work is being investigated. Negative attitude towards the interlocutor is associated with negative assessment of the way he uses the language, and yet both sides make an effort to listen to each other and even decode non-verbal signals. Thus, in the case of communication standstill, we are also dealing with active listening, the signals of which are changes in facial expressions, nodding, eye contact, paraphrasing the interlocutor's words – these are irrefutable evidence of involvement in the conversation. The host and the guest want to take responsibility for the substantive scope of the interview, direct its course, manage the dispute, and thus strive in their unique style to maintain the continuity of the conversation.

However, the disintegration progresses: the interlocutors want to maintain contact, but are unable to integrate the language in the meaning of 'languaging as practice' (Love 2017, p. 115). Additionally, when communication crisis situations arise, each participant exposes their own experiences related to words and meanings, and therefore each uses the language differently. Despite belonging to a specific language community (e. g., *lingua materna*), differences related to, for example, the ideological context create problems with the acceptance of the interlocutor's language:

> Although the language we use may be understandable to others within a particular language community, it may be incomprehensible to those outside – and those people may interpret our language in ways other than we intend (Morreale / Spitzberg / Barge 2007, p. 98).

Then, there are techniques such as commanding, warning, moralizing, suggesting only the right solutions, instructing, judging, showing compassion, distracting attention from the problem, changing the subject, etc., which contribute to the 'language of non-acceptance' (Gordon 2003, p. 54f). It is one of the products of the breakdown of natural language in public debate.

Although the purpose of the presented analysis was to trace the symptoms of the communication crisis in the public debate in Poland, its conclusions are also of a methodological dimension. Considering the common conceptualizations of natural language in the interpretive framework apparatus, the triangulation of research approaches was applied – each of the frames allowing to illuminate the natural language in common perceptions from a different angle: mutual relations with material and social reality, legitimizing the power of common ideas, conventions regulating linguistic behaviour in direct interaction and in the media environment. In this way, it was possible to reconstruct the idea of natural language updated in the analysed media meeting in a more in-depth way and taking into account the contextual nature of meanings.

It is also worth emphasizing that each framework, i. e., *lingua nativa, lingua receptiva, lingua fracta*, refers to different values and belief systems about language. Just as it is difficult to fully define the meaning of a simple concept of 'breakfast' without reference to the cultural order of the day regulating the appropriate times of meals, it will be impossible to grasp the semiotic richness of the concept of natural language without reference to the literary tradition – especially the era of Romanticism, in which the relation of language to reality was questioned, placing the 'world of spirit' in the foreground. Just as it is difficult to understand the idea of 'weekend' without knowing the seven-day cycle of the week and the order of the five-day working week and two days of rest established in social practice, it is difficult to understand the idea of the mother tongue without reference to the nation as an ethnic community and monolingualism as something natural in social life (as in the slogan: 'You only have one mother'). Just as the ontological status of a verbal contract ('oral agreement') requires placing legal discourse in a broader background, explaining why two people who do not want to talk to each other are engaged in an hourly discussion in front of the cameras can be found in the convention of journalistic interviewing and principles of public communication in general.

Additionally, the innovative path (Koller 1999) was adopted in the search for what is unspoken and assumed in the communication between the participants of the analysed conversation. The point was not only to juxtapose the conceptualizations of language referred to by the interlocutors, but also to reveal the 'framework conflict' (Fillmore 1982, p. 127), which results from adopting different notions about the essence of language. As the analysis proved, the unspoken 'idioms' framing the asymmetric pragmatically and discursively disproportional conversation between Lis and Kaczyński are three colloquial expressions that refer in various ways to the situation of speaking: (1) find a common ground with someone [In Polish we find a common 'tongue'], (2) pure language, (3) drawl something through one's teeth. The idiomatic expression to find a common ground means, as defined in the Oxford Dictionary (in electronic version): shared interests, beliefs, or opinions between two people or groups of people who disagree about most other subjects. When the visions of reality are completely different, there is no language serving as a common ground. On the other hand, the belief that the language should be 'pure' controls not only the selection of native lexis, but also presupposes the anchoring of public debate in one national culture (Abizadeh 2002). Going beyond it carries the risk of exclusion. Then, 'drawling through the teeth' suggests anger, aversion, irritation –

all the negative emotions that accompany unwanted contacts in interpersonal communication. As the analysis at a deeper level of interpretation suggests, the symptoms of the communication crisis are revealed not so much in the struggle for words or arguments in a specific worldview discussion, but in various projections or interpretive frames of the language behind them.

References

Albury, N.: 'Introducing the folk linguistics of Language Policy', in: INTERNATIONAL JOURNAL OF LANGUAGE STUDIES 2014/8, p. 85–106.

Anderson, Benedict: Imagined Communities. Reflections on the Origin and Spread of Nationalism. London-New York 2006.

Bourdieu, Pierre: Language and Symbolic Power. Cambridge 1991.

Boyd, Andrew: Broadcast Journalism. Techniques of Radio and Television News. Oxford 2001 [1988].

Brooke, Collin: Lingua Fracta. Towards a Rhetoric of New Media. New Jersey 2009.

Czyżewski, Marek / Kowalski, Sergiusz / Piotrowski, Andrzej: Rytualny chaos. Studium dyskursu publicznego. Kraków 1997.

Fillmore, Ch.J.: 'Frames and the semantics of understanding', in: QUADERNI DI SEMANTICA 1985/6, p. 222–254.

Gal, Susan: 'Migration, minorities and multilingualism: language ideologies in Europe', in: Mar-Molinero, Clare / Stevenson, Patrick (eds.): *Language Ideologies, Policies and Practices. Language and the Future of Europe.* London 2006, p. 13–29.

Gellner, Ernest: Nations and Nationalism. London 2006.

Gordon, Thomas / Burch, Noel: Teacher Effectiveness Training: The Program Proven to Help Teachers Bring Out the Best in Students of All Ages. New York 2003.

Grzegorczykowa, Renata: Wstęp do językoznawstwa. Warszawa 2007.

Heinz, Adam: Dzieje językoznawstwa w zarysie. Warszawa 1978.

Hobsbawm, Eric J.: Nations and Nationalism since 1780: Program, Myth, Reality. Cambridge 1990.

Kiklewicz, Aleksander: Znaczenie a prawda. Fantomy semantyczne. Olsztyn 2017.

Koller, H.-Ch.: 'Lesarten. Über das Geltendmachen von Differenzen im Forschungsprozeß', in: ZEITSCHRIFT FÜR ERZIEHUNGSWISSENSCHAFT 1999/2, p. 195–209.

Langacker, Ronald: Wykłady z gramatyki kognitywnej. Translation and edition: Kardela, Henryk. Lublin 1995.

Love, N.: 'On languaging and languages', in: LANGUAGE SCIENCES 2017/61, p. 113–147.

Marcjanik, Małgorzata: W kręgu grzeczności. Wybór prac zza zakresu polskiej etykiety językowej. Kielce 2001.

Markowski, Andrzej: Kultura języka polskiego. Teoria. Zagadnienia leksykalne. Warszawa 2006.

Matthes, J. / Kohring, M.: 'The content analysis of media frames: Toward improving reliability and validity', in: JOURNAL OF COMMUNICATION 2008/58, p. 258–279.

McLuhan, Marshall: 'Playboy interview: A candid conversation with the high priest of popcult and metaphysician of media,' March 1969. Reprinted in: McLuhan, Eric / Zingrone, Frank (eds.): *Essential McLuhan*. New York. 1995, p. 233–269.

Mikoś J.M. (ed.): Polish Romantic Literature: An Anthology. Bloomington 2002. [J. Słowacki, 'Beniowski': excerpts, p. 85–88; C.K. Norwid, 'Generalities', p. 134].

Morreale, Sherwyn P. / Spitzberg, Brian H. / Barge, Kevin J.: Human Communication: Motivation, Knowledge and Skills. Wadsworth 2007.

Nowicka-Franczak, M. / Kumięga, Ł.: 'Analiza dyskursu a prawda o dyskursie', in: PRZEGLĄD SOCJOLOGII JAKOŚCIOWEJ 2020/16, p. 6–17.

Partee, M.H.: 'Plato's theory of language', in: FOUNDATIONS OF LANGUAGE 1972/8, p. 113–132.

Schiffman, Harold: 'Language policy and linguistic culture', in: Ricento, Thomas (ed.): *An Introduction to Language Policy: Theory and Method*. Malden 2006, p. 111–125.

Steciąg, M.: 'Od lingua nativa do lingua fracta: kulturowe wymiary dyskursu w analizie lingwistycznej', in: TEKST I DYSKURS – TEXT UND DYSKURS 2019/2, p. 49–63.

Steciąg, M.: 'Struktury konceptualne w różnych politycznych orientacjach dyskursywnych (na przykładzie exposés premierów)', in: OBLICZA KOMUNIKACJI 2009/2, p. 109–117.

Wąsik, Elżbieta: Język – narzędzie czy właściwość człowieka? Założenia gramatyki ekologicznej lingwistycznych związków międzyludzkich. Poznań 2007.

Yildiz, Yasemin: Beyond the Mother Tongue: The Postmonolingual Condition. New York 2012.

Łukasz Kumięga / Przemysław Gębal

From autonomy to inclusion. Discourse studies and constructivist teaching of Polish as a second language in the 'pretext' of Tomasz Lis' interview with Jarosław Kaczyński

Abstract

The following article transfers Tomasz Lis' interview with Jarosław Kaczyński into the area of reflection on teaching and learning Polish as a foreign language in Poland, in the context of migration. It does so by referring to cognitive constructivism and its implications for language didactics (concerning, among others, the processes of construction, reconstruction and deconstruction), while thematizing the autonomy and agency of learners and moving away from the instructional role of teachers. At the methodological level, it employs the tools of action didactics and expands them to include the analytical categories of discourse studies. By defining intercultural competence and extending this optic to include transcultural topics, and with reference to the concept of education for democracy, it indicates avenues for the use of interviews in the linguistic training of migrants, taking into account the social, political and cultural context of the host country. In addition, the text may be treated as a contribution to the discussion of systemic solutions for the education of migrants in a subjective-inclusive spirit, as well as a contribution to the methodological discussion of the relationship of discourse research with constructivist intercultural and transcultural didactics.

Keywords: constructivism, foreign and second language didactics, discourse research, intercultural education, education for democracy, interdisciplinarity

Preface: where did the idea for this text come from?

Contemporary language education against a background of migration invites undertaking a range of pedagogical activities and didactic interactions aimed at developing linguistic, but also non-linguistic competences. They should be perceived as a space in which participants are prepared to engage in a variety of linguistic activities while at the same time supporting the development of their

Łukasz Kumięga, University of Gdańsk (Poland), ORCID: 0000-0002-8034-3593, Lukasz.Ku miega@ug.edu.pl.

Przemysław Gębal, University of Gdańsk (Poland), ORCID: 0000-0002-4335-5886, Przemyslaw. Gebal@ug.edu.pl.

psycho-social competences to facilitate progressive acculturation processes. As this type of education should primarily aim pedagogically to prepare the participants for their social inclusion and integration into their new cultural environment, the content implemented during language classes needs to incorporate a range of issues covering every-day, social and political life. In line with the concept of social teaching and education for democracy, these consist of aspects related to the development of civil society, and ought to be implemented in the classroom in a concrete action dimension. This involves incorporating open forms of learning and teaching in the form of projects of a socio-cultural character. Their implementation ensures personal experience of cooperation with other participants initiated in the spirit of equality, as well as the formation of autonomous attitudes, preparing learners for the conscious assumption of responsibility for the cooperation undertaken and its tangible results. All this is carried out in order for the participants to consciously shape their own linguistic and cultural development in the new educational environment and to understand the social and cultural conditions of the new living space, recognize it and try to find the best possible place for their existence in it. The above-mentioned assumptions should also constitute a fundamental point of reference for programs teaching Polish as a second language to people with migration experience, in which the hierarchy of didactic objectives is arranged in the reverse order to previous glottodidactic approaches. Essentially, contemporary language courses aim at the development of cultural and psychosocial competences, ranking linguistic skills further down, treated as a kind of means of achieving superior competences of a transversal nature.

Domain-related contexts of Tomasz Lis interview with Jarosław Kaczyński

When we consider in terms of cognitive and methodological scope the academic contexts into which Tomasz Lis interview with Jarosław Kaczyński can be written, what imposes itself first are, among others, the fields related to linguistics, sociology, political science or media studies. Pedagogy would be a less obvious association, although, on the one hand, one might pose questions related to the presence of the discourse on education in the said interview, or, on the other hand, examine the role of educational activities (understood somewhat ironically in the context of the interview itself, as well as outside of it) within the sphere of media pedagogy. One could also look for perspectives contained within or intersecting various domain encounters (in line with the popular approach referred to as interdisciplinary), such as, for example, conversation analysis or (critical) discourse analysis. The following text will follow a completely different path, emphasizing the didactic perspective which, after all, refers to a certain extent to pedagogical viewpoints, but situating it within the currently relevant context related to the teaching and learning of Polish as a second language, i.e. in the context of migration. Lis interview with Kaczyński is thus didactically inscribed in the process of teaching our language to foreigners in Poland, i.e. in the implementation of language classes in an endolingual and endocultural environment in which the understanding of socio-political circumstances is one of the key elements accompanying the progressive acculturation processes. The other added value of the presented considerations will be embedding them in the current of modern didactic concepts related to constructivism, intercultural and transcultural optics, and education for democracy. The text will be complemented by a critical look at the apparently experienced reality in the field of migrant education, that is, that of German as a second language, which is oriented in its integrational dimension (because not in the inclusional one) on the transfer and evaluation of the acquired factual knowledge as a measurable determinant of the degree of integration of migrants in Germany. It is precisely with reference to this limiting context that Lis' interview with Kaczyński will serve as one of the numerous albeit specific examples of understanding migrant education in the spirit of supporting their own construction of knowledge about the world, related to autonomy and agency. This context also unambiguously indicates the connections of this kind of didactic, migration and inclusion-related optics and this kind of social problem with discourse research. The methodological question about the construction of productive interdependence of these two perspectives will be the subject of further considerations which will indicate the possibility of complementing and expanding the study of discourse with reflections of didactic and inclusionary nature.

Discourse constructivism vs. educational and didactic constructivism

Indeed, the volume in which we publish the following text explicitly concerns discourse optics (because, to be terminologically precise, it refers to discourse theory), which only seemingly has little to do with foreign or second language didactics, for the common denominator of both approaches is constructivism.

Broadly defined, discourse studies (some attempts to classify this heterogeneous field can be found in Czyżewski 2013, Kumięga / Nowicka 2012 or Kopytowska / Kumięga 2017) treat reality as a construct produced in the process of negotiating meanings through communicative practices and, in their most radical iterations, attribute totality to discourse, meaning that everything non-discursive is unreal. And although the study of discourse derives from linguistics it is primarily the constructivist inspirations that become apparent even at a first glance. The opening of linguistics to such currents has led to a redefinition of language and even a transformation of its concept, moving away from the colloquially (although not only) invoked instrumentality of language to its agency in constructing the social reality[1]. Discourse studies themselves, therefore, have a primarily semantic dimension, as they reconstruct and unmask the mechanisms of negotiation and domination of meanings. The adoption of this perspective is not limited to linguistics and, importantly, has also triggered a whole range of meta-scientific debates. The thesis that there is no objective reality, i. e. that it is intersubjective (produced through the meanings and beliefs shared by the subjects), has opened the way to a new view of reality constructed within the framework of scientific discourse. To summarize (for the purposes of this text): discourse research based on constructivism has led to at least three changes: a shift in thinking about (1) the mechanisms that construct social reality; (2) language and its active participation in this process; and (3) the status of scientific knowledge that is part of the relativist trend.

Taking a further step to reflect on the reception of constructivism within the framework of educational research in its broadest sense, which focuses on educational constructivism (Klus-Stańska 2020), it is impossible not to draw attention to its ambiguity. This ambiguity is due to at least two reasons. First, it is oncontextualized, and often re- or even decontextualized for the purposes of different disciplinary or empirical areas. Second, it concerns the extent of its reception, i.e., the question of on what stretch of the constructivist road individual researchers stop to proceed or, in the most radical variety, do not do so at all. Hence all the resulting ambiguities, as well as tensions in the perception of constructivism as a thought figure within individual attempts to incorporate it into scientific reflection.

Just as in the framework of discourse optics, also in education, those researchers who lean towards constructivism take the position that it has led to a transformation at least in cognitive and ontological terms. Klus-Stańska (2020, p. 8) writes in this context about "a revolutionary change in the understanding of the phenomena played out in the classroom, in school programs and educational outcomes" Żylińska (2009, p. 10–12), on the basis of the reflections of Reich (2006), identified the main determinants of "constructivist/postmodern didac-

---

1 Czachur (2020) mentions five paradigms that have fundamentally influenced the modeling of language within linguistics. These include the pragmalinguistic, cognitivist, constructivist, cultural and communicological paradigms.

tics", that is, the perspective relevant to our text[2] . Their multiplicity can be grouped around the following themes:

- Contextuality, i. e., taking into account changes related to postmodernism and the knowledge society in the didactic process, and responding to current social contexts within the educational process (open curricula and open ways of planning classes);
- Variability in the applied models, methods and techniques of education;
- Learners as autonomous individuals, critical of the reality around them, expressing and realizing their educational needs, making strategic choices;
- Teachers as autonomous individuals, open to learners (their interests and ideas in relation to the activities being implemented during classes);
- Symmetrical relations between learners and teachers, striving to reduce the dependence of learners on teachers, as well as to facilitate cooperation between them and belief in the influence of emotions on the educational process;
- Diversity regarding the teaching materials used, de-textbooking, de-conceptualization of classes, dominance of open communication, interplay of symbolic and imagination-related elements, problem orientation of the teaching process.

The optimism resulting from, among other things, attempts to define educational and didactic areas through the prism of constructivism is tempered by numerous critical voices (especially those coming from objectivist currents, cf. e. g. Pondiscio 2021) and, much more importantly, a certain disjunction between the theoretical constructivism and the educational theory derived from it on the one hand, and the didactic reality on the other. Thus, the openness of a certain group of teachers or even researchers to constructivist "innovations" often collides with difficult attempts to implement them in the teaching process itself (cf. Gołębniak 2014 and a critical analysis of Dernowska's work 2008 in Klus-Stańska 2020, p. 14f). In conclusion: systemic (top-down educational strategies) and cognitive (didactic behaviorism) constraints will dilute the potential of constructivism and, at the same time, invite reflexive attempts to translate its difficulty into concrete didactic actions.

This brief reconstruction of the key elements of discourse constructivism, educational constructivism and didactic constructivism invites domain-oriented and methodological considerations that are the subject of this volume. Thus, it encourages reflection on the connections between discourse research and didactics. These connections (for the purposes of this text and for the purpose of

---

2 For the sake of terminological order, it is worth distinguishing between educational constructivism as a broad cognitive perspective in education and didactic constructivism referring to solutions of a didactic nature, which also has methodological implications.

facing its main research and didactic problem, formulated as proposing an offer of subjective and inclusive migrant education) refer us to at least three levels of (inter)disciplinary and methodological reflection. They will be: the meta-scientific level, the contextual level, and, to name it in a terminologically neutral manner, the interdisciplinary level. Thus, the constructivism invoked at the beginning of our text, should be regarded as a perspective that coheres the discursive and didactic encounter, which, at the meta-scientific level, has led to the transformation of concepts in the specific domain areas. For example, it is present in the aforementioned linguistics and, further, in the interdisciplinary studies of discourse derived from it – with regard to the concept of language, or in didactics, redefining, for example, teachers as 'those who teach' or students as 'those who learn' within the processual stream. Constructivism should be treated as a paradigm that specifies in a meta-scientific manner the perception of science and objects of its study. On the second – or contextual – level, we treat Lis' interview with Kaczyński as a "pretext" (cf. Nowicka / Kumięga in this volume: p. 21–22) for reflection not only methodological, but also problem-centric, i.e. the one related to the question of the visions of social, political and cultural education of migrants, moving away from the transmission-oriented and factual methodology. Finally, at the interdisciplinary level, we will view the discourse and didactic encounter (according to the interdisciplinarity models of van Leeuwen [2005] cited in the introduction to this volume) in an integrative variant. Neither the discourse research nor the constructivist didactics can independently solve the research and didactic problem formulated in this text. The methodology of discourse research (cf. Kopytowska / Kumięga 2017) might uncover the mechanisms of constructing socio-political reality within the framework of Lis' interview with Kaczyński and serve as one of the methodological tools (from the perspective of the didactics of discourse research), but it is unable to design tools for subject-inclusive education. Conversely, constructivist didactics and the methodology based on it will not reach the deep and hidden structures and elements of the interview in question without the tools of discourse research.

Relating further methodological reflections to the challenges formulated by Koller (1999) (cf. the introduction to this volume) and with reference to the addition of intercultural and transcultural dimensions to constructivist didactics (cf. the fourth chapter of this text), another perspective opens up. On the one hand, it will be related to the "maximization of interpretation" (Koller 1999) in the didactic process itself, since the action- and project-based methodology offered to migrants in the context of using Lis' interview with Kaczyński as the didactic material overseen by a reflective and open-minded teacher and in the context of their diverse experiences in constructing socio-political reality does not favor a one-sided and Polish-centric interpretation of the interview. In the dimension of "dispute understood as contradiction" (ibid.), working with that interview also has the potential of a didactic nature for the realization of a specific variant: not scientific, but inter- and transcultural; not only "skeptical", but also "innovative". It may consist in the search – here within the framework of the inter- and transcultural outlook – for an "idiom" to define the unspoken; that is, what from the analytical perspective, but also, as we can see, from the didactic perspective, appears most cognitively opening.

Cognitive and discourse constructivism and its implications for didactics and methodology (of second languages)

Since the core of the constructivist approach in the educational context is the reflection on knowledge arising in the mind of learners[3], we will focus in this part of the text on this thread and derive implications of an identity-related nature (i. e., concerning the definition of learners and teachers and the relationship between them), methodological nature (referring to action didactics of foreign and second languages, and discourse studies) and implications of an empirical nature in relation to Lis' interview with Kaczyński.

From a didactic point of view referring to cognitive constructivism, the essence of the learning process consists in not only the acquisition of knowledge and the development of relevant skills and competencies, but first and foremost in the reinforcement of learners' personalities. Constructivist teaching offers them an educational environment conducive to discovery, independent construction, survival and reflection, including the reflection of a critical nature. It forms a move away from transmissive forms of teaching in favor of open-ended, task-based, project-based and action-oriented activities. It is the orientation of teaching activities not only towards the content of education, but first and foremost on the relationship between the various participants in the teaching process; importantly, not only between learners themselves, but also between learners and teachers. This is due to the redefinition of teachers, who in this trend do not control the learning process, but accompany it. Thus, this furthers the primacy of interaction and pedagogical mediation over the traditional monologic communication in the relationship between teachers and learners. The quality of the relations prevailing in the unique community of learners constitutes one of the factors determining not only the assimilation of new educational content, but, above all, the development of psychosocial competence.

---

3 Bunge (2001) distinguishes ontological constructivism, which assumes that the cognizer creates the world by questioning the reliability of knowledge from cognitive constructivism interested in the human mind and the individual constructs created within it.

According to the concept of the German didactician Kersten Reich, learning and teaching in the constructivist movement consists of three phases of the critically oriented cognitive process: construction, reconstruction and deconstruction (Reich 2010). Here again the didactic perspective and the discourse perspective become mutually consistent, since the listed elements of the cognitive process in constructivist didactics correspond to the operations of an analytical nature within the framework of discourse studies.

Thus, in the process of construction, learners become inventors of sorts and creators of their own world. Construction denotes creating knowledge from scratch. The learning process at this stage is accompanied by experiencing, discovering, trying and experimenting. It takes place with the use of techniques that support autonomous linguistic action, ensuring the development of all linguistic skills including reception, production, interaction and both oral and written mediation. Reconstruction is the rediscovery of given knowledge, its further testing and experiencing. What is more important in constructivist didactics than its acquisition is the process of discovery itself and the lessons it provides for the learners themselves and the development of their self-awareness, in our context: of linguistic, social, political and cultural awareness. The last level of constructivist teaching marks the process of deconstruction, that is, the examination, disclosure and rejection of previous knowledge. This is the time for self-evaluation of acquired skills and reflection on one's own learning process, which is supposed to protect against uncritical worship of one's discoveries, further becoming one of the main determinants of modern critically oriented didactics (cf. Kumięga 2020). Deconstruction is a time for learners to form a critical attitude towards their previous constructions. It is also an encouragement to examine one's actions from different perspectives. It denotes seeing oneself and one's linguistic prowess in a group, becoming aware of the learning strategies, attitudes, values and accompanying emotions adopted and used. These translate directly into the formation of openness and good relations in the group, which facilitates and supports a critical view of one's own and other learners' achievements and the perception of learning as an endless process of working on one's own development and its impact on the development processes of others.

Relating these considerations to the context of interest in this text related to Lis' interview with Kaczyński, the interview should be defined – from the perspective of constructivist didactics – as a teaching material by way of which learners gain the opportunity to construct their own knowledge of socio-political-cultural reality in Poland. This perspective will be supported by the tools of action-oriented didactics of foreign and second languages (about which more later in this text), such as project work, task-based method or other creative and open forms of learning and teaching. The teacher, in turn, will act as a facilitator of the entire knowledge construction process, stepping in only when necessary for substantive and politically or culturally sensitive reasons. Following Reich (2010), construction will involve, in the context of teaching and learning Polish as a second language with the use of the interview in question, pointing out those elements that are foreign to migrants and attempting to interpret them in accordance with their experience. Reconstruction is the moment of discovering those elements of the interview that come from the culture – for example, political culture – of the country of origin, and transferring them to contexts that are relevant today (for Poland, Europe and the World), including those located outside of Lis' interview with Kaczyński itself. It also means comparing this interview with other contemporary political interviews, designing our own interviews, and consequently strengthening political and social awareness in the spirit of civic education. Finally, deconstruction is a time for critical reflection on social and political reality, constructed on the basis of the interview, and a time for allowing multiple perspectives, including those that compete with or exclude each other, thus encouraging learners to reflect in more depth.

The spectrum of possible ways to didacticize Lis' interview with Kaczyński – those formulated above, based on the phases of the cognitive process (ibid.) and in accordance with the didactic-discourse encounter postulated in this text – might be supplemented with analytical categories from the field of discourse studies (cf. Kopytowska / Kumięga 2017) to deepen its cognitive and analytical potential, such as: the category of Self and Stranger/Us and Them, the analysis of inconsistency and internal contradiction of the interview elements, the interdiscursive analysis or, more broadly, recontextualization, discursive strategies, such as denotation and naming, predicating, argumentation, perspectivization or discursive representation, amplification and toning, or the strategy of intended ambiguity.

The didactic project sketched in this way, dedicated to migrants in the context of teaching and learning Polish as a second language, shows that educational goals can become identical with social goals, which is one of the basic determinants of modern didactics of foreign and second languages, and which gives particular importance to the introduction of open forms of teaching and didactic materials into the didactic process, especially those that are not obvious, such as the interview in question.

Thus, the constructivist approach in language didactics will be a certain theoretical basis of a primarily cognitive nature (here in relation to the process of learning and teaching), which is further encapsulated by methodological reflection implemented under the banner of action didactics, which, incidentally, also draws on sociological theories of action. It focuses on the development of interaction skills, shaped through the personal involvement of learners in the implementation of specific tasks, the result of which is each time a specific product of communicative activities, presented and, importantly, evaluated on the forum of the whole group. Like the traditional communicative approach, action didactics proclaims the primacy of the spoken language over the written one, thus becoming a part of social (including professional) expectations, with social interaction, cooperation and collaboration playing an increasingly important role and contributing to the development of key social competencies.

The aim of classes in the action approach is to develop action competence, understood as the learner's ability and readiness to act independently, responsibly, expertly and professionally, which is a dynamic and lifelong process. Increasingly important in the context of the action approach is the process of acquiring knowledge and skills, in particular, as related to the results that spring from it. This belief stems from the assumption that procedural knowledge is becoming of greater value within modern education in comparison with declarative knowledge. Increasingly more attention is being paid to the process of transforming acquired knowledge into skills and competencies. Process-oriented didactics focuses on development, and development is understood as a continuous change that enhances the creation of new opportunities. Experiencing "novelty" not only broadens horizons, but also fosters an attitude of openness to new perspectives and trends and the ability to undertake various tasks. Learners should, therefore, be provided with an opportunity to set and realize goals for their own development. In the development described above, a specific support may be formed by the introduction of socio-political content into the content of the teaching materials used in the classroom, such as, for example, Lis' interview with Kaczyński, which is the basis of our considerations, and the pedagogical impact of which will consist in encouraging the implementation of tasks and reflection on not only linguistic, but also civic reflection. The two-voiced nature of the interview in question might encourage self-reflection; through redefining and updating the perspectives contained in it and expanding them based on the current socio-political context[4].

Intercultural teaching with education for democracy

On a theoretical level, the following text is complemented by turning to concepts related to intercultural teaching and education for democracy. Intercultural teaching in language classes has been, and still is, an essential concept for pedagogically developing in the learners an openness to the cultural and social diversity of Europe and the world. The product of intercultural teaching has become the

---

4 Naturally, the development of this type of competence does not exclude the teaching of elements of the language subsystems, which in the action approach greatly affects the way grammar, vocabulary and correct pronunciation are taught. The introduction of new linguistic constructions in classes each time refers to specific social linguistic activities that impose a progression of grammatical, lexical and phonetic material.

formation of intercultural competence, understood as one of the elements conditioning the effectiveness of the process of communication with representatives of different cultural realities. One of the first Polish definitions of this competence, introduced into academic circulation by Zawadzka (2000), describes it as:

> a complex of analytical and strategic skills in the relations with representatives of other nationalities. Through knowledge of other cultures and culturally conditioned forms of behavior, by analyzing them without prejudice, intercultural competence enables sensitization towards culturally conditioned otherness, as well as changing the existing attitudes, and thus broadens the possibilities for interpretation and action of a given individual (ibid., p. 451).

Intercultural competence is closely related to linguistic competence and communicative competence. Wilczyńska, Mackiewicz and Krajka (2019) state that they form the linguistic-communicative-cultural competence of individuals. According to definitions derived from the fields of language and communication, linguistic competence includes norms and formal rules governing the functioning of autonomous systems of the languages in question. Communicative competence, on the other hand, concerns social norms and rules that control the use of language in specific communicative situations. Since culture plays an important role in communication (the reverse relationship also functions), the resulting interdependence between the two is made apparent in the mental-intellectual activity of individuals, acting in a social context on the basis of their resources and competencies. The common axis of all the components of such expanded competence is:

> their orientation towards socially constituted symbolic meanings, expressing more or less directly the values relevant to a given community. Meanings are not exhausted only in language, only in communicative action or only in culture (…). This important property of competence as a collective regulator of our communicative actions is linked to the rest of our psycho-intellectual resources, which is vividly revealed both in the acquisition of L1 and subsequent L2, and in specific acts of linguistic communication (ibid., p. 371)[5].

The above reconstruction showed the passage from strictly linguistic, to communicative approaches, to strictly discourse-oriented approaches, i.e. those related to the main elements of discourse research, albeit strongly immersed in language. Seeking to operationalize these paths – for the purposes of didacticizing Lis' interview with Kaczyński – it is worth examining Byram's (1997) concept of intercultural communicative competence, which is particularly in-

---

5 Other Polish definitions of intercultural competence note the close relationship between language and culture in the didactic process and emphasize the importance of one's own culture as a reference point for the concept described (Miodunka 2004, Torenc 2007, Gębal 2010, 2018 and 2019).

teresting because of its integrative cognitive nature. Emerging from linguistics, it also includes a pedagogical and didactic-methodical dimension. The linguistic field of intercultural communicative competence, as defined by Byram, consists of three sub-competencies: linguistic, sociolinguistic and discursive (cf. the CEFR concept of linguistic communicative competence). On the pedagogical level, this definition differentiates between five goals of teaching activity, which include: transmission of cultural knowledge, ability to discover the unknown and interact with it, critical cultural awareness and political education, as well as ability to interpret and establish interrelationships. All of the aforementioned goals shape learners' attitudes, which, in terms of competence, should lead to openness to cultural difference and curiosity about diversity. Byram's concept also locates intercultural learning, placing it in a traditional didactic context within the framework of research and field exercises, and based on self-directed learning.

Referring to Byram's vision, a number of specific concepts of intercultural competence have been formulated. These include the popular conceptualization of definitions of intercultural sub-competencies by Erll and Gymnich (2013). It consists of cognitive competence, affective competence and pragmatic-communicative competence (Erll / Gymnich 2013, p. 11–14) (see Table 1).

Table 1. Intercultural sub-competencies according to A. Erll and M. Gymnich (2013)

INTERCULTURAL COMPETENCE		
Cognitive competence (knowledge of)	Affective competence (attitudes and mindsets)	Pragmatic-communicative competence (know-how, self-activity)
1. Knowledge of other cultures (knowledge of the cultural peculiarities of other countries). 2. General, theoretical knowledge of culture (knowledge of the ways in which cultures function, the existence of cultural differences and their impact on communication processes taking place in intercultural contexts). 3. Self-reflection (analysis of one's own ways of perceiving reality, one's own attitudes, modes of behavior and communication patterns).	1. Interest in and openness to other cultures. 2. Empathy (ability to empathize with behaviors and attitudes that differ from our own). 3. Ability to understand what is foreign/different from our own. 4. The ability to deal with contradictions/ differences between our own system of values and norms and those characteristic of our communication partners' cultures.	1. Using communication patterns appropriate to the situation. 2. Using effective conflict resolution strategies.

A detailed presentation of the partial scopes of intercultural communicative competence highlights the broad spectrum of skills whose development requires various teaching activities undertaken by language teachers.

Looking at the structure of Lis' interview with Kaczyński, it is not difficult to observe that it invites the above-mentioned goals of intercultural teaching, here in the context of Polish as a second language. This applies first of all (abstracting from the purely linguistic and factual level of the interview) to the symbolic meanings and values addressed by the intercultural perspective, which, it is worth noting at this point in particular, demonstrate the relationship of intercultural and didactic optics with discourse perspective, preliminarily operationalizing the didactization of discourse analysis (cf. Czachur / Kulczyńska / Kumięga 2014)[6]. More broadly, this will include strategies that can be embedded on two levels: on the one hand, reading and interpreting the strategies used in the interview itself, and on the other hand, transferring them also to the learners' communicative and discursive practice in relation to the surrounding socio-political reality, i.e. the host country. Finally, the biculturality of the interview actualized within the framework of different contexts, which is inscribed in the ever-present political disputes with a reach beyond the reality of Poland enables, from the perspective of learners of Polish as a second language, the discovery of what is different. It also opens up the search, in a reflective spirit, for contradictions and, in a mediating spirit, for (strategic) connections between the aforementioned biculturality and the interview itself and/or the reality beyond the interview. The levels designated within the framework of this reflection comprise: 1. linguistic-factual, 2. axiological, and 3. strategic-intercultural. They correspond to intercultural sub-competencies according to Erll and Gymnich (2013) when it comes to 1. "knowledge about", 2. "attitudes and attitudes", 3. "knowledge how".

In the context of the last level immersed in the intercultural perspective, it is impossible not to extend it to include the transcultural perspective (regarding teaching Polish as a foreign language, cf. e.g. Nawracka 2020), which is also implicitly revealed by Lis' interview with Kaczyński itself. Welsch (1998) distinguishes three perspectives on cultural processes in the modern world, i.e., the multicultural, intercultural and transcultural perspectives. The first two can be characterized, in this sense, as enclosing, in that they view cultures in the separatist trend as homogeneous and are thus inadequate in the face of modernity, characterized by the crossing of cultural boundaries due to progressive migration processes, the influence of communication systems and dependencies, and subordinations of an economic nature. Instead of separating and unifying cultures, Welsch advocates within his concept of transculturalism a view that takes into account the formation of cultural networks, by viewing cultures as inter-

---

6 Here opens another methodological perspective regarding intercultural research on discourse.

twined and interrelated, and influencing the formation of specific identities: "transcultural identities include a cosmopolitan aspect, but also local filiation. Transcultural people combine these two aspects" (ibid., p. 221 f). A transcultural look at Lis' interview with Kaczyński will therefore refer learners (and teachers) to an in-depth reflection on the search for elements of a socio-political nature not only characteristic for Polish reality, but on their basis also beyond this context. They will be interpreted in two ways: firstly, as a (re)contextualization of European and, more broadly, global socio-political tendencies within the public discourse in Poland (e. g., within the framework of the interview in question, this will be an inward perspective), and, secondly, as an exemplification of the socio-political shifts characterizing modernity (whether in the direction of (re)defining liberal democracy or in the direction of strengthening of tendencies which might be diplomatically referred to as peri-democratic, forming an outward perspective).

The "political education" in cross-cultural teaching, revealed in the framework of the above reflections, is a contribution allowing to extend this perspective to include a didactically relevant topic related to education for democracy.

Tolerance, respect and empathy toward others are values that are part of the concept of education for democracy, understood in terms of a certain lifestyle, which is relevant to the process of language education. Dewey (1972), a proponent of education for democracy, speaks of a way of life based on honesty, fair play, tolerance, solidarity and social cooperation. Democracy is seen here as a way in which people behave and form interpersonal relationships, and as the interacting activity within small communities and groups. The learning environment belongs to such communities where democracy is formed at the "face to face" level. Democracy is also a "creative democracy", as Dewey calls it, because the system grows on the grounds of liberty, creativity, involvement, protest, and resistance to injustice. An important element of education is the experience at the level of social relations, not only prevailing between learners, but also, between teachers and learners. These relationships should be based on mutual respect, tolerance and trust. They contribute to the formation of attitudes of harmonious coexistence in the group by solving common problems, for example, during the implementation of project method work. Projects are a method of shaping social competencies needed in a democracy, such as arriving at common solutions, making compromises, mitigating conflicts, dealing with emotions, self-awareness and self-control. All of these values are an important part of classes – including language classes – that are communication and action-oriented.

Second or foreign language classes, whose primary goal is to support learners in developing their communication skills via specific action, present a number of contexts in which democratic values influence the process of learners' linguistic development. This is because they get to know languages that are foreign to them in order to build specific bridges of understanding between representatives of different cultures and languages in the future, with respect for their differences and recognition of their achievements and contributions to the development of civilization. Each language is a value in itself. Knowledge of languages makes it possible to establish contacts with Others through conversation and dialogue, and to build transnational and transcultural democratic relations based on respect and cooperation.

Transferring the pedagogical principles of education for democracy into the field of language education implies a number of didactic possibilities and activities. These are illustrated in Table 2.

Table 2. Education for democracy and its implications for language didactics according to Męczkowska-Christiansen 2014 (own work)

Pedagogical assumptions of education for democracy	Implications of education for democracy for foreign language didactics
building democratic relations through conversation, dialogue, respect for the other person, other cultures	dialogue-oriented discussions with other class participants, respect for representatives of other cultures (intercultural teaching)
recognition of socially approved norms and values with non-violation of the right to explore the fields of one's own freedom	discovery of values hidden in other cultures, development of communication skills in an intercultural context (intercultural teaching)
involving learners in the decision-making process	supporting learner autonomy
use of democratic methods of work in classes, including agreements, contracts (without constant exposure of the teacher as the sole decision-maker)	implementation of open forms of work, including projects (with particular attention to issues of participation) setting and signing the rules of the contract governing the course of classes,
trustful, curious and empathetic attitude of teachers to learners	democratic style of work of the teacher, supporting the development of learners' strengths

To be able to take full advantage of the resources of education with respect to democratic values, it is necessary to use its three didactic dimensions: education about democracy, education for democracy itself, and education in democracy (Męczkowska-Christiansen 2014).

Education about democracy is the process of teaching on how democracy is defined, what types of democracy there exist, in what values it manifests itself. Education for democracy comprises teaching social responsibility, expressed, for instance, by fostering patriotism understood in a number of different ways, participating in elections, teaching tolerance and dialogue. Much of the above overlaps with the principles of intercultural teaching in the context of language classes. The third strand, education for democracy is a teaching process that uses methods and forms of work that support community behavior, enhancing the unique potential of an individual while understanding and supporting the common good, promoting activities in cooperation with others, embedded in peaceful relations. This involves teaching participation and criticism, as well as independent thinking and self-reflection. These elements are part of the main demands of linguistic critical didactics (cf. Kumięga 2020).

Applying these considerations to Lis' interview with Kaczyński, the said interview has the potential to proceed through the three paths mentioned above:
- both in its implicit and explicit form, the interview opens up a discussion around the condition of democracy in both the Polish context and in a context far beyond it. It also opens up a discussion about redefining democracy and its bicultural and/or polyvocal nature.

Example No. 1 will concern the condition of Polish democracy in the pre-election context and, specifically, the question regarding the debate between Jarosław Kaczyński and Donald Tusk:

> TL: Mr. Chairman, do you know of a European country where the leader of the opposition refuses to debate the head of the government, where debates between the prime minister and the head of the opposition are not held on the eve of very important parliamentary elections? Could you point us to such a country?
>
> JK: Well, what I can tell you is that the debates, as far as Poland is concerned, were held, with probably only one exception on the occasion of the presidential elections, so I know such a country, that is, of Poland.
>
> TL: I thought that four years ago you were in the studio next door together with Donald Tusk.
>
> JK: Well, yes, but... Agreed. But that was only once and before that I don't recall such debates, although...
>
> TL: You did not come to like this tradition.
>
> JK: Although, perhaps, although I might be wrong. So there is at least one such country, Poland.
>
> TL: Yeah.
>
> JK: Sir, do you know a country where the Prime Minister says about large social groups that they are mohair berets? In which they say that grandmothers – and now they are talking about young people – that things have to be taken away from them, their ID cards stolen? When people are referred to as 'cattle'? It is said by a well-known politician... or 'cemetery hyenas'? (...)

- education for democracy means to recognize, on the basis of the interview, the dangers of increasingly expansive attempts to redefine democracy, looking at these trends in a reflective spirit, thereby awakening among learners the responsibility for and a sense of influence on various peri- and anti-democratic tendencies.

An illustration of education for democracy from Lis' interview with Kaczyński can be found, for instance, in the following passage introduced by Lis in the context of Beata Kempa, a Law and Justice MP who vouched for Piotr "Staruch" Staruchowicz in 2011. In this passage, an interesting topic that opens the context of education for democracy concerns freedom of speech:

(...)

JK: I would like to remind you that the stadium area is the territory of the Republic of Poland and freedom of speech shall apply there.

TL: Is Jihad Legia also included in this freedom of speech?

JK: There were incidents...

TL: Hooked noses, sir, is this freedom of speech too? Is Widzew-Żydzew also included in this freedom of speech? JK: There were incidents...

TL: These are the fans who support you. On mutual terms, unfortunately.

JK: There are examples of such behaviours which exceed the scope of freedom of speech. We have such cases very often when it comes to the attitude towards our political formation. I haven't noticed much outrage on your side in response to this. But, generally speaking, freedom of speech undoubtedly exists in football stadiums, and of course it is not permitted there to shout out such anti-Semitic slogans, and I do not condone this in any way, however, one is allowed to criticize the current government. (...)

– education in democracy, using action didactics methods in the work on the interview, will support the moments of taking different perspectives on this didactic material, trying to understand them and searching for solutions that support community building.

Example No. 3 is an excerpt from the interview regarding Jarosław Kaczyński's strategy while addressing Prime Minister Donald Tusk during the interview, which can be discussed as an anti-example in the context of education for democracy:

TL: Again, why do you keep referring to Donald Tusk as "this man"?

JK: I speak as I see fit.

TL: And I ask as I see fit.

Instead of a summary

Referring to the title of our article it is worth concluding our text with a reflection on the language education of migrants, which is or should denote social and civic education. The dispersion of education-migration policy in Poland does not serve to strengthen it and poses a major challenge within the framework of widely understood migration research with an educational slant.

Moreover, in this regard, even those frequent references to "Western" solutions do not direct us towards concepts worthy of imitation, or even reflexive imitation, if we are to take into account the Polish context. And so, looking at the solutions applied in Germany, we find an institutionalized offer of so-called integration courses, comprising 300 hours of basic language course, 300 hours of extended language course (leading ultimately to level B1 according to the language proficiency scale of the Common European Framework of Reference for Languages) and 100 hours of orientation course on the social, political and cultural aspects of life in Germany, culminating in the acquisition of an integration course certificate (Deutschtest für Zuwanderer – DTZ). Thus, the very concept of integration courses takes into account the theme of social, political and civic education of migrants, which is relevant to our text, but its implementation (as exemplified by the analysis of textbooks approved for use in the orientation course) and, above all, its testing involve primarily the factual knowledge. Systemic solutions, therefore, block the possibility of referring to constructivist didactics that also draws on interdisciplinary discourse studies.

Thus, an important didactic task in the context of migration seems to be the formulation of the foundations and components of discourse competence, which once again highlights the connections and potentials of constructivist-didactic and discourse optics. An outline of "discursive" competence appears in the Polish literature on academic didactics. Pędzisz (2016) defines two pillars of discursive competence, which are: multifaceted analysis of the text embedded in the structure of the discourse, starting with the key words through the reconstruction of the thematic-rhetorical structure to the argumentative structure, and influencing through the text another participant in the discourse. In the end, this definition takes up a number of important aspects (including those taken into account in some variants of broadly understood discourse studies), but the specifics of discursive competence are not entirely clear, especially when we think about the definitions of communicative competence and action causation. By seeking a broader specification and modifying the terminology adopted in favor of discursive competence (here with reference to education in the context of migration, as far as it concerns Lis' interview with Kaczyński), we hope to have provided inspiration within this text from areas related to educational-didactic and discourse constructivism, action didactics, intercultural teaching that also takes into account the transcultural dimension, the concept of education for democracy and, finally, also the analytical background of discourse studies, thus offering a basis for the implementation of language classes, including those with a social, political and cultural slant in endolingual and endocultural settings.

References

Bunge, Mario: 'Relativism: Cognitive', in: Smelser Neil J. / Baltes, Paul B. (eds.): *International Encyclopedia of the Social & Behavioral Sciences*. Oxford 2001, p. 13009–13012.

Byram, Michael: Teaching and Assessing Intercultural Communicative. Competence Multilingual Matters. Clevedon 1997.

Czachur, Waldemar: Lingwistyka dyskursu jako integrujący program badawczy. Wrocław 2020.

Czachur, Waldemar / Kulczyńska, Agnieszka / Kumięga, Łukasz (eds.): Jak analizować dyskurs? Perspektywy dydaktyczne. Kraków 2016.

Czyżewski, Marek: 'Teorie dyskursu i dyskursy teorii', in: KULTURA I SPOŁECZEŃSTWO 2013/2, p. 3–25.

Dernowska, Urszula: Działania nauczyciela a wiedza pojęciowa uczniów. Warszawa 2008.

Dewey, John: Demokracja i wychowanie. Wprowadzenie do filozofii wychowania. Wrocław-Warszawa-Kraków-Gdańsk 1972.

Erll, Astrid / Gymnich, Marion: Interkulturelle Kompetenzen. Erfolgreich kommunizieren zwischen den Kulturen. Stuttgart 2013.

Gębal, Przemysław E.: Podstawy dydaktyki języka polskiego jako drugiego. Podejście integracyjno-inkluzyjne. Kraków 2018.

Gębal, Przemysław E.: Dydaktyka języków obcych. Wprowadzenie. Warszawa 2019.

Gębal Przemysław E.: Dydaktyka kultury w kształceniu językowym cudzoziemców. Podejście porównawcze. Kraków 2010.

Gębal, Przemysław E. / Miodunka, Władysław T.: Dydaktyka i metodyka nauczania języka polskiego jako obcego i drugiego. Warszawa 2020.

Gołębniak, Bogusława D.: 'O "upedagogicznianiu" szkoły poprzez akademicki dyskurs edukacyjny: ku autoetnografii', in: FORUM OŚWIATOWE, 2014/2(52), p. 147–169.

Klus-Stańska, Dorota: 'Konstruktywizm edukacyjny – niejednoznaczność, kontrowersje, dylematy', in: PROBLEMY WCZESNEJ EDUKACJI / ISSUES IN EARLY EDUCATION 2020/4(51), p. 7–20.

Koller, H.-Ch.: 'Lesarten. Über das Geltendmachen von Differenzen im Forschungsprozeß', in: ZEITSCHRIFT FÜR ERZIEHUNGSWISSENSCHAFT 1999/2, p. 195–209.

Kopytowska, Monika / Kumięga, Łukasz: 'Krytyczna analiza dyskursu: konteksty, problemy, kierunki rozwoju', in: Czyżewski, Marek / Otrocki, Michał / Piekot, Tomasz / Stachowiak, Jerzy (eds.): *Analiza dyskursu publicznego. Przegląd metod i perspektyw badawczych*. Warszawa 2017, p. 177–207.

Kumięga Łukasz: 'Discourse, Critique and Subject in Vocational Language Education in Germany: An Outline of the Concept of Critical Foreign Language Didactics', in: PRZEGLĄD SOCJOLOGII JAKOŚCIOWEJ 2020/16(4), p. 126–145.

Kumięga, Łukasz / Nowicka Magdalena: 'Dyskurs o badaniach nad dyskursem w Niemczech', in: OBLICZA KOMUNIKACJI 2012/5, p. 129–154.

Męczkowska-Christiansen, Astrid: 'Edukacja dla demokracji jako demokracja w edukacji. Wokół podstawowych pojęć', in: Gawlicz, Katarzyna / Rudnicki, Paweł / Starnowski, Marcin / Tokarz, Tomasz (eds.): *Demokracja i edukacja. Dylematy, diagnozy, doświadczenia*. Wrocław 2014, p. 13–25.

Miodunka, Władysław T. (ed.): Kultura w nauczaniu języka polskiego jako obcego. Stan obecny – programy nauczania – perspektywy. Kraków 2004.

Nawracka, Monika: Nauczanie języka polskiego jako obcego w perspektywie refleksyjnej i kulturowej. Kraków 2020.

Pędzisz Joanna: 'Kompetencja dyskursywna a rozwój sprawności językowych: możliwości, perpektywy, wyzwania', in: Czachur, Waldemar / Kulczyńska, Agnieszka / Kumięga, Łukasz (eds.): *Jak analizować dyskurs? Perspektywy dydaktyczne*. Kraków 2016, p. 119–136.

Pondiscio, Robert: Explicit teaching vs constructivism: The misadventures of Bean Dad. https://fordhaminstitute.org/national/commentary/explicit-teaching-vs-constructivis m-misadventures–bean-dad. 2021.

Reich, Kersten: Konstruktivistische Didaktik: Lehr-und Studienbuch mit Methodenpool. Weinheim und Basel 2006.

Reich, Kersten: 'Erfinder, Entdecker und Enttarner von Wirklichkeit', in: PÄDAGOGIK 2010/ 1(10), p. 42–47.

Torenc, Marta: Nauczanie międzykulturowe – implikacje glottodydaktyczne. Wrocław 2007.

Welsch, Wolfgang: 'Transkulturowość. Nowa koncepcja kultury', in: Kubicki, Roman (ed.): *Filozoficzne konteksty koncepcji rozumu transwersalnego. Wokół koncepcji Wolfganga Welscha*. Poznań 1998, p. 195–222.

Wilczyńska, Weronika / Mackiewicz, Maciej / Krajka Jarosław: Komunikacja interkultur-owa. Wprowadzenie. Poznań 2019.

Zawadzka, Elżbieta: Nauczyciele języków obcych w dobie przemian. Kraków 2004.

Zawadzka, Elżbieta: 'Glottodydaktyczne aspekty interkulturowości', in: Kielar, Barbara / Krzeszowski, Tomasz / Lukszyn, Jurij / Namowicz, Tadeusz (eds.): *Problemy komuni-kacji interkulturowej – lingwistyka, translatoryka, glottodydaktyka*. Warszawa 2000, p. 451–465.

Żylińska, Marzena: 'Konstruktywistyczna dydaktyka języków obcych', in: JĘZYKI OBCE W SZKOLE 2009/1, p. 5–14.

Van Leeuwen, Theo: Introducing Social Semiotics. London 2005.

Violetta Kopińska

The potential of interdisciplinarity in Discourse-Historical Approach. The example of the interview of Tomasz Lis with Jarosław Kaczyński in educational perspective

Abstract

The principal aim of this paper is to recognize and describe a potential for inter-disciplinarity in Discourse-Historical Approach (DHA) in relation to two categories: a research problem and a context. Therefore, two research questions were constructed: What potential of interdisciplinarity can be recognized at the level of a research problem formulation? What potential of interdisciplinarity can be recognized in the concept of the four-level context of Ruth Wodak? The basis for this recognition is the three models of interdisciplinarity of Theo van Leeuwen: centralist, pluralist, and integrationist. The second aim of this paper is to identify and describe the potential for interdisciplinarity that the pedagogical perspective brings based on a specific case study, namely Tomasz Lis' interview with Jarosław Kaczyński – the leader of the conservative Law and Justice (Prawo i Sprawiedliwość; PiS) political party. Since the topic of the interview is not education, the education perspective of analysing this interview is a good example to show its analytical potential within the framework of an integrationist model of interdisciplinarity.
Keywords: interdisciplinarity, DHA, discourse, education, interview

Introduction

Discourse analysis, regardless of approach, is associated with interdisciplinarity. However, interdisciplinarity can be implemented in various ways, which is related not only to the characteristics of the approach in question but also with other factors, both dependent and not dependent on the researchers themselves.

In the article, I focus on Critical Discourse Analysis, specifically on the Discourse-Historical Approach (DHA). I do not intend to enter into a discussion of the critique of CDA (Kopytowska / Kumięga 2017, p. 194–195), nor do I intend to analyse the relationship between different approaches within CDA (ibid., p. 177–207). I treat DHA as one of the proposals a that allows for the another exploration of the case potential analysed both in this article, and in this book. The article is

Violetta Kopińska, Nicolaus Copernicus University in Toruń (Poland), ORCID: 0000-0002-5255-9995, violetta.kopinska@umk.pl.

structured according to inductive logic. I do not assume at the outset what DHA's potential for interdisciplinarity is, but arrive at it through analysis. The same is true for the educational perspective of the analysed interview. I do not assume that this perspective is useful for analysing this case. I formulate the question of its usefulness in the case of the exemplary problems posed in the article. To sum up, I do not justify my choices at the outset. I do not pose theses, I pose questions and on the basis of the analysis I come to certain conclusions, thus adding one more reading of the analysed case.

Therefore, two aims are constructed in the article. The first is to identify and describe the potential for interdisciplinarity in DHA. The concept of Theo van Leeuwen's three models of interdisciplinarity serves as a criterion for this recognition. The analysis of interdisciplinary potential will focus on two categories: problem and context.

Accordingly, two research questions were constructed: (1) What potential for interdisciplinarity can be recognised in DHA at the level of research problem formulation? (2) What potential for interdisciplinarity can be recognised in Ruth Wodak's concept of the four-level context?

The second aim of this article is to identify and describe the potential of interdisciplinarity brought by the pedagogical perspective based on a specific case, namely Tomasz Lis's interview with Jarosław Kaczyński. Since education is not the topic of the interview, in this case, the question will be formulated from the perspective of the integrationist model of interdisciplinarity, i.e., what pedagogy can contribute to the solution of an exemplary, extra-disciplinarily formulated research problem.

The order of the paper will be as follows: first, I will characterise the three models of interdisciplinarity identified by Van Leeuwen, followed by an analysis of the potential of interdisciplinarity in DHA, and finally, I will refer to the example of Lis' interview with Kaczyński, to indicate what potential interdisciplinarity brings to the pedagogical perspective of discourse analysis of this material.

Three models of interdisciplinarity by Theo van Leeuwen

Theo van Leeuwen (2005) lists three models of interdisciplinarity: centralist, pluralist, and integrationist. The centralist model assumes that each discipline perceives itself as constituting the centre. Theories, methodologies, and focus areas are closely related to this discipline. They simultaneously flow out of it, as well as reflexively form its core (Van Leeuwen 2005, p. 3f). Though the other disciplines are treated as autonomous, the centralist discipline perceives itself as "more important" than the other ones (ibid., p. 10) (Fig. 1). This understanding of scientific disciplines is historically well established. As Leeuwen argues, a centralist approach fosters the development of specific methodologies applied within disciplines, but conversely, leads to the neglect or omission of problems interpreted as not falling within a discipline (ibid., p. 5).

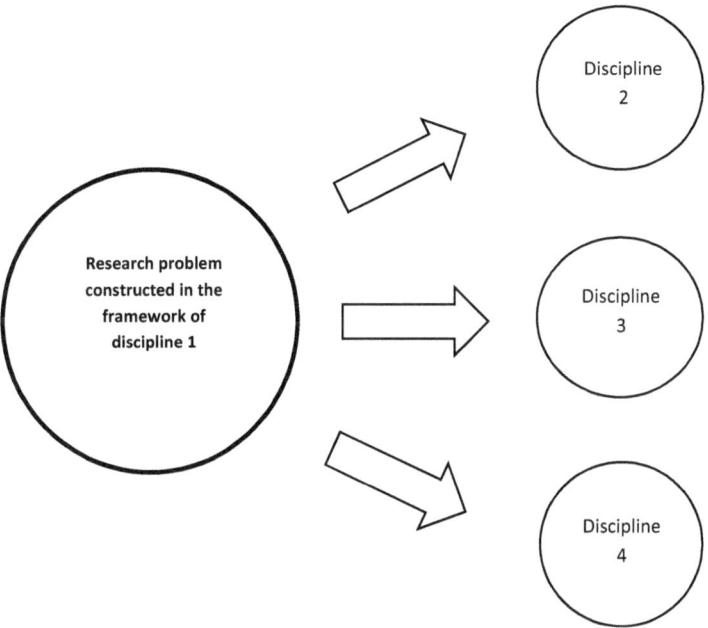

Figure 1. Centralist model of interdisciplinarity. Source: Own elaboration based on Van Leeuwen, 2005.

The pluralist model means focusing on the problem. This problem can be solved by different scientific disciplines, with each of these solutions being autonomous and capable of functioning independently of the others (Fig. 2). None of these disciplines claims to be "central", or more important than others (Van Leeuwen 2005, p. 6).

The integrationist model, like the pluralistic one, assumes a problem orientation and that the problem can be solved by various disciplines. Unlike the pluralist model, however, these disciplines are not perceived as independent of each other. Further, this model points out that it is not possible to solve a problem with just one discipline, meaning that a particular discipline can only offer part of the solution (ibid., p. 7f) (Fig. 3).

In Poland, the centralist understanding of disciplines is still supported by the legal and organisational regulations in higher education. I am referring not only to the internal structure of universities and colleges but also to the fact that academic degrees are awarded in specific scientific disciplines. In addition, rel-

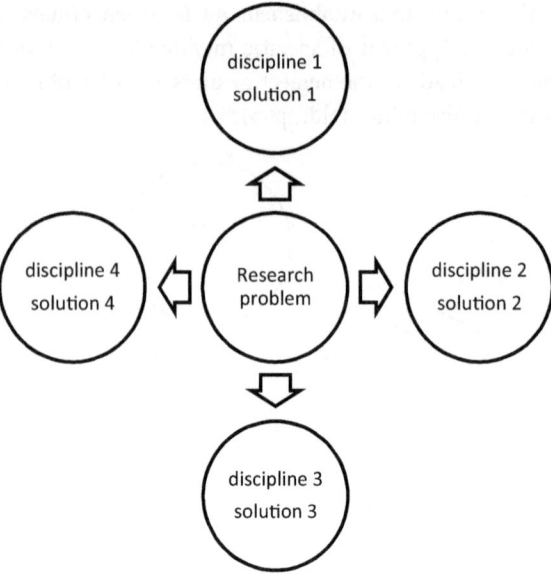

Figure 2. Pluralist model of interdisciplinarity. Source: Own elaboration based on: Van Leeuwen, 2005.

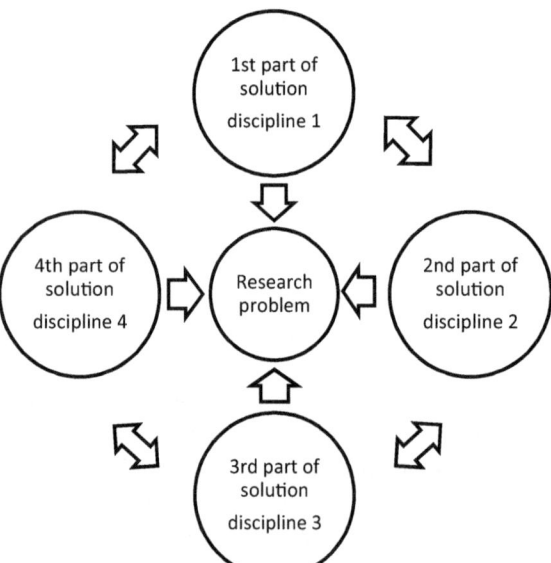

Figure 3. Integrationist model of disciplinarity. Source: Own elaboration based on: Van Leeuwen, 2005.

atively new legal regulations contribute to the entrenchment of the centralist model in science. Act of 20 July 2018 – Law on Higher Education and Science (consolidated text, Journal of Laws of 2021, item 478 as amended) and related executive acts introduced in Poland the evaluation of higher education units based on disciplines and, consequently, enforced the necessity for researchers to declare the discipline in which they conduct research and publish scientific texts resulting therefrom. These declarations, by design, take the form of an individual's entitlement to a percentage of the (at most two) disciplines (once every two years) that he or she represents, are in practice, because of the regulations related to the evaluation of units, closely linked to the place of work (in the sense of a specific department and/or institute) and the policies of the university. As a result, declaring more than one discipline is interpreted as a problem because it implies limited possibilities for those responsible for the development of these disciplines within a particular university to control the effects. Researchers are urged to make declarations indicating one discipline, even if their scientific activity clearly goes beyond that. The above regulations do not imply a *de facto* impossibility of transgressing the "declared" discipline but nevertheless contribute to perpetuating the divisions between disciplines rather than abolishing them, and to entrenching the perception of one discipline as "more important" than another.

The potential of interdisciplinarity in DHA

In this section, I will attempt to recognise the potential for interdisciplinarity in DHA, vis-a-vis the two categories of the research problem and the concept of a four-level context.

The potential for interdisciplinarity at the level of research problem formulation

As mentioned, a rather crucial element that differentiates models of interdisciplinarity is the research problem. Both the pluralist and integrationist approaches are problem-oriented, which distinguishes them from the centralist model. Undeniably, every research process is initiated by the posing of a research problem that determines the subsequent course of action. This is the case regardless of whether interdisciplinarity is involved or not. The above comments raise the question: in what sense does Van Leeuwen define the centralist model of interdisciplinarity as not problem-oriented? I feel this is more about the perspective from which the research problem is constructed. Two approaches can be distinguished at this point. The research problem can be constructed from the perspective of a particular discipline. This means that it is identified as a problem, e. g., pedagogical, psychological, legal, or other, closely related to a particular discipline. Therefore, it could be said that the scientific discipline in question plays a fundamental role here. On the other hand, a problem can be constructed beyond a discipline, which means that, by its very nature, it is not linked to one particular scientific discipline.

Assuming that each of these approaches requires an interdisciplinary approach to problem-solving, however, it should be noted that the first approach is associated, as a rule, with a centralist model of interdisciplinarity, while the second results in a pluralist or integrationist model (Fig. 4).

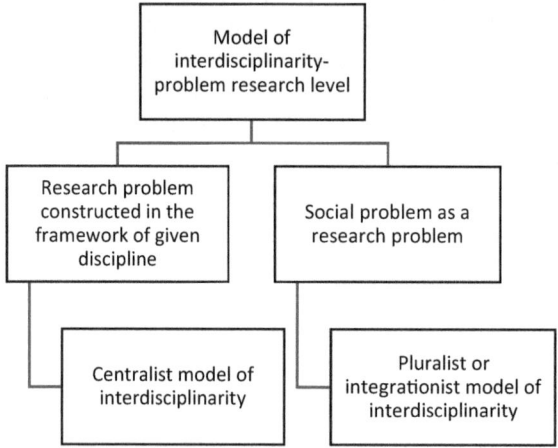

Figure 4. Relationship between the research problem and the interdisciplinarity model. Source: Own elaboration.

On the contrary, a social problem, as a research problem, by its very nature, cannot be located in a particular scientific discipline, although it is obvious that its specificity may be related to a particular discipline to a greater extent than to another. Interdisciplinarity in this case does not mean moving out of a particular discipline towards others, as is the case with the centralist model. This applies rather to moving from the problem towards solutions in different disciplines. These solutions can be autonomous, that is, formulated independently of each other within different scientific disciplines, with each solution being interpreted as independent of the remaining ones, without denying the rationale of others, but at the same time, without claiming to be the "most important" solution. This results in a collection of autonomous, by definition unrelated, solutions (Fig. 5). On the other hand, solutions can be treated as inherently dependent, which means that researchers contribute only a specific part to the solution of the problem while being aware of the fragmentary solution and the need to complement this solution in other disciplines. These can be independent parts of the solution, that is, parts that make sense independently of awareness of complementing the solution within other disciplines. These may also be dependent parts of the solution (Fig. 5), which, already at the level of their construction, assume the "use" of several disciplines, perhaps related to the competence of either individual researchers or potential of the research team.

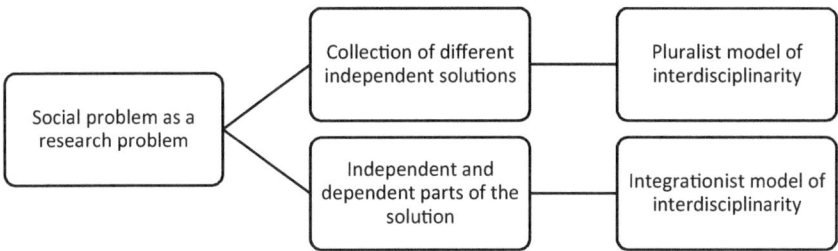

Figure 5. The relationship between the social problem as a research problem and models of interdisciplinarity. Source: Own elaboration.

Critical Discourse Analysis (CDA), as a group of approaches, focusses on social problems. However, this does not mean that the analysis of these problems does not occur within the framework of theories or paradigms (Van Dijk 1993, p. 252). Those researching the CDA perspective are concerned with revealing hidden power relations (Meyer 2001, p. 15f), mechanisms, exclusions/inclusions of specific social actors, or meanings. By definition, CDA has an interdisciplinary character, which translates into a broad and diverse description of the object of investigation (ibid., p. 16). One approach that fits within the CDA umbrella is DHA by Ruth Wodak. Among the program assumptions of the DHA, Wodak mentions the interdisciplinary approach located at diverse levels: "in theory, in the work itself, in teams, and in practice" (Wodak 2001, p. 69). Further, it indicates that the approach is problem-oriented and theories, as well as methods, are integrated to understand and explain the research object (ibid.). The aforementioned features direct attention towards a pluralistic and integrationist model of interdisciplinarity. Does this mean that there is no place for a centralist model of interdisciplinarity? Given the assumptions of the DHA and CDA in general, the answer to this question is negative. However, it should be emphasised that the three models of interdisciplinarity identified by Van Leeuwen are mere constructs that, for analytical reasons, have a so-called "pure form." This means that, in research practice, their characteristics can blend. The historical and organisational entrenchment of the centralist model may therefore be reflected in the approach to interdisciplinarity, and features of this model may still be evident in the pluralist model generally pursued, for instance. As Van Leeuwen points out, these models do not represent "a kind of menu choice from which researchers can choose according to their needs" (Van Leeuwen 2005, p. 3). This does not mean, however, that researchers are unaware of how they operate and what this behaviour entails.

The potential of interdisciplinarity at the level of Ruth Wodak's concept of a four-level context

Discourses should be analysed in relation to the context in which they occur. Context is also crucial to all approaches within the CDA umbrella, including historical, social, cultural, psychological, political, and other components in the research process (Meyer 2001, p. 15). The concept of a four-level context of Ruth Wodak is to provide a triangulation that Meyer describes as theoretical (ibid., p. 29). According to Wodak, the context includes the following levels: "(1) the immediate language- or text-internal co-text; (2) the intertextual and inter-discursive relationship between utterances, texts, genres, and discourses; (3) the extralinguistic social/sociological variables and institutional frames of a specific context of the situation (middle-range theories) (4) the broader sociopolitical and historical contexts which the discursive practices are embedded in and re-lated to" (Wodak 2001, p. 67). Analyses at each of these levels require inter-disciplinarity. Opportunities to realise a pluralistic and integrationist model of interdisciplinarity arise especially at levels three and four. It is at these stages that the principle of the interdisciplinarity of this approach declared in the program assumptions, is most clearly demonstrated (Kopińska 2017a). Focussing on a social problem requires a multidisciplinary approach that can generate both solutions that are autonomous but – by definition – do not claim to be the only ones and recognise the equivalence of other autonomous solutions. On the other hand, it is possible and most desirable to apply an integrationist model of in-terdisciplinarity, since we are discussing the integration of theory to understand and explain the object under study (Wodak 2001, p. 63).

The first level of analysis – descriptive – is the most problematic. DHA requires the incorporation of linguistic categories, and this means going outside the discipline unless the researcher themselves represents linguistics. A certain limitation of the interdisciplinarity of discursive analysis, including DHA, results from its application to a specific approach within CDA (besides, a similar con-clusion could also apply to the whole group of approaches referred to as CDA), i. e., a certain method which, although problem-oriented, has some characteristic features. Correspondingly, is a pluralistic or integrationist model of inter-disciplinarity possible, if the methodology is at least to some extent established? In my view, it is this point of the DHA that proves that features of inter-disciplinarity models can intersect in practice. It cannot be argued that DHA is disciplinary-embedded or that the only model possible here is the centralist one. This would contradict the main assumption of the DHA. Nonetheless:

(1) Firstly, the issues addressed here must have their discursive reference, which in effect, at the starting point, means making an assumption about the relationship between language and society. Such a limitation applies, of course, to all approaches associated with discursive analysis, and, consequently, the relationship can be understood differently (Meyer 2001, p. 15). In the case of DHA, the theoretical background is argumentation theory, rhetoric, system-functional linguistics, social theories of Michel Foucault, Pierre Bourdieu, and Niklas Luhmann (ibid., p. 20–29; Kopińska 2016, p. 320).

(2) Secondly, the different social problems that become the subject of research using DHA are analysed according to a specific procedure. This does not obstruct the possibility that features of a pluralistic or integrationist model may emerge, but the solutions to the social problems explored in the DHA flow from following a particular procedure of treatment.

Both comments point to features of the centralist model of interdisciplinarity in DHA, which is particularly evident at the first two levels of the analysis. On the other hand, already at level two, when interdiscursive analysis emerges, more space opens up for a pluralistic and integrationist model of interdisciplinarity. This is in fact about seeking a relationship with other discourses, and this, in turn, means triangulating data, methods, theories, or even researchers (Flick 2007). The relationship between the perspective, within which the research problem is formulated, and the model of interdisciplinarity, is also evident at this point (Fig. 4). If the problem is formulated within a specific discipline, then the interdiscursive analysis is severely limited in terms of the selection of discourses and discursive analyses that can be included in this analysis. The range of discourses and discursive analyses conducted by different researchers, who represent different approaches that differ at the programmatic level and therefore make different choices at the level of macro-theory, middle-range theory, and micro-theory, which subsequently translates into the use of specific methods (Meyer 2001), is after all determined by the scope of the problem. And since the problem is formulated within a specific discipline, the delimitation of this scope not only cannot reach beyond the centralist model of interdisciplinarity but is also subject to considerable limitations. On the other hand, the fact that the research problem is formulated beyond a discipline opens the gates for the inclusion of discourses and discursive analyses in a much wider ambit.

In sum, therefore, it can be concluded that DHA, as an interdisciplinary approach to discourse analysis, is by definition directed towards the application of a pluralistic and integrationist model. Nevertheless, this is an approach that has a well-established theoretical background and developed methods of analysis at the descriptive level, which in effect reorientates it, at least to some extent, towards a centralist model.

Tomasz Lis's interview with Jarosław Kaczyński – the analytical potential of an integrationist model of interdisciplinarity: Educational opening

In the previous sections, I have focussed on analysing the interdisciplinary potential of DHA. Here, I intend to reverse the optics of the problem. I will therefore not seek answers about the interdisciplinary potential of DHA. I will ask what an integrationist model of interdisciplinarity implemented through DHA can contribute to solving a specific research problem. As an example, I will use Tomasz Lis' interview with Jarosław Kaczynski, broadcast on TVP2 on 3 October 2011 in the "Tomasz Lis na żywo" program. The interview took place just before the parliamentary elections in Poland. Based on this material, I will formulate a sample problem and show what an educational perspective can contribute to solving it. This procedure should be seen as a kind of exercise since, in practice, it is the problem that determines the selection of genres and texts that will eventually constitute the research corpus. Consequently, this is a problem that determines the search for solutions in different scientific disciplines. In this particular case, the situation, for analytical reasons, is reversed. The interview is the starting point. The choice of pedagogy/education as a discipline that can contribute to solving the exemplary problem is mainly because I myself am a representative of this discipline. However, an additional value is that this interview, at the level of what was said, is not about education. A literal reference to education is made once, and it concerns nursery schools, which are mentioned in the context of statements about the cost of election promises.

An exemplary problem that can be posed here is that of the polarisation of Polish society. This is a socially relevant problem, as the consequences of this polarisation are manifest in many areas of social functioning. Polarisation means the construction of a WE which remains in opposition to a THEY. Since the relationship between WE and THEM is one of opposition, the boundary must be clearly defined, along with WE and THEM, to be clearly valued. In the case of WE, it is a clearly positive valuation, with a simultaneous effort to create homogeneity of this group by diminishing or ignoring the differences within WE. It will be similar in the event of THEY, with the difference that the valuation will be unambiguously negative. This is an issue with a discursive dimension and means that some descriptions and explanations can be offered by discourse analyses within different approaches, including within DHA. The choice of the problem arises from the criteria for selecting the interview as the case analysed in this book. The idea is that this interview immediately precedes a period of strong and impassable political and media division and, on the other hand, is still relevant because the themes and dividing lines it delineates are still present in political discourse (see Introduction).

Answering the question of what pedagogy can contribute to the solution of the problem I constructed as an example, I will take the perspective of the integrationist model of interdisciplinarity, assuming that examples of the pedagogical opening of the problem lead to partial solutions (Fig. 3) and are linked to other disciplines, at the level of both the analysis process itself and its effect.

Referring to the relationship between discourse and education, as well as considering ontological, generic, thematic and functional relationships, Ostrowicka (2017) distinguishes diverse types of educational discourse. In the following paragraphs, I will focus on the ontological relationship between education and discourse in the context of the problem under analysis. The remaining relationships will be outlined only in the next section.

Discourse as education, or citizenship education in an interview between Tomasz Lis and Jarosław Kaczyński

The relationship between discourse and education can be considered in ontological terms (Ostrowicka 2017). Education in the broad sense is the totality of diverse kinds of conditions and interactions that may or may not be institutionalised, planned or not, intentional or not, and which, as a result, contribute to identity formation (Ostrowicka 2017, Kwieciński 1995). If, on the other hand, discursive practices are understood as those that form the objects/subjects of which they speak (Ostrowicka 2017), then practices understood in this way fit into the definition of education.

I interpreted Lis' interview with Kaczyński as citizenship education. Citizenship is not understood here as a formal-legal status (Isin / Turner 2002, Isin et. al. 2008) but as a social construct, one of the basic elements of which is a sense of belonging to some group, a community, whereby this community can be understood in different ways (Abowitz / Harnish 2006, Lister 2007, Morelli 2019), as a national, state, ethnic, linguistic, community of values, cultural, historical, community of closed, exclusive or inclusive character. The sense of belonging to a community understood in a certain way translates into a specific conception of citizenship education that aims to shape certain types of citizens (Westheimer / Kahne 2004, Abowitz / Harnish 2006, De Groot / Veugelers 2015, Kopińska 2017). How are WE and THEY discursively shaped in the interview analysed?

Kaczynski constructs WE in two spaces that overlap at some points in the interview. WE is the party, although the word 'party' does not appear even once:

> "We must win the elections", "We want a coalition", "And that is what we will work on. I hope our voters will give us that chance."

The transition from WE-the party, to WE-our supporters, the people who support us, and WE-Poland, for example, can be seen in the following points:

> JK: And, excuse me, hasn't someone said various words about us than I don't even want to quote here? Isn't it the case that Donald Tusk constantly, and by the way he is coming back to it now, says something that constantly refers to those famous mohair berets[1]?

> JK: You belong to a certain formation, which is, unfortunately, very popular in Poland, which is harmful to us.
> TL: Harmful to you? And who is this 'you'?
> JK: Well, harmful. Harmful to Poland. Those who are so terribly afraid of those in Berlin, of those in Moscow, are harmful. They are still overwhelmed by this Polish history. (...)

> JK: However, those who..
> TL: Uhm.
> JK: ...they have a different approach to it, one that is full of fear, just like you, these are the ones who make others completely ignore us, that Mrs. Steinbach[2] can say such things about Poles that if she said such things about French people or Jews, she would be thrown out of German politics.

At the same time, the shift from WE-the party to WE-Poland has a value judging character, because it means that the political option represented by Kaczyński's party is identified here with what is good for Poland. Positive value judgement of WE is constructed by building an oppositional YOU, which in turn is unambiguously negatively valued, i.e., in turn, provides an argument for positive valuing of WE. YOU constructed from Kaczyński's perspective is "a certain formation," "the other group", which is harmful to Poland, afraid of "those in Berlin" and "those in Moscow", "is overwhelmed by history", those who " fear Poland becoming a big, strong nation", have no "Polish self-confidence". YOU is also Prime Minister Donald Tusk and the Civic Platform (PO) party:

---

1 Initially ironically, then clearly negatively value judging, a term for people who support conservative, national Catholic politics. The term comes from the stereotypical image of such a person, i.e., an old lady who wears this type of headgear (mohair beret). The term became popular in the language of politics from 2005 and began to be often associated with the electorate of the Law and Justice party (PiS) and the League of Polish Families (Liga Polskich Rodzin; LPR), which targeted the conservative and Catholic part of society with their message broadcast on the Polish Catholic radio station Radio Maryja.

2 The statement refers to Erika Steinbach, German politician, and the leader of the Federation of Expellees in Germany.

> JK: Sir, do you know a country where the Prime Minister says about large social groups that they are mohair berets? In which they say that grandmothers – and now they are talking about young people – that things have to be taken away from them, their ID cards stolen?[3] When people are referred to as 'cattle'? It is said by a well-known politician... or 'cemetery hyenas'?

or

> JK: For six years, there has simply taken place an unprecedented campaign of defamation, or insult, against a large part of the society. There is something going on that should end, and it can only end in such a way that we win the elections because we do not need this social engineering. It is the Civic Platform that needs such social engineering to govern. It is the Civic Platform that has to tell tales ... about our governing. They have to tell tales about us in order to be in power.

YOU also refers to Polish journalists and publicists, whom Kaczyński identifies with the interviewer Lis, and whom he assesses negatively, ascribing to them a frivolous attitude and a lack of courage in defending Polish interests:

> JK: You are saying it with a type of irony which, I must admit, I do not appreciate very much. Because a truly Polish journalist should display a serious attitude toward their own nation.

> JK: I would like to see insults to Poles treated in the same way as insults to French people or Jews are treated in Germany. Imagine that I would like to see this. But I understand that you are from a different formation, that you wouldn't want this, that you are too shy. (...) But I would also very much like Polish publicists and journalists to be bolder. And I encourage you to do so with all my might (...).

Lis, on the other hand, refers directly to WE only twice, saying:

> TL: We, the citizens have the right to know it (...)

> TL: Because you, the party leader, when you are saying, "YOU are in our way," then I am thinking, the election day has not come yet and you are already dividing us.

In both cases, the WE constructed by Lis refers rather to the Polish society in general, and Kaczyński himself is constructed as the one who does not provide information, the one who divides. One can conclude that Lis' questions and statements during the interview construct Kaczyński as someone threatening the interest of WE, understood as Polish society. Lis repeatedly points out that Kaczyński pretends to be the leader/prime minister of a 40-million-people country and refers to responsibility for his word, for his people, for foreign policy.

---

3 A reference to a post which appeared in 2007 during the election campaign on the website www.trwam.net: "Election coming up. Save the country. Confiscate your grandmother's ID card." The author has indicated that this was a joke. The post became very popular within a few days. The author quickly backed away from it.

In most of his statements, however, Lis does not use the term YOU. He does so, however, clearly in this part of the interview, which concerns the personal guarantee given in 2011 by Beata Kempa (one of the well-known members of the PiS at that time) for one of the so-called pseudo-fans nicknamed "Staruch" [an old man], who, on the anniversary of the Warsaw Uprising, was detained by the police and arrested for three months for committing a robbery[4]:

> JK: Well, sir, we are in favour of zero tolerance for ...
> TL: Zero tolerance?
> JK: ...for disorder of all kinds both inside and outside sports stadiums.
> TL: You keep saying that these hooded figures, who mothers with baby strollers give a wide berth, are the essence of patriotism
>
> JK: (...) I would like to remind you that the stadium area is the territory of the Republic of Poland and freedom of speech shall apply there.
> TL: Is "Jihad Legia[5]" also included in this freedom of speech?
> JK: There were incidents...
> TL: "Garbate nosy" [hooked noses], sir, is this freedom of speech too? Is "Widzew[6]-Żydzew" [Widzew-Hebrew] also included in this freedom of speech[7]?
> JK: There were incidents...
> TL: These are the fans who support you. On mutual terms, unfortunately.

In both cases, Lis constructs YOU, which is unambiguously negatively valued through arguments that refer to support for groups that express racist and anti-Semitic views. He uses intensification by referring to the most glaring examples of this type of behaviour, by repeating the question and using hyperbole. This passage also shows that Lis remains in opposition to the YOU.

If we assume that Lis' interview with Kaczyński is citizenship education, then citizenship is understood here from the respective perspectives of Kaczyński and Lis. These perspectives are constructed as adversarial to each other so that what can be reconstructed as a goal of citizenship education in Lis' statement is diagnosed as a problem by Kaczynski, and inversely. It is also characteristic that the aims of education are built precisely based on negative evaluation of the other interlocutor's behaviour, with the difference that Lis refers in this evaluation to Kaczyński and people from his party, while Kaczyński refers to Lis as a representative of journalists, publicists on the one hand, and on the other, as a representative of those who are discursively excluded by Kaczyński from the "WE" category. Since the two interlocutors' visions of citizenship are basically in conflict, let us examine the one constructed by Kaczyński. From Kaczyński's

---

4 Kempa claimed at the time that the detention was for made for "show".
5 Legia is Polish football club from Warsaw.
6 Widzew is Polish football club from Łódź.
7 Lis refers here to racist and anti-Semitic banners at football matches in Poland.

perspective, citizenship appears to be a sense of belonging to a community that, on the one hand, is identified with Poland, but in fact is a community of specific views and shared values. It is therefore a community of those who support Kaczyński's party, who are his votaries, and who differ markedly from "other groups" to the detriment of the latter. Kaczyński's diagnosis of the situation indicates that the problem is the current shape of foreign policy, which puts Poland in the position of a client state. Kaczyński blames the Civic Platform (PO), Donald Tusk, journalists, and publicists who, in his opinion, lack courage, and an unspecified other group that is harmful to Poland. The normative layer builds an image of a sovereign, independent, strong, large, and self-confident national community, which is respected by other states, and which forms its international position not by creating constructive relations with its neighbours, but through its strength and courage. The conception of citizenship that can be reconstructed from Kaczynski's speech, by glorifying the state, thus clearly refers in its normative layer to conservative concepts (Rheindorf /Wodak 2018) with elements of civic republican concept (Abowitz / Harnish 2006, p. 657–690). It is characteristic that in the normative layer, Kaczyński's pedagogy is constructed primarily by negatively valuing those who do not share Kaczyński's vision, who are opposed to it. It is therefore not only a matter of highlighting one's own nation and its position vis-à-vis other states but also of explicitly excluding from the "WE" community those who do not share such a vision of citizenship.

Generic, thematic and functional links between discourse and education in the example of Tomasz Lis' interview with Jarosław Kaczyński

The generic relationship between discourse and education in Lis' interview with Kaczynski can be considered here in that the relationship between the interlocutors can be analysed in terms of pedagogisation, an asymmetrical relationship between the interlocutors (Ostrowicka, 2017) that can shift and reverse at different points in the conversation, as well as in references to practices or terminology from school. This is evident in several places in the interviews analysed in this book. In the case of Lis, this takes the form of, for example, of:
– disciplining:

> TL: I only have one request to you, the several dozen people who came with the chairman, to reward him with an applause, but maybe not while he's speaking, because then you're making it difficult for Mr. Chairman to speak.

– correcting errors:

> JK: …on Angela [ˈandʒela] (*he pronounces her name incorrectly*) Merkel. Do you think that a German publicist asking Mrs. Angela (*again, he mispronounces her first name*) Merkel about her possible…
> TL: Angela [ˈaŋgela] (*the journalist corrects Kaczyński's pronunciation*)
> JK: Well, let it be Angela [ˈaŋgela] (*this time pronounced her name correctly*), well, let it be Angela, I am very sorry. (…)

– correcting the rules on appropriate addressing:

> TL: Why do you keep saying, "this man", and not "the prime minister"? (…) Again, why do you keep referring to Donald Tusk as "this man"?

or

> JK: Well, doctor, you are simply telling untruths.
> TL: I am not a doctor; I am a redactor.

– correcting the understanding of answers by referring to grammar:

> TL: Do you think anyone will want to form any kind of coalition with you?
> JK: It is the case that if someone wins the elections, which is what we are talking about … and I am very pleased that you believe that this will be the case.
> TL: The conditional, Mr. Chairman, the conditional sentence.

In the case of Kaczyński, on the other hand, the following can be observed:
– explaining:

> JK: (…) And these are the rules of arithmetic. You seem not to know how certain fees are collected, so I'm trying to explain this to you.

– assessing your preparation/knowledge of the subject:

> JK: You are really completely unprepared for today's broadcast. I'm sorry. I'm really sorry. Really sorry.

or

> JK: (…) because at this point you are reaching the level of really terrible disgrace. Because, to refer to such newspapers, really [he shakes his head].

Both Lis and Kaczyński take on the role of teacher-educator at various points during the interview, instructing their interlocutor, adopting a moralising tone, and constructing normative statements, e.g.:

- Lis in the role of teacher-educator:

  TL: Because you know, there is an insinuating tone in this sentence, which is not befitting a person who wants to be the Prime Minister of Poland.

  or

  TL: But Mr. Chairman President, I just wanted to verify this. Can you elaborate on your thought? Because it is a matter of responsibility for words, which should be proper to people who want to lead great nations.

- Kaczyński in the role of teacher-educator:

  JK: You are saying it with a type of irony which, I must admit, I do not appreciate very much. Because a truly Polish journalist should display a serious attitude toward their own nation.

In contrast, the thematic relationship between discourse and education in the example of this interview is difficult to grasp insofar that, as I pointed out earlier, education in the literal sense is not its subject. On the other hand, it is this fact that shows us the position of education in political discourse. Lis, in his last interview before the elections, did not ask a single question about education to the leader of the party who could potentially soon be the Prime Minister and form the Polish government. Kaczynski, on the other hand, also makes no reference to education in his extended statements. He does so only once when asked about the cost of election promises, he mentions nursery schools (min. 7:18). This noted exclusion of education from the topics of conversation allows to conclude that it is not an issue perceived as important and relevant.

The analysed interview can also be understood in terms of discourse in education. The potential of this case has its functional educational references because it is a representative example of a broader political discourse that draws normative ideas that are then translated at the level of political solutions, including those concerning education policy. The exemplary problem of the polarisation of society that I have indicated, evident in this interview when juxtaposed with the changes in schooling that have occurred and continue to occur after PiS came to power in 2015, provides the basis for an examination of discursive change in education. Vivien Schmidt's (2008) concept of discursive institutionalism can provide an analytical tool in this regard. The ideas underlying institutional discourses are shaped at three levels: philosophies, programs, and policies (Schmidt 2008, p. 306 ff). In this case, it is about analysing how ideas from the programmatic level translate into the "policy solutions" level. The ideas constructed in the general program discourse of the party cannot be expected to find a straightforward translation even into the program discourse on educational policy, not to mention the fact that they would determine the discursive construction of practical political and legal solutions in the field of education. However, this does not mean that the connection is lacking. Thus, the question is how the discursive nomination, predication, argumentation and intensification/mitigation categories "WE" and "YOU"/"THEY" are then applied to the aims and tasks of school, both at the level of announcements of changes, justifications of introduced reforms, as well as at the level of the specific content of teaching (core curricula, programs, textbooks), on the one hand, and, on the other, the construction of the school's position in the system of educational authorities and the internal school system: What is the relationship of the categories "WE" and "YOU"/"THEY" constructed by Kaczyński in the analysed interview with analogous categories reconstructed from discursive changes in school education (e.g., concerning core curricula, textbooks, competences of school superintendents and justifications accompanying these changes).

Summary and conclusions

The analyses conducted in this article lead to the following conclusions:
1. On the potential level of the interdisciplinary DHA:
   - Interdisciplinarity is inherent in DHA at both the problematic and contextual levels; hence, it is possible here to pursue all models of interdisciplinarity distinguished by Van Leeuwen.
   - The problem orientation inscribed as a program assumption of DHA implies the location of this approach within a pluralistic and/or integrationist model of interdisciplinarity.
   - The analysis of the four-level context concept, however, leads to the conclusion that the well-established theoretical background and the developed methods reorient the analyses conducted at the descriptive level towards a centralist model.
2. On the level of the analytical potential of Tomasz Lis' interview with Jarosław Kaczyński analysed from a pedagogical perspective and assuming an integrationist model of interdisciplinarity:
   - Starting from the perspective of the thematic relationship between the discourse on education broadens the analysed problem by what has been excluded from the subject matter of an interview conducted a few days before the parliamentary elections with the head of one of the most important political parties in Poland.
   - The perspective of the ontological relationship between discourse and education enables us to understand the analysed interview as citizenship education, whose aims can be reconstructed based on the statements of the

two interviewer and the interviewee. The statements of both Lis and Kaczyński imply a normative layer of this education, which, interestingly, is created mainly based on the negative result of the diagnosis of "YOU" actions (with visible differences in the discursive construction of the "YOU" category).

- The generic link between discourse and education enables capturing in the interview analysed the dynamics of the changing position of the interlocutors and the discursive interventions that aim to achieve an asymmetry in this relationship, which are compared to the strategies used in school between student and teacher.
- A functional understanding of the relationship between discourse and education allows us, in turn, for example, to analyse the interview as an example of a discourse outlining certain general curricular ideas, which are then translated into changes in educational policy and through this, applied to political and legal solutions.

References

Abowitz, K.N. / Harnish J.: 'Contemporary discourses of citizenship', in: REVIEW OF EDUCATIONAL RESEARCH 2006/76(4), p. 653–690.

De Groot, I. / Veugelers, W.: 'Why we need to question the democratic engagement of adolescents in Europe', in: JOURNAL OF SOCIAL SCIENCE EDUCATION 2015/14(4), p. 27–38.

Flick, Uwe: Managing Quality in Qualitative Research. London-Thousand Oaks-New Delhi-Singapore 2007.

Isin, Engin / Turner, Bryan: 'Citizenship Studies: An Introduction', in: Isin, Engin F. / Turner, Bryan (eds.): *Handbook of Citizenship Studies.* London 2002, p. 1–10.

Isin, Engin / Brodie, Janine / Juteau, Danielle / Stasiulis, Daiva, K: 'Recasting the social in citizenship', in: Isin, Engin (ed.): *Recasting the Social in Citizenship.* Toronto 2008, p. 3–17.

Kopińska, V.: 'The concept of four-level context by Ruth Wodak as an expression of interdisciplinarity in Discourse Analysis', in: KULTURA-SPOŁECZEŃSTWO-EDUKACJA (CULTURE – SOCIETY – EDUCATION) 2017a/2(12), p. 157–169.

Kopińska, V.: 'Krytyczna Analiza Dyskursu – podstawowe założenia, implikacje dla badań pedagogicznych, zastosowanie', in: ROCZNIK ANDRAGOGICZNY 2016, p. 311–334.

Kopińska, V.: Edukacja obywatelska w szkole. Krytyczna analiza dyskursu podręczników szkolnych. Toruń 2017.

Kopytowska, Monika / Kumięga, Łukasz: 'Krytyczna analiza dyskursu: konteksty, problemy, kierunki rozwoju', in: Czyżewski, Marek / Otrocki, Michał / Piekot, Tomasz / Stachowiak, Jerzy (eds.): *Analiza dyskursu publicznego. Przegląd metod i perspektyw badawczych.* Warszawa 2017, p. 177–207.

Kwieciński, Zbigniew: Socjopatologia edukacji. Olecko 1995.

Lister, R.: 'Why citizenship: Where, when and how children?', in: THEORETICAL IN-QUIRIES IN LAW 2007/8(2), p. 693–718.

Meyer, Michael: 'Between theory, method and politics: positioning of the approaches to CDA', in: Meyer, Michael / Wodak, Ruth (eds.): *Methods of Critical Discourse Analysis*. London-Thousand Oaks-New Dehli 2001, p. 14–31.

Morelli, U. (2019). 'From national cultural paradigms to European/global cultural paradigms: A Copernican revolution', in: JOURNAL OF SOCIAL SCIENCE EDUCATION 18 (3), p. 2–40.

Ostrowicka, H.: 'The educational discourse, veredictions and pedagogies. From the constellations of the relations between discourse and education to the alethurgic analysis of the educational practice', in: KULTURA-SPOŁECZEŃSTWO-EDUKACJA (CULTURE – SOCIETY – EDUCATION) 2017/2(12), p. 123–142.

Rheindorf, M. / Wodak, R: 'Borders, fences, and limits. Protecting Austria from refugees: Metadiscursive negotiation of meaning in the current refugee crisis', in: JOURNAL OF IMMIGRANT & REFUGEE STUDIES 2018/16(1–2), p. 15–38. https://doi.org/10.1080/15562948.2017.1302032.

Schmidt, V.A.: 'Discursive institutionalism: The explanatory power of ideas and discourse', in: ANNUAL REVIEW OF POLITICAL SCIENCE 2008/11, p. 303–326.

The Act of 20 July 2018: Law on higher education and science (consolidated text), in: JOURNAL OF LAWS 2021, item 478 (as amended).

Van Dijk, T.A.: 'Principles of Critical Discourse Analysis', in: DISCOURSE & SOCIETY 1993/4(2), p. 249–283.

Van Leeuwen, Theo: 'Three models of interdisciplinarity', in: Wodak, Ruth / Chilton, Paul (eds.): *A New Agenda in (Critical) Discourse Analysis. Theory, methodology and interdisciplinarity*. Amsterdam-Philadephia 2005, p. 3–18.

Westheimer, J. / Kahne, J.: 'What kind of citizen? The politics of educating for democracy', in: AMERICAN EDUCATIONAL RESEARCH JOURNAL 2004/41(2), p. 237–269.

Wodak, Ruth: 'The discourse-historical approach', in: Meyer, Michael / Wodak, Ruth (eds.): *Methods of Critical Discourse Analysis*. London-Thousand Oaks-New Delhi 2001, p. 63–94.

Agnieszka Kampka

The eyes, the smile, the audience. A multimodal analysis from a rhetorical perspective

Abstract
The object of analysis is the rhetorical delivery in two media contexts: the television interview and the recording of this programme published on YouTube. The author pointed out how the journalist and the politician used non-verbal means to construct ethos and how the audience reads these actions. The theoretical basis is multimodal discourse analysis, combining the semiotic approach and digital rhetoric. The analysis consisted of two stages: a description of the elements of a rhetorical situation in two media contexts (television, Internet) and an analysis of YouTube comments on the non-verbal elements of a conversation (mainly body language). The interdisciplinary perspective allowed for a better understanding of the context of the communication situation, goals and participants' persuasive strategies (e.g. ethos construction by the interlocutors, framing of the situation by the media sender, reading of non-verbal behaviour by the audience).
Keywords: multimodality, rhetorical situation, non-verbal, ethos, YouTube

This chapter answers how changing the media context changes the rhetorical situation. The object of analysis is the rhetorical delivery considered in two media contexts: the interview aired on television and the recording of this program published on the YouTube platform. The subject of analysis is only a selected aspect of discourse – all non-verbal elements accompanying the transmission of a given text. Thus, in the analysed case, we consider the participants' behaviour, gestures, facial expressions, scenography and camera work. It is also essential to ask which of these elements are considered significant by the audience.

The theoretical basis is multimodal discourse analysis, combining the semiotic approach and reflection on the changing conditions of rhetorical delivery in digital communication. The analysis used the methods of rhetorical criticism, and the analysis itself consisted of two stages. At first, attention was focused on the rhetorical action taking place in the television studio. All non-verbal elements

Agnieszka Kampka, Warsaw University of Life Sciences (Poland), ORCID: 0000-0002-9732-6482, agnieszka_kampka@sggw.edu.pl.

that could have a persuasive meaning were extracted. Then, based on a diagram of the rhetorical situation, these factors were compared in two media contexts: television and the Internet.

The second stage of the analysis involved the examination of selected comments posted under the video on the YouTube platform. Out of more than 1200 comments, several dozen were selected, which referred to the previously identified non-verbal elements (mainly body language). The final stage was reconstructing the audience's perceptions of the interviewees' ethos.

Thus, three issues are essential: 1) what non-verbal means participants in an interaction use to construct their ethos; 2) how the audience perceives these tools; 3) how their persuasive potential changes depending on the medium and what theoretical concepts help understand this.

The chapter will begin with a brief discussion of the rhetorical perspective in political discourse studies, the concept of the rhetorical situation, and its variations depending on the media context. An indication of the persuasiveness of non-verbal elements in various media will follow this. In the last section, the comments of internet users on delivery will be presented.

The rhetorical approach in discourse analysis

The rhetorical perspective in discourse studies is used in analyses concerning political discourse due to its indisputably persuasive nature (Gill / Whedbee 1997). Rhetoric distinguishes five canons (and at the same time stages of speech preparation): *inventio* (choice of topic and collection of materials), *dispositio* (composition, arrangement of content), *elocutio* (choice of style and form of expression), *memoria* (ways of remembering the prepared speech) and *actio* (delivery, choice of appropriate verbal and non-verbal strategies). In the present analysis, only the last canon will be of interest.

While ancient rhetoric involved direct contact between sender and receiver, modern research into mediated texts explores ways to influence a distant (in time and space) receiver. However, the critical question in rhetorical analysis remains the context, the rhetorical situation that determines the shape of an utterance. An essential concept in the rhetorical analysis is, among others, the category of appropriateness (*decorum*), i.e., the adaptation of an utterance to the circumstances, external conditions, expectations of the audience, and the reason for which one takes the floor. At the same time, it is worth remembering that a rhetorical statement may change the context. In the analysed case, uploading the recording of the TV program on the YouTube channel and giving it a specific title was intended to change the perception of the whole situation. The TV interview was replaced by a duel, the winner of which was made clear to viewers before they even watched the whole thing. The TV program was one of a series of conversations under the title: "Tomasz Lis na żywo" [Tomasz Lis live]. The recording posted on YouTube was entitled: "Jarosław Kaczyński masakruje Tomasza Lisa" [Jarosław Kaczynski massacres Tomasz Lis].

Other vital issues (and in the analysed case – key ones) are the credibility of the rhetor and the implied audience, i.e., the audience imagined by the speaker, whose characteristics can be discovered by analysing the given speech. We can say that the participants of the television program assumed that certain groups of viewers would watch them, and they directed their message to them. However, the journalist and the politician did not influence the audience for this conversation recording on YouTube. In the latter case, we can instead wonder about the audience the channel owner imagines. The expression of his assumptions is the title he gave to the recording and its description.

The chosen object of analysis – rhetorical *actio* – resonates with the themes addressed in multimedia discourse analysis, which deals with visual, spatial, aural and linguistic elements (Jewitt 2014, Kampka 2017, Kress 2009, Norris / Maier 2014). Research on multimodal communication from a rhetorical perspective can take many forms, including using digital tools for qualitative discourse analysis (see Rossolatos 2014). New forms of online communication have created opportunities for new explorations. Jay Lemke (2005) uses the notion of heteroglossia about online content, showing differences in speech due to differences in social position. The analysis then concerns which groups identify with a given media artefact and how the meanings of cultural (media) multimodal texts are produced. Discursive content and ideological functions are not permanently assigned to a text but result from the use of these texts by different audiences, as is perfectly evident from the recording analysed in this chapter.

Lemke (2005, p. 16f) discusses a model of "multiplicative" multimedia meaning effects, according to which successive meanings do not so much overlap or complement each other as "multiply". The basis, in turn, is cross-contextualisation – the intersection of contexts through which "the meaning of any word becomes more specific in the context of the words (and situations) around it" (Lemke 2005, p. 16). This remark applies, of course, to words and images and the relationship between words and images. However, at the same time, it is necessary to remember the incommensurability of the individual semiotic codes. The image, word, gesture, and spoken argument will never perfectly match; one cannot replace the other; each will always have a different meaning.

Analysing non-verbal elements combines rhetorical approaches and semiotics, especially social semiotics (Leeuwen 2017). For both perspectives, the context of using specific signs is important. Their meaning always derives from a specific situation. Multimodal discourse analysis involves studying and interpreting the different modes of communication used in a given text or interaction.

In rhetorical terms, multimodality concerns the rhetorical action, the form and manner in which the message is presented. These interdisciplinary connections between discourse, rhetoric and semiotics are obvious when online communication becomes the object of analysis (Bogost / Losh 2017).

All issues of hypertext, remediation, and new participatory practices require a focus on the delivery and negotiation of meanings of particular forms, styles and symbols. However, the persuasive power of representation, identification and signification remains unchanged (Kampka 2021). Rhetoric is a dynamic process. By constructing their ethos and responding to the emotions of their audience, the speaker creates a particular image of the world, and the audience must respond to this vision of reality created by the sender and take action as a result of accepting or rejecting it.

The interdisciplinarity of the approach presented here lies primarily in the interweaving and complementarity of perspectives. The fundamental assumption of the persuasiveness of the studied discourse steers towards the concept of the rhetorical situation. This concept becomes a valuable framework for structuring the analysis process and highlighting the differences between persuasion in two media contexts. Multimodal discourse analysis makes it possible to identify all the non-verbal elements influencing the audience and to include audience reactions in the analysis. Finally, social semiotics helps to understand and interpret the meaning of the elements indicated.

Rhetorical situation

The terms 'television context' and 'Internet context' will be used in describing the analysed situation. The former referred to a situation in a television studio and broadcasted on television. On the other hand, the Internet context refers to a new situation that has been created by putting this recording on YouTube.

Analysing a persuasive message requires considering the rhetorical situation, i.e., all the circumstances in which a given message reaches its audience. It is always about a specific situation and a specific goal of the message (Bitzer 1968). The number of elements of a rhetorical situation indicated by researchers varies from three to seven.

The three essential elements of a rhetorical situation are 1) the exigence, the problem, and the issue to which the text refers; 2) the audience, the persons addressed by the sender; and 3) the constraints, persons, events, objects, relations that affect the speaker and the audience. The sources of these constraints are views, attitudes, documents, facts, traditions, interests, motives and preferences. The discussion of the components of a rhetorical situation shows how much creating, understanding and interpreting a message depends on sometimes minor changes in the context of the utterance. Audience, target, medium and context is a four-part view of the rhetorical situation. Subject and writer (speaker), audience, target and context appear in five-element descriptions. On the other hand, the most elaborate definition points to seven elements of the rhetorical situation: writer (rhetor); audience; purpose; exigence; topic; context (including constraints) and genre.

The crucial aspect of a rhetorical situation is the sender, whether an individual, a group or an institution (including a media broadcaster). In what social role is the sender speaking at this moment? From what social position is he speaking? How does his communication relate to his past appearances, goals, values, and past and present image? How does his identity (race, gender, ethnicity, education) determine what he says (writes, shows)? All these questions are related to the ethos of the speaker.

Contemporary reflections on ethos and its importance in persuasion can be found in many scientific disciplines and diverse theories (Załęska 2012). These reflections concern the individual, his or her identity, different types of self, group identities, media representations or marketing image creation. Researchers distinguish different dimensions and types of ethos. In this case study, the distinction proposed by Patrick Charaudeau (2005) is valid. He writes about the ethos of credibility (when a politician appears serious, honest and competent) and the ethos of identification (when a politician is an intelligent, empathetic, strong leader).

Maria Załęska (2012) analyses three levels of politicians' ethos: pre-textual, textual and meta-textual. Pre-textual is everything a politician is, regardless of the speech (here: the interview). Textual is the ethos created through the message, during the speech, in response to the audience or interlocutor. Finally, meta-textual is reputation. The comments of Internet users analysed below show that all these dimensions of ethos were important in the reception and evaluation of behaviour by Lis and Kaczyński.

The pre-textual ethos is independent of a particular speech. On the contrary, textual is always linked to a given rhetorical situation and is most dependent on the speaker, inventive, argumentative, stylistic choices that the politician (or another speaker) uses when addressing a particular audience.

In this case, we are dealing with three senders: 1) the interlocutors, i.e., a journalist and a politician who talk to each other in a TV studio, 2) the institutional media broadcaster – the TV station which prepared and broadcasted the program, 3) the individual media broadcaster – the owner of a YouTube channel who posted the recording of the program on the Internet.

Since the elements of rhetorical action are the subject of analysis in this text, let us focus only on them, comparing these three senders. Tomasz Lis and Jarosław Kaczyński have experience as public actors, accustomed to public appearances due to their professions. Both have clearly defined roles and precise goals (which are another element of the rhetorical situation): self-presentational (e.g., the journalist wishing to present himself as an inquisitive exposer, the politician wishing to present himself as a charismatic and rational leader) and directed against their interlocutor (e.g., the journalist wishing to 'expose' the politician, the politician wishing to ridicule the journalist). Furthermore, both actors have the same tools: their appearance, body movements, gestures, mimicry, and way of speaking.

The institutional media sender (television context) wants to attract and maintain the audience's attention. This attention is possible by making the message more attractive and making it easier for the audience to interpret. Therefore, the means at the sender's disposal are mainly the studio's decoration, the way the meeting participants are shown, i.e., the camera work, additional visual elements that appear on the screen – projected recordings, subtitles and captions.

The individual media sender (internet context) has the most limited scope for action. He could have interfered with the message itself, edited the recording differently, and added some elements, but he did not do so. His action was limited to giving a title and description. The name of the channel and the avatar are also part of the rhetorical *actio*.

The sender's role also derives from the circumstances of the time. In the analysed situation, there is a time inconsistency. While the actions of the interviewees and the TV station took place simultaneously, posting the recording on YouTube took place several years after the program broadcast. While the rhetorical action presented by the interlocutors and the TV station was a one-off and was presented once, the publication of the recording online made the situation a repeatedly played message.

Another element of the rhetorical situation is the audience. In the analysed situation, we are dealing with three groups of receivers. The first is the audience gathered in the studio (TV context), the people invited by the two interlocutors. They are the only group that can react to the message directly, using the same means at the disposal of the senders – interlocutors: body movements, gestures, mimicry, and voice. Their reactions are visible to all participants in the situation. The second group consists of television viewers watching a live program. Their possibilities of reaction seem to be the most limited. Apart from sending a text message, as the media broadcaster encourages, they may comment on what they see and interrupt their viewing, but these actions will be invisible to others. The third group of viewers are YouTube users (online context) who can comment on the posted video and the statements of other viewers. They can use words, emojis and post links.

Referring to the next element of the rhetorical situation, the purpose, we can reflect on whether the goals of the different senders coincide. Similarly, we should consider the exigence to which the actions of the different participants respond. Divergences may relate to the main topic that the participants are addressing. What is it? If there are several important themes, what is their hierarchy? Divergences may be about what the participants consider important and whether they think other topics are essential and not raised. However, answering these questions is beyond the scope of this analysis, as it would require an analysis of the verbal message itself.

In considering the elements of a rhetorical situation, the genre to which a speech can be classified is also significant. Traditionally in rhetoric, three types of speech are distinguished: judicial oratory (or forensic), deliberative oratory (or legislative) and epideictic oratory (ceremonial or demonstrative). Political discourse, by definition, belongs to the deliberative genre, in which people consider the pros and cons of solutions. Nowadays, the genre in rhetorical studies is related to situational context. Genre in a rhetorical approach links to specific situations and social action (Harrell / Linkugel 1978, Miller 1994). It is crucial to assume that certain types of social situations create similar needs and expectations of the audience and that a particular type of rhetoric is the response. Therefore, the rhetorical situation becomes the primary determinant of the genre, and specific circumstances determine its exigence. At the same time, very high flexibility of genres is also assumed, their ability to dynamic change. Genres in this approach are not classes or categories into which a text can be included but forms of action or ways of acting. For example, a television interview is not just a text but an element of a social ritual, in this case – an election campaign.

Genres are constantly ready for transformation and modification. This sociocultural approach focuses on the dialectical relationship between a genre's permanent and dynamic (Kamberelis 1995). The relationship between genre and ideology is also emphasised. Genres are the carriers of ideology; ideology is assimilated through immersion in genre frameworks in learning and socialisation. In this approach, the focus shifts from the formal features of the text to the people, institutions, goals, and themes, i.e., the whole rhetorical situation. This understanding of genre is helpful with the analysed case. On the one hand, we deal with a fairly established interaction, such as a TV interview with a politician. On the other hand, putting the recording on YouTube creates a new genre framework that is much less defined.

Based on the characteristics of the profile, it can be assumed that the account owner has particular political views. He gave the title: "Jarosław Kaczyński massacres Tomasz Lis" and the description: "PiS president crushes resort[1] journalist hyene of the year in TVP program *Tomasz Lis na żywo*". It suggests that making the recording available is not simply archiving but an expression of appreciation for Kaczyński or a desire to ridicule Lis. Admittedly, sharing the recording from several years ago makes it a symbolically important event. Situational, rhetorical understanding of the genre, however, also requires taking into account the audience's expectations because their understanding of the situation also co-creates the framework of the genre.

Can we clearly define what these expectations are in this case? Concerning a specific group of viewers, yes – we can assume that these people with right-wing views appreciate Kaczyński and do not appreciate Lis. Nevertheless, this is not, after all, the only group of potential receivers. The comments show a significant predominance of people who agree with the video's title's interpretation. However, there are some critical comments: "It would be good if the founder of the channel changed the title of this video because no one is massacring anyone here, you can see moments of the stress of both participants of the conversation and the title shown is at least unfair... wouldn't it be better to call it 'Kaczyński-Lis conversation'? They attack each other nicely, it's a pity that the channel broadcaster is biased in setting such a title of the proposal on yt. It's not a reliable broadcaster!"; "I forced myself to watch this program, and somehow I didn't notice any crushing". These are just a few examples from over a thousand comments, but they nevertheless confirm the ideological heterogeneity of the audience.

Context change

Let us consider how the change in context has altered two fundamental aspects of the analysed discourse: linguistic and social. Putting the recording of the TV interview on YouTube changed the scope of the language. It allowed new participants (viewers commenting on the video) and new linguistic styles – which is characteristic of internet commentaries. Thus, a certain linguistic inconsistency has emerged. Lis and Kaczyński speak in an official language, typical for political and media discourse. However, Internet users commenting on the conversation use a different register. Any linguistic interaction between the interviewees and the viewers can occur, so this linguistic inconsistency is not a communication problem. However, it can be a research challenge, especially if we want to socially characterise the viewers based on the comments.

---

1 This word ('resortowy' in Polish) refers to a popular right-wing discourse term for journalists accused of a privileged position due to their parents' merits in the communist system.

In some cases, it would be relatively easy to determine their ideological profile, e. g., by recognising phrases and expressions typical of right-wing media messages. At the same time, we can observe a paradox related to the possibility of participating in the discourse and speaking out. The journalist and the politician were the active actors in the television context. They decided on the course of the interaction; they spoke and acted. In the online context, these actors were somehow incapacitated; their statements became the object of viewers' discursive activity.

As far as the social context is concerned, even more has changed. The program "Tomasz Lis na żywo" broadcast on TVP on 3 October 2011, was one of many publicist programs. The program could not be biased even if Lis' political sympathies were widely known. The journalist's critical attitude towards the Law and Justice party was also known, and the journalist was repeatedly criticised in the right-wing media. For many Law and Justice voters, he was a symbol of a hostile media, journalists who owe their careers to their parents – beneficiaries of the communist regime. Therefore, one can assume that viewers watching the program on television are both Kaczyński and Lis sympathisers. It is not easy to define their specific expectations from the interview. However, it was an exceptional event, as the Law and Justice president generally does not interview the unfriendly media.

The social context for the YouTube recording is quite different. The recording was posted several years after its original broadcast: on 9 January 2016. The title added and the video's description is very explicit, suggesting the nature of the conversation and the roles played by the interviewees. At the same time, the characteristic of the profile (other content posted on the channel) allows us to assume that the message is addressed to a rather right-wing audience.

The social situation involves the participants' identities, which are both social (telling who is who, what status they have) and discursive (constructed through the linguistic act) (Charaudeau 2002). These dimensions are close to the two ethos approaches mentioned earlier – what the audience already knows about the speaker and how he presents himself in the speech. The authority that a speaker acquires is dependent on both of these dimensions.

Discourse memory is the shared knowledge and beliefs circulating in a discursive community, expressed in representations (ibid.). In the analysed case in the Internet context, elements of such memory may be attributed to the journalist named Lis ('fox' in Polish) characteristics culturally attributed to the figure of the fox: cunningness and deceitfulness. The memory also concerns perceptions of journalistic professionalism (asking questions in a non-aggressive manner, not attempting to ridicule the guest, controlling one's emotions) or of a politician winning an argument (in control of the situation, relaxed, intelligent).

Semiotic communities (ibid.) use the same signs: words, images, and gestures. Discursive memory binds the community together; these are shared value systems, moral judgements or political views. The participants of an interview (and its recipients) remember specific ways of speaking and behaving; they recognise routinised behaviours (e.g., Kaczyński's smile, the way Lis asks questions). Memory is one of the 'filters' through which discourse participants perceive each other and the situation, referring to knowledge and perceptions, giving meaning to statements and behaviour. The context of the discourse is socialised; the reading of signs is part of the discourse itself and simultaneously creates the conditions in which it functions (Grzmil-Tylutki 2007, p. 29).

The social frameworks of the interaction limit each participant in various communication situations. Social norms regulate the scope of acceptable behaviour for journalists and politicians. These rules also apply to rhetorical action: speaking, body posture, gesticulation, and mimicry. On the other hand, the participant can choose the discursive strategies. Lis chose a particular way of asking questions, gestures and body positions. Kaczyński chose such and no other mimic reactions or speaking pace.

Both used these means to pursue strategies ethos of legitimacy and credibility (Charaudeau 2002). Lis used the attitudes described by Charaudeau in his analysis of the media discourse: neutrality and distance; he asked questions on behalf of the Poles, referred to other people's statements and asked his interlocutor to refer to them. In the non-verbal layer, these attitudes were manifested, among others, by the seriousness in the tone of voice and facial expressions, but also by showing on the screen, in graphic form, quotations and playing back fragments of recordings.

Kaczyński pursued a captation strategy by resorting to a controversial attitude, which manifests itself, for example, in 'destroying the opponent', ridiculing him, and questioning his ideas and his person in general while gaining the support of his listeners. Such behaviours include Kaczyński's ironic remarks that Lis is unprepared for the interview or asks stupid questions, remarks to which part of the audience reacted with applause and laughter.

However, it is worth remembering that in the case of non-verbal elements, the meanings attributed to them by recipients may be highly different. Kaczyński's smile could be interpreted as victorious, proving the politician's superiority, or mocking or contemptuous. Lis' leaning towards the interlocutor could be interpreted as a sign of involvement, attentive listening, or as a form of aggression or attack. Understanding a sign depends on the community of interpretation to which the recipient belongs. It is visible in the comments when, among a dozen statements declaring admiration for Kaczyński, the comments mentioned above negate the interpretation imposed by the video's title.

Rhetorical *actio*

The ancients distinguished between a rhetor and an actor. The rhetor should not act, but at the same time, he should be proficient in *hypocrisis*, the ability to use the voice and the body. It was about pretending, but it was an art – not nature and not spontaneous, ruleless behaviour. Moderation and composure were the qualities that distinguished rhetorical *actio* from acting. Rhetorical *actio* is different from stage performance. This remains a valid assumption even in the age of the theatricalisation of political life, associated with the increasing visuality of politics.

Rhetorical treatises pointed to two types of *pronuntiatio* (delivery): *naturalis* (natural) and *artificiale* (learned). In analysing non-verbal means of persuasion, it is sometimes difficult to determine which of the speaker's behaviours result from a conscious choice dictated by the desire to influence the recipient and which are reflexive. In ancient rhetorical texts, natural gestures resulted from the character or age and learned conventional ones but should be consistent with the speaker's personality. They were generally divided into informational and emotional. Also crucial in *pronuntiatio* is the timbre of the voice, accent, intonation, adapting the voice to the subject, body movements, *cultus* (neatness of dress, but also social propriety), gestures, and mimicry.

Contemporary questions about *actio* are related to the specificity of different media. In the described case, both interviewees – as has already been mentioned – have extensive experience in public appearances; they are familiar with the rules of performing in front of an audience and behaving in a TV studio. Therefore, we can assume that their behaviour is close to *hypocrisis* – they perform in a public role, are aware of their behaviour, and use it on purpose. However, based on the analysed material, it is difficult to determine to what extent the viewers are aware of the theatricality of their scenes. Do they realise they are watching a performance rather than a natural interaction?

The opposition leader's television interview broadcast before the elections is a carefully directed and acted political performance. Moreover, although this theatricality does not have to mean artificiality and untruth, it is undoubtedly not spontaneous and natural. The studied gestures and facial expressions have clearly defined persuasive purposes. However, it is challenging to distinguish which behaviours are spontaneous and independent of the speaker's will in rhetorical analysis. They are consciously 'played' by him to influence his interlocutor or listeners.

The gestures are ambiguous. Lis repeatedly props up his head or chin. It may be a sign of attentive listening to the interlocutor and negative assessment of him, or even a signal of decision-making (e.g., what the next question should be). Since the stakes of this conversation are high for both interlocutors and each is keen to construct an ethos, it can be assumed that most behaviours (poses, gestures, facial expressions) are deliberate, conscious, planned actions. However, it should be remembered that some are typical of the speaker and are not uniquely connected to the particular situation. In contrast, others may be unplanned reflexes (e. g., the journalist's impatient leaning towards the interlocutor when the politician again avoids answering a question or Kaczyński's tightening of his lips when talking about the attacks on his dead brother).

"People who have power do not need to make many gestures" (Pease / Pease 2007, p. 413) – this general truth is confirmed when we analyse the situation of the clash between two actors fighting for dominance. The men differ in height, but the scenery does not emphasise this difference. Both are dressed in dark suits (black and grey). Both use a somewhat limited repertoire of gestures. Kaczyński is more static, often resting his forearms on the back of his chair and gesturing with his hands alone. Sometimes he leans back, sometimes not, but he does not lean towards Lis. On the other hand, the journalist takes a more offensive stance, improves his armchair more energetically, and leans towards the politician.

Two types of gestures predominate. In Lis' case, it is the already mentioned propping up of the chin or head, which can be generally interpreted as a sign of attentive listening (although not only), while in Kaczyński's case – illustrative gestures of spreading the hands, emphasising the clarity and obviousness of the statements made. They also make gestures regarded as attacking or accusing – they point at the interlocutor with their hand or finger. Tomasz Lis uses the sheets of paper he is holding in his hands; he looks into them to construct a strategy of distance; the quotations or data referred to are supposed to give the impression of the journalist's neutrality. Lis also significantly folds those pieces of paper, symbolically putting them aside, as if Kaczyński's behaviour forced him to ask questions other than the ones he had prepared earlier.

According to rhetorical textbooks, mimicry serves two purposes: to show the speaker's commitment and deep conviction of the truthfulness and rightness of the sentences proclaimed (Tuszyńska 2016, p. 236). If we look at the facial expressions of the two interlocutors, we notice repeated and similar reactions. Kaczynski's slight smile, slight closing of the eyes, raising of the eyebrows, wrinkling of the eyebrows. An intensive stare of Lis, a severe face, an ejection of the chin. There is no doubt that mimicry in both interlocutors was an element of their ethos strategy. It was supposed to support the image of a professional, inquisitive journalist and a balanced, experienced politician. At the same time, both interlocutors tried to undermine the ethos of their opponent. One could have the impression that they tried to bring each other out of balance. Lis tried to 'discover' the true face of the Law and Justice president, while Kaczyński tried to ridicule the journalist, showing him as unprepared, unserious and biased.

The media broadcaster reinforced this aggressive side of the interaction (taunting can also be a form of attack). The studio scenography and camera work suggested the confrontational nature of the conversation. The participants sitting opposite each other were often shown as competitors in the ring. The camera went around them and showed their mutual reactions. Shots of the whole studio were alternated with close-ups, which is one way of constructing the program's dynamics. Additional visual elements were quotations and photos shown on the screen against which the interviewees were sitting. All of this made the message more visually attractive and stimulated emotions.

In televised discourse, emotions are of exceptional importance, and camera close-ups on participants' faces allow these emotions to be shown (Lorenzo-Dus 2009, p.184). Moreover, it is one of the signs of the emotionalisation of mediatised politics. Semiotic (and rhetorical) means of showing negative emotions on television include, apart from verbal insults or accusations, para-linguistic (raising the voice, interrupting the interlocutor, persistent repetition of a phrase or question) and non-verbal (entering the physical space of the other, finger-pointing) behaviour. On the other hand, the media broadcaster has at his disposal "the rapid interweaving of camera angles that juxtaposed close-up shots of angry performers and long-range shots of amused audiences" (Lorenzo-Dus 2009, p. 185). Television interviews with politicians resemble hunts with journalists aiming to get the politician to say something he did not intend. At the same time, the journalist tries to maintain the role of a neutral, objective provocateur. As a result, researchers observe an increase in the frequency of hostile questions and antagonising answers (Lozenzo-Dus 2009, p. 135). The analysed conversation is a perfect illustration of just such behaviour. The journalist must not grimace or roll his eyes to reveal his attitude towards the interlocutor; the politician must not show that he treats the journalist's questions as a personal attack.

Non-verbal behaviour seems more reliable, so observers often refer to it in political scandals, assuming that unconscious gestures or facial expressions will betray the truth. One of the most famous examples of this inconsistency between words and non-verbal behaviour is President Clinton's statement denying his relationship with Monica Levinsky (Lorenzo-Dus 2009, p.145).

It is also worth remembering that audiences may tend to detect insincerity, especially in a disliked politician, even when the gesture is not explicit. Besides, online communication has also provided deliberate (sometimes involuntary) manipulation opportunities. For reading non-verbal signals, it is necessary to put them in context; when a single image is cut out of a video recording, it can completely change the interpretation of the behaviour in question. A brief, casual glance caught on a photograph can become 'evidence' of hostility, an unhealthy interest or an affair. So nowadays, the non-verbal behaviour of public figures is also planned in detail, and training in this area is a regular feature in the schedules of politicians. They need it for credibility, a valuable currency today (cf. Thompson 2000). Body language is supposed to be consistent with the verbal message. Politicians are aware that cameras will catch every movement and gesture.

In ancient textbooks, there were many indications about how a speaker should use his body and voice to stimulate emotion and enhance persuasion. We find such remarks in Aristotle, Cicero and Quintilian. The latter links delivery with ethos, with the speaker's character (Quintilian 1922, book XI), and although he describes in some detail various paralinguistics and non-verbal means, he emphasises that everything depends on the context: who the speaker is, the audience he is addressing, in what circumstances, what his goal is, and finally – what genre he uses. In antiquity, delivering a speech was considered the action of an individual actor; today, it is increasingly seen as a cultural practice (discursive practice). The new communication circumstances require a rethinking of all the conditions of a rhetorical situation.

Rhetorical *actio* changes with the spread of mass media. Different skills were needed when the speaker reached the audience gathered at a rally, others when they listened to him on the radio, and others when the message was mediated by television. The last analyses concern what changes when the message reaches the audience via the Internet. What are new elements of *pronuntiatio?*

Kurniawan Ildi (2021) analysed comments posted online under Ken Robinson's speech (TED Talks) recording. The results show that the audience paid attention to two aspects of the rhetorical action. First, they focused on the speaker's high level of competence, which made the speech perceived as attractive, sincere, knowledgeable, fluent, accurate, effective, and efficient. Secondly, the audience also noticed specific speaker's tricks, above all, the use of humour. Similar reactions were presented by Internet users commenting on the Lis-Kaczyński conversation. However, it should be noted that in Robinson's case, this was an online recording of a speech delivered directly to an audience, face to face, so the speaker was using classical rather than digital means of persuasion.

Much research is now also concerned with technology, such as visual elements in rhetorical action. For example, the visual setting of a politician's press conference and the slide presentations used during official speeches by public figures raise questions about the importance of delivery in the age of television, media spectacles, performativity and the increasing visuality of politics (Welch 1990).

Delivery in a digital media context can be considered a specific type of mediation. It involves using all available technological solutions that allow the speaker to reach the audience. The speaker's choices are related to the specific medium but also timing and synchronisation. James E. Porter (2009), who deals with rhetoric in digital media, proposes that the following elements should be included in the analysis of digital delivery: body/identity, distribution/circulation, access/accessibility, interaction, and economics. Thus, we can see the classical rhetorical *actio* elements directly related to the participants. It is about the body, gestures, clothes, gender, race (body/identity), and possibilities of audience response (interaction, distribution – options for reproducing, distributing, and circulating digital information). However, there are also technological issues (accessibility, i.e., conditions of Internet access) or legal issues (economics, i.e., copyright, ownership and control of information, fair use, authorship). In the analysed case, the latter can be more relevant, as the interaction of the main actors was not directly intended for dissemination on the web.

Erving Goffman writes in the introduction to his book *Forms of Talk*:

> Everyone knows that when individuals in the presence of others respond to events, their glances, looks, and postural shifts carry all kinds of implication and meaning. When in these settings, words are spoken, then tone of voice, manner of uptake, restarts, and the variously positioned pauses similarly qualify. As does manner of listening. Every adult is wonderfully accomplished in producing all of these effects, and wonderfully perceptive in catching their significance when performed by accessible others. Everywhere and constantly this gestural resource is employed, yet rarely itself is systematically examined (Goffman 1995, p.1ff).

It is important to emphasise that this cultural training in understanding signs applies to speaking and listening. Goffman, analysing various forms of everyday interaction, points out that gestures, glances, para-linguistic sounds, which are initially "an unintended by-product of speaking and listening" (ibid., p. 2) in the process of ritualisation, quickly acquire their meaningful consequences and cease to be unintentional or merely expressive. In turn, one of the purposes they can serve is persuasion. However, whether they can perform this function depends on the "participation framework" adopted by the message recipients.

Although each medium changes visual language, it is still possible to analyse the message by referring to the essential functions of semiotics indicated by Halliday: ideational, interpersonal, and textual (Kress / van Leeuwen 1996). The non-verbal behaviour observed by the audience becomes a semiotic message. They are read as a representation (ideational function): a malicious/professional journalist or a threatening/responsible politician. The chosen adjective is an effect of the interpersonal function based on the relation between the producer and receiver of the sign (signs complex). The combination by the recipients of individual elements, individual gestures or faces into a coherent whole (he is smiling, relaxed, victorious/he is angry, helpless) is a textual function.

The traditional perception of the speaker and audience is insufficient in a media interaction. Double articulation is characteristic for television discourse; communicative interaction occurs between people in the studio and between them and 'absent audiences' (Lorenzo-Dus 2009, p. 5). Goffman (1995) proposes a more complex model, well describing the situation we deal with, for example, in news programs. He presents production (sender) and participation (receiver) dimensions. He identifies three roles that the broadcaster can play: the animator (the transmitter, the resonance box), the author or the principal (the reported party). As for the recipients, Goffman describes ratified (official or intended, which can be either addressed or not) and unratified (overhearers, eaves-droppers). The fluidity of the roles of senders and receivers is essential and enlarged by new media.

Audience reactions

Lis and Kaczyński, talking in a TV studio, probably did not plan to record this conversation on the Internet. Therefore, it would be a methodological mistake to consider the non-verbal means they used in terms of online *pronuntiatio*. Hence, the decision was only to analyse comments that referred to the appearance and body language of the interviewees. In which roles are the politician and the journalist perceived? How do para- and non-verbal elements create the ethos of the interlocutors?

Opinions on the behaviour of both interviewees are automatically linked to evaluating their attitudes. General comments on Tomasz Lis' appearance were often based on non-visual associations. In one of the comments, the journalist is described as "Rudy pół lis-pół hiena"[2] [Redheaded half fox-half hyena], which shows the overlapping of several plans of meaning. Firstly, there is the association – the fox is red. The fox figure is associated with malice and deceit in fairy tales and proverbs. Negative stereotypes associated with red hair are also linked to malice. Thus, the journalist's name evoked a series of negative connotations, the apparent reference to outward appearance having a purely metaphorical meaning – the journalist is blonde. In turn, 'half-hyena' refers to the title of "Hyena of the Year", which the Association of Polish Journalists awarded Tomasz Lis in 2015 for his unreliable and unethical conduct in one of his programs.

The comments varied considerably in style or level of aggression. The comments concerning Tomasz Lis were mainly about his hateful looks, rage and fear: "Ale ten Lis ma wredne spojrzenie" [What Lis has a mean look]; "Lis wygląda jak [...] moczymorda [...], której założyli garnitur.Eurocwel" [Lis looks like a juicer dressed in suit. EU-faggot]; "lis sprawa wrażenie psychopaty do tego ta nordycka uroda Breivika, mam wrażenie, że ma duże problem z nerwami" [Lis seems like a psychopath, plus that Breivik's Nordic beauty, I have an impression that he has big problems with nerves]; "Lis.... wściekły i zarazem przystojny..."[Lis... fierce

---

2 Original spelling in all quoted comments.

yet handsome...]; "Jak wiele mówi postawa redaktora, jego spojrzenie, jego postawa ciała, jego marsowa mina. Szkoda, że się ten człowiek tak zamyka w sobie i w tych emocjach, które niekorzystnie rzutują na efekty jego pracy na antenie. Oby się potrafił rozluźnić i nabrać dystansu :D" [The editor's attitude, his look, his body posture, his frown say a lot. It is a pity that this man is so closed in on himself and in his emotions that they negatively influence the effects of his work on the air. Let's hope he can relax and get some distance :D]; "Widać nienawiść w oczach Lisa do Kaczyńskiego :D" [You can see the hatred in Lis eyes towards Kaczynski:D].

The sign that attracted the audience's attention in Kaczyński's case was his smile, unanimously read as a symbol of derision, superiority or falsity. "Ten uśmiech prezesa :))))), rewelacja!" [That president's smile :))))) revelation!]; "Ten obłudny fałszywy uśmieszek" [That hypocritical fake smile]; "TEN IRONICZNY uśmieszek Jarka na samym początku:P mistrz" [Jarek's[3] IRONIC smile at the very beginning:P master]; "Kaczyński rzeczowo, profesjonalnie i z uśmiechem na twarzy" [Kaczynski factual, professional and with a smile on his face]. Comments expressing admiration for Kaczynski's smile have several times prompted counter-comments: "Zajebisty uśmieszek Kaczyńskiego przez cały program" [Kaczynski's cool smirk throughout the program]; reaction: "chujowy jak on cały" [as dick as he is].

It was characteristic to contrast the behaviour of the two interviewees. "Redaktor Lis niepewny i emocjonalny, Jarek racjonalny, skupiony i dowcipny" [Editor Lis uncertain and emotional, Jarek rational, focused and witty]; "Lis to szuja. Butny, atakujący (...) Kaczynski? odprezony,usmiechniety" [Lis is a scumbag. He's arrogant, attacking (...) Kaczynski? Relaxed, smiling.]; "Pięknie patrzeć jak się lis gotuje z wkurwienia ale nic nie może zrobić i musi udawać niewzruszonego a Kaczyński na naturalnym luzie i niesamowitej pewności siebie, jego mowa ciała dobitnie do pokazuje" [It's beautiful to see Lis boiling with piss, but he can't do anything and has to pretend to be unmoved, while Kaczynski is naturally relaxed and incredibly confident, his body language clearly shows it]; "Łał,Kaczyński może nie ma prezencji i takiej typowej charyzmy, ale niszczy Lisa niemal na każdym polu" [Wow, Kaczyński may not have the looks and typical charisma, but he destroys Lis in almost every field]; "Kaczyński cyframi sypie z pamięci jestem w szoku a lis z kartki czyta i jeszcze się myli" [Kaczyński is spitting numbers from memory, I am shocked, while Lis is reading from a sheet of paper and is still wrong].

"Dla mnie TOP komedia pierwszej wody przecież widać jak sobie robi jaja po kilku minutach bo nie ma o czym gadać z biednym Liskiem[4] hehe Biedny sie poci

---

3 Jarek – diminutive of the name Jaroslaw.
4 Lisek – diminutive from "lis" [fox].

czeka na dyrektywke ze słuchawki" [For me TOP comedy of the first water, after all, you can see him pull of tricks after a few minutes because there is nothing to talk about with poor Lisek hehe Poor guy is sweating, waiting for a directive from the earphone] – this is one of the few comments drawing attention to the theatricality of the scenes being watched. The earphone was noticed several times; the viewers interpret it with the sheets of paper held by the journalist and consider it a sign of his dependence and awkwardness. This opinion can be regarded as a symptom of low media competence because the earphone in the presenter's ear is natural and necessary for technical and organisational reasons. The dominant interpretation of the textual ethos is that Kaczyński presented himself as a professional, matter-of-fact, composed, charismatic politician, while Lis is nervous, aggressive, unprofessional, and frightened.

Internet users also noticed secondary characters, pointed to particular people: "Ten w okularkach najlepszy Xd" [The one with the glasses is the best xD]; "xD ta mimika tej kobiety po prawej Lisa haha:D" [xD that facial expression of that woman on the right Lisa haha:D]. And in this case, the interpretations of the audience are based on previous assumptions and the belief that there is an interpretative community to understand, for example, such an undefined statement: "Ja myślę, że wystarczy spojrzeć na ludzi za Panem Kaczyńskim i za Panem Lisem:)" [I think it is enough to look at the people behind Mr Kaczyński and behind Mr Lis:)] or: "Nawet bez fonii mowa ciała adwersarzy mówi właściwie wszystko o tym kto po tej debacie leżał na deskach" [Even without the audio, the body language of the opponents says virtually everything about who was down after the debate].

Conflicting readings of the same signs result from several factors. Firstly, the ambiguity of non-verbal messages themselves. Secondly, there seems to be a more substantial bias (personal, ideological, media), which determines the perception of the actions of both actors. Finally, the viewers' opinions confirm the importance of the emotional dimension of ethos. Calmness or yielding to emotions is significant for the perception of the sender.

Conclusion

The interdisciplinary perspective allows for a broader understanding of the context of the communication situation. Thus, further aspects can be identified, which allows for a better understanding of the participants' interaction dynamics, goals and persuasive strategies (e.g., ethos constructing by the interlocutors, framing of the situation by the media sender, reading of non-verbal behaviour by the audience). At the same time, this research approach can serve a supportive function by indicating, for example, critical moments of interaction or ideological interpretations of participants' behaviour.

As the rhetorical situation analysis has shown, a change in the media context fundamentally changes the roles of the individual participants in the discourse. However, one cannot assume that a medium – television or the Internet – predetermines the possible forms of participation, the signs used, the nature of the audience or the freedom of action of individual actors. Everything depends on the specific situation. Focusing on non-verbal elements in this analysis allowed us to show changes independent of discourse's linguistic and ideological dimensions. At the same time, the analysis of selected comments proved how much the reading of these non-verbal messages is shaped by language and ideology.

The rhetorical perspective makes us focus on the persuasive dimension of communication. The semiotic approach allows us to see and understand the social embeddedness of signs serving this persuasion. The multimodal discourse analysis helps to analyse the functioning of complexes of these signs in online communication. The term ethos, which is crucial in the analysed situation, can be explained by referring to many concepts explaining how discourse participants' positions are constructed and how processes of legitimation or representation occur.

The analysis presented here, although it concerns only a fragment – the non-verbal dimension of discourse – shows how many possibilities arise when we begin to define the situational context.

References

Bitzer, L.F.: 'The rhetorical situation', in: PHILOSOPHY & RHETORIC 1968/1, p. 1–14.

Bogost, Ian / Losh, Elizabeth: 'Rhetoric and digital media', in: MacDonald, Michael J. (ed.) *The Oxford Handbook of Rhetorical Studies*, Oxford 2017, p. 758–771.

Charaudeau, P.: 'A communicative conception of discourse', in: DISCOURSE STUDIES 2002/3, p. 301–318.

Charaudeau, Patrick: Le discours politique. Les masques du pouvoir. Paris 2005.

Gill, Ann M. / Whedbee, Karen: 'Rhetoric', in: van Dijk, Teun A. (ed.) *Discourse as Structure and Process: Discourse Studies: A Multidisciplinary Introduction*. London 1997, p. 154–184.

Goffman, Erving: Forms of Talk. Philadelphia 1995.

Grzmil-Tylutki, Halina: Gatunek w świetle francuskiej teorii dyskursu. Kraków 2007.

Harrell, J. / Linkugel, W.A.: 'On rhetorical genre: An organising perspective', in: PHILOSOPHY & RHETORIC 1978/4, p. 262–281.

Jewitt, Carey (ed.): The Routledge Handbook of Multimodal Analysis. London 2014.

Kamberelis, G.: 'Genre as institutionally informed social practice', in: MARYLAND JOURNAL OF CONTEMPORARY LEGAL ISSUES 1995/6, p. 115–171.

Kampka, Agnieszka: 'Multimodalna analiza dyskursu – ujęcie semiotyczne', in: Czyżewski, Marek / Otrocki, Michał / Piekot, Tomasz / Stachowiak, Jerzy (eds.) *Analiza dyskursu publicznego. Przegląd metod i perspektyw badawczych.* Warszawa 2017, p. 95–122.

Kampka, A.: 'Retoryka identyfikacji online. Na przykładzie koreańskiego zespołu BTS', in: RES RHETORICA 2021/3, p. 91–110.

Kress, Gunther / Leeuwen, Theo van: Reading Images. The Grammar of Visual Design. London 1996.

Kress, Gunther: Multimodality. A Social Semiotic Approach to Contemporary Communication: Exploring Contemporary Methods of Communication. Los Angeles 2009.

Kurniawan, I.: 'A rhetorical analysis of comments and delivery strategy on TED Talks', in: JOALL (JOURNAL OF APPLIED LINGUISTICS AND LITERATURE) 2021/1, p. 149–161.

Leeuwen, Theo van: 'Rhetoric and semiotics', in: MacDonald, Michael J. (ed.) *The Oxford Handbook of Rhetorical Studies.* Oxford 2017, p. 673–682.

Lemke, Jay: 'Critical Analysis across Media: Games, Franchises, and the New Cultural Order', in: Labarta Postigo, M. (ed.) *Approaches to Critical Discourse Analysis.* Valencia 2005 (CDROM edition).

Lorenzo-Dus, Nuria: Television Discourse. Analysing Language in the Media. Basingstoke 2009.

Miller, Carolyn R.: 'Genre as Social Action', in: Freedman, Aviva / Medway, Peter (eds.) *Genre and the New Rhetoric.* Bristol 1994, p. 23–42.

Norris, Sigrid / Maier, Carmen Daniela: Texts, Images, and Interactions: A Reader in Multimodality. Boston 2014.

Pease, Allan / Pease, Barbara: Mowa ciała. Poznań 2007.

Porter, J.E.: 'Recovering delivery for digital rhetoric', in: COMPUTERS AND COMPOSITION 2009/26, p. 207–224.

Quintilian: Institutio oratoria (H.E. Butler, Trans.). Cambridge 1922. available at: https://penelope.uchicago.edu/thayer/e/roman/texts/quintilian/institutio_oratoria/home.html [30.09.2021].

Rossolatos, G.: Conducting multimodal rhetorical analysis of TV ads with Atlas.ti 7, in: MULTIMODAL COMMUNICATION 2014/3(1), p. 51–84.

Thompson, John B.: Political Scandal: Power and Visibility in the Media Age. Cambridge 2000.

Tuszyńska, Krystyna: Oratorstwo i retoryka grecka z wyborem tekstów źródłowych. Od oralnej kultury retorycznej Homera do konceptualizacji retoryki przez Arystotelesa. Poznań 2016.

Welch, K.E.: 'Electrifying classical rhetoric: Ancient media, modern technology, and contemporary composition', in: JOURNAL OF ADVANCED COMPOSITION 1990/1, p. 22–38.

Załęska, Maria: 'Rhetorical patterns of constructing the politician's ethos', in: Załęska, Maria (ed.) *Rhetoric and Politics: Central/Eastern European Perspectives.* Newcastle upon Tyne 2012, p. 20–50.

Łukasz Kumięga / Magdalena Nowicka-Franczak

Weighing discourse in a single-case study. An attempt at an appraisal

Abstract

The following is an attempt at an overview of the research goal which this volume's contributing authors collectively pursued. The variants of interdisciplinary analyses of a single case presented in the introduction are discussed in greater detail. The authors of this book decided to follow interdisciplinary approaches in their analyses, which helped demonstrate the productivity of studying discourse in this way, but has also highlighted the resulting methodological challenges. Strong focus was given to the centralist model of interdisciplinarity (Theo van Leeuwen's approach) in discourse studies, as well as to mechanisms related to the semantics of such studies. The cognitive value of the present volume has to be emphasized, the publication bringing together a number of approaches to studying the mechanisms which govern public communication in Poland and beyond. Keywords: discourse analysis, interdisciplinarity, Polish public discourse, single case analysis

An appraisal of our research endeavor may reveal an ostensibly "old-school", micro-analytic approach, although one referring to a primarily macro-analytic category, i.e. discourse. Critics of this perspective could raise doubts as to the selection of the text for the analysis – all the more that any such choice and the reasoning behind it will be inherently arbitrary and subjective. It may be rightly argued that there are many other theoretical and methodological angles which this volume has not considered, and which could be well-suited to approaching this text. Finally, a basic but important question could be asked: what is the purpose of this micro-analytic effort?

We would be preaching to the choir arguing that insights into public discourse are not solely intended to perpetuate academic discourse (in the sense of engaging in it just for the sake of it), but are, first and foremost, of cognitive value – both with regard to academic discourse itself, and more broadly, with reference

Łukasz Kumięga, University of Gdańsk (Poland), ORCID: 0000-0002-8034-3593, Lukasz.Kumiega@ug.edu.pl.

Magdalena Nowicka-Franczak, University of Łódź (Poland), ORCID: 0000-0002-4535-4246, m.nowicka_franczak@uni.lodz.pl.

to understanding the nature of communicative and discursive practices, which exist beyond it and in relation to it. At this point, a question arises as to the extent of the impact of academic discourse on its surroundings. This is an important question, but one which is outside the scope of this volume. Still, the materials collected may serve as an inspiration to inter-discursive efforts, which in this case would amount to translating the mechanisms of public debates expressed in the language of discourse studies into a language closer to the participants of these debates and their audiences. In line with the positions of a number of critical discourse approaches which insist that research should have impact on social reality (see e.g. Jäger / Maier 2009), this research initiative, too, may be a step toward bringing together the researchers of public discourse and its practitioners (such as journalists).

But the main focus of this volume is on researcher's own work, that is, the self-reflection of the academic circles on the direction for research projects concerning significant substantive and methodological challenges which surround communication, discourse, and the role of the symbolic elites (journalists, politicians, and others, see e.g. Van Dijk 1993, Wodak / Januschek / Czyżewski / House / Duszak 2010). It is not a coincidence that the volume opens with a text by Marek Czyżewski, which combines – in the context of a single-case study – two classical research perspectives: quantitative and qualitative, the latter being closer to a discursive approach, although frequently just as critical of single-case analyses.

Thus, in the spirit of a wise maxim that "words should be weighed, not counted", the present volume is clearly aligned with an approach which reveals the significance of discourse studies, including those conducted on the basis of a single text. Under this perspective, micro-analyses identify instances of particular communicative and discursive practices which create social processes being debated in public. Therefore, this is a strictly empirical insight, which departs from abstract theorizing, as well as from theorizing based on formally attractive numbers and figures. Capturing both patterns within, and changes of, the linguistic, communicative, and material embodiment of discourse is the overarching goal of this perspective. This goal is inextricably connected with another critical-analytical task: studying the relations between the discourse of power and power in discourse (discursive power, i.e. the mechanisms of exercising power through discourse), as well as analyzing the role of discourse in the social transmission of knowledge (see e.g. Foucault 1972, Keller / Schneider 2020, Czachur 2021). Discourse scholars, including the authors of this volume, treat knowledge as yet another instrument of power, seeing as the former provides the explanations behind particular visions of social, economic, and political order. Moreover, focusing on one fragment of discourse – here, an interview between Tomasz Lis and Jarosław Kaczyński – encourages scholars to take a closer look at its many contexts, some of which are still relevant to the present-day public debate.

Noticing various possible ways of presenting a research problem is the departure point for discourse-oriented analyses. In the subsequent chapters of this volume, the authors, following different methods and approaches, attempt to fulfill the aforesaid goals. First, on the strength of particular statements and sequences of statements taken from the interview, they perform a micro-analytic reconstruction of the interactional order, the multimodality of the message, or the rhetorical and argumentative modes employed throughout. Second, they pay particular attention to various contextual levels in which the analyzed interview is embedded, such as immediate, situational, intertextual and interdiscursive, institutional, sociopolitical, and historical (see Reisigl / Wodak 2009: 93). On this basis, the authors point to asymmetries present in certain discursive practices and retrace the system of interdependencies which had culminated in the interview. Third, by dissecting a political interview which appeared in the Polish media, they are scouring individual speech acts for reflections of general mechanisms of public communication. Discursive analyses pursuing these three chief goals do not preclude the possibility of complementing the picture with a quantitative perspective, on condition that it is well thought-out, i. e. as long as it is employed following the establishment of a methodological and cognitive logic that would justify this move. Thus, aside from the suggested potential meeting of public discourse researchers with its practitioners, a follow-up to the methodological medley we have proposed may also include a discursive-quantitative approach, much as this may appear contradictory (see e. g. Baker 2012).

On the one hand, a scenario where a group of scholars from various fields analyzes a single text will inevitably lead to theoretical, empirical, and cognitive polyvocality. On the other hand, it offers an opportunity to appreciate the elements which different analytical approaches share or on which they apparently disagree. This observation points to the primary goal of our workshop and of this volume, which is to consider the nature of interdisciplinarity, understood as the gathering of various disciplines around one empirical moment (here, the Lis-Kaczyński interview).

In the following part of this summary, we are trying to capture what, from the aforesaid perspective, are this volume's key aspects, as manifesting on four levels: theoretical, conceptual, inter(sub)disciplinary, and cognitive.

On the theoretical level, and invoking Theo van Leeuwen's (2005) centralist model of interdisciplinarity, one may conclude that the present volume is in a way dominated by approaches which originated in linguistics and social sciences. Both constitute the basic reference point for discourse-oriented analyses. The former arise from the linguistic roots of the concept of discourse, in the sense of the use of a language system, as well as with regard to the structuralist division into *langue* and *parole* and the inclusion of discursive approaches (which represent some of the obvious choices for such studies from today's perspective) in language studies. The latter serve as the background for perspectives focused on the linguistic construction and perpetuation of social processes, social identities, and social change.

On the conceptual level, the analyses making up this volume display some of the semantic mechanisms which are typical of interdisciplinary approaches and/ or of situations where they concern – as they do in this case – a shared conceptual background, that is, discourse. One of them is competing terminology, while another is competing meanings. The single-case analysis has the potential to resolve this competition, if one considers terms crucial to this volume, such as language, text, genre, political interview, or discourse itself. Attempts at this resolution took two basic directions: toward limiting the superfluity of seman-tically-overlapping terms, and toward working out detailed definitions of terms on account of their discursive dimension.

On the inter(sub)disciplinary level, i.e. pertaining to the relations between different fields and approaches concerned with discourse, a number of inter-disciplinary propositions has been offered. This aspect is the book's added value in times when interdisciplinarity is treated in reductionistic fashion: either as a catchphrase aimed to boost the appeal of research grants applications, or as something plain obvious and not accompanied by any sort of meta-scientific insight. The first proposition focuses on attempts to find methods of imposing structure on the analytic material. Necessarily, this attempt lays bare certain methodological deficiencies of broadly defined discourse studies, e. g. a tendency to concentrate on the verbal message at the expense of a more thorough analysis of the non-verbal, emotional, and material aspects of communication. Said methods are understood as a certain preliminary stage paving way for further analytical steps. The second proposition concerns the multidimensional process of constructing the study subject, i.e. the political interview, as representing an invitation for enlisting various methodological and/or cognitive strategies. The third proposition is searching for contexts which may encourage inter-disciplinarity. Here, inter(sub)disciplinary challenges may also arise if the in-terdisciplinarity of discourse studies themselves is considered, or if discursive perspectives previously existing separately are being combined. A special type of interdisciplinarity is confronting a single case with other genres or texts. The present volume also touches upon such issues as the maximalization of inter-pretations or attempts to find linguistic embodiment for what has remained unexpressed in the analysis for now. The authors contributing to this book prove that the interdisciplinarity of discourse studies may be pursued in many ways.

Finally, on the cognitive level, the present volume offers original approaches to the issue of public communication. The conclusions arrived at by the authors may be applied not just to the Polish public discourse, but also – for the best part – to the mechanisms governing public and media discourse in general. Some of the most important findings concern the following:

1. The priority of media-based rules of a polarized conflict over conventional forms and norms of public communication;
2. The violation of genre-specific norms for the purposes of achieving particular interactional goals and occupying particular positions in discourse;
3. The strategic manipulation of the interactional order so as to enhance the rhetorical impact of a statement;
4. The fluid inclusion and exclusion of oneself and others into and from particular language and discourse communities;
5. The instrumentalization of specialized and common knowledge in order to validate statements and counter-statements and to discredit one's interlocutor more efficiently;
6. The media-based re- or de-contextualization of the material dimension of social conflicts, which sees them reduced to the status of symbolic competition.

The analyses included in this volume display a tension between the theoretical and methodological framework of this study on the one hand, and its subject, that is, the Polish public discourse – situated on the global or even local European periphery – on the other. The contributing authors readily draw upon the German and Anglophone critical linguistics, critical discourse analysis, the analysis of interactional order in media interviews, the semiotic tradition, classical rhetoric and a new theory of digital rhetoric, Western critical theory, post-structuralism, and post-Marxism. These forays inevitably result in a certain universalization of the study subject and the related phenomena. However, it has to be remembered that in the Polish public discourse, and in Polish society alike, the stakes still involve the direction of social modernization and the communicative means for its expedition.

On the level of micro discourse, i. e. in the statements analyzed, this manifests in the fact that both Jarosław Kaczyński and Tomasz Lis elevate the act of speaking and the language they want to use to the status of one of the main themes of their conversation. They invest a lot of effort into enforcing their respective stances on what scholars would label as interactional order and the order of discourse. They argue over who should be speaking and what turns they should take, who is obligated to answer, and who has the right to refuse to speak. One subject channeling the conflict between the interlocutors is also the issue of the language which they use addressing each other and other social actors. For that reason, some of the chapters of this volume are explicitly concerned with the evolution of the public language and communicative norms on display in the interview, or the latter's meta-dimension (an interview seen as "speaking about speaking", as a competition over the right to speak, or as a platform for shaping the polarized images of ostensibly impartial speakers). Other chapters explore the issue of the media interview as a genre and of its impact on what is said in public and how it is said – or rather, what was said in the Poland of 2011 and how it was said.

For discourse scholars, an interview of a well-known Polish journalist with an equally well-known Polish politician, in which the interlocutors stand for the conflicting political and social stances, is a microcosm of local strategies of conducting an argument and deciding on the issue of who is Poland's elite, and who is an ordinary but decent citizen; of who can lead the nation, and who is its enemy. The authors of this volume demonstrate that these are matters significant for the collective identity, whose shape is decided in the sphere of public communication. Hence the title of this volume: "Analysing discourse, analysing Poland", because it is discourse that guides us through the Polish public sphere.

References

Baker, Paul: 'Acceptable bias? Using corpus linguistics methods with critical discourse analysis', in: CRITICAL DISCOURSE STUDIES 2012/9(3), p. 247–256, https://doi.org /10.1080/17405904.2012.688297.

Czachur, Waldemar: 'Czy dyskursy negocjują wiedzę', in: Knieja, Jolanta / Krajka, Jarosław (eds.): *Teksty, komunikacja, translacja w perspektywie antropocentrycznej. Studia dedykowane Panu Profesorowi Jerzemu Żmudzkiemu.* Lublin 2021, p. 133–145.

Foucault, Michel: The Archeology of Knowledge and the Discourse of Language. New York 1972.

Jäger, Siegfried / Maier, Florentine: 'Theoretical and Methodological Aspects of Foucauldian Critical Discourse Analysis and Dispositve Analysis', in: Wodak, Ruth / Meyer, Michael (eds.): *Methods of Critical Discourse Analysis.* London 2009, p. 34–61.

Keller, Reiner / Schneider, Werner: 'Wissenssoziologische Diskurs- und Dispositivforschung: Zur machtanalytischen Rekonstruktion der Vorauslegung der alltäglichen Auslegung', in: Hitzler, Ronald / Reichertz, Jo / Schröer, Norbert (eds.): *Kritik der Hermeneutischen Wissenssoziologie.* Weinheim 2020, p. 52–66.

Koller, H.-Ch.: 'Lesarten. Über das Geltendmachen von Differenzen im Forschungsprozeß', in: ZEITSCHRIFT FÜR ERZIEHUNGSWISSENSCHAFT 1999/2, p. 195–209.

Reisigl, Martin / Wodak, Ruth: 'The Discourse-Historical Approach (DHA)', in: Wodak, Ruth / Meyer, Michael (eds.): *Methods for Critical Discourse Analysis.* London 2009, p. 87–121.

Van Dijk, Teun: Elite Discourse and Racism. Newbury Park 1993.

Van Leeuwen, Theo: Introducing Social Semiotics. London 2005.Wodak, Ruth / Januschek, Franz / Czyżewski, Marek / House, Juliane / Duszak, Anna: 'Perspektiven der Kritischen Sozialwissenschaften im Allgemeinen und der Kritischen Diskursanalyse im Speziellen', in: Duszak, Anna / House, Juliane / Kumięga, Łukasz (eds.): *Globalization, Discourse, Media: In a Critical Perspective.* Warsaw 2010, p. 559–596.

Notes on Contributors

Artur Lipiński is Associate Professor in the Department of Political Science and Journalism, Adam Mickiewicz University, Poznań. Currently, he is involved in the H2020 consortium project DEMOS "Democratic Efficacy and the Varieties of Populism in Europe". His main research interests are focused on right wing politics in Poland, discourse analysis and populist political communication.

Agnieszka Budzyńska-Daca is Associate Professor at the Institute of Applied Polish Studies, University of Warsaw, Chair of Department of Rhetoric and Media, and Centre for Applied Rhetoric. Currently serves as Vice President of the Polish Rhetoric Society. She is the author of "Retoryka debaty. Polskie wielkie debaty przedwyborcze 1995–2010" ("The Rhetoric of Debate. Polish Great Pre-Election Debates 1995–2010", 2015). She has also co-edited textbooks of rhetoric, including "Retoryka" ("Rhetoric", 2008) and "Ćwiczenia z retoryki" ("Exercises in Rhetoric", 2010). Her research interests revolve around rhetoric in public communication, rhetorical genre studies, and rhetorical criticism.

Waldemar Czachur is Professor at the Institute for German Studies, University of Warsaw. His research interests include discourse linguistics, textual linguistics, comparative discourse analysis, linguistic research on collective memory, history of German-Polish relations. His recent publications are books: "*Nigdy więcej wojny!* 1 września w kulturze pamięci Polski i Niemiec w latach 1945–1989" in cooperation with Peter Oliver Loew ("*No More War!* 1 September in the Culture of Memory of Poland and Germany in 1945–1989", 2020); "Lingwistyka dyskursu jako integrujący program badawczy" ("Discourse Linguistics as an Integrative Research Programme", 2020, author), "Diskursive Weltbilder im Kontrast. Linguistische Konzeption und Methode der kontrastiven Diskursanalyse deutscher und polnischer Medien" ("Discursive Worldviews in Contrast. Linguistic Concept and Method of Contrastive Discourse Analysis of German and Polish Media", 2011, author).

Marek Czyżewski is Professor at the Institute of Sociology, University of Łódź. His main interests include: discourse analysis, public and mass communication, public opinion, and democracy, hate speech, "governmentality", intercultural and international communication, social theory (especially interpretive approaches, sociology of knowledge, and Foucault). Editor-in-chief of "Przegląd Socjologiczny" ("Sociological Review"), editor of the series "Biblioteka Dyskursu Publicznego" ("Library of Public Discourse"). Among his publications are: "Öffentliche Kommunikation und Rechtsextremismus" ("Public Communication and Right-wing Extremism", 2005, author), "Dyskurs elit symbolicznych. Próba diagnozy" ("Discourse of Symbolic Elites. An Attempt at Diagnosis", 2014, co-editor and co-author), and "Analiza dyskursu publicznego. Przegląd metod i perspektyw badawczych" ("Analysis of Public Discourse. Review of Methods and Approaches", 2017, co-editor).

Przemysław E. Gębal is Professor at the Institute of Applied Linguistics, University of Gdańsk, involved in research and practice of foreign language teacher training. His research interests include multilingualism and cross-cultural communication with a particular focus on their pedagogical and didactic aspects. He is the scientific editor of the publishing series "Foreign Language Didactics", PWN publishing house, and "Interdisciplinary Localisations of Applied Linguistics", Vandenhoeck & Ruprecht Verlage.

Agnieszka Kampka is Assistant Professor in the Department of Sociology at Institute of Sociological Sciences and Pedagogy, Warsaw University of Life Sciences. She is the author of journal articles and book chapters in the fields of political and visual rhetoric, and the author, editor, and co-editor of 10 books and monographs, including "Perswazja w języku polityki" ("Persuasion in Political Language", 2009, author), "Debata publiczna: zmiany społecznych norm komunikacji" ("Public Debate. Changes in Social Communication Standards", 2014, author), "Rhetoric, Knowledge, and the Public Sphere" (2016, co-editor). She is the chief editor of the journal "Res Rhetorica" (https://resrhetorica.com).

Violetta Kopińska is Associate Professor, Deputy Director of the Institute of Education Sciences at the Faculty of Philosophy and Social Sciences, Nicolaus Copernicus University in Toruń, Vice Editor-in-Chief of "Przegląd Badań Edukacyjnych" ("Educational Studies Review"). She focuses her research interests on citizenship education, civic participation, and anti-discrimination education. She studies discourse of citizenship education from the perspective of critical pedagogy, and the relationship between politics and education in a discursive approach. Author of over 60 academic publications, including the monograph: "Edukacja obywatelska w szkole. Krytyczna analiza dyskursu podręczników szkolnych" ("Citizenship Education at School. Critical Discourse Analysis of the School Textbooks", 2017).

Marcin Kosman is a PhD candidate at the University of Warsaw, holds MA degrees and Linguistics and Psychology, and works at the University of Economics and Human Sciences in Warsaw. A two-time recipient of the scholarship of the Minister of Science and Higher Education for outstanding achievements. His research interests include corpus linguistics, sociology of translation, multimodal discourse analysis, and political discourse analysis.

Łukasz Kumięga is Assistant Professor at the Institute of Applied Linguistics, University of Gdańsk. He is a linguist, discoursologist, interested in relationships between language and social processes. Author of a monograph on street demonstrations of extreme right-wing movements in Germany: "Rechtsextremistischer Straßendiskurs in Deutschland" ("Right-wing Extremist Street Discourse in Germany", 2013), co-editor of 10 multi-author monographs from the area of interdisciplinary relationships of linguistics with other humanities and social sciences (for example: "Pädagogisch-fremdsprachendidaktische Verortungen der Lehrerforschung. Konzepte, Herausforderungen, Perspektiven" ("Pedagogical-Foreign Language Didactic Localisations of Teacher Research. Concepts, Challenges, Perspectives", 2021) and "Sprache und Gesellschaft. Theoretische und empirische Kontexte der Linguistik" ("Language and Society. Theoretical and Empirical Contexts of Linguistics", 2020). Currently conducting research at the intersection of language, discourse, education and migration.

Magdalena Nowicka-Franczak is Assistant Professor of Sociology at the Institute of Sociology, University of Łódź. Her academic interests focus on the current public debates in Poland, the collective memory of Shoah and WWII, symbolic elites, post-Foucauldian discourse analysis, and postcolonial studies. She is the author of the monograph "Niechciana debata. Spór o książki Jana Tomasz Grossa" ("The Unwanted Debate: Jan Tomasz Gross' Books in Poland", 2017).

Kaja Rostkowska-Biszczanik has a PhD in humanities and adjunct position at the University of Zielona Góra. She is the head of the Journalism Studio in the Department of Journalism and New Media. Her PhD thesis concerned the works of the Polish master of interviews – Teresa Torańska. The dissertation was published in the form of a book entitled "One. Wywiady Teresy Torańskiej w ujęciu genologicznym" ("They. Interviews of Teresa Torańska in Terms of Genre", 2019). In scientific research, she is interested in the methodology of media studies and media genres. Deputy editor-in-chief of academic media at the University of Zielona Góra (radio station, cable and Internet television).

Jerzy Stachowiak is Assistant Professor in the Department of the Sociology of Culture at the University of Łódź. His research interests include discourse analysis, culture of capitalism, public sphere and social theories. He is the author of the book "Czynnik ludzki. O cywilizowaniu uprzedmiotowienia" ("The Human Factor. On Civilizing of the Objectification", 2020).

Magdalena Steciąg is Associate Professor of Polish Linguistics at the University of Zielona Góra. Her main research interests lie in the fields of genre studies, discourse analysis, and ecolinguistics. Her last book was dedicated to ecological discourse in Polish public debates: "Dyskurs ekologiczny w debacie publicznej" ("Ecological Discourse in Public Debate", 2012. Currently she is leading a research project "Lingua Receptiva or Lingua Franca? The Linguistic Practices in the Borderland Area Between Poland and the Czech Republic in the Face of English Language Domination (Ecolinguistic Approach)" financed by National Science Centre, Poland. A member of the International Ecolinguistics Association and Polish Linguistic Society (Polskie Towarzystwo Językoznawcze).

Marta Wójcicka is Professor at the Institute of Social Communication and Media Sciences, Maria Curie-Skłodowska University, Lublin. Her research interests include collective memory, discourse, text, genre of speech. Publications: "Dawno to temu, już bardzo dawno… Formuły ramowe w tekstach polskiej prozy ludowej" ("A Long Time Ago, a Long Time Ago. Framework Formulas in the Texts of Polish Folk Prose", 2010), "Pamięć zbiorowa a tekst ustny" ("Collective Memory and Oral Text", 2014, in English 2020), "Mem internetowy jako multimodalny gatunek pamięci zbiorowej" ("Internet Meme as a Multimodal Genre of Collective Memory", 2019).